Countermobilization

Chicago Studies in American Politics

A series edited by Susan Herbst, Lawrence R. Jacobs, Adam J. Berinsky, and Frances Lee; Benjamin I. Page, editor emeritus

ALSO IN THE SERIES:

Countermobilization

Policy Feedback and Backlash in a Polarized Age

ERIC M. PATASHNIK

The University of Chicago Press
Chicago and London

The University of Chicago Press, Chicago 60637
The University of Chicago Press, Ltd., London
© 2023 by The University of Chicago
Published 2023
Printed in the United States of America

32 31 30 29 28 27 26 25 24 23   1 2 3 4 5

ISBN-13: 978-0-226-82987-6 (cloth)
ISBN-13: 978-0-226-82989-0 (paper)
ISBN-13: 978-0-226-82988-3 (e-book)
DOI: https://doi.org/10.7208/chicago/9780226829883.001.0001

Library of Congress Cataloging-in-Publication Data

Names: Patashnik, Eric M., author.
Title: Countermobilization : policy feedback and backlash in a polarized age /
    Eric M. Patashnik.
Other titles: Chicago studies in American politics.
Description: Chicago : The University of Chicago Press, 2023. | Series: Chicago
    studies in American politics | Includes bibliographical references and index.
Identifiers: LCCN 2023020238 | ISBN 9780226829876 (cloth) | ISBN 9780226829890
    (paperback) | ISBN 9780226829883 (ebook)
Subjects: LCSH: Opposition (Political science)—United States. | Polarization (Social
    sciences)—United States. | United States—Politics and government—21st century.
Classification: LCC JC328.3 .P38 2023 | DDC 328.3/6909730905—dc23/eng/20230501
LC record available at https://lccn.loc.gov/2023020238

For my family—Debbie, Michael, and Josh

Contents

Figures and Tables

Figures

Tables

Introduction

On June 26, 2009, the House of Representatives passed the American Clean Energy and Security Act to tackle climate change.[1] The measure featured an innovative "cap-and-trade" program. Power plants and other emitters were required to hold pollution permits for every ton of greenhouse gas they released but could buy and sell the permits in a market. Companies would thus be incentivized to find the most cost-effective ways to produce and use clean energy.

While economists argued that making polluters pay was the most efficient way to address climate change, the proposal died in the Senate after igniting a backlash among defenders of the fossil fuel status quo.[2] Americans for Prosperity, an antiregulatory group funded by the billionaire brothers Charles and David Koch, held public events across the country to galvanize opposition. Many ordinary citizens—including enthusiastic Tea Party supporters—participated in the countermobilization. During summer 2009, Democrats faced a barrage of criticism over their support for the bill.[3] When Congressman Tom Perriello, a first-term incumbent from Central Virginia, attempted to explain his position at one town hall, "he was unable to be heard over the chants of 'drill, drill, drill.'"[4] Opponents claimed that cap-and-trade would kill jobs, raise taxes, and destroy freedom.[5] Polls showed that a bare majority of Americans favored the measure, and that support fell below 50 percent when citizens learned it would raise electricity prices.[6] In 2010, Democrats lost sixty-three seats (and their majority) in the House—the largest midterm blowout for a party since 1938. Voting for the cap-and-trade bill damaged Democrats from moderate districts like Perriello, who was defeated.[7] And the negative feedback from the bill's failure was a contributing factor in the lack of legislative progress on climate change for over a decade.

Cap-and-trade is not the only policy to spark a high-profile backlash in recent years. In spring 2018, the Donald Trump administration began separating migrant parents from their children to deter illegal border crossings. No previous administration had split apart families as a matter of official policy. In an address announcing the new "zero tolerance" regime, Attorney General Jeff Sessions stated, "If you are smuggling a child, then we will prosecute you, and that child will be separated from you as required by law."[8] When media outlets disseminated heart-wrenching images of children in cages, outraged Americans began holding protests across the country, many at Immigration and Customs Enforcement (ICE) facilities. The single largest event—organized by progressive groups like the National Domestic Workers Alliance—was the nationwide "Families Belong Together" protest, which took place in more than seven hundred cities.[9] Surveys show that only about one in four Americans supported family separations, making it one of the most unpopular policies of recent decades.[10] World leaders, business executives, and Pope Francis denounced the policy as immoral. On Capitol Hill, Democrats amplified the public backlash. Most Republican lawmakers initially held back, refusing to support Democratic measures to end separations at the border. As the public outcry reached a crescendo, however, some Republicans broke ranks with the administration. Trump finally caved and signed an executive order rescinding the policy.[11]

At first blush, the cap-and-trade and family separation cases would seem to have little in common. And yet, at a deeper level, both episodes are illustrative of a common pattern in governance: the politics of policy backlash. Policy backlashes occur when a change (or attempted change) in the policy status quo stimulates widely noticed resistance. Backlashes come in many forms, from voter blowbacks and spontaneous grassroots protests to elite-led countermobilizations. All arise within what David Mayhew calls the "public sphere"—the realm of politics featuring "uncertainty, open deliberation and discussion, opinion formation, strutting and ambition, surprises, endless public moves and countermoves by politicians and other actors, rising and falling issues, and an attentive and sometimes participating audience of large numbers of citizens."[12] As Mayhew argues, what occurs within the public sphere encompasses a great deal of what anyone would consider politically important. To be sure, strategic actors can also exercise power at the subterranean level. But while backlashes are only a subset of power relations, they are an important one. Backlashes shape the prospects for policy adoption and sustainability. They can affect policy agendas, the sustainability of reforms, and the alignment of political coalitions. Conspicuous, contentious, and at times enormously consequential for governance, policy backlashes are an integral part of American politics, and they merit close attention.

What policy attributes tend to produce backlashes in U.S. government? Which actors have participated in major backlashes in U.S. politics in recent years, and what have been their objectives? What roles do both elites and mass publics play in backlash politics? Do policy backlashes in American politics have a dominant ideological direction? What happens *after* backlashes occur? How do backlashes shape ensuing rounds of policymaking? Why do loss-bearing constituencies sometimes *fail* to countermobilize? How has backlash politics shaped battles over the size and scope of the policy state? Finally, how can strategically oriented policymakers manage the risk and potency of backlashes in order to promote the durability of their accomplishments?

The Contemporary Backlash Moment

These questions are urgent ones for scholars, journalists, activists, and citizens. Backlash politics is at the heart of the contemporary U.S. policy state. A selective list of issues that have stimulated counterreactions since the 1960s includes the conservative backlashes against abortion, same-sex marriage, and civil rights; the labor union and environmentalist backlash to the North American Free Trade Agreement (NAFTA); the populist backlash against the government's "bailout" of Wall Street through the Troubled Assets Relief Program (TARP); the senior citizen backlash against the Medicare Catastrophic Coverage Act (MCCA); the public backlash against managed care plans in the 1990s; the consumer backlash against a 1970s federal mandate that new cars include a seatbelt interlock mechanism (which prevented drivers from starting their vehicles if they weren't buckled up); the parental backlash against "high-stakes" testing in public schools; the conservative backlash against the Affordable Care Act (ACA); the protests against COVID-19 restrictions issued by governors and state public health agencies; and the public backlash against the Supreme Court's decision in *Dobbs v. Jackson Women's Health Organization* eliminating the national right to abortion.

Policy backlashes can be sparked by decisions that never were popular or had organizational support, such as Jimmy Carter's standby gasoline-rationing plan or the Ronald Reagan administration's proposal to cut the Social Security benefits of early retirees. Backlashes can be set off by a recent action, as occurred in 2005 when Amtrak executives announced—without alerting Congress beforehand—that there would be a massive fare hike for commuters. The intense blowback forced Amtrak's executives to postpone the increase.[13]

Backlashes can also be triggered by a series of developments that finally cross a threshold.[14] For example, the backlash stimulated by the adoption of a liberal civil rights plank in the Republican Party's 1960 platform was a response to the pent-up anger among racial conservatives about the "growing disconnect" between the Republican Party's leadership and the views of "rank-and-file party activists and officials on civil rights."[15] Finally, backlashes can occur when a policy produces new costs due to a failure to update its rules to reflect a changing external context (a process called "policy drift").[16] For example, homeowners sometimes mobilize against increases in property taxes based on assessed market value, even when underlying property tax rates remain stable.[17]

Policy backlashes are not a new phenomenon in American democracy. The early republic featured countermobilizations against attempts by the national government to assert its authority. In 1791, Treasury Secretary Alexander Hamilton proposed to fund the debts that states had incurred during the Revolutionary War by imposing a federal excise tax on distilled spirits. The plan sparked protests and violence from farmers and citizens living in the nation's western frontier. The controversy continued for four years until President George Washington mobilized a militia to put down the insurrection.[18]

The Alien and Sedition Acts of 1798 also spurred backlash. A Federalist-dominated Congress feared that enemy spies would weaken national security as war with France loomed. Accordingly, lawmakers passed these notorious acts to outlaw antigovernment speech, increase residency requirements for citizenship, and empower the president to deport aliens deemed to be a threat.[19] The measures incensed ordinary citizens, newspaper editors, and leaders of the Democratic-Republican opposition. Thomas Jefferson and James Madison secretly drafted resolutions for the Kentucky and Virginia state legislatures criticizing the laws as unconstitutional usurpations of power. Jefferson warned that if the acts were allowed to stand, it would drive the states into "revolution and blood and [would] furnish new calumnies against republican government, and new pretexts for those who wish it to be believed that man cannot be governed but by a rod of iron."[20] Protests took place in many states and voter backlash contributed to the Federalists' defeat in the 1800 election. Both political elites and everyday citizens participated in this counterreaction. As historian Douglas Bradburn writes, "This mobilization cannot be completely seen as either a bottom-up or a top-down story; it must be seen as a process of politics in motion in the early Republic, a representative politics before the institutionalization of a party system. Newspaper editors were key actors, yet so were the elites, and none of them could function or gain influence without the participation of hundreds of local citizens giving voice to their complaints in formal petitions."[21]

The most tragic backlash episode in American history occurred during and after the First Reconstruction. Hundreds of thousands of previously enslaved persons cast ballots for the first time, and some Black Republicans were elected to public offices. While these developments brought the nation closer to achieving its democratic ideals, they also triggered a reactive sequence of acts of paramilitary violence and white supremacist countermobilization. The backlashers included both ordinary citizens who participated in terrorist groups like the Ku Klux Klan and political elites who served on a commission that agreed to withdraw federal troops in the South in exchange for the Democrats conceding the disputed 1876 presidential election to Republican nominee, Rutherford B. Hayes.[22] As Richard M. Valelly writes, these backlash processes were protracted, but they ultimately "reduced black voting and black elected office-holding in the ex-Confederacy to approximately zero."[23] Black Americans in the South were virtually shut out of the democratic process until the enactment of the Voting Rights Act of 1965.

While there are many differences between the nineteenth century and contemporary American politics, we are living in another contentious era. What makes the contemporary period distinctive is less the intensity of the backlash forces it has unleashed than the *range* of policy sectors in which counterreactions are occurring. Backlash politics has penetrated into virtually every domestic arena, from education and the environment to immigration and trade.

My analysis develops a policy-centered framework for exploring the politics of backlash and countermobilization. My central thesis is that backlash politics is partly an endogenous response to the attributes of public policies themselves. Not all attempts to shift the policy status quo carry major risks of backlash. It makes an enormous difference how and when policies distribute perceived benefits and costs, whether they are in synch with the preferences and priorities of voters, and whether they bolster or disrupt existing arrangements to which people are strongly attached. These factors help explain why some policy moves are much more likely to trigger adverse reactions than others. Yet backlashes are not a product of policy feedback effects alone. They are also shaped by the incentives for countermobilization created by the evolving political context.

Backlash politics has become a common pattern in the modern U.S. policy state for three key reasons. The first is hyperpolarization. Whether driven by ideological differences over the role of government or strategic incentives to win elections in an era of razor-thin majorities, today party leaders increasingly engage in backlash politics. Participating in backlash politics enables them to activate their base supporters, direct attention away from party positions that expose fissures within their coalitions (or that are unpopular with swing voters), and battle their partisan rivals on more favorable terrain.[24] To be sure, policy backlashes are not always partisan. For example, the Joe Biden administration's proposal to make it harder for charter schools to qualify for federal funds sparked backlash from leaders of both parties, as well as from charter school operators and angry parents.[25] Backlashes can also occur *within* parties. For example, conservative Republicans revolted against President George H. W. Bush in 1990 for breaking his "read my lips" pledge not to raise taxes.[26] Yet partisan backlashes are easily triggered in a polarized age, especially when major policy reforms like the ACA are adopted on party-line votes.

Second, and relatedly, American culture and society have changed dramatically since the early 1960s. As a result of large-scale immigration, the U.S. population has become more racially and ethnically diverse.[27] Black Americans, the LGBTQ community, and other marginalized groups have gained rights and acceptance. Millions of people have embraced these changes in American society, and public opinion has moved leftward on many issues like same-sex marriage and women's equality.[28] Yet many noncollege graduates, religious conservatives, and white residents of rural communities who hold traditionalist values have felt threatened by the growing secularism and diversity of American society.[29] Some everyday citizens have found the changes disorientating and claim they feel like "strangers in their own land."[30] The political divide between urban and small-town America has become a chasm.[31] The culture wars exacerbate policy backlash by focusing debates over issues like immigration and education less on whether specific government interventions would solve concrete problems and more on what they signal about the relative status of identity groups in a rapidly changing polity.

The final trend spurring backlash politics is the policy feedback from the expansion of activist government itself. As Bryan D. Jones, Sean M. Theriault, and Michelle Whyman discuss in their superb book *The Great Broadening*, the federal government significantly widened the range of its responsibilities between the late 1950s and mid-1970s.[32] The expansion of national policymaking activity generated powerful interest-group feedbacks. Many programs offered money and other resources to a host of constituencies, including senior citizens and health care providers. These groups possess the capacity to mobilize when their benefit flows are threatened.[33] At the same time, the broadening of the federal government's role imposed costs on actors such as business corporations, stimulating their countermobilization. As a result of these dynamics, the U.S. interest-group system grew larger and more complex. As Beth Leech and colleagues argue, the growth of the federal government functioned like a magnet, "pulling groups of all kinds to become active."[34]

As a general matter, the expansion of the policy state has been a liberal project. As I show in chapter 2, when policy backlashes have an ideological orientation, they disproportionately involve adverse reactions from the right. I find that conservative backlash intensifies as the number of liberal laws increases. And yet liberals—alarmed by the increasing radicalism of the Republican Party—have become increasingly active participants in backlash politics as well. In a comprehensive study of congressional efforts to repeal major statutes, Jordan M. Ragusa and Nathaniel A. Birkhead show that the volume of repeal bills proposed by Republican members of Congress *doubled* between the 1950s and 2016.[35] To be sure, many domestic programs are protected by supportive constituencies. The conservative effort to kill the welfare state has largely failed, at least so far.[36] As Matt Grossmann and David A. Hopkins argue, "Republican politicians are often much more effective at fomenting popular backlash to the perceived overreach of Democrats than they are in dismantling Democratic policies."[37] Nonetheless, liberals are having to countermobilize against attacks on their past achievements. As Karen Orren and Stephen Skowronek argue, "Progressives have been playing defense, fighting on all fronts to repel policy encroachments on victories seemingly won—labor's right to bargain collectively, African Americans' right to vote, women's 'right to choose,' everyone's right to health care and security in old age."[38]

The legal and social science literatures on civil rights and abortion, gay rights, immigration, and business countermobilization contain scattered empirical insights, but these insights have not been brought together in a unified framework that foregrounds the politics of policymaking. Policy backlash requires an integrated, *political* analysis. Providing such an analysis is the aim of this book.

The Literature on Backlash

The literature on backlash politics contains two distinct strands. The first analyzes backlash as an intrinsically conservative (reactionary) response. A major focus is the history of white backlash as a brake on racial progress. The second body of research adopts a more inclusive, neutral definition of backlash, analyzing it as a negative reaction to *any* challenge to the status quo. My analysis builds primarily on the latter strand, which accommodates the investigation of different types of backlash across multiple issues.[39]

Accounts of reactionary backlash argue that it is the product of resentment among privileged groups whose status is eroding. For example, in their

1970 history of right-wing extremism in the United States, *The Politics of Unreason*, Seymour Martin Lipset and Earl Raab defined backlash as the "reaction by groups which are declining in a felt sense of importance, influence, and power, as a result of secular endemic change in the society."[40] In a 2020 essay, historian Lawrence Glickman argues that white backlash is a "reactionary tradition, one that is deeply woven into American political culture and that extends back to the era of Reconstruction, at least." Glickman identifies the "constituent elements of white backlash to the civil-rights movement: its smoldering resentment, its belief that the movement was proceeding 'too fast,' its demands for emotional and psychological sympathy, and its displacement of African Americans' struggles with its own claims of grievance."[41] This is a discerning body of work. It highlights continuities in the rhetoric of reactionary backlash over time and provides a reminder that conservative backlashers possess agency, even when they cast themselves as victims.[42]

While the literature on reactionary backlash offers potent insights into the psychology of conservative resentment, it has also generated critical scholarly engagement. Vesla Weaver's assessment and recasting of this literature is especially creative and penetrating.[43] Defining backlash as "the politically and electorally expressed public resentment that arises from perceived racial advance, intervention, or excess," Weaver raises a number of excellent points that any framework for understanding the politics of backlash in general should address.[44] First, she suggests that the backlash thesis fails to elucidate its "unique characteristics."[45] Second, she argues that research assumes that backlash is automatic (like a "bungee cord that snaps when stretched too far"), yet not all policy changes provoke adverse reactions.[46] Finally, she argues that research on backlash tends to attribute agency solely to mass publics, downplaying the entrepreneurial role of political elites in steering backlashes.

Weaver develops the alternative concept of "frontlash," meaning "the process by which formerly defeated groups may become dominant issue entrepreneurs in light of the development of a new issue campaign."[47] She argues that the emergence of punitive crime policy during the mid- to late 1960s originated in the efforts of elite opponents of civil rights and the legal norm of racial equality to reassert their power and agenda control after policy setbacks. "Aided by two prominent focusing events—crime and riots—issue entrepreneurs articulated a problem in a new, ostensibly unrelated domain—the problem of crime. The same actors who had fought vociferously against civil rights legislation, defeated, shifted the 'locus of attack' by injecting crime onto the agenda," she writes.[48] Weaver persuasively demonstrates the coalitional linkages between contestation over civil rights and crime policy. Her analysis places less emphasis, however, on the agency of ordinary citizens. While political elites play a critical role in amplifying—and sometimes instigating—backlashes, they cannot always foresee public backlashes or manage their effects. As Monica Prasad argues, the lesson of the 2016 U.S. presidential election is that "policies that leave behind significant segments of the population will generate a backlash that cannot be controlled, even by those who promote those policies or who benefit in the short term from the backlash."[49]

A subtle but critical distinction between frontlash and many of the counter-reactions discussed in this book is that the segregationists and racial conservatives in Weaver's account recognized that they had lost the legislative battle. While the civil rights movement generated a ferocious backlash, the losing actors knew that the landmark Civil Rights Act of 1964—which passed with bipartisan support in Congress—would not be repealed. Accordingly, conservative opponents of civil rights shifted tactics, seeking out more favorable policy terrain—the crime control domain—in which to reclaim their lost power. Yet backlashers do not always regard policy losses as irreversible nor feel compelled to move to a new issue arena. For example, conservative backlashers were unwilling to concede that the ACA would stick. On the contrary, they invested substantial political resources in a decade-long campaign to dismantle the law and won the repeal of several of its key provisions, including the individual mandate, the "Cadillac tax," and the Independent Payment Advisory Board.

Another limitation of this literature for understanding the politics of policy backlash is that many participants in backlash episodes are vested interests (such as business corporations, trade associations, professional societies, and labor unions) that are motivated to countermobilize less by status anxieties or trepidation about cultural change than by a desire to maintain their existing material benefits and organizational prerogatives.[50] Finally, not all ideologically tinged backlash is conservative. Attempts to withdraw social rights or scale back public benefits can also provoke counterreactions among organized groups and voters, as the public backlash to the overturning of the *Roe v. Wade* decision suggests. *Right-wing identity politics and policy backlash are frequent traveling companions, but they are not synonymous.*

A second group of social scientists, while recognizing that most backlash empirically comes from the right, argue that the phenomenon of backlash cannot be reduced to conservative resentment. They have opted for a more inclusive definition of backlash that permits an analysis of the similarities and differences in political dynamics across a wider range of cases. My study builds on this line of scholarship. In seeking to "carve out an analytically useful term from the cluster of its common political associations," Jane Mansbridge and Shauna L. Shames define backlash as the "use of coercive power to

regain lost power as capacity."[51] Their definition has three components—a reaction (a lashing back), the instrumental exercise of power, and the objective
of regaining power (meaning the capacity to turn preferences into outcomes).
More recently, Karen J. Alter and Michael Zürn offered another inclusive,
neutral definition of backlash. Viewing backlash as a type of contentious politics, their definition includes the "following three necessary elements: (1) a
retrograde objective of returning to a prior social condition, (2) extraordinary goals and tactics that challenge dominant scripts, and (3) a threshold
condition of entering mainstream public discourse."[52] The Alter and Zürn
definition is helpful, but for my purposes it cuts too deeply by requiring backlashes to involve "extraordinary" goals or tactics. This stipulation excludes
voter blowbacks, letter-writing campaigns, and many other "ordinary" forms
of backlash that regularly occur in American politics.

A key distinction between mobilization and countermobilization is the
relationship of actors to the status quo. Without this reference point, it becomes difficult to distinguish analytically (not substantively) between movements seeking to bring about social transformation (e.g., Black Lives Matter)
and countermovements seeking to resist it (e.g., Blue Lives Matter). To be
sure, the conceptual distinction between mobilization and countermobilization can be a bit fuzzy in practice. Once a large policy regime is in place,
political advocacy will inevitably have to take past policies into account. Yet
there is a fundamental difference between mobilizing to resist permanent
losses and mobilizing to achieve durable gains. Backlashers can be preemptive, acting before a formal policy change has been enacted. Even when backlashers are early movers, however, they are reacting to what they *perceive* to
be a threat to their interests, values, or power resources. For example, in 2023
a comment by the commissioner of the Consumer Product Safety Commission that his agency might consider banning gas stoves over health concerns
generated a firestorm from the oil and gas industry and Republican lawmakers.[53] Many observers argued this was an overreaction, pointing out correctly
that a federal ban on gas stoves was not about to happen—the agency was not
even considering putting a proposal on its agenda. Yet there is a politically
engaged network of environmentalists who aim to regulate gas stoves, and
New York state and some cities have already begun to ban gas hookups in
new buildings. Countermobilization to block the diffusion of such policies
is a predictable response by industry actors and conservatives who seek to
prevent this movement from gaining momentum.

Another complication is that the location of the status quo changes over
time. Prolife groups were countermobilizing during the 1970s and 1980s when
abortion rights were liberalizing (relative to the baseline of the 1950s and

early 1960s), but today prochoice groups (reacting to the loss of reproductive rights) are the ones lashing back. Another wrinkle is that backlash movements rarely are *completely* backward-looking; they often seek to reclaim a lost past (as they remember it) in order to construct a better future.[54] Yet, as Alter and Zürn argue, even when countermovements have positive goals for reform, "backlash politics necessarily contains a retrograde objective."[55]

Research Approach

Most of the research on U.S. policy backlash has focused only on select issues like civil rights and abortion. These are critical topics for study, but they provide a truncated picture of the politics of backlash and countermobilization. When have adverse reactions among mass publics, organized groups, or political elites occurred in the modern U.S. policy state, and in what policy sectors? Which actors have been involved in them? Are conspicuous backlashes occurring more frequently now than in the 1960s? Unfortunately, no database exists to answer questions like these. My research strategy is to combine empirical analysis of media-identified backlashes and detailed case studies of key domestic arenas.

As high-profile events in the public sphere, backlashes receive extensive media coverage. I created a database on backlash episodes using *New York Times* (*NYT*) articles. My research assistants and I coded articles mentioning the term *backlash* between 1960 and 2019. The result is a data set of nearly two thousand articles. We analyzed the articles across multiple dimensions, including whether the backlashes had already materialized or were anticipated, the major actors involved, and the ideological directions of each counterreaction. Many important events appear in this data set, including the backlash against civil rights in the 1960s; business countermobilization against the environmental and consumer legislation of the 1970s; the conservative backlash against women's rights and abortion rights; the public backlash against immigration during the 1980s; the managed care backlash in the 1990; the backlashes against education reform, government surveillance, gay rights, and free trade during the 2000s; and the countermobilization against the ACA and immigration control policies during the 2010s. It would be difficult to recount modern U.S. political history without reference to these episodes. Any account of how policies create a new politics needs to acknowledge them.

Using *NYT* articles to identify and measure backlash trends does have several limitations, however. The articles describe negative reactions to policy developments but do not necessarily indicate whether these views are broadly shared. The data set thus captures opposition thrusts, not public opinion. For example, many *NYT* articles report on the backlash of social and religious conservatives against gay rights during the 2010s, a period during which the overall public was becoming much more accepting of gay people.[56] The database is also not a reliable source on policy resistance that occurs under the radar. The media skews toward issue areas that are highly salient to voters, such as civil rights, health care, and education. In addition, the *NYT* is only one source, and its portrayal of backlash politics could be idiosyncratic. I address these concerns in a number of ways in chapter 2. For example, I show that the *NYT* measure captures prominent backlashes mentioned by historians and that it is not simply a reflection of changes in the use of the term *backlash* in the language.

A deeper concern about analyzing media-identified backlashes is that journalists have a bias for conflict. In order to pique the interest of their audiences (while maintaining professional norms of objectivity and balance), journalists often portray policymaking as a battle between combatants rather than an exercise in collective problem-solving. Using a conflict frame to portray public affairs clearly influences political elites' incentives and ordinary citizens' attitudes. Indeed, Mary Layton Atkinson demonstrates that the media's focus on the contentiousness of the legislative process contributes to public backlash against important enactments.[57] This empirical finding is consistent with Mayhew's argument that "society's preference formation" is "substantially endogenous" to the public sphere, of which the media is an essential part.[58] This is not a major problem for this part of my study, however, as my main research goals here are descriptive. I seek to identify episodes in which counterreactions have entered the consciousness of political elites and politically attentive citizens since 1960 and to explore when they occurred, what sectors they occurred in, and who the key players were. *NYT* coverage is a reasonable source for questions like these. How backlash dynamics would change if media coverage were more focused on policy substance and less on political conflict is a fascinating counterfactual question that lies beyond the scope of my analysis.

The most serious limitation of the *NYT* database for understanding the politics of backlash is that news articles only provide "snapshots" of reactions to policy changes or threats at single moments of time. Yet, as Paul Pierson has persuasively argued, what we really need in order to understand political life are not snapshots but "moving pictures."[59] To investigate how policy dynamics unfold over extended periods of time, I conducted detailed case studies of policy development in the following areas: health care, immigration, trade, civil rights (the efforts to withdraw tax subsidies from segregated schools and to recognize transgender rights), and gun control. I selected these areas for three reasons. First, they include policy sectors that my analysis of *NYT* articles identifies as high-backlash domains. Second, they illustrate how backlashes can be generated by a range of policy attributes, including concentrated costs and challenges to settled arrangements. Finally, they include cases that political scientists and historians have identified as substantively important.

Drawing on the secondary literature, I analyze the politics of each backlash along several dimensions, including what specific policy attributes and contextual factors encouraged it, when the backlash occurred (before, during, or after policy enactment), what forms it took, and whether it followed a change (or anticipated change) in the scope or scale of government activities or a shift in the distribution, timing, or salience of benefits and costs. I also explore the major consequences of the backlashes for ensuing patterns of governance.

A Preview of the Argument

While government policies can build supportive coalitions, they can also mobilize powerful opposition forces. Backlash politics is a core pattern in contemporary American democracy for several reasons. First, the U.S. political system provides many venues for redress, which enables defenders of the status quo to "shop" for an institutional setting where they can block change.[60] In addition, public opinion is "thermostatic": on many issues, citizens' attitudes become more liberal when conservatives are in power and more conservative when liberals control the government.[61] The public often responds to major changes in the direction of policy not by demanding more of the same but rather by increasing its support for politicians who promise to slow things down or reverse course. Finally, the amplification of backlashes is an attractive strategy for the management of partisan coalitions in an era of polarization.

My central thesis is that policy backlashes are not random or wholly unpredictable events but rather the product of motives, means, and political opportunities. I operationalize this claim by examining the influence of three factors. The first is *policy attributes*. By virtue of their design elements, some policies contain the potential to produce negative feedback because they impose costs on constituency groups, overreach public opinion, or fail to respect reliance interests (commitments that people have made in expectation that an existing policy or arrangement will continue). The second factor is the *internal capacity of constituencies for civic participation and engagement*. Whether by voting, protesting, or petitioning government officials, groups require the participatory means to resist challenges to the status quo. Not all constituencies possess such mobilization capacities, however. Some loss-bearing or threatened groups are unable to defend their interests or values due to a lack of resources or an inability to overcome the barriers to collective action, which is one reason why backlashes are not automatic.[62] Finally, the *political opportunity structure* supplies external incentives for countermobilization. Key elements of the opportunity structure include the level of partisan conflict, the existence of divisions among elites, and the presence of influential allies who can provide support and negotiating leverage to loss-bearing constituencies.[63]

The role of these factors can be seen in this introduction's two opening vignettes. In the cap-and-trade episode, backlashers possessed both material and ideological motives for countermobilization. Everyday citizens worried that the cap-and-trade bill would raise their electricity prices. Industry groups wished to maintain the policy status quo, which involved producing energy without having to internalize the cost of pollution. And Tea Party conservatives viewed the cap-and-trade bill as a threat to individual freedom. In contrast, Trump's family separation policy was a clear case of overreach. The overwhelming majority of Americans considered the separation of migrant children from their parents to be an unacceptably cruel solution to the problem of unauthorized immigration, even if they favored stronger border security. The policy simply went too far. In both cases, the political opportunity structure was conducive to backlash politics. The presence of divided elites helped to amplify and legitimate the grassroots countermobilizations. And backlashers in both cases received crucial support and organizational assistance from key allies in their institutional networks.

My analysis suggests that both political elites and mass publics play important roles in backlash politics. Political elites choose whether to stoke, amplify, or suppress public backlashes based on their incentives. Elites can also shape mass opinion, especially on novel issues where everyday citizens lack direct experience. For example, if President Trump had been promask from the beginning of the COVID-19 pandemic, it is likely many of his followers would have been on board with mask wearing rather than railing against it. Yet on many issues such as electricity prices and religious service restrictions imposed during the pandemic, everyday citizens develop their own perceptions of policy effects. These perceptions can fuel grassroots protests and other types of popular countermobilization that elites cannot always control.

Policy backlashes per se are not good or bad. At times, backlash politics can strengthen democratic accountability by punishing officeholders who support measures that fail to reflect the priorities and preferences of ordinary voters. Indeed, *without* the possibility of backlash and countermobilization, slippages of political representation would be far less likely to be corrected.[64] Backlashes can even promote political learning by helping policymakers discover what types of policy solutions are acceptable to the public—and thus more likely to be enacted and sustained. As I discuss in the conclusion, Democrats passed landmark climate legislation in 2022 without generating a public backlash by abandoning the policy design strategy they had used to craft the cap-and-trade bill. Rather than making polluters pay for their emissions, they provided subsidies to industry and consumers to switch to clean-energy technologies. In sum, they learned that carrots are more palatable than sticks.[65]

Yet it would be incorrect to suggest that backlash politics guarantees either smooth equilibration or the promotion of the public good. Backlashers sometimes mobilize against policies that provide large net benefits to society, promote equality, or deliver assistance to marginalized groups. Just the mere expectation of triggering backlash can cast a shadow over governance, narrowing the set of policy options that are considered in the first place. It can even lead policymakers to neglect their duty to safeguard democratic rights. Backlash politics can result in the adoption of policies designed as much to minimize pushback as to solve problems. Yet if policymakers plunge ahead without taking heed of backlash risks, they may fail to ensure the political feasibility and sustainability of their reform proposals. The targeted beneficiaries of the reforms could even be left worse off. These are complex governance dilemmas, and different actors, such as elected officials, advocates, and political organizers, may choose to accept different trade-offs based on their goals, incentives, and time horizons. Regardless of its normative consequences, policy backlash should be recognized as a fundamental pattern in governance, which is as central to the politics of policymaking as increasing returns and self-sustaining processes.

The Plan of the Book

In the chapters that follow, I explore the politics of policy backlash in modern American politics. Chapter 1 is a conceptual chapter. It draws on the literatures on policy feedback, postloss power-building, and political opportunity structures to provide a framework for understanding the conditions that are most conducive to backlash. In addition, the chapter discusses how backlashes shape downstream outcomes by producing either self-undermining or reactive sequences.

Chapter 2 presents the core findings of my analysis of the *NYT* database on articles about backlash since 1960. The analysis shows that backlash forces have diffused across issue arenas over time. While backlash was mainly confined to civil rights in the 1960s, today it impinges on nearly every domestic arena. Chapters 3 through 6 feature detailed case studies of the politics of backlash in a number of sectors. Chapter 3 examines health care. Chapter 4 looks at immigration and trade, the two issues at the heart of the antiglobalization backlash. In chapter 5, I examine three cases in which conservatives countermobilized against perceived threats to their interests, institutions, and values: withdrawal of the tax-exempt status of private, segregated schools; the threat of tighter gun restrictions (the rise of "Second Amendment sanctuaries"); and the recognition of transgender rights. And in chapter 6, I examine three instances where policymakers imposed losses on constituencies or provided benefits to negatively constructed clienteles yet backlash forces were muted: the savings and loan bailout, Reagan's firing of striking air traffic controllers, and the provision of social benefits like food stamps to convicted drug felons.

In the conclusion, I pull together my main findings about the causes and consequences of backlash politics in the policy state. I discuss how backlash dynamics may change going forward now that conservatives possess a Supreme Court supermajority and have a greater ability to attack liberal policy accomplishments that had long been considered safe. In addition, I offer practical suggestions for how advocates of activist government can recognize backlash risks and take steps to design policies to manage or prevent them. The takeaway lesson is *not* that policy backlash should be avoided at all costs. Making good policy decisions may require taking politically perilous actions, such as imposing losses on powerful constituencies. Nonetheless, strategic policymakers are more likely to retain power and to preserve their policy legacies if they confront the possible adverse reactions to their projects without illusions rather than simply hope they will not happen.

Understanding Policy Backlash

Social Security demonstrates that public policies can experience dramatic growth without stimulating public opposition. The number of Social Security recipients climbed from about three million in 1950 to more than twenty-five million twenty years later.[1] Congress increased Social Security benefits significantly over the postwar era, which built a large, supportive constituency. Remarkably, workers and retirees today are "equally supportive" of the program.[2] Both groups favor *more* spending on Social Security, not less. Social Security is a classic demonstration of E. E. Schattschneider's observation that "new policies create a new politics."[3]

Yet public policies do not always cultivate clienteles, generate increasing returns, or stimulate reliance interests. Some policies do not create positive feedback because their designs are flawed (e.g., they fail to confer substantial, visible benefits on a mobilizable constituency) or because they were enacted at the wrong moment.[4] And some policies produce adverse reactions, generating self-undermining feedback that energizes opposition coalitions and impairs the policies' own entrenchment and expansion.[5] What types of policies tend to cause people to lash back at government? When are threatened groups likely to countermobilize—and when will they absorb material losses or attacks on their values without mounting a resistance? What happens *after* backlashes begin? This chapter addresses these questions by synthesizing insights from the literatures on self-undermining policy feedback, legislative politics, postloss power-building, vested interests, and social movements.[6] As a preface to this discussion, I discuss broader patterns facilitating backlash and countermobilization in the American political system.

The U.S. Political System as a Setting for Backlash Politics

Policy backlashes are not unique to the United States. They can occur in any polity in which people can mobilize against government decisions. European democracies experienced a wave of backlash politics during the 2010s. For example, in 2018 French President Emmanuel Macron was forced to abandon a planned increase in the fuel tax in response to pressure from protesters called the *gilets jaunes* (yellow vests).[7] In 2017, a furious public backlash led British prime minister Theresa May to ditch a Tory proposal to change the way residential long-term care is funded. Under the plan—which critics dubbed a "dementia tax"—long-term care patients would have been required to "forfeit all but 100,000 pounds (around $130,000) of their assets, including the value of their property."[8] And Chancellor Angela Merkel faced right-wing backlash in 2015 for waiving a European Union law that required refugees to apply for asylum in the first European country they entered, which led to the influx of hundreds of thousands of refugees into Germany.[9]

But while backlash is not uniquely an American phenomenon, several features of the U.S. political system confer advantages on actors seeking to defend the status quo. First, the Madisonian system is fragmented. Congress and the presidency share governing powers and the federal government and the states exercise overlapping public authority in many policy domains.[10] The implementation of national policies frequently requires cooperation from the states, and presidents regularly struggle to obtain buy-in. For example, many conservative states rejected Medicaid expansion during the Barack Obama administration, while the Trump administration "encountered strong opposition from Democratic-leaning states challenging administration policy on immigration, environment, and health policy."[11] In addition, U.S. courts play a much more expansive role in governance than their counterparts abroad, which allows actors who lose in other venues to challenge their opponents in court.[12] As Terry M. Moe argues, "The American government system is literally designed, therefore, to make blocking—and thus defending the status quo—far easier than taking positive action. The advantage always goes to the side that wants to keep things as they are."[13]

Second, U.S. public opinion is thermostatic on many (though not all) issues.[14] When liberals are in power and policy moves to the left, public opinion typically becomes more conservative. And when conservatives are in power and policy moves to the right, public opinion typically becomes more liberal.[15] Ordinary citizens react negatively when politicians overshoot. As Matt Grossmann and Christopher Wlezien write, "Rather than reward ideological ambition, voters appear to check the incumbent party with more votes for the opposition when they go beyond voters' expectations."[16] To be sure, thermostatic backlash is a short-run negative feedback. It remains a matter of scholarly debate whether and under what conditions policy changes provoke *enduring* public opinion backlashes.[17] But quick, negative public responses to the direction of public policy are an empirical regularity.[18] When leaders of the out-party, organized groups, or other elite actors challenge a president's agenda items, they often have the winds of public opinion at their backs.

Finally, the U.S. electoral system is distinctive. The United States holds more elections, for more offices, than many other wealthy democracies.[19] Whether due to thermostatic public opinion or greater motivation among opponents of the president's party, midterm voters usually "balance ideologically against the party controlling the White House by trimming its seat shares on Capitol Hill."[20] Over the postwar era, the president's party has lost an average of twenty-two House seats and three Senate seats in the midterms.[21] As Frances Lee observes, "In the polarized era, midterm elections have resulted in repeated, severe backlashes against sitting presidents, including a loss of majority control for the president's party in one or both chambers in 1986, 1994, 2006, 2010, 2014, and 2018."[22] The 2022 midterms (in which the Democrats retained their Senate majority and barely lost the House) is a fascinating partial exception to this pattern, and one that backlash politics helps to explain. This was the first election after the Supreme Court overturned *Roe v. Wade*. Voter anger over the decision (along with Republican nomination of extremist candidates and election deniers) helped Democrats beat historical expectations.[23] It is rare, however, for a party that controls both Congress and the presidency to suffer a policy defeat on the scale of the loss of the constitutional right to abortion.[24]

The drivers of midterm election results are voters' partisan identities, economic conditions, and presidential approval ratings.[25] Policy feedback is usually of secondary importance in determining election outcomes. But voter reactions to specific policy moves can sometimes have a significant impact as well. In some midterms, voters punish legislators who supported unpopular items on the president's agenda. As Mayhew observes:

> In focus here are particular policy initiatives of the previous two years that raise a storm. The midterm penalty [for the president's party] takes a special jump. Good cases recently are 1994, 2006, and 2010, when the Clinton legislative program, the Iraq war, and the Obama legislative program stirred blowback. These effects were apparently general—that is, overall net sags—but they can be seen cross-sectionally in the greater penalties suffered by House members of the president's party who cast roll calls *for* certain White House measures as opposed to those who voted *against* them.[26]

In analyzing the electoral margins of House Democrats in the 2010 midterms, David W. Brady, Morris P. Fiorina, and Arjun S. Wilkis show that Democrats might have saved their House majority if members from moderate districts had not supported the ACA and cap-and-trade.[27] This is not to suggest that Democrats were wrong to support these policies (the ACA has expanded health coverage for millions of Americans—a long-sought liberal accomplishment), but there was clearly a political cost to these decisions.[28]

Why would the in-party support policies that endanger its electoral majority? There are several possible reasons. First, policymakers may not recognize the likelihood of backlash. They can fall prey to the optimism trap, believing that voters will reward them for delivering change or that if there is opposition to policy moves, it will quickly die down. Based on interviews with congressional staffers, political scientist Eileen Burgin discovered that congressional Democrats in 2009–2010 were so consumed with the congressional battle to enact health reform that they gave inadequate attention to "venomous post-enactment partisanship, problems that delegated governance might generate, and the importance of cultivating supportive constituencies."[29]

In other instances, policymakers are aware that their proposals will provoke blowback but believe that the substantive gains will outweigh the political costs. A case in point is the Kansas-Nebraska Act, which enraged the North by reopening the bitter national debate over the spread of slavery. The vast majority of the northern Democrats who voted for the act lost their seats in the congressional elections of 1854 and 1855. Violence broke out between pro- and antislavery forces at Bleeding Kansas, killing more than fifty people. While these precise consequences may not have been foreseen, some scholars argue that "much of the nation understood with remarkable sophistication what perils lay ahead should Congress enact the Kansas-Nebraska legislation."[30] "I know [the measure] will raise a hell of a storm," Senator Stephen A. Douglas (D-IL) said.[31] Yet Douglas pressed forward, believing the act would advance his priorities: "national expansion, a Pacific railroad, and local self-government."[32]

Motives, Means, and Opportunities for Backlash Politics

When will policy developments elicit adverse reactions among citizens, organized groups, or political elites? As the product of politics in motion, backlashes are subject to contingency. How and when unique events unfold can affect the reactions that policies generate among members of the public.[33]

Yet backlashes are not random events. Whether actors react (or fail to react) negatively to policy developments depends on both policy substance and the context in which the policies are established. Consider the lack of backlash to the U.S. diplomatic overture to China in 1972. It is commonly agreed that "only Nixon could go to the China." The implication is that if a president without Nixon's reputation as an anticommunist hawk had tried to pull off the same foreign policy maneuver, there would have been ferocious blowback. But is this really true? By the time Nixon made his famous trek, the political situation was highly favorable to improving relations with China. U.S. policymakers of both parties were calling for rapprochement. There was relatively little conflict among foreign policy elites over this strategy. If Nixon "had not visited the People's Republic, other American politicians could have, and would have," writes one scholar.[34] In sum, contingent factors play a role in backlash politics (or its absence), but the influence of chance elements can be overstated. *When a policy backlash occurs, it is typically more like a rocket crashing due to design flaws than lightening striking out of a clear blue sky.*

Indeed, backlash risks can often be identified in advance, at least in their broad parameters.[35] My analysis stresses that policies are more likely to produce adverse reactions when *policy attributes* impose costs or threats that give affected groups motivations for resistance; when such groups possess the *internal capacities for civic participation and engagement*; and when the *political opportunity structure* supplies external incentives for countermobilization (figure 1.1). These factors are neither necessary nor sufficient conditions for backlash politics. My analysis presumes probabilistic, not determinative, causation. But they do help explain both the strength and the timing of backlash politics. Policies are more likely to elicit strong backlashes when all three factors are present. When one or more of the factors is missing, backlash forces are more likely to be anemic—or to gain strength only after the other factors come into play. I discuss each of these factors in more detail next.

MOTIVES: POLICY ATTRIBUTES

The risk of backlash politics is elevated when one or more of the following five policy attributes are present: concentrated costs; salient general costs; threats to the status of constituencies that are highly reliant on or strongly attached to existing arrangements; the provision of benefits to "undeserving" constituencies; and policymaking that fails to represent the preferences and priorities of voters (see table 1.1).[36]

Several preliminary points should be made. First, policy costs and threats are matters of *perceptions*, which may not correspond to the actual incidence of policy effects.[37] While cues from the media and opinion leaders are very important, people may also develop views about policy effects based on their

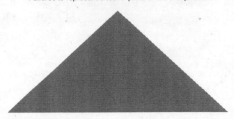

Motives (policy attributes)
– Concentrated costs
– Highly salient general costs
– Threats to existing arrangements to which people are strongly attached
– Provisions of benefits to "undeserving" groups
– Failures to represent citizens' preferences and priorities

Means (internal capacities of groups for participation and engagement)
– Resources
– Shared identities
– Interest-group representation

Political opportunities (external incentives for countermobilization)
– Divided elites
– Influential allies
– Partisan polarization

FIGURE 1.1. Motives, Means, and Opportunities for Backlash Politics

TABLE 1.1. Policy Attributes and Conditions Associated with Backlash

Policy Attribute	Favorable Conditions for Backlash
Concentrated costs	• Geographic costs • Group costs • Near-term costs
Salient general costs	• Large, visible costs • Shocks that increase the salience of policy effects • Presence of "instigators" who communicate with and educate mass publics
Threats to the status of people reliant on or strongly attached to existing arrangements	• Reforms that threaten the power and prerogatives of citizens and vested interests • Policies that expand the role of government in sectors dominated by private interests • Challenges to the autonomy of professional groups
Provision of benefits to the "undeserving"	• Provision of benefits to recipients not seen as needy, subject to forces beyond their control, and striving to become independent • "Last-place aversion"
Failures to represent the preferences and priorities of voters	• Incentives for policy overreaching due to close party balance and uncertainty of future control • Influence of party activists due to partisan sorting and polarization

experiences, their intuitions, and what others in their social networks believe.[38] Once the role of perceptions is acknowledged, it becomes reasonable to assume that citizens' *subjective* beliefs about how policies affect their self-interest will have a large influence on their policy preferences. This is true not only on issues where causal pathways are straightforward, like a gas tax hike, but also on more complex issues that affect people's interest along multiple dimensions, such as immigration.[39] Second, the five policy characteristics are analytically distinct but can occur together. Third, as Jonathan Oberlander and R. Kent Weaver observe, policies can generate both positive and self-undermining feedbacks simultaneously, and it is the balance between these effects "that matters politically."[40] Finally, backlash risk analysis is not a substitute for normative analysis. The fact that a mobilizable constituency views a policy as a loss from its perspective may be extremely important politically, but this does not imply that the policy would be harmful to society or to other groups.

Concentrated Costs

Building on work by James Q. Wilson and R. Douglas Arnold, my framework allows costs to be either economic or noneconomic.[41] Costs can be concentrated in two ways—cross-sectionally and temporally.[42] Cross-sectional concentration refers to costs that accrue disproportionately to people living in a particular area (*geographic concentration*) or to groups who share social identities, interests, or values, such as small business owners, evangelicals, or ethnic groups (*group concentration*).[43] An example of a backlash triggered by geographic costs is the building of clean-energy infrastructure. Leah Stokes has shown that citizens punish incumbent politicians for constructing nearby wind turbines.[44] Costs are also more likely to be noticed when they are concentrated in time. As Alan Jacobs and R. Kent Weaver observe, people are much more likely to become aware of policy costs when they are temporally concentrated than when "they take the form of a 'slow drip' of policy losses."[45] Imposing concentrated costs has a high probability of triggering backlashes for two reasons. First, as Arnold argues, concentrated costs are usually "traceable," meaning that affected constituencies can perceive the costs and link them back to identifiable government actions and to the decisions of specific actors (unless policymakers take steps to break traceability chains, preventing citizens from understanding how they are being harmed and whom to blame).[46] The second reason is the psychological phenomenon known as *loss aversion*—the tendency for people to react more intensely to a given amount of costs than to the same level of benefits.[47] Even when a policy delivers offsetting benefits, the losses will usually count more politically.

Highly Salient General Costs

In contrast to concentrated costs, general costs fall on all members of society and include "across-the-board tax increases, economic decline, inflation, health epidemics, and those losses of liberty associated with a bureaucratic state and a regulated economy."[48] General costs often escape public detection since they are not borne by a particular segment of society but rather dispersed broadly. Yet general costs can trigger intense negative public reactions under some conditions, such as when they become salient due to the economic or social context, the persuasion efforts of political elites, or policy attributes such as their magnitude.[49] Citizens are unlikely to notice a 3 percent cut in the budget of the Environmental Protection Agency (EPA), but they are likely to become incensed if their monthly internet service bill climbs by thirty dollars due to the implementation of a new tax. Various kinds of economic or political shocks can also increase the salience of general costs. For example, the adoption of the McKinley Tariff shortly before the 1890 midterm elections generated a sharp voter backlash due its association with a "sudden spike in consumer prices."[50] As Arnold points out, citizens may become aware of general costs when an "instigator" is available to help them understand their stakes in an issue.[51] For example, in 1973 an oil company attempted to "create a consumer backlash" against federal emission control requirements by taking out advertisements warning consumers that new federal pollution controls would be very expensive for car owners.[52]

Challenges to the Status of People Reliant on or Strongly Attached to Existing Arrangements

A third way that policies can trigger backlash is by threatening the status of people who depend on existing arrangements and wish to see them continue. For example, fears that the ACA would drain funds from Medicare and reduce the program's ability to meet the needs of existing beneficiaries engendered a backlash among senior citizens.

When groups organize to preserve their stakes in existing institutions, they become what Terry M. Moe calls "vested interests."[53] Vested interests may receive direct governmental benefits, such as a business that receives government contracts. In other instances, preexisting arrangements permit vested interests to manage their own affairs with a minimum of interference. The backlash to the growth of federal environmental regulations during the 1970s is an illustrative example. Many vested interests that were strongly attached to the prereform status quo viewed an expanded government role as a threat to their autonomy. As David Brian Robertson writes, "American farmers, ranchers, mine owners, and others became accustomed to exceptionally broad prerogatives over their environmental domains over two centuries."[54]

The new environmental laws challenged the long-accepted right of these actors to manage private lands and natural resources as they saw fit. By taking advantage of their institutional resources in a federal system, "those interests accustomed to insignificant interference with their control of the environment mobilized against these initiatives and enjoyed success in a number of states."[55] Some of the most powerful vested interests in the American policy state are professional associations, such as medical societies. For example, physicians countermobilize whenever policymakers cast a skeptical eye on the appropriateness of their clinical decisions and suggest that a common medical procedure may not be cost-effective.[56]

Provision of Benefits to the "Undeserving"

A fourth policy attribute that can provoke backlashes is the provision of benefits to a constituency that is constructed by policy as "undeserving."[57] As Theda Skocpol argues, "Institutional and cultural oppositions between the morally 'deserving' and the less deserving run like fault lines through the entire history of American social provision."[58] Research suggests that people define the deservingness of constituency groups using multiple criteria, including need, whether recipients are responsible for their particular situations, and whether they are striving be independent. The greater the level of need, the more recipients are believed to be subject to forces beyond their control, and the more they are seen as trying hard to make it on their own, the more they will be seen as deserving.[59] At the same time, beliefs about deservingness "are also strongly shaped by the construction of beneficiaries as belonging to particular gender, race, and class groups."[60] For example, the backlash against welfare spending has been fueled by racial stereotypes about Black Americans' commitment to the work ethic.[61]

Perceptions of deservingness are also shaped by people's relative position in the income distribution. Some research suggests that low-income individuals oppose redistributive programs that would seem to be in their self-interest because they fear they could assist a group just beneath them "to whom they can currently feel superior."[62] "Last-place aversion" helps explain the initial backlash against the ACA among the working poor. Some workers who both earned more than the threshold for Medicaid eligibility and faced high deductibles and copays for their own health insurance plans resented the fact that people who were unemployed could sign up for Medicaid, which offered better and cheaper insurance coverage than they themselves could obtain or afford.[63]

Failures to Represent the Preferences and Priorities of Voters

Finally, ordinary citizens may react negatively to policies that they believe are *not responding to their preferences and priorities.* While policymakers' electoral incentives might be expected to prevent this representational slippage from happening, Morris Fiorina argues that the combination of party sorting (the movement of voters into the party that matches their ideologies) and the closeness of the electoral competition between the Democrats and Republicans in recent decades has encouraged a "go-for-broke" mindset.[64] Knowing that their hold on authority may be temporary, partisan leaders may seek to leverage their power before it dissipates, prioritizing issues that are important to their party's base but much less important to others or adopting proposals and positions that are more extreme than those favored by their party's marginal supporters.

For example, when the House passed the cap-and-trade bill, only 30 percent of Americans said that addressing global warming was a priority.[65] Moreover, after the House vote, Democrats privately acknowledged that it would be a liability in the 2010 midterms.[66] Had Democrats been more confident that they would retain their majority, they might have chosen to wait until after the economy recovered from the Great Recession to advance such an ambitious bill, but they believed that if they did not act quickly, they might not have another chance. In sum, today's polarized parties possess incentives to "overreach," advancing proposals that contain the seeds of their own destruction. As Grossmann argues, "Partisans tell themselves that this time will be different, that the final vanquishing of their opponents is just around the corner. But even maintaining a narrow majority for more than four years would be unprecedented of late—much less winning a long-term partisan war. Rather, the historical record suggests that the price for enacting a large ideological policy agenda may be losing the very power that made it possible."[67]

Party sorting and the influence of party activists can also lead to overreaching that sparks backlashes. An example occurred when the Democrats unexpectedly picked up five House seats in the 1998 midterm elections—the first midterms since 1934 in which the president's party *gained* seats. Voter backlash against the GOP's impeachment of Bill Clinton for his affair with Monica Lewinsky was the major cause of this result.[68] While the Republicans who voted to impeach Clinton were responding to the preferences of Republican activists, the impeachment drive failed to reflect the preferences of the overall electorate. Most voters wanted Clinton to remain in office. As a result, while the impeachment drive did not harm Republican incumbents who held safe seats, it damaged those from marginal districts.

MEANS: INTERNAL CAPACITIES FOR CIVIC
PARTICIPATION AND ENGAGEMENT

The internal capacities of groups for civic participation and engagement comprise the second overarching factor that shapes backlash politics. Backlashes cannot gain momentum unless constituencies can exercise influence through participatory acts such as voting, contacting government officials, and joining rallies and protests. Such acts require time, money, and political knowledge. Groups whose members are wealthier and better educated, other things being equal, are much more likely to participate in backlashes than members of less advantaged constituencies, *even when the latter are disproportionately harmed*. In sum, the more the costs of policy changes are concentrated on marginalized groups, the less likely the policies are to trigger significant adverse reactions. This is a deeply troubling conclusion. Consider reactions to the Supreme Court's overruling of *Roe v. Wade*. As David A. Hopkins argues, whether the *Dobbs* decision will lead to a sustained, ferocious backlash in the coming years will depend in part on whether and how much antiabortion enforcement regimes at the national and state levels affect the middle class and those with political power who expect to be treated with respect:

> Will married thirty-something women of the bourgeoisie be left with permanent physical damage as a result of medical complications that could have been avoided with access to abortion procedures? Will their miscarriages be subjected to criminal investigation? Will they be denied fertility treatments, such as in-vitro fertilization, that involve the destruction of embryos? Will they be sent to prison for procuring illicit mifepristone pills, or face lawsuits for driving their daughters to clinics across state lines? The more the answer to these questions is yes, the more that dissatisfaction is likely to build across these women's well-connected social networks and provide fodder for news media stories and campaign commercials that portray them as victims of injustice.[69]

While the capacity of constituency groups to participate in backlashes is usually exogenous to particular battles, it can be endogenously strengthened over time by positive policy feedback. For example, senior citizens today are able to countermobilize against threats to their government benefits because Social Security has enhanced their ability to participate in the democratic process. As Andrea Campbell explains, while seniors "were once the least active age group in politics," they are now the most highly engaged. Social Security has given older Americans significant financial and political resources. In so doing, the program has enhanced their level of political interest and efficacy and created "incentives for interest groups to mobilize them by creating a political identity based on program recipiency."[70]

But some policies *do not* enhance the capacity of constituency groups to mobilize against threats.[71] For example, the U.S. welfare programs for families with dependent children, Aid to Families with Dependent Children and Temporary Assistance for Needy Families (AFDC/TANF), provide limited financial resources (the benefits are stingy) and send negative messages to recipients about their value to society. Research shows that these programs actually *lower* the political participation of enrollees.[72] The contrast between Social Security and welfare is even more stark with respect to interest-group representation. The national interest group for seniors, AARP, has millions of members and a multibillion-dollar annual budget. In contrast, while the National Welfare Rights Organization had around twenty-five thousand dues-paying members by the late 1960s, it disbanded in the mid-1970s due to conflicts over strategic direction and financial difficulties.[73] When Clinton signed legislation ending AFDC in 1996, there was no national interest group to mobilize a public backlash.

The most effective organizational leaders build the capacity of their groups to wage future battles. Over the past several decades, few membership-based interest groups have had more success in this regard than the National Rifle Association (NRA). As Matthew Lacombe argues, while the NRA has suffered some significant policy defeats, such as the Brady Act and the assault weapons ban during the 1990s, "the organization used these losses to strengthen shared identity among gun owners, which in turn boosted its membership and enhanced its mobilizational capacity in future contests."[74] By drawing their members' attention to the concentrated costs of gun regulations on its members (e.g., diminished freedom, waiting periods, additional paperwork, and higher fees), leaders of the NRA "actively cultivated shared grievances among its supporters, pointing to features of the new policies as evidence that they were being based on their status as gun owners."[75] These policy losses were not devastating for the NRA because they did not strip the organization of critical resources or undercut its mobilization capacity. But postloss power-building does not always happen. As Lacombe stresses, some political losses introduce collective action problems that undermine a group's capacity to maintain its influence and political engagement.

An example of a policy that permanently weakened the mobilization capacity of a loss-bearing group is airline deregulation. Prior to 1978, the government limited the entry of airlines into the market and regulated passenger fares to stabilize industry profits—a classic instance of what James Q. Wilson calls "clientele politics."[76] After deregulation, a bevy of discount carriers entered the market. Some legacy carriers were unable to compete and went bankrupt. While many of the surviving firms continued to favor government interventions that would insulate them from market pressures, they now confronted airlines that exerted counterpressure on transportation policy-makers. The political cohesion of the airline industry declined, making its countermobilization more difficult.[77]

POLITICAL OPPORTUNITIES:
EXTERNAL INCENTIVES FOR COUNTERMOBILIZATION

Finally, the prospects for backlash politics are shaped by the *political opportunity structure*, meaning "dimensions of the political environment or of change in that environment that provide incentives for collective action by affecting expectations for success or failure."[78] Many factors shape political opportunities, from the institutional rules of the game and public opinion to the level of partisan polarization. In his insightful account of how political opportunities influence social movement activities, Sidney G. Tarrow emphasizes two factors that are particularly relevant to backlash dynamics. The first is the presence of divisions among elites.[79] When political elites reach a strong consensus on the need to move policy in a given direction, it becomes difficult for defeated constituencies to mount a resistance since the odds of success are so long. However, when conflicts arise within and among elites over policy changes, loss-bearing groups gain confidence that at least some powerful actors will amplify and legitimate their grievances. The second key factor is the availability of influential allies. Groups are more likely to countermobilize when allies within their networks provide resources and leverage. For example, when social conservatives resist proposed expansions of the welfare state, they often receive support from the business community.

Partisan polarization is the major factor shaping the opportunities for countermobilization in American democracy today. Polarization provides incentives for elite actors to stoke backlashes (or amplify ones that are already building grassroots momentum) to activate base voters.[80] Backlash politics allows partisan leaders to highlight the costs and unintended consequences of the other side's proposals, thereby directing attention away from the tensions or conflicts over policy priorities within their own coalitions. As Jacob S. Hacker and Paul Pierson observe, "Partisan opponents and their allies have powerful incentives to make new initiatives a focal point for countermobilization. . . . They will draw on perceived fiscal constraints, low trust in government, and heightened polarization (with its attendant partisan media, culturally insulated voter blocs, and team-oriented politician and interest group alignments) to generate backlash."[81]

To be sure, partisan backlashes are not guaranteed to deliver electoral gains. In an era of hyperpolarization, the number of people who are willing to defect to the other side when they are unhappy with a party's performance or disagree with its positions is relatively small. Yet swing voters have not vanished entirely. They are critical to election outcomes, given the tight partisan competition for control of national institutions, and partisan loyalty does not always trump economic interests or values. As a result, partisan backlashes can backfire. For example, Suzanne Mettler, Lawrence R. Jacobs, and Ling Zhu have shown that the GOP's attempt to repeal the ACA, while initially a useful political strategy, led to increased support for the law among Republican voters by raising the salience of its benefits and reminding people what would be lost if the repeal drive actually succeeded.[82]

One way that polarization reinforces backlash politics is by tightening alliances between parties and organized groups. The evolution of the abortion issue is illustrative.[83] During the 1970s, there was little difference between the two parties on abortion. The 1976 Republican convention platform acknowledged a lack of consensus on abortion within the party, stating that it is "undoubtedly a moral and personal issue."[84] While the 1976 Democratic platform opposed a constitutional amendment to overturn *Roe*, it recognized "the religious and ethical nature of the concerns which many Americans have on the subject of abortion."[85] Not until the mid- to late 1980s did the two parties sharply polarize on abortion. As Linda Greenhouse and Reva B. Siegel argue, the entanglement of abortion in partisan politics is due to a "complex mix of top-down and bottom-up forces."[86] New Right strategists, seeking winning issues for the Republican Party, "seem to have recognized—and indeed to have helped create—abortion as a vivid symbol to motivate political participation."[87] At the same time, as Neil O'Brian has shown, there was already support for prolife views among evangelical Protestants at the grassroots level. When evangelical leaders shifted right on the issue and amplified the anti-abortion backlash, they were, in many ways, catching up with their followers.[88]

Finally, as the sociologist Donald Black has argued, each actor in a conflict creates a "gravitational field."[89] Third parties are more likely to be pulled into the conflict and to be become partisans when they are relationally and culturally close to one of the combatants (on whose side they will align) and remote from the other.[90] For example, I show in chapter 5 that major national corporations became allies of the LGBTQ community in the backlash against North Carolina's effort to prevent transgender people from using bathrooms aligned with their gender identities. While this conflict was not directly tied to the firms' business interests, major corporations are increasingly led and staffed by well-credentialed cultural liberals who reject the traditionalist values of social conservatives.[91] In an era of intense polarization, third parties find it difficult to remain on the political sidelines and not assist their cultural allies.

Understanding When Backlashes Occur

One way to understand the conditions under which backlash politics occurs is by recognizing that the internal capacities of loss-bearing groups to participate in the democratic process and the external incentives for countermobilization can each vary in strength. This implies a simple two-by-two matrix outlining four types of responses by constituencies to unwelcome changes in the policy status quo (figure 1.2).

The top left quadrant of the figure captures highly favorable conditions for backlash politics: loss-bearing or threatened constituencies possess the ability to resist policy changes through protests, rallies, voting, lobbying, and other participatory acts and their grievances receive support from political elites and influential allies in their organizational networks. An example is the backlash of Tea Party conservatives against the ACA. Mainstream Republican politicians amplified the backlash and leveraged it to score political gains in the 2010 midterms. Another example is the backlash of teachers' unions in response to school accountability mechanisms, such as the use of standardized test scores to evaluate student performance and then use this information to hold teachers or schools responsible for poor results. As Moe argues, while school accountability gained national momentum through the enactment of the No Child Left Behind Act (NCLB), teachers' unions attempted to water down its consequences at every turn. Among other responses, they "launched public relations campaigns that loudly criticized accountability— claiming that students were over-tested, teachers were teaching to the test, and so on—to convince Americans that NCLB was fatally flawed."[92] Over the next decade, the backlash widened to include unions' allies in the Democratic Party, conservatives who feared the NCLB act could lead to a national curriculum, and parents who were unhappy with the amount of testing or with assessments that gave poor marks to the schools their kids attended.[93]

The remaining three quadrants in the matrix display responses to distinct challenges that loss-bearing groups may face. In the lower left quadrant, a loss-bearing group can win attention and support from actors in its political network but lacks the internal capacity for effective countermobilization in the short run. This is broadly the position legal conservatives

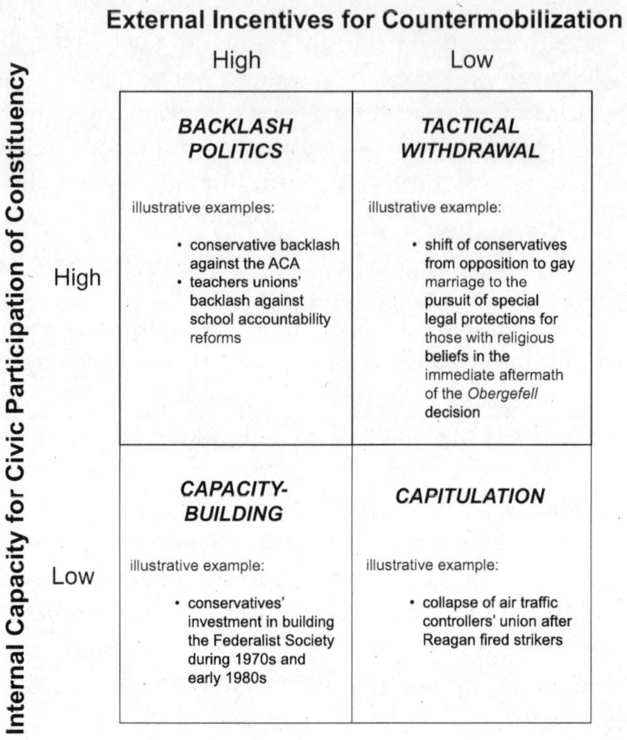

External Incentives for Countermobilization

	High	Low
High	**BACKLASH POLITICS** illustrative examples: • conservative backlash against the ACA • teachers unions' backlash against school accountability reforms	**TACTICAL WITHDRAWAL** illustrative example: • shift of conservatives from opposition to gay marriage to the pursuit of special legal protections for those with religious beliefs in the immediate aftermath of the *Obergefell* decision
Low	**CAPACITY-BUILDING** illustrative example: • conservatives' investment in building the Federalist Society during 1970s and early 1980s	**CAPITULATION** illustrative example: • collapse of air traffic controllers' union after Reagan fired strikers

(vertical axis label: Internal Capacity for Civic Participation of Constituency)

FIGURE 1.2. Responses to Losses, Internal Group Capacities, and External Incentives for Countermobilization

found themselves in from the 1970s through the early 1980s. As Steven Teles shows in his excellent account of the rise of the conservative legal movement, ideological conservatives had largely captured the Republican Party by this point, pushing GOP moderates to the sidelines.[94] But while conservatives were increasingly winning the day on issues like taxes, they were frustrated by their inability to reverse deeply embedded liberal accomplishments in the law. When scanning the landscape, they were dispirited by the scarcity of conservative faculty in top law schools, which serve as the pipeline for Supreme Court appointments. They also recognized that they could not match the vast network of public-interest lawyers in liberal advocacy organizations. As a result, they recognized the need to build up their organizational capacity. As Teles argues, dislodging legal liberalism required conservatives to make strategic investments in "a broad range of activities designed to reverse their elite-level organizational weakness."[95] Only after the establishment of organizations like the Federalist Society was the conservative legal movement in a position to build the "intellectual and network resources to challenge legal liberalism in the courts."[96]

A constituency falling in the upper right quadrant possesses the internal resources and capacity necessary for countermobilization but lacks negotiating leverage because the external environment is unfavorable. As a result, the group has little chance to restore the status quo ante in the near term. The best response for a loss-bearing group (to use a military analogy) is a "tactical withdrawal"—retreating to safer ground while continuing to use the means at its disposal to impede an enemy's progress. This dynamic captures the way in which religious and social conservatives responded in the immediate aftermath of the Supreme Court's *Obergefell v. Hodges* decision that gay couples have a constitutional right to marry. While many in the Christian right hoped to see *Obergefell* reversed, conservatives recognized that political elites were broadly supportive of the decision and that they had few influential allies. Even Donald Trump said he accepted same-sex marriage. "It's law. It was settled in the Supreme Court. I mean, it's done," Trump said in 2016.[97] By 2021, 70 percent of the public (including 55 percent of Republicans) expressed support for same-sex marriage.[98] Rather than seeking to mobilize support for the restoration of traditional marriage rules, the Christian right made a tactical decision to seek special exemptions in the law, such as the right of religious bakers to refuse wedding cake orders from same-sex couples. As political scientist Andrew R. Lewis argues, religious conservatives argued "that they're vulnerable like other minorities and they need protections from the broader culture."[99]

To be sure, conservative activists have continued to push an anti-LGBTQ agenda in red states. Activists focused initially not on reversing gay marriage but rather on edge issues where there is not yet a social consensus, such as allowing transgender women to compete against other women in high school and college sports, the discussion of gender identity in elementary school classrooms, and gender-affirming care for transgender minors. By 2023, conservatives escalated their attacks to energize base voters. For example, some red states have sought to deny gender-affirming care to adults and restrict drag performances. Social conservatives have been empowered by the growing radicalism of the GOP and the recent emergence of a conservative supermajority on the Supreme Court. Citizens in many red states are supportive of anti-trans legislation, suggesting that state legislators face little immediate risk of voter backlash. It remains to be seen, however, how successful social conservatives will be in their effort to relitigate past conflicts and reestablish traditional gender hierarchies in American society. Public opinion on transgender issues is complex and still evolving. In 2022, opinion surveys showed that a clear majority of Americans believed that transgender people should not face discrimination in areas such as jobs, housing, and public spaces, but

the public's views on many specific policies related to people who are transgender were divided.[100] The public's attitudes have become significantly more
liberal on many cultural issues, including race, women's equality, and the
rights of gay Americans. As Atkinson and colleagues point out, "Large swaths
of the American public [are] adopting new, pro-equality positions" on these
issues (and older Americans who hold antiequality views are being genera-
tionally replaced).[101] If public opinion ultimately follows a similar course on
transgender issues, support for the enactment of anti-trans laws could become an electoral liability in many states.

Finally, in the lower right quadrant, a shift in the policy status quo fails to
trigger backlash because the relevant constituency group lacks both critical
support from external allies and the internal capacity for countermobilization.
As I show in chapter 6, this describes the situation in which air traffic controllers found themselves in 1981 when their effort to win contract concessions
by going on strike backfired. Not only did the controllers fail to receive better
terms, but President Reagan fired them and broke their union. The controllers' most influential potential network ally, airline pilots, declined to provide
critical support, instead siding with the administration. The American public lacked sympathy for the controllers' cause, and Reagan's tough stance did
not trigger a backlash despite the risks to the performance of the air traffic
control system. Under these unfavorable conditions, postloss power-building
became impossible for the union.[102] Lacking the capacity to perform basic
organizational maintenance tasks, the controllers' resistance collapsed.

The Aftermaths of Backlashes

A final conceptual issue that requires attention is the downstream consequences of backlashes. After a backlash, what happens next? Some backlashes
slow the expansion or entrenchment of a policy initiative. For instance, in 1982
the Reagan administration triggered a backlash when it proposed to close 75
of the federal government's 348 weather stations.[103] The constituencies that de-
pended on the early warnings from local weather forecasts for their economic
planning—farmers, citrus growers, and timber growers—made certain that
Congress and the administration knew about their distress, and the administration ultimately gave 45 stations a reprieve. Backlashes can even reinforce
policy stability. For example, the public and legislative blowback against the
Reagan administration's 1981 proposal to cut the Social Security benefits of
early retirees—the Senate passed a resolution against the plan by a vote of
96–0—helped keep initiatives for welfare state retrenchment off the agenda.[104]

Yet other policy backlashes take on a life of their own, causing outcomes to wind up, not back where things started, but in a different place from where the reactive sequence began.[105] An example is the conservative backlash to the ACA. Some Republican governors of Medicaid expansion states managed the push-back from conservative voters by adopting work requirements for Medicaid recipients. These work requirements then diffused to other conservative states that had never adopted Medicaid expansion in the first place. As a result, for a period of time during the Trump administration, Medicaid eligibility became "even more restrictive in these states than it was before passage of the ACA."[106] As Robert Jervis argues, "In many cases one change leads to others, but these neither reinforce nor dampen the initial one. They move the system sideways, so to speak."[107] In sum, policy backlashes can *transform* patterns of governance.

A useful way to understand the varying aftermaths of backlashes is to construe them as events that occur early within sequences of events that unfold over time. These sequences, in turn, can follow either a "self-reproducing" logic or a "reactive" logic. In a self-reproducing sequence, the initial events move the process in a single direction, whereas in a reactive process, the events are subject to reversals or changes of direction. This analysis draws on a framework for analyzing sequences developed by Tulia G. Falleti and James Mahoney.[108] Table 1.2 modifies their framework to present three distinct sequences that can embody backlash forces: *self-eroding, oscillating*, and *transformative*.

In a *self-eroding* process, events reproduce themselves and move in the same direction, but "each event in the sequence serves to weaken, diminish, or undermine the configuration found in the early stages of the sequence. Each step down the path moves away from the established outcome associated with the early process and makes it increasingly less likely that the outcome or the process itself will be sustained. The status quo becomes harder and harder to maintain."[109] An example is the erosion of abortion rights and access in many conservative states following the 1973 *Roe v. Wade* decision. In response to the backlash against abortion, conservative state legislatures began passing increasingly stringent restrictions on abortion. Even before the *Dobbs v. Jackson Women's Health Organization* decision, abortion services were already largely unavailable to women in many conservative states.[110]

In contrast to self-reproducing processes, in which the events that occur after backlashes all move in the same direction, backlashes that generate *reactive processes* lead to changes in direction. In a reactive process, each event "is a cause of each subsequent event because it triggers a reaction or a response to the prior event."[111] Two types of reactive processes should be distinguished.

TABLE 1.2. Backlash Outcomes and Sequences

Type of Process	Definition	Description and Diagram of Process	Example
Self-reproducing	Events in a particular direction induce subsequent events in the same direction.	*Self-eroding process* Countermobilizations generate a sequence in which each event weakens the configuration found in the initial stages of the sequence. A →A→A→A→A	Erosion of abortion rights and access to reproductive services in red states in the decades prior to the overturning of *Roe v. Wade*
Reactive	Events are linked via reaction/counterreaction dynamics.	*Oscillating process* Countermobilizations induce other countermobilizations, causing movements to swing back and forth. A →B→A→B→A	Swings between federal and state control over K–12 education standards and school accountability
		Transformative process Backlashes transform events and move the process in a new direction. A ~A→ B ~ B→Y	Development of punitive crime policy following the civil rights movement

Source: Modified from Falleti and Mahoney 2015, 221.

The first is an *oscillating* process. In this sequence of events, a backlash occurs when policy moves too far in one direction and the losing constituency countermobilizes. The policy then reverses, but because of frictions and delays, it then moves too far in the other direction, triggering a countermobilization from another disfavored group.[112] Education policy again offers an instructive example. In response to the backlash over school accountability reforms, Congress passed the Every Child Succeeds Act in 2015, which significantly returns education power to the states and local districts.[113] The federal government will no longer require students' performance on standardized tests to be part of teachers' evaluations or decide what should be done if schools fall short of their goals. In the event that public school performance does not show improvements over the coming decades, however, the accountability pendulum could swing back to Washington again.

Reactive processes become *transformative* when "the initial event and the final event seemingly bear little relationship to one another, yet they are connected by virtue of the reaction/counterreaction dynamics that compose the overall causal chain."[114] A backlash that generates a transformative sequence of events does not restore the status quo ante; rather, it creates new politics and reconfigures political outcomes. The shift toward punitive crime policy is an example. As Vesla Weaver has shown, following the inability of conservatives to block the Civil Rights Act of 1964 and the Voting Rights Act of 1965, states pushed for the death penalty, largely abolished parole, and imposed mandatory minimum sentences. In addition, the federal government massively expanded its role in crime control.[115]

A detailed investigation of cases is necessary to understand why policy losses and threats have trigged backlashes in some instances while barely generating a reaction in others. As the starting point for this investigation, the next chapter provides an overview of instances of backlash in American national policymaking since the 1960s.

An Overview of Backlash Politics

When have policy backlashes happened in recent American history? In what issue arenas have they happened? What actors have participated in them? And what were these actors' objectives? In the remainder of the book, I address these questions through detailed case studies, but first I take a bird's-eye view. In this chapter, I describe how I coded *New York Times* articles to uncover patterns of backlash politics in the U.S. policy state since 1960. Using these data, I show that backlashes have mobilized many different actors, from businesses and unions to consumers and senior citizens. While backlash forces were largely confined to the civil rights arena in the 1960s, they now penetrate virtually every sector.

I find that backlash politics is strongly associated with partisan polarization. As the partisan divide has widened, backlash politics has become a compelling strategy for galvanizing base voters. My analysis further shows that different forms of backlash—including electoral, public, and organizational—have somewhat different organizing dynamics. I also find that ideologically infused backlash politics has been disproportionately conservative. Conservative backlash has focused on turning back liberal policy and making government's role less expansive. In contrast, liberal backlash—which has come to the fore as Republicans in Washington have moved right—has been mainly about preservation, seeking to prevent the erosion of previous gains.

Research Approach

As events that unfold in the public sphere, backlashes receive extensive media attention. My research assistants and I searched for the word *backlash* in *New York Times* (*NYT*) articles' titles or text, including news articles, news analysis

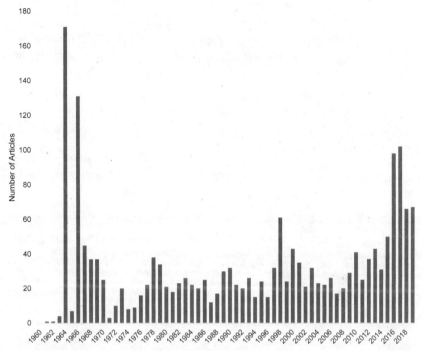

FIGURE 2.1. *New York Times* Articles about Policy Backlash, 1960–2019
Source: Author's compilation of *New York Times* articles.

articles, op-eds, and letters to the editor. I included both articles about Washington politics and *NYT* articles about backlashes at the state, local, and international levels that were directly related to U.S. public policies, such as white backlash in southern states against the Civil Rights Act of 1964. I excluded articles about backlashes in defense and international affairs unless there was a direct linkage to trade, immigration, or a domestic policy area such as veterans' affairs or civil rights. I also excluded articles about backlash in nonpolicy contexts, such as backlashes against fashion styles or music trends. Finally, I excluded articles about backlashes against groups that were not directly connected to a proposed or enacted U.S. policy, such as hate crimes against Muslim-Americans following the 9/11 attacks.[1]

This canvasing produces a total of 1,932 articles, of which 1,700 (88 percent) are news or news analysis articles (the remaining 12 percent are opinion pieces, editorials, and letters to the editor). The measure includes 786 unique bylines, including coauthored articles. The median byline appeared only once (mean = 2.0). The *NYT* measure is thus not driven by a very small number of authors.[2]

Figure 2.1 displays the annual number of articles published between 1960 and 2019. The five years with the highest article counts are 1964 (171 articles),

1966 (131), 2017 (102), 2016 (98), and 2019 (67). While the 1960s are widely recognized as a key backlash moment, the *NYT* measure points to an upsurge in countermobilization activity during the 2010s as well. Backlashes against the drive to protect the civil rights of Black Americans dominated *NYT* coverage in 1964 and 1966. The three high-count years between 2016 and 2019 featured articles about liberal backlashes against state-level proposals to limit the access of transgender persons to public bathrooms, the GOP's effort to repeal the ACA, and the Trump administration's treatment of migrants at the southern border.

Limitations of the *NYT* Measure

The *NYT* measure produces a fascinating portrait, revealing backlash-related activity to be a far more routine pattern than is typically acknowledged. Quite simply, a great deal of American politics consists of voters and groups countermobilizing against enacted or anticipated changes in public policy.

As noted in the introduction, the *NYT* measure had several important limitations that should be acknowledged. First, it only covers the 1960–2019 period. Prior to the 1960s, journalists occasionally described adverse political reactions to policy moves as "backlashes." For example, a 1950 article predicted that President Harry Truman would face backlash if he signed a bill to exempt some natural gas producers from federal regulation, thus undercutting his campaign pledge not to yield to special interests.[3] (He vetoed the measure.) But it was not until the 1960s that the term *backlash* became part of the popular lexicon. As Lawrence Glickman notes, while the term originally referred to the white backlash, it soon began to be used to refer to counterreactions to all manner of political and social developments.[4] The *NYT* measure thus omits many important earlier backlashes, such as the backlash of conservative elites against the New Deal, the public's thumbs-down reaction to Franklin Roosevelt's court-packing plan, and the massive resistance to school integration in the 1950s. The tendency to countermobilize is baked into American democracy and it clearly predated the civil rights era, but a different data source would be needed to catalog instances of backlash in the public sphere during earlier periods of U.S. history.

Second, the *NYT* measure reflects the journalistic biases of the paper's writers and editors. If the *NYT* failed to frame particular events as backlashes, the data set will replicate these omissions. A third limitation is that each article in the *NYT* database counts as a single entry even though some backlashes are far more consequential than others. Backlash intensity registers through the total number of articles coded in a policy sector within a given time period.

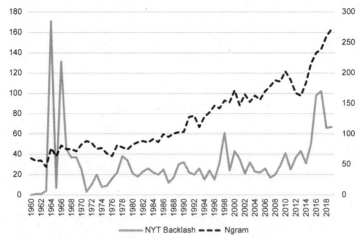

FIGURE 2.2. Google Ngrams Mentions of "Backlash" and *New York Times* Measure, 1960–2019
Sources: Google Ngrams and author's compilation of *New York Times* articles.

Another potential concern is that the *NYT* measure might reflect changes in the use of the word *backlash* in the language. I examined Google Ngrams (which searches for phrases used in books by publication year) to investigate this issue. As figure 2.2 shows, the term *backlash* has become more common in American English since the 1960s. Is the *NYT* measure simply a reflection of changes in language? It does not appear so. I find that the *NYT* measure is only moderately correlated with the Ngrams trend ($r = .33$).[5] I also compared the *NYT* measure to trends of mentions of backlashes in other media outlets. Using NexisUni and Proquest Historical Newspaper databases for the available years, I searched for articles or broadcast transcripts about U.S. political news with the term *backlash* in the title. In general, the *NYT* measure tracks these other sources fairly well. The media source with the strongest correlation with the *NYT* measure is *CBS Evening News* ($r = .84$) over the full 1960–2019 period. The correlations between the *NYT* measure and use of the term *backlash* by other media outlets is also fairly strong, including the *Washington Post* ($r = .66$ for 1960–2019), the *Christian Science Monitor* ($r = .60$ for 1960–2008), and *Fox News* ($r = .59$ for 1998–2019). Taken together, these findings suggest that the *NYT* measure is more strongly associated with the way other media outlets cover backlash events than with general shifts in language since 1960.

As an additional check of the *NYT* measure's reliability, I examined whether it picks up backlashes that are recognized for their historical significance. I examined a selection of monographs and edited volumes that offer studies of events that occurred during presidential administrations from John F. Kennedy through Obama. Table 2.1 displays a list of backlash episodes

TABLE 2.1. Backlashes and Countermobilization Episodes Mentioned in Presidential Histories

Backlash Episode
(All cases were mentioned in one or
more articles included in the NYT
measure except for those shown in
italics.)

| | Mentioned in Source? | | |

Barack Obama

	Zelizer (2018)	Chait (2017)	Levin, Disalvo, and Shapiro (2012)
Economic stimulus	x	x	x
Affordable Care Act	x	x	x
Cap-and-trade bill	x	x	x
Auto bailout		x	
"Race to the Top" education reform	x		x

George W. Bush

	Kruse and Zelizer (2019)	Mann (2015)	Levin, Disalvo, and Shapiro (2012)
No Child Left Behind	x	x	x
Stem cell research		x	
Sarbanes-Oxley Act		x	
Social Security privatization	x	x	x
Troubled Assets Relief Program	x	x	x
Federal takeover of Fannie Mae and Freddie Mac bailout		x	
Federal intervention in Terri Schiavo case	x		x
Immigration reform	x		x

Bill Clinton

	Kruse and Zelizer (2019)	Tomasky (2017)	Patterson (2005)
Gays in the military	x	x	x
Crime bill		x	
North American Free Trade Agreement	x	x	x
Health reform	x	x	x
National history standards			x
GOP'S impeachment of Clinton over the Monica Lewinsky scandal	x	x	x
World Trade Organization/ globalization			x

TABLE 2.1. *(continued)*

Backlash Episode
(All cases were mentioned in one or
more articles included in the NYT
measure except for those shown in
italics.)

	Mentioned in Source?		
	George H. W. Bush		
	Naftali (2007)	*Sinclair (1991)*	*Patterson (2005)*
Immigration			x
Breaking the "no new taxes" pledge	x	x	x
Nomination of Justice Clarence Thomas	x		x
	Ronald Reagan		
	Weisberg (2016)	*Dallek (1999)*	*Brands (2016)*
Cuts in domestic spending	x	x	
Proposed cut in Social Security benefits		x	x
Lax environmental enforcement			
Interior Secretary James Watt's plans to sell federal lands to private bidders along with his controversial statements	x	x	x
	Jimmy Carter		
	Zelizer (2010)	*Dumbrell (1995)*	*Patterson (2005)*
Proposed cuts in federal water projects	x	x	x
Comprehensive energy proposal		x	x
IRS denial of tax-exempt status to discriminatory private schools			x
Affirmative action		x	x
Equal Rights Amendment		x	x
	Gerald Ford		
	Reichley (1981)	*Brinkley (2012)*	*Patterson (1996)*
Environmental regulation			x
Nixon pardon	x	x	x
Transportation deregulation	x		
	Richard Nixon		
	Reichley (1981)	*Drew (2007)*	*Patterson (1996)*
Roe v. Wade decision		x	x
Family Assistance Plan	x	x	x
Affirmative action in employment and education			x
Busing	x	x	x

(continues)

TABLE 2.1. *(continued)*

Backlash Episode *(All cases were mentioned in one or* *more articles included in the* NYT *measure except for those shown in* *italics.)*	*Mentioned in Source?*		
	Lyndon Johnson		
	Peters (2010)	*Dallek (1998)*	*Patterson (1996)*
Civil Rights Act of 1964	x	x	x
Voting Rights Act of 1965	x	x	x
Model Cities (provisions related to school integration)		x	
War on Poverty legislation		x	x
	John F. Kennedy		
	Brinkley (2012)	*Dallek (2003)*	*Patterson (1996)*
JFK's pressure on the House Rules Committee to enlarge its membership		x	
Civil rights	x		x
Federal aid to education		x	x
Medicare proposal		x	

Source: Author's compilation.

that received some attention in these books (whether or not the word *back-lash* was used to describe them). The vast majority of these events mentioned in these sources also appear in the *NYT* database, with the exception of those in italics. Items range from the federal aid to education bill during the Kennedy administration to George W. Bush's Social Security privatization proposal. The list also includes backlashes to executive actions such as Clinton's pledge to lift a ban on gays and lesbians serving in the armed forces. Overall, the *NYT* measure does a reasonable job of capturing counterreactions that make it into the history books.

Diffusion of Backlash Politics across Policy Sectors

A key pattern captured by the *NYT* measure is the diffusion of backlash politics across policy sectors. Figure 2.3 displays the count of articles about backlash across fourteen policy sectors during the decades of the 1960s, 1970s, 1980s, 1990s, 2000s, and 2010s.[6] While during the 1960s, *NYT* coverage focused almost exclusively on white backlash to civil rights, backlash forces began to penetrate other domestic arenas over time. By the 1980s, six different

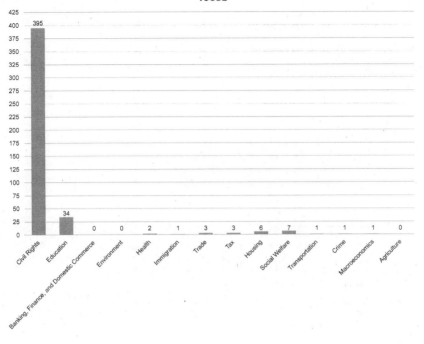

1960s

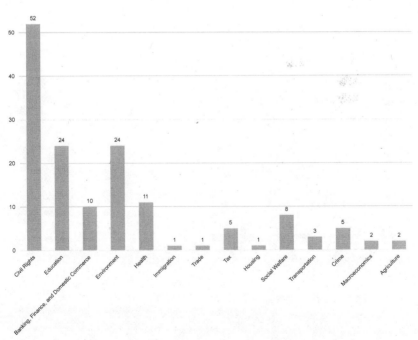

1970s

FIGURE 2.3. *New York Times* Articles about Backlash in Domestic Policy Areas by Decade
Source: Author's compilation of *New York Times* articles.

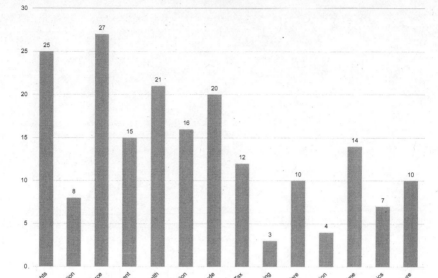

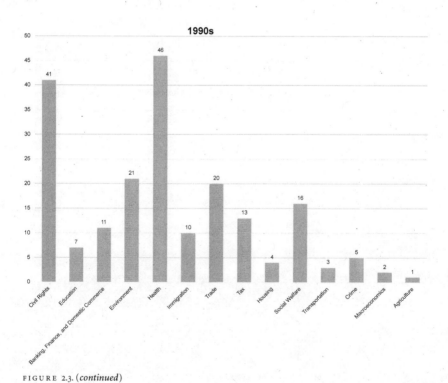

FIGURE 2.3. (*continued*)

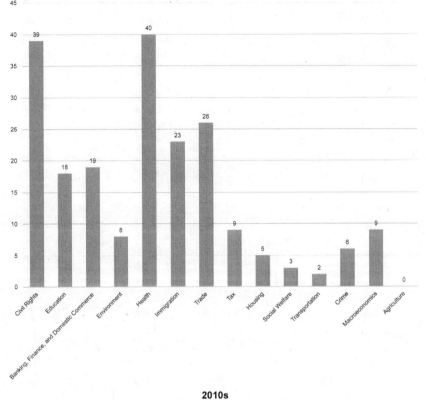

2000s

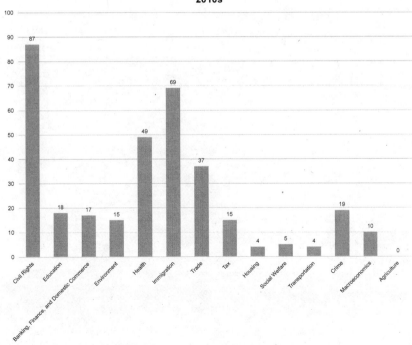

2010s

FIGURE 2.3. (*continued*)

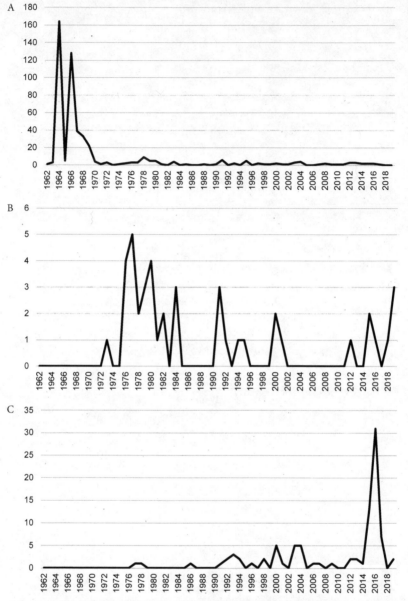

FIGURE 2.4. *New York Times* Articles about Backlash in the Civil Rights Arena Focused on Black Americans, Women, and LGBTQ People, 1962–2019
Source: Author's compilation of *New York Times* articles.
A.   Black Americans
B.   Women
C.   Gays, Lesbians, and Transgender Persons

policy sectors could be classified as major backlash sites (15 or more articles each): banking, finance, and domestic commerce (27 articles), civil rights (25), health (21), trade (20), immigration (16), and the environment (15).

Overall, the seven policy areas with the highest number of articles between 1960 and 2019 are civil rights (639 articles), health (169), immigration (120), education (109), trade (107), banking, finance, and domestic commerce (84), and the environment (83). The two sectors with the lowest counts are agriculture (13) and transportation (17).[7] The correlations across the policy sectors are generally low, suggesting that most sectors remain weakly coupled. However, backlash trends have moved in tandem in two pairs: immigration and trade ($r = .52$) and civil rights and housing ($r = .43$). These patterns can be explained by programmatic and constituency linkages. For example, labor unions—seeking to protect workers' wages in an era of globalization—have countermobilized against both unrestricted immigration and free trade deals. And many of the conservative groups that countermobilized against civil rights and affirmative action also opposed fair-housing laws and antipoverty programs.

Since civil rights backlash is such a large part of *NYT* coverage, I split out the various groups mentioned in the time series. Figure 2.4 shows trends for articles about backlashes affecting three key populations: Black Americans; women; and gays, lesbians, and transgender persons. (Note that each figure is plotted on a different scale.) *NYT* coverage of backlash with respect to the civil rights of Black Americans peaked in 1964 (164 articles), the year in which Congress passed landmark civil rights legislation and Barry Goldwater (who opposed the law) was the Republican Party's presidential nominee. Another high-coverage year was 1966 (128 articles), which featured articles about the unexpected Democratic primary election victory of Maryland gubernatorial candidate George P. Mahoney, an arch opponent of open-housing laws; a violent attack on children by a white mob opposed to the integration of schools in Grenada, Mississippi; and the Senate elimination of fair-housing legislation because of white backlash following riots in Watts and Cleveland. Coverage of backlash politics with respect to women and gender equality peaked in 1977 (five articles), focusing on the conservative mobilization against the Equal Rights Amendment led by antifeminists like Phyllis Schlafly. More recently, the *NYT* has focused on battles over the civil rights of gays, lesbians, and transgender people.

Predictors of Policy Backlash

What factors are associated with patterns of backlash politics? To address this question, I estimate a statistical count model in which the dependent variable

TABLE 2.2. Descriptive Statistics

Variable	Mean	Std. Deviation	Min.	Max.
Backlash	32.74	29.92	1.00	171.00
Polarization	0.69	0.12	0.54	0.88
Policy mood	60.06	4.49	50.70	69.80
Divergence from partisan parity	3.16	6.15	−6.39	15.64
Divided government	0.62	0.49	0	1.00
Election year				
Unemployment	5.97	1.60	3.50	9.70
Civil rights era	0.10	0.31	0	1.00
Ngrams trend of the term *backlash* (three-year moving average)	1.53e-06	2.33e-06	5.27e-07	0
Federal budget outlays (2012 dollars)	2,134.14	954.34	720.10	4,036.60

is the number of articles about policy backlash published in the *NYT* per year. While this analysis is descriptive rather than causal, it illuminates the relationship between backlash politics and explanatory variables.[8] Table 2.2 presents descriptive statistics for the variables included in the analysis. The first independent variable is *partisan polarization*.[9] To measure polarization, I use the first difference in House of Representatives party means, (first dimension NOMINATE). Because NOMINATE scores are calculated on the basis of legislators' voting records in each two-year Congress, I coded both years of each biennium (e.g., 1977–1978) with the same polarization scores. Partisan polarization in Congress has increased significantly since the 1980s. Legislative polarization has been asymmetric. The Republican Party's movement to the right has been responsible for most of the divergence between the two parties in roll call voting.[10]

The model also includes an independent variable for *the divergence from partisan parity*. The closer the partisan parity variable is to 0, the more evenly balanced are the two parties in the competition for the control of national institutions.[11] As Lee argues, "The period since 1980 stands out as the longest sustained period of competitive balance between the parties since the Civil War. Contemporary American politics is distinctive for its narrow and switching national majorities. Nearly every recent election has held out the possibility of a shift in party control of one institution or another."[12] Democrats held seemingly permanent majorities in both chambers of Congress (and the presidency most of the time) during the decades after the New Deal. Stuck in the minority, the GOP's best response during this era was to negotiate for half a policy loaf. After the Democrats lost their permanent majority status during the 1980s, however, party competition became much more intense. Lee argues persuasively that this shift in competitive circumstances has transformed lawmakers' incentives. "When control of national institutions hangs in the balance, no party wants to grant political legitimacy to its opposition by voting for the measures it champions," she writes. "After all, how can a party wage an effective campaign after supporting or collaborating with its opposition on public policy? Instead, parties in a competitive environment will want to amplify the differences voters perceive between themselves and their opposition. They will continually strive to give voters an answer to the key question: 'Why should you support us instead of them?' "[13]

I explore thermostatic opinion by including the *public policy mood* as a variable in the models. The public policy mood is an aggregate measure of the public's preferences on a left-right scale, based on public opinion surveys.[14] In addition, I investigate the impact of *divided government*.[15] Some models include the following controls: *Ngrams trend* (three-year moving average) of the term *backlash* to capture changes in language; *unemployment rate* to capture the role of macroeconomic conditions; and *federal budget outlays* (adjusted for inflation) to capture the dramatic expansion of the federal government.[16] The scope of many other forms of policy activity, including regulations and tax expenditures, has also broadened over time.

I also explore the influence of a dummy variable for the *civil rights era* (1963–1968). Finally, my preferred specifications include a *lagged dependent variable* to account for the effect of the level of backlash in the previous year (thus the time series begins in 1961), but I also present models in which I control for the time trend.[17]

KEY FINDINGS

Table 2.3 presents the results. The main finding is that partisan polarization has a positive, statistically significant relationship with media-identified backlash politics in every model in which this variable is included.[18] Both Democrats and Republicans initially supported the broadening of the policy state during the 1950s and 1960s. As Bryan Jones and colleagues argue, however, over time Republicans "began to see electoral advantages in moving right," and thus aligned themselves with groups such as business, social conservatives, and other opponents of a liberal policy state.[19] Conservative countermobilization became central to GOP coalition-building. Democrats, in turn, pushed for policy expansions. As the two parties moved further apart, increasing numbers of policy sectors became subject to backlash forces. Significantly, the association between polarization and backlash has persisted into the present era, even though the Great Broadening process was largely complete by the late 1970s.[20]

TABLE 2.3. Factors Influencing Count of *New York Times* Articles about Policy Backlash, 1961–2019

	[1]	[2]	[3]	[4]	[5]
Polarization	9.107*	10.826*	4.654***	4.611***	
	(4.164)	(3.945)	(0.929)	(0.906)	
Divergence from partisan parity					−.056*
					(.018)
Policy mood	0.018	−0.001	−0.038#	−0.039#	0.009
	(0.026)	(0.027)	(0.022)	(0.022)	(0.022)
Civil rights era (1963–1968)			1.443***	1.259***	1.116*
			(0.299)	(0.330)	(0.392)
Divided government				−0.164	−0.285
				(0.180)	(0.212)
Election year				0.159	0.186
				(0.156)	(0.175)
Budget outlays		0.001*			
		(0.001)			
Unemployment			−0.084	−0.089#	−0.031
			(0.052)	(0.051)	(0.059)
Ngrams of term *backlash* (three-year moving average)	−193,180**	−205,513**	−107,509#	−110,958#	−122,515*
	(67,248)	(66,936)	(60,818)	(61,267)	(61,822)
Time trend	−0.517#	−0.139**			
	(−0.028)	(0.044)			
Lagged dependent variable			−0.001	−0.001	0.002
			(0.003)	(0.003)	(0.004)
Constant	−2.127	−2.559	3.001*	3.133*	3.241*
	(2.388)	(2.323)	(1.250)	(1.262)	(1.397)
Pseudo R^2	0.022	0.033	0.073	0.076	0.050
N	59	59	59	59	59

Note: Table entries are negative binomial regressions, with standard errors in parentheses.
#$p < .1$; *$p < .05$; **$p < .01$; ***$p < .001$.

To be sure, partisan polarization is not a necessary condition for backlash politics. During the 1960s, *social polarization* on issues like civil rights and the Vietnam War was intense, but this social divide occurred *within* the two parties rather than between them.[21] As figure 2.5 shows, partisan polarization did not begin to increase until the late 1970s. As the ideological distance between the two parties has grown, however, party leaders have gained an incentive to mobilize their coalitions against the policy moves of their rivals. Political parties are certainly not the only institutional actors that can activate backlashes and build their energy over time. Interest groups and cross-party coalitions can also perform these tasks. But parties are exceptionally well situated to mobilize opposition forces. As Mayhew writes, "A party (as opposed to a cross-party coalition) is an organization built exactly to generate messages and mobilize voters. A party that loses on a congressional issue, if it was united in that confrontation and stays angry, may have an incentive to keep the conflict going."[22] (The GOP's ten-year crusade against the ACA is a case in point.)

While polarization began as an elite phenomenon, it diffused to ordinary citizens over time. In 1994, only about two in ten partisan identifiers had a very unfavorable view of the other party. By 2016, however, 58 percent of Republicans and 55 percent of Democrats viewed the other party in highly negative terms.[23] As Lilliana Mason observes, people's "partisan, ideological, religious, and racial identities" are currently moving into "strong alignment."[24] In a world of hyperpolarization, people come to see their partisan rivals' policies not just as misguided but as a threat to their status and way of life.

What makes polarization an even more potent catalyst for backlash politics is that today the two parties are evenly matched. The negative relationship between backlash and the divergence from party parity (model 5 in table 2.3) is consistent with Lee's argument that the growing closeness of party competition has intensified the incentives for partisan combat.[25] *In sum, the rise of polarization in the context of a tight partisan struggle for the control of national power has institutionalized backlash as a fundamental pattern of political mobilization and constituency engagement.*

The results of table 2.3 also show a positive association between backlash politics and the level of federal spending, and they provide suggestive evidence ($p < .10$) of an inverse relationship between backlash politics and the liberalism of the policy mood, meaning that the number of *NYT* articles about backlash politics rises when public opinion becomes more conservative. In

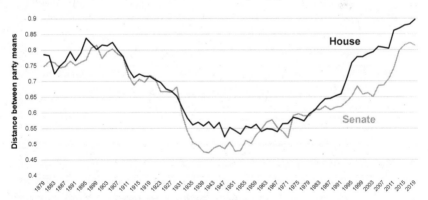

FIGURE 2.5. Partisan Polarization by Chamber, 1879–2019

Source: Jeffrey B Lewis et al., 2022, *Voteview: Congressional Roll-Call Votes Database*, https://voteview .com/.

Note: Figure shows the distance between party means (measured with NOMINATE ideological scores).

addition, the results suggest that the civil rights era was distinctive. The coverage of backlash politics increased during the 1963–1968 period, controlling for polarization and other factors. Finally, the results provide no evidence of a relationship between backlash and divided government.

Ideological Direction of Backlashes

Next, I investigate the ideological direction of backlashes. Building on the pioneering work on the ideological orientation of public policies by Robert S. Erikson, Michael B. MacKuen, and James A. Stimson and follow-up work by Matt Grossmann,[26] I coded backlashes (in the *NYT* article database) as *conservative* if they focused on backlashes against policies or proposals that expand the size or scope of government responsibility, such as the backlash to the ACA. I coded backlashes as *liberal* if articles referred to backlashes against policies or proposals that contract the size or scope of government responsibilities, such as the backlash to the Republican Party's proposals to reduce Medicare spending. Articles were coded as *both* if they described a mix of liberal and conservative opposition to complex policies (such as the teachers' unions and conservative backlashes to the NCLB act) or highlighted opposing backlashes on a single issue (e.g., an article about political reactions to a proposed free trade pact that discussed a conservative backlash to the inclusion of environmental regulations in the agreement and a progressive backlash to the exclusion of strong labor protections). Finally, backlashes against policies that involved no clear change in government's size and scope (such as the backlashes to rules balancing the rights of mountain bikers and hikers on federal trails and those to the George H. Bush administration's decision to give certain health care workers a smallpox vaccine in the case of terrorist attack) were coded as *neither*. Similar to Grossmann, in cases where the ideological character of backlashes had a different understanding in contemporary political discourse, I used the commonly understood direction.[27] For example, I coded the backlash to the promotion of domestic nuclear power as liberal and the backlash to needle exchange programs as conservative.

There were nearly twice as many articles about conservative backlash (1,031 articles) than liberal backlash (518 articles) over the 1960–2019 period. This is not surprising. As Grossmann observes, most new policies "expand existing government programs, establish new endeavors, or exchange new responsibilities for old ones."[28] It is difficult to terminate or scale back existing government programs due to positive feedback, constituency building, and the status quo bias of American political institutions. When new policies are under consideration, conservatives usually have greater reason for distress.

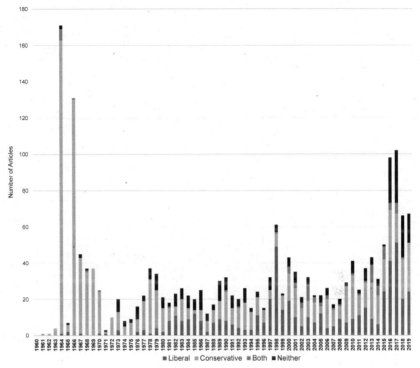

FIGURE 2.6. Ideological Character of Backlashes, 1960–2019
Source: Author's compilation of *New York Times* articles.

Yet as conservative Republicans have gained power in recent decades and become more ambitious in their reform goals, the threat to preexisting policy accomplishments has increased, strengthening incentives for the countermobilization of liberal constituencies.

Figure 2.6 displays trends in the ideological direction of the backlashes covered in the *NYT* since 1960. The early part of the time series is dominated by conservative backlash, while liberal backlash rises in the 1980s. This finding somewhat complicates the standard view about how the battle over activist government has unfolded. In the conventional account, conservatives countermobilized by the end of the liberal era of policymaking (1960s through mid-1970s) and stopped its positive momentum. In fact, however, conservative backlash was an almost immediate response to the civil rights movement and social reform thrust of the 1960s. *NYT* articles focused on the anticipation and manifestation of backlash of white voters against civil rights as well as the pushback against the federal government's growing role in domains that had long been viewed as subject to state and local control, such as education and housing.

TABLE 2.4. Factors Influencing Count of *New York Times* Articles about Conservative and Liberal Backlash, 87th to 115th Congresses

	[1] Conservative Backlash	[2] Liberal Backlash
Policy mood	0.050	−0.016
	(0.033)	(0.045)
Net liberal laws	0.083*	−0.060
	(0.042)	(0.037)
Democratic president	0.250	−0.102
	(.297)	(.323)
House Democrats' party mean	−5.070	
	(4.600)	
House Republicans' party mean		10.463***
		(2.416)
Lagged dependent variable	0.002	0.007
	(0.004)	(0.010)
Constant	−2.184	−0.121
	(2.476)	(3.012)
Pseudo R²	0.070	0.143
N	29	29

Note: Table entries are negative binomial regressions, with standard errors in parentheses.
#$p < .10$; *$p < .05$; **$p < .01$; ***$p < .001$.

By the mid-1980s, liberals were clearly on the defensive. Reagan won the White House twice, and congressional Republicans were beginning their sharp movement to the right. Finding themselves less well situated to advance further expansions of activist government, liberal advocates for antipoverty programs, civil rights, women's equality, and environmental programs began countermobilizing against conservatives' efforts to cut domestic spending, narrow affirmative action requirements, promote traditional social values, and extend the deregulation projects that had begun in the late 1970s. *In sum, conservatives rose to national power on a wave of backlash politics, while liberal backlash was largely a response to the loss of agenda control following Republican victories and the rightward turn of the GOP.*

During the 2010s, conservative and liberal backlashes often occurred in the same year on contested issues such as immigration, gun control, and health care. In addition, the number of backlashes without a clear ideological direction climbed, such as backlashes against actions by President Trump that triggered broad opposition.

Table 2.4 uses negative binomial regressions to explore the predictors of media-identified conservative and liberal backlashes from the 87th through 115th Congresses. The models control for the *policy mood, the president's party* (a dummy variable coded 1 for Democratic), *mean party positions of House*

Democrats and Republicans, and a measure of the *net number of liberal laws* (the number of important liberal laws minus the number of important conservative laws) passed in each Congress.[29]

The results suggest that conservative and liberal backlashes are responsive to different forces. Conservative backlash is associated with lawmaking activity. The net number of liberal laws variable is positively associated with conservative backlash and is statistically significant at the .05 level. When the policy products that emerge from Congress become more liberal, conservatives become more energetic backlashers.[30] In contrast, liberal backlash is associated with the ideological position of House Republicans ($p < .001$). As the GOP has moved right, the annual count of articles about liberal backlashes has increased. In sum, over the 1960–2019 period, conservative backlash has been associated with the liberal thrust of lawmaking whereas liberal backlash has been correlated with the growing radicalism of the GOP.

Who Are the Backlashers?

Many different actors have participated in backlashes since the 1960s. Here I highlight three prominent ones: business, labor unions, and Congress.

BUSINESS BACKLASH

The business community has been an active player in backlash politics. Drawing on the *NYT* measure, table 2.5 provides a select list of backlash episodes in which business interests have been prominently featured. During the early 1970s, business backlash focused on narrow policy targets; for example, the automobile industry fought new environmental regulations. In addition, white businessmen countermobilized against the Small Business Administration's minority loan program, and the advertising industry battled the consumer regulations of the Federal Trade Commission (FTC).

By the middle of the 1970s, the focus of business countermobilization widened to oppose "big government" more generally.[31] Under its ambitious director Michael Pertschuk, the FTC issued regulations targeting used car dealers, optometrists, life insurance companies, vocational schools, vendors of hearing aids, and advertisers who hawked sugared cereals on children's television shows.[32] Between 1981 and 2000, corporate backlash ebbed. This was a neoliberal era in which the federal government regulated markets and corporate activities with a lighter touch and there were fewer regulatory threats on the horizon. The business community again became highly involved in policy backlashes when the political climate shifted left in the 2000s. Key triggers of

TABLE 2.5. Selected *New York Times* Articles about Backlashes and Countermobilizations by Business Interests

Date	Issue	Article Summary
November 18, 1970	Environment and consumer safety	Backlash against the environment and consumer movements is emerging in the automobile industry.
May 16, 1971	Small business loans for minorities	There has been backlash from white businessmen who are unhappy with the Small Business Administration's emphasis on providing loans to minority-owned businesses.
May 30, 1972	Proconsumer positions of Federal Trade Commission (FTC)	The FTC's emergence as an aggressive consumer advocate has triggered backlash from advertisers and broadcasters.
July 18, 1978	Expanded federal role	There is a growing backlash against the federal bureaucracy among New Right conservatives, big businesses, and the Republican Party.
April 16, 1980	FTC authority	The FTC has been taking on a more active role in regulation, drawing backlash from businesses, who have lobbied Congress to restrict the FTC's power.
February 11, 1983	Financial regulation	There is backlash from financial institutions against the new requirement to withhold 10 percent of income from interest or dividends.
June 3, 1984	FTC regulations	The FTC's adversarial relationship with businesses has drawn significant corporate backlash, leading many firms to join the U.S. Chamber of Commerce.
December 9, 1984	Railroad deregulation	Shipper groups claim railroad deregulation has gone too far. Some railroad executives fear backlash against them and are seeking an accommodation with shippers to prevent Congress from intervening.
July 25, 2003	Sarbanes-Oxley Financial Regulations	There is a backlash among some business groups that believe the Sarbanes-Oxley financial reforms went too far.
January 28, 2010	Populist calls for tighter regulations of Wall Street	Wall Street brokers and traders have countermobilized against "fat cat" criticisms about Wall Street and calls for more regulation.
April 23, 2012	Employee rights	The National Labor Relations Board issued a new rule requiring employers to post notices of employee rights, generating business backlash.

Source: Author's compilation of *New York Times* articles.

corporate backlash during this period included the Sarbanes-Oxley Act (a reform intended to prevent fraudulent financial reporting by firms) and the requirement that firms give workers a more visible notice of their labor rights.

The major participation of corporate interests in high-visibility backlash politics is somewhat surprising. A great deal of literature emphasizes that the business community exercises "quiet influence."[33] Why drag conflicts over public policy into the public sphere? It can often be more effective for powerful actors to mask their influence from the public. For example, conservative Republicans employed sub rosa tactics to undercut enforcement of the Voting Rights Act (VRA) of 1965. As Jesse H. Rhodes shows, Republican members of Congress repeatedly voted *for* legislative expansions of the VRA between 1970 and 2006 because they believed that openly opposing voting rights could harm their electoral prospects. Seeking to avoid voter backlash, conservatives "exploited periods of control of one or more branches of the federal government to *incrementally advance* the project of limiting federal voting rights enforcement via the executive branch or the judiciary."[34] The conservative backlash against the VRA largely escaped public notice. Indeed, no articles about this topic appear in the *NYT* measure until the Supreme Court's landmark 2013 decision in *Shelby County v. Holder*, which struck down a key part of the law.

There are several reasons why the business community followed a much more public countermobilization strategy than voting rights opponents. First, the business sector has often *needed* the public's backing to achieve its legislative objectives. While businesses certainly want judges and regulators to support their interests, they also seek a favorable legislative environment. As Mark A. Smith has demonstrated, businesses are often defeated in legislative battles unless they have public opinion on their side. As a result, business groups have incentives to influence lawmakers' decisions indirectly by working through the citizenry using strategic alliances with think tanks and other actors to mold Americans' beliefs about public policy.[35]

A second reason why the business community has often chosen to use a public backlash strategy rather than quiet influence is that it has often lacked the power necessary to nip offending policies in the bud. This was especially true prior to the ascendancy of conservatives in contemporary American politics. As David Vogel argues in his book *Fluctuating Fortunes*, business leaders found themselves on the defensive in the 1960s and early 1970s (relative to their strength in the 1950s) due to the dramatic expansion of federal policy in areas like consumer protection, affirmative action, the environment, occupational health and safety, and energy.[36] To reverse their losses, corporate elites had little choice but to build up their capacity for democratic engagement.

The executives of major companies "hired large numbers of lobbyists and lawyers, opened Washington offices, established and funded political action committees (PACs), expanded the size of their governmental relations staffs, developed sophisticated strategies for influencing public opinion, and learned how to mobilize the 'grass roots.'"[37] The countermobilization of the business sector during this period has had a massive impact on American politics. As Alexander Hertel-Fernandez has shown, groups like the American Legislative Exchange Council (ALEC), which was established in 1973, came into their own between the 1980s and 2000s, "precisely the juncture when the threat to business had diminished."[38] In other words, the liberal policy enactments of the 1960s and 1970s did not simply generate negative feedback that restored the status quo ante. Rather, they instigated the business sector to build durable organizations that reshaped the policy terrain.

Finally, business actors sometimes miss the implications of new policies for their interests. As Leah C. Stokes has argued, "Interest groups and politicians can struggle to forecast policies' likely consequences because of the fog of enactment."[39] When policies impose unexpected costs, businesses may countermobilize to reverse their losses during the critical implementation stage.

LABOR UNION BACKLASH

Like the business community, organized labor has also been a vigorous backlasher in the public arena (see table 2.6). One of the main triggers for participation in backlash politics by private-sector unions since the 1960s has been the enactment of free trade agreements. As chapter 4 shows, unions mobilized against the adoption of the North American Free Trade Agreement (NAFTA) and granting China permanent normalized trade relations, believing these measures would impose concentrated costs on their members in the form of lower wages. This countermobilization did not produce policy reversals, however. Not only had private-sector union membership shrunk, but during the neoliberal era, politicians as diverse as Clinton and Newt Gingrich shared a belief that removing trade barriers would promote widely shared prosperity and that it was futile to resist market forces. As historian Gary Gerstle argues, "By 2000, the institutional matrix that had brought labor such important gains during the New Deal order had been largely wiped out."[40] Labor unions pushed back against neoliberalism but were unable to recoup their previous economic gains.

In contrast to private-sector unions, public-sector unions have not been concerned about free trade and globalization. (State and local governments,

TABLE 2.6. Selected *New York Times* Articles about Backlashes and Countermobilizations by Labor Unions

Date	Issue	Article Summary
June 17, 1980	Trade liberalization	The Carter administration has triggered labor union backlash by resisting protectionist demands by the auto and steel industries.
September 9, 1984	Education reform	There is backlash among teachers' unions to a slew of education reforms, such as testing teachers' competency.
February 4, 1994	Trade liberalization	The Clinton administration anticipates union backlash to its plans to expand the North American Free Trade Agreement.
May 19, 2000	Trade liberalization	President Clinton and the Democratic Party are fighting with their labor union base over giving China permanent normalized trade relations.
July 4, 2000	Education reform	The heads of two national teachers' unions harshly criticized the national push for student testing.
February 1, 2002	Globalization	More than five hundred union members demonstrated against the Gap's use of low-wage factories overseas.
April 21, 2005	Education reform	Backlash to the No Child Left Behind Act is brewing across the nation.
April 5, 2011	Collective bargaining rights	Labor unions and civil rights groups held rallies and teach-ins to protest Republican-led efforts in Wisconsin and Ohio to curb collective bargaining for public employees.

Source: Author's compilation of *New York Times* articles.

unlike private employers, could not threaten to offshore their operations to hire cheaper workers, giving public-sector unions greater bargaining leverage.) Nonetheless, public-sector unions have faced serious threats to their interests, which have stimulated their countermobilization. This is especially the case for teachers' unions. One of the biggest threats to the vested interests of teachers' unions was the attempt to impose greater accountability on public schools. Following the publication of a 1983 blue-ribbon report ("A Nation at Risk") that concluded that America's public schools were failing, many states and localities began adopting reforms that contained penalties for poor learning outcomes. The federal government got in the school accountability game with the passage of the NCLB Act under President George W. Bush in 2002. The NCLB required public schools receiving federal funding to administer nationwide standardized tests to students in certain grades each year, track the performance of various student subgroups, including minorities, and demonstrate that they were making "adequate yearly progress." Schools that did not meet their benchmarks were potentially vulnerable to tough sanctions, including the possibility of being closed. Moreover, teachers in core areas were required to demonstrate proficiency in their subject matter.[41]

The NCLB passed with the endorsement of both the business community and civil rights groups, but the law's implementation alienated many stakeholders, including conservatives, who bristled at the expanded federal role in primary education; parents, who disliked being told that the schools their children attended were failing; and teachers' unions, which viewed accountability as a threat to the jobs, wages, and professional autonomy of their members.[42] The *NYT* database includes twelve articles about the NCLB, which is one of the largest counts of backlash against any law outside of the civil rights arena. The American Federation of Teachers "engaged in an aggressive (and ultimately successful) lobbying campaign" against regulations "that would have restricted collective bargaining rights to contracts under NCLB."[43] In 2015, President Obama ended the accountability reforms at the heart of the NCLB by signing bipartisan legislation (the Every Student Succeeds Act) that eliminated federal penalties for states and districts that perform poorly. This was a major policy reversal, which shifted education power from the federal government back to the states.[44] As Moe argues, teachers' unions largely achieved their goals through the politics of blocking.[45]

CONGRESSIONAL BACKLASH

Congress is a key institutional actor in backlash politics. By legislating, investigating, or taking stands, lawmakers can initiate backlashes—or amplify countermobilizations by their constituencies and organized groups. Many of the clusters of congressional activity that Mayhew catalogs in his book *America's Congress: Actions in the Public Sphere* can be understood as legislative backlashes against policy moves, such as the opposition of Henry Clay (W-KY), Daniel Webster (W-MA), and John C. Calhoun (W-SC) to the policies of the Andrew Jackson administration; the disapproval of Thaddeus Stevens (R-PA), Charles Sumner (R-MA), and Benjamin F. Wade (R-OH) of Reconstruction policy; and the "assault" of conservative Democrats like Martin Dies (D-TX) and Howard Smith (D-VA) on the New Deal and the operations of war agencies.[46]

Table 2.7 highlights select congressional backlashes included in the *NYT* measure. One irony is that when Congress instigates backlashes against policy changes, it is not infrequently opposing its own legislative handiwork. For example, Congress passed landmark reforms in the 1970s to curb pollution but then reinforced the industry backlash against these policies by advocating for weaker environmental protections. By participating in backlash politics,

TABLE 2.7. Selected *New York Times* Articles about Backlashes by Congress

Date	Issue	Article Summary
October 9, 1966	Civil rights	Congress is responding to white backlash by considering amendments to federal school aid legislation to weaken desegregation efforts.
June 13, 1977	Environment	Congressional backlash to environmental policy is leading to a weakening of the Clean Air Act and strip-mining controls, the watering down of offshore oil development regulations, and other policy changes.
September 8, 1985	Trade	President Reagan announced plans to move against unfair trading practices from Japan and other trading partners in response to surging protectionist backlash in Congress.
March 23, 1996	Agriculture	In a backlash to the free-market principles of a 1996 agriculture reform bill, a House-Senate conference committee inserted a provision to allow a New England milk cartel to raise prices.
May 26, 1997	Health	Congress passed the Newborns' and Mothers' Health Protection Act in response to concerns that hospitals have been rushing new mothers out of hospitals in twenty-four hours, which marked the beginning of a legislative backlash against managed care.

Source: Author's compilation of *New York Times* articles.

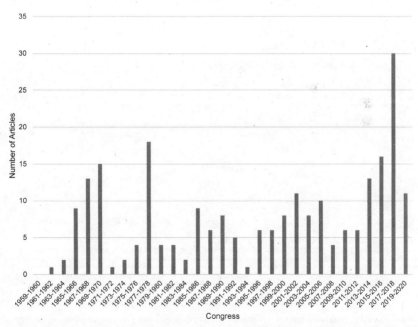

FIGURE 2.7. *New York Times* Articles Mentioning Congressional Backlash, 87th to 115th Congresses
Source: Author's compilation of *New York Times* articles.

lawmakers can both take electorally rewarding stands and advance policy goals, such as when Congress passed legislation to prevent health maintenance organization (HMO) managers from discharging new mothers from the hospital the same the day they gave birth and when it forced President Reagan to crack down on Japan's unfair trading practices.

Figure 2.7 displays trends in the amount of coverage of congressional backlash between the 87th and 115th Congresses. In appendix 2.1, I explore the corelates of the level of media-identified legislative backlash in each biennium and find that it is associated with polarization, the civil rights era, and the start of presidential terms.

Trends in Different Types of Backlash Politics

The *NYT* measure highlights the fact that backlash comes in many forms. After reading each article, I coded the type or types of adverse reactions described therein. Categories included electoral backlash (543), public backlash (536), organizational countermobilization (264), legislative backlash (239), boycotts (32), and violence (7 articles). The vast majority of articles were coded in a single category, but articles that specifically mentioned more than one type of backlash were coded in multiple categories, such as a boycott mobilized by an organization. Examples of each type of backlash are shown in table 2.8.

TABLE 2.8. Examples of Different Types of Backlashes Captured in the *New York Times* Measure

Type of Backlash	Date	Issue	Article Summary
Electoral	October 9, 1966	Civil rights (Black Americans)	White backlash is threatening the political viability of southern Republicans.
	February 17, 1970	Lowering the voting age to eighteen	Witnesses at a congressional hearing stated that television coverage of disruptive college students is creating a backlash among adults that contributed to the defeats of recent referenda in Ohio and New Jersey for lowering the voting age.
	November 5, 1998	Clinton impeachment	Joseph M. Hoeffel III defeated incumbent Jon D. Fox. Hoeffel attributed his victory to voter backlash to the GOP's impeachment of President Clinton.
	May 23, 2011	Health care	There is voter backlash in western New York to Republicans' plans to overhaul the Medicare program.

TABLE 2.8. (*continued*)

Type of Backlash	Date	Issue	Article Summary
Public	January 11, 1976	Civil rights (women)	There is a male backlash in the workplace as women enter traditionally male bastions such as assembly lines.
	July 1, 1986	Immigration	A new public opinion survey suggests that Americans see allowing large numbers of immigrants as damaging job prospects and a strain on the welfare system.
	July 14, 2013	Education	There is backlash from parents to the recent emphasis on testing to promote school accountability.
Public and legislative	October 26, 1989	Environment	The *Exxon Valdez* oil spill has led to huge public protests, and the backlash led Congress to reject Chevon's request to drill in the Arctic National Wildlife Refuge.
Organizational	January 12, 1970	Health	A freeze on the fees doctors can charge under Medicaid has sparked a physician backlash against the program.
	February 12, 1996	Family policy	There is backlash from conservative Christian groups against no-fault divorce laws.
	July 25, 2003	Banking, finance, and commerce	A number of companies and Wall Street firms are lobbying Congress and the Security and Exchange Commission to roll back the Sarbanes-Oxley reforms.
Boycotts	April 13, 1993	Civil rights (gays and lesbians)	After Colorado passed a ballot measure repealing local ordinances banning discrimination against gays, national gay rights groups called for a boycott of the state.
	April 1, 2015	Civil rights (gays and lesbians)	There has been a wave of corporate boycotts over an Indiana law that would allow Christians to refuse to provide services to same-sex couples.
Violence	September 18, 1966	Civil rights for Black Americans	There was mob violence in Grenada, Mississippi, over school integration.
	March 12, 1993	Civil rights for gays	Hate crimes against gays have increased following the debate over allowing gays to serve in the military and efforts to promote gay awareness in the public schools.

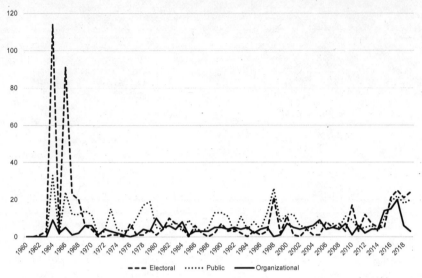

FIGURE 2.8. Count of *New York Times* Articles Mentioning Voter, Public, and Organizational Backlash, 1960–2019

Figure 2.8 displays trends in *NYT* articles mentioning voter, public, and organizational backlashes. The earlier part of the time series is dominated by articles reporting on the anticipation and manifestation of backlash among white voters to civil rights law, the civil rights movement, and Great Society programs that were seen as targeted at cities and minority groups. Over the full time period (1960–2019), public and voter backlashes have tended to move together ($r = .68$). The associations between the counts of articles about both organizational backlashes and voter backlashes ($r = .22$) and the counts of articles about organizational backlashes and public backlashes ($r = .36$) are much weaker.

In appendix 2.2, I use negative binomial regressions to explore the predictors of each type of backlash. The main findings are that all three types of backlash are positively associated with polarization. Voter backlash increases during election years, and public backlash increases when the public mood becomes more conservative.

Anticipated Backlash

Backlash can shape the incentives of policymakers even when it does not materialize. Just the threat that a policy move will trigger backlash can constrain policymakers' behavior, foreclosing alternatives that might otherwise be attractive. Anticipated backlashes are a prime example of the "second face of power" (the mobilization of bias), while backlashes that materialize are an example of the "first face" (open contestation over policy alternatives).[47] Anticipated backlashes play an important role in leading accounts of American politics. For example, in R. Douglas Arnold's theory of congressional policy-making, legislators attempt to predict whether a policy could rouse an inattentive public.[48] Figure 2.9 displays the annual count of *NYT* articles about anticipated and materialized backlashes.

Table 2.9 provides a selective list of episodes in which future backlash was characterized as a clear possibility. What can be learned from this list? At least four points can be made.

First, anticipated backlashes do not always occur, but they often do. Anticipated backlash is a fairly good statistical predictor of materialized backlash the following year.[49] For example, a July 1973 article stated that the Department of Transportation (DOT) feared that a new car safety device—an "interlock" system that prevents the engine from starting if front-seat occupants haven't buckled their seatbelts—would generate mass protests. The DOT officials were right to be apprehensive about the reception the interlock system

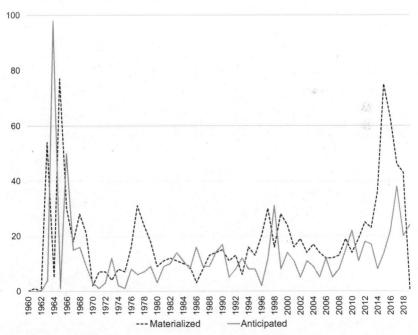

FIGURE 2.9. Count of *New York Times* Articles Mentioning Anticipated and Materialized Backlash, 1960–2019
Source: Author's compilation of *New York Times* articles.

TABLE 2.9. Selected Instances of Anticipated Backlash

Date of NYT article	Policy Area	Type of Backlash	Instance
March 21, 1965	Civil rights	Voter	Democrats fear that a surge of white backlash in southern states in the 1966 elections is likely.
October 26, 1966	Civil rights	Voter	The leaders of the AFL-CIO are nervous that white backlash may reduce votes for prolabor candidates.
May 2, 1972	Environment	Legislative	There is emerging legislative backlash to the National Environmental Policy Act, and some people fear that opponents will blame the law for blackouts.
July 15, 1973	Transportation	Public	The Department of Transportation is concerned about public backlash to a requirement that 1974 model year cars will have an interlock system that prevents the engine from starting unless front-seat occupants have buckled their seat belts.
June 21, 1974	Energy and environment	Public	Some environmentalists fear that utilities will provoke an environmental backlash by passing on to consumers the costs of compliance with the Clean Air Act.
July 12, 1978	Postal service	Public	The president of the American Postal Workers Union sees a possibility of a backlash against public employees.
May 12, 1979	Energy	Public	The House rejected President Carter's gasoline-rationing plan out of fear of backlash from constituents.
September 1, 1981	Agriculture and trade	Public	Agriculture Department economists are concerned that the high level of grain exports will increase domestic prices. They fear that the next time prices increase, public backlash may lead to embargoes.
March 6, 1983	Civil rights	Voter	A group of Black Republicans was invited to the White House to discuss the potential for backlash against the Reagan administration's record on race.
October 6, 1983	Banking, finance, and domestic commerce	Public	The Federal Communications Commission decided to set a monthly fee on access to long-distance calls, but Congress is considering overruling the decision, fearing public backlash.
July 1, 1986	Immigration	Public	Members of Congress warn that public backlash against immigration is possible if tighter controls are not adopted.
August 27, 1986	Labor and social welfare	Economic	The Chamber of Commerce warned that passage of a parental leave bill could lead to employer backlash against men and women of childbearing age.

TABLE 2.9. (*continued*)

Date of NYT article	Policy Area	Type of Backlash	Instance
January 31, 1987	Government ethics and reform	Voter	The Senate has rejected pay increases for senators and government workers due to fear of voter backlash.
September 27, 1989	Education	Public	Some states are hesitant to participate in the National Assessment of Educational Progress standardized test system out of fear of public backlash should the results show their schools are lagging.
March 30, 1994	Social welfare	Public	The Clinton administration is passing significant antipoverty legislation but has remained quiet about these efforts out of fear of backlash from middle-class people.
April 11, 1997	Social welfare	Organizational, Voter	President Clinton let a proposal to pare back cost-of-living adjustments for Social Security and other programs die out of fear of backlash from senior citizens.
September 20, 2004	Immigration	Public	A new influx of immigrants could revive the immigration backlash of the early 1990s.
April 26, 2006	Energy	Organizational	President Bush took steps to stem the increase in energy prices, risking backlash from business leaders and conservatives who were opposed to government interventions.
September 30, 2006	Immigration	Voter	Fearing a voter backlash, House Republicans have abandoned any bill that could be considered to provide amnesty for illegal immigrants.
February 22, 2008	Housing	Voter	Providing relief to homeowners whose mortgages are underwater scares both parties as it could trigger backlash from homeowners who are in better shape.
October 21, 2008	Civil rights	Public	Former Ku Klux Klan leader David Duke has predicted that an Obama victory would lead to white backlash and an increase in the number of white supremacists.
February 6, 2012	Tax, social welfare	Voter	Republicans agreed to extend the payroll tax cut and federal jobless benefits through 2012 due to fear of voter backlash, although they had been opposing these measures.
November 6, 2017	Tax	Voter	Republican proposals to undo or limit federal tax write-offs for state and local taxes could generate voter backlash and jeopardize the Republican majority in Congress.

would receive; the public *hated* it. In response to a consumer revolt, Congress repealed the mandate that car makers install the interlock mechanism.[50]

Second, politicians worry about backlashes arising from many places. In the *New York Times* articles, U.S. politicians are depicted as constantly looking over their shoulders, reflecting on whether the positions they take might create problems with some politically relevant constituency and, if so, whether the resulting trouble would be worth any offsetting gains.

Third, the anticipation of future backlash is a key mechanism by which business firms influence the policy process, by threatening to exercise their structural power over hiring and investment decisions.[51] For example, the Chamber of Commerce warned in 1986 that employers might refuse to hire workers of childbearing years if Congress enacted a family and medical leave bill.[52] Business opposition to family and medical leave remained steadfast over the next four years. The delegates to the White House Conference on Small Business not only opposed a national family and medical leave policy but urged Congress to bar states from enacting their own measures.[53] When Congress finally overcame business opposition and passed a family and medical leave bill in 1990, President George H. W. Bush vetoed the measure, arguing that businesses should provide this benefit voluntarily.[54] Not until Clinton became president in 1993 (with a unified Democratic Congress) did a policy of family and medical leave win adoption.

Finally, anticipated backlash casts a shadow not only over what goals politicians support, but also over *how* politicians design and sell policies. Consider the Clinton administration's "quiet war" against poverty. The administration made large investments in social programs that offer assistance to poor and low-income Americans. However, as it was concerned about the potential for backlash from white, middle-class voters, the Clinton administration leaned heavily on "submerged" policies such as expansions of the Earned Income Tax Credit rather than more direct means of benefit delivery. Further, the administration decided not to make a straightforward moral appeal about the need to provide assistance to Black and Hispanic Americans, who made up a disproportionate share of the beneficiaries. Administration officials assumed (correctly or not) that white backlash could be easily triggered by bringing attention to these constituencies. "You have to use some elliptical language," said Henry G. Cisneros, secretary of housing and urban development.[55] While Clinton's backlash-avoidance strategy may have been encouraged by the antigovernment political climate of the 1990s, it may have made future progressive policymaking more difficult by increasing the disconnect between citizens and government.[56]

Concluding Observations

This chapter has reviewed the trend in backlash politics over the past six decades, as captured by *NYT* coverage. An intriguing finding is that the 2010s were a period of significant backlash activity that was clearly surpassed in intensity only by the 1960s. Both the similarities and differences between the two eras are important. In the 1960s, backlash forces were tremendously powerful but largely confined to the civil rights arena. Back then, the Democratic and Republican parties were internally divided over civil rights and the Vietnam War. As a result, the political impact of counteractions was often dampened rather than amplified by elected officials. *Society* was polarized in the 1960s, but the two parties overlapped a great deal on many domestic issues.

By the 1980s, however, the political terrain had shifted.[57] Backlash forces had diffused from civil rights into other domestic sectors, including health care, trade, education, and immigration. A key difference between the 1960s and the contemporary era is that the policy state became much larger. As Bryan Jones and colleagues argue, the federal government dramatically broadened the scope of its activities, penetrating nearly every aspect of civil society.[58] As the policy state widened its reach, it not only built supportive constituencies but also mobilized opponents who viewed activist government as a threat to their interests or values. While this development was unfolding, partisan polarization was rising, and electoral competition between the two parties was intensifying. As a result, political battles today are increasingly policy battles fought on numerous fronts, and entrepreneurial party leaders and issue advocates continually test to determine which ones can help them gain a strategic advantage.[59]

In reviewing the full data set of nearly two thousand *NYT* articles, I am struck by the diversity of backlashing actors. Businesses, unions, legislators, religious conservatives, environmentalists, and many other actors have participated in countercoalitions at one point or another. Behind the cataloging of events and players, however, my analysis reveals key empirical regularities. Conservative backlash is associated with the production of liberal laws. Liberal backlash is associated with the rightward shift of the GOP. Public backlash climbs when the public mood becomes more conservative. Moreover, the level of legislative backlash rises at the start of presidential terms, when presidents are most disruptive of the status quo.

This chapter provides insights into the overall patterns of backlash politics, but many questions remain unanswered. When have specific policy losses and threats instigated backlashes, and when have they produced quiescence? What have been the consequences of backlash moments? To gain

insight into these questions, a detailed comparison of cases is necessary. The
following chapters turn to that task.

Appendix 2.1

Table A2.1 shows the results of a binomial regression model that predicts the
level of reported legislative backlash in each biennium. The independent variables are partisan polarization in the House, (first dimension NOMINATE), the
policy mood, a "start of term" variable for the first two years of each presidential
term, chamber switch (a dummy variable that takes the value of 1 when partisan
control of the House and/or Senate switches), and divided government.

The key finding is that partisan polarization is strongly associated ($p <$
.01) with media-identified congressional backlash. As the partisan divide has
widened, Congress's participation in backlash politics has increased. In addition, the variable for the start of the presidential term is positive and statistically significant ($p < .05$). In a regression analysis of the number of laws
enacted per Congress, Mayhew found that more laws could be expected to
pass during the first two years of a presidential term than during the second
two years.[60] The results presented here suggest that Congress is not only a
busier legislator early in presidential terms but is also a more active amplifier

TABLE A2.1. Factors Influencing Count of *New York Times* Articles
about Congressional Backlash, 87th to 115th Congresses

Partisan polarization	2.420**
	(1.091)
Policy mood	−0.031
	(0.030)
Divided government	0.047
	(0.255)
Start of presidential term	0.635*
	(0.249)
Chamber switch	0.052
	(0.289)
Civil rights era	0.996*
	(0.470)
Lagged congressional backlash	0.068**
	(0.025)
Intercept	1.339
	(1.866)
Pseudo R^2	0.098
N	29

Note: Table entries are negative binomial regressions, with standard
errors in parentheses.

#$p < .10$; *$p < .05$; **$p < .01$; ***$p < .001$.

of backlashes during this period. Congressional backlash increased during the civil rights era ($p < .05$). The other variables are not significant.

Appendix 2.2

Table A2.2 displays the results of models predicting counts of each of these three types of backlash politics. I again employ negative binomial regressions. Taken together, the results confirm that partisan polarization is a predictor of backlash politics, but they also suggest that each of the three forms of backlash has a somewhat different organizing principle. The polarization variable is positive and significant for all three types of backlash. As expected, the count of articles about voter backlash rises in election years. In contrast, there is little evidence that public and organizational backlashes are responsive to the election cycle. The policy mood variable has a negative and statistically significant influence on the count of articles about public backlashes, suggesting that public backlash activities increase when public opinion becomes more conservative. The civil rights era has a strong association with voter backlash, but not with the other two types. Finally, public backlash has a negative relationship with the unemployment rate, suggesting that protests and other forms of public countermobilization against policy changes tend to be lower during bad economic times.

TABLE A2.2. Factors Influencing Count of *New York Times* Articles about Voter, Public, and Organizational Backlash, 1961–2019

	Voter Backlash	Public Backlash	Organizational Backlash
Polarization	6.121***	2.165*	2.648**
	(1.538)	(1.019)	(0.995)
Policy mood	−0.192	−.0518*	−0.036
	(0.038)	(0.254)	(0.242)
Civil rights era (1963–1968)	3.200***	0.430	0.455
	(0.592)	(3.963)	(0.403)
Election year	0.624*	−0.061	0.139
	(0.286)	(0.181)	(0.178)
Divided government	0.195	−0.208	−0.127
	(0.315)	(0.210)	(0.204)
Unemployment	−0.120	−0.179**	−0.038
	(0.079)	(0.063)	(0.613)
Lagged dependent variable	−0.001	0.000	0.474#
	(0.009)	(0.015)	(0.026)
Constant	−2.078	4.921**	1.778
	(2.247)	(1.495)	(1.484)
Pseudo R^2	0.125	0.044	0.061
N	59	59	59

Note: Table entries are negative binomial regressions, with standard errors in parentheses.
#$p < .10$; *$p < .05$; **$p < .01$; ***$p < .001$.

3

First Do No (Political) Harm:
Backlash Forces in U.S. Health Policymaking

This chapter explores the politics of backlash in federal health policymaking. As is well known, the United States spends substantially more on health care than other wealthy countries yet leaves millions of people without coverage and ranks at or near the bottom on many population health outcomes, such as infant mortality.[1] Any effort to understand the evolution of U.S. health care policymaking—and the reasons why alternative roads were not taken—must recognize how backlash politics, and its anticipation, have constrained policymakers' behavior. There have been backlashes against proposals to restructure the health care system, such as Clinton's health reform proposal and the Affordable Care Act (ACA). There have been backlashes against efforts to dismantle safety-net protections, such as the Republican Party's attempt to retrench Medicare and Medicaid in 1995. And there have even been backlashes against proposals to expand benefits for an organized constituency, such as the attempt to offer senior citizens new benefits through the ill-fated Medicare Catastrophic Coverage Act (MCCA). Neither liberals nor conservatives have discovered a sure-fire approach to moving health policy in their preferred direction without risking or experiencing blowback. Attention to the interaction between policy design elements, the participatory capacities of stakeholder groups, and the incentives created by rising polarization helps explain why health reform proposals frequently trigger backlashes even when they aim to improve the system's performance.

The remainder of this chapter proceeds as follows. I first canvas the *New York Times*'s articles mentioning health policy backlash between 1960 and 2019. Next, I use Mayhew's list of landmark enactments to identify which major health policy changes have aroused negative reactions. Finally, I examine how backlash dynamics shaped the struggle over the passage and entrenchment of the ACA.

Trends in Health Policy Backlash since 1960

Figure 3.1 displays the annual count of *New York Times* articles mentioning "backlash" in health care since 1960. While there have been swings from year to year, the coverage of health policy backlash has remained fairly high since the 1980s. The three years with the highest counts of articles were 2017 (fifteen), 2009 (fifteen), and 1997 (thirteen). Articles during 2017 and 2009 mainly focused on the backlashes against ACA repeal and enactment, respectively. Articles about the "managed care" backlash—the public outcry over restrictions that HMOs and other insurance plans were imposing on patients' access to medical care to contain cost increases—dominated coverage in 1997. In appendix 3.1, I show that the annual count of articles is associated with partisan polarization, the percentage of Americans naming health care as the nation's most important problem, and Democratic presidencies.

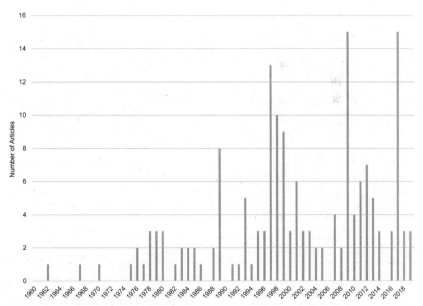

FIGURE 3.1. Count of *New York Times* Articles about Health Policy Mentioning Backlash, 1960–2019
Source: Author's compilation of *New York Times* articles.

Clusters of Health Policy Backlash

In what issue areas of health policy have backlashes been concentrated? Based on an analysis of articles in the *NYT* database, I identify four clusters: national health insurance and coverage expansion, spending restraint and cost control, managed care, and public health (table 3.1).

TABLE 3.1. Clusters of Backlash Politics in Health Policy, 1960–2019

Cluster: Coverage Expansion and National Health Reform

Date	Administration	Issue	Backlash Episode
May 30, 1989	Bush	Growing number of uninsured	Business leaders fear that the growing number of uninsured Americans could provoke a political backlash that will harm industry.
July 24, 1989	Bush	Medicare Catastrophic Coverage Act	Due to the power of senior citizens, Congress is moving to either repeal the Medicate Catastrophic Coverage Act or terminate the surtax paid by some beneficiaries.
September 2, 2009	Obama	Affordable Care Act	Democrats cannot pass health care reform without the support of Blue Dogs elected in conservative districts, who have the most to lose if the bill triggers backlash.
March 1, 2010	Obama	Affordable Care Act	Favors provided to Senator Ben Nelson to gain his support for health reform have generated backlash.
November 16, 2011	Obama	Affordable Care Act	During the 2008 primary campaign, Barack Obama opposed the health insurance mandate, recognizing that it could generate backlash, but once in office he reversed his position.
December 18, 2009	Obama	Medicare buy-in	The Obama administration's decision to scrap language allowing people as young as fifty-five to buy into Medicare in order to appease moderate Democrats has led to progressive backlash.
February 10, 2012	Obama	Birth control coverage in Affordable Care Act	The Obama administration announced its decision to require religiously affiliated hospitals and universities to cover birth control in their insurance plans, triggering backlash from Catholic institutions.

TABLE 3.1. (*continued*)

Cluster: Coverage Expansion and National Health Reform

Date	Administration	Issue	Backlash Episode
November 15, 2013	Obama	Affordable Care Act	President Obama announced a policy reversal that would allow insurance companies to temporarily keep people on health plans that were to be canceled under the new law, calming fear of a backlash among congressional Democrats.
November 17, 2013	Obama	Affordable Care Act	The ACA keeps facing backlash in new places, and now another backlash is occurring over the website's glitches and canceled insurance plans.
October 27, 2014	Obama	Affordable Care Act	Politically, the ACA has not served President Obama or the Democrats well, fueling the anger that helped give rise to the Tea Party movement.
March 29, 2017	Trump	Affordable Care Act repeal	Republicans are grappling with whether they should revive the deeply unpopular ACA repeal bill close to midterm elections and risk angering a broad set of voters.

Cluster: Health Care Cost Control

Date	Administration	Issue	Backlash Episode
February 25, 1967	Johnson	Rising Medicaid spending in New York	The backlash against Medicaid spending reflects the sloppiness with which the program's eligibility rules were drafted.
January 12, 1970	Nixon	Federal efforts to control health care costs	The Nixon administration proposed a freeze on physician fees under Medicaid, which has caused a backlash among doctors.
February 1, 1984	Reagan	Medicare spending	President Reagan will not propose Medicare cuts due to fear of voter backlash.
April 26, 1992	Bush	Rising health care costs	Backlash against rising health insurance costs has led fourteen states to adopt a community-rating system.
September 22, 1995	Clinton	Medicare spending cuts	Democrats hope the Republicans will push their plan for extracting $270 billion from Medicare in seven years so hard that it will prompt a public backlash.

(*continues*)

TABLE 3.1. (*continued*)

Cluster: Health Care Cost Control

Date	Administration	Issue	Backlash Episode
July 6, 2000	Bush	Drug prices	Genentech is producing Avastin, a $100,000/year drug with marginal effects on cancer. Some in the pharmaceutical industry fear a backlash.
April 22, 2011	Obama	Independent Payment Advisory Board	There is a congressional backlash against the Independent Payment Advisory Board, which is intended to curb Medicare spending.
May 22, 2011	Obama	Proposed Medicare cuts	House Republicans who voted to restructure Medicare failed to recognize that the plan will generate voter backlash.

Cluster: Managed Care and Health Maintenance Organizations

Date	Administration	Issue	Backlash Episode
September 29, 1995	Clinton	Maternity patients	There has been a growing backlash against the policies of many HMOs and insurance companies to cover only up to twenty-four hours of hospital care after normal vaginal births.
May 19, 1996	Clinton	Managed care cost control	A backlash of criticism against managed care is forcing health plans to abandon cost-cutting practices.
June 5, 1997	Clinton	HMOs and managed care	Texas will become the first state where consumers will explicitly be allowed to sue HMOs on grounds of medical malpractice or negligence, one of the sharpest reactions yet in the backlash against HMO power.
July 14, 1997	Clinton	HMOs and managed care	State legislatures have introduced over one thousand managed care bills this year, some of which require HMOs to authorize hospital stays after mastectomies and pay for avoidable emergency room visits.
February 16, 1998	Clinton	HMOs and managed care	The debate over managed health care and consumer rights has been stirring a populist backlash in state capitals, shattering long-standing alliances among doctors, business leaders, and probusiness Republicans.

TABLE 3.1. (*continued*)

Cluster: Managed Care and Health Maintenance Organizations

Date	Administration	Issue	Backlash Episode
January 13, 1999	Clinton	HMOs and managed care	Managed care abuses have caused legislative backlash, resulting in laws such as the Newborns' and Mothers' Health Protection Act of 1996 and the Patients' Bill of Rights Act pending in Congress.

Cluster: Disease, Vaccination and Public Health

Date	Administration	Issue	Backlash Episode
July 31, 1978	Carter	Flu immunization	The House voted against spending fifteen million dollars for a flu immunization program in a legislative backlash to the 1976 swine flu vaccine, which resulted in deaths and injuries due to side effects.
September 25, 1998	Clinton	AIDs	State legislatures are increasingly passing laws that make it a crime to transmit or expose others knowingly to AIDS. This reflects a backlash from earlier laws that protected the civil liberties of people infected with HIV.
December 14, 2002	Bush	Smallpox vaccination	The Bush administration announced the nation's first smallpox vaccination campaign and is willing to accept the potential backlash from complications of the vaccine.
February 12, 2007	Bush	Vaccination to prevent cervical cancer	Administration of the new vaccine for human papilloma virus (HPV) has been mandated in twenty states, causing a backlash among religious conservatives and others.
March 2, 2008	Bush	Vaccination	As states require more vaccines for school-age children, a backlash is growing.
June 18, 2019	Trump	Vaccination	The nation is facing a serious measles outbreak, yet curbing religious and philosophical exemptions to vaccination has proved difficult. In Oregon, a push for limiting nonmedical exemptions provoked a furious backlash.

Source: Author's compilation of *New York Times* articles.

NATIONAL HEALTH INSURANCE
AND COVERAGE EXPANSION

The United States stands out from other wealthy democracies in lacking national health insurance. Many Americans fall through the cracks when seeking insurance coverage, especially those too young for Medicare or too rich
to be eligible for Medicaid based on their state of residence. While the ACA
has expanded coverage substantially, it did not replace America's patchwork
system. Why is there no national health insurance in the United States? What
explains American health care exceptionalism? A large body of scholarship
investigates the impact of a range of factors, including institutional fragmentation, political culture, and path dependence.[2] My focus here is on a
narrower set of questions; namely, when have efforts to expand health care
coverage or benefits sparked backlashes and how has the desire to forestall
backlashes shaped policymakers' decisions?

The senior citizen mobilization against the MCCA is a canonical example
of backlash politics in the health care arena.[3] Enacted by large bipartisan majorities in 1988, the attempt to offer seniors coverage for catastrophic care
grew out of concerns that policymakers had failed to update the Medicare
benefit package to reflect changes in medical services and costs since the mid-
1960s.[4] The Reagan administration and Congress agreed to expand Medicare
to cover prescription drugs and limit enrollees' out-of-pocket payments for
covered services. Public opinion surveys taken shortly before the act's passage showed that seniors overwhelmingly approved of the measure.[5] But as
Richard Himmelfarb observes in his excellent analysis of the MCCA, only a
few months after the law was enacted, seniors "were in open revolt" against
the program, a reaction that caught lawmakers by surprise.[6]

Both policy attributes and the participatory capacities of beneficiary
groups facilitated this backlash. In order to win Reagan's approval, the new
benefits were financed though income-related premiums. Making affluent seniors pay for their own benefits constituted a departure from the traditional
funding sources used for Social Security and Medicare (payroll taxes and general revenues). These concentrated costs were highly visible for those older
Americans who were subject to the mandatory additional charges. Beyond
their direct economic costs, the supplemental premiums fostered the perception that better-off seniors were being forced to support others who had
lacked the foresight to save for their retirement.[7] While the premiums were
collected up-front, the new benefits were phased in over time. These policy
attributes weakened the law's capacity to build a supportive constituency.[8] In
addition, strong reliance interests were at stake. Many seniors already had

supplemental, private insurance policies (called Medigap) to cover gaps in Medicare's coverage. Policymakers failed to recognize how strongly attached the elderly were to their existing Medigap plans and that many people were not interested in switching to a government program.[9] Finally, interest-group countermobilization played a major role in the backlash. Organizations like the National Committee to Save Social Security and Medicare, along with firms that sold Medigap policies and some unions, attacked the law, sending misleading mailings that created the impression that all seniors, regardless of income, were subject to the surtax. Political support for the MCCA collapsed in the face of the uprising.[10] In a remarkable policy reversal, Congress repealed the law nearly in its entirety in 1989.[11]

Policymakers drew important lessons from the MCCA backlash that influenced the design of Medicare Part D, the prescription drug bill enacted as part of the Medicare Modernization Act (MMA) of 2003.[12] One lesson is that seniors resist paying for their own drug benefits. Policymakers thus subsidized the prescription drug program through general revenues. A second lesson is that people resent being forced to pay for coverage they believe they do not need. Policymakers therefore made participation in Medicare Part D voluntary. Finally, the MCCA backlash convinced policymakers that they needed to quickly phase in some benefits in order to cultivate a constituency.[13] The MMA almost immediately gave beneficiaries a prescription drug discount card and a lower deductible.

HEALTH CARE SPENDING RESTRAINT AND COST CONTROL

A second backlash cluster consists of health care spending restraint and cost control.[14] Growth in health care spending began to generate concern among national policymakers during the late 1960s. The initial fear was that spending for programs like Medicare and Medicaid was crowding out other budgetary priorities. In more recent years, policymakers have worried about the impact of rising health care spending on the overall economy. In 2019 the United States spent a total of 17 percent of gross domestic product (GDP) on health care (including spending by governments, businesses, and households), far more than the share of GDP devoted to health care spending in other rich democracies, even though the United States performs much less well on health outcome measures like infant mortality.[15] While there is an expert consensus that the American health care system costs too much and delivers too little, policymakers have generally not embraced the tools employed in other wealthy nations to control medical costs, such as global budgets, supply-side controls on the diffusion of medical technology, and the use of cost-effectiveness analysis in coverage decisions. Many factors explain why the United States has chosen to follow a distinctive path on health care cost-containment, including the fragmentation of U.S. health care financing.[16]

However, the simplest explanation for why U.S. policymakers have eschewed the most aggressive cost-control strategies is that they have sought to avoid provoking backlashes. Policymakers have been at pains not to antagonize two sets of stakeholders. The first consists of what Paul Starr calls "the protected public"—middle-class and older Americans who, as a result of previous reforms, enjoy reasonable insurance coverage through their jobs, the Veterans Administration (VA), or programs like Medicare.[17] Members of the protected public are the relative winners in the American health care system. As Starr argues, they believe they have earned their coverage, are highly attached to existing arrangements, and react negatively to threats to their privileged status. The second set of stakeholders includes doctors, hospitals, pharmaceutical firms, medical device companies, and health insurance companies. Any effort to reduce health care spending or lower costs harms the financial interests of these stakeholders, which hold substantial lobbying advantages over taxpayers and other diffuse interests, and policy outcomes broadly reflect this balance of forces. As Jonathan Oberlander observes, "American health politics are littered with failed efforts to pass robust cost controls, hyped reforms that did not live up to their promise, and potentially effective policies that were enacted only to be weakened in implementation or discontinued."[18]

This is not to suggest that policymakers have done nothing to curb health care spending. In fact, policymakers have taken meaningful steps to control the spending growth of Medicare. Congress adopted a prospective payment system for hospitals and a fee schedule for physicians, and it included Medicare savings in many deficit reduction laws during the 1980s. But Congress has generally avoided imposing large, visible losses on Medicare beneficiaries, attacking the profits of the medical products industry, or challenging physicians' professional autonomy.[19] When policymakers have moved in these directions, they have frequently encountered resistance from stakeholder groups. Backlashes have at times been sparked by even modest efforts to control spending. For example, in 1970 the Nixon administration triggered a backlash among physicians when it froze the fees that could be charged under the Medicaid program. The provider backlash intensified the next year when the administration issued an executive order that temporarily capped hospital prices and physicians' fees. The hospital industry countermobilized against legislative proposals to extend the duration of the cap, which then died in Congress.[20]

Efforts to weed out inappropriate or low-value medical services have invariably been met with provider resistance. For example, in 1989 Medicare administrators proposed a coverage rule that would allow the denial of services found to be cost-ineffective. Doctors, hospitals, and industry groups mobilized against the proposal, and the agency subsequently withdrew it.[21] In a similar vein, the Agency for Health Care Policy and Research (AHCPR) provoked a doctor backlash during the mid-1990s when it questioned the clinical benefits of spinal-fusion surgery for back patients. The report concluded that the surgery was not based on reliable evidence and caused many complications. Back surgeons reacted angrily to this challenge to their professional sovereignty. In response to pressure from medical societies, Congress cut AHCPR's budget by 21 percent, removed the word "policy" from the agency's name, and forced it to get out of the guideline-writing business.[22] When Medicare was enacted in 1965, the program's designers made large concessions to obtain the support of physicians.[23] First, "the federal government surrendered direct control of the program and its costs," allowing providers to nominate private insurers, rather than government bureaucrats, to process claims and reimbursements.[24] Second, it made no attempt to use its bargaining leverage to obtain good terms for taxpayers, instead agreeing to pay doctors whatever was standard and customary for their services.[25] These accommodations ensured that physicians would develop a vested interest in the program, thus contributing to its political sustainability. But the concessions would prove to be terribly expensive ones.

Proposed cuts to Medicare benefits have also mobilized opposition. In 1995, the new House Republican majority, led by Speaker Newt Gingrich (R-GA), attempted to change Medicare's fundamental character by shifting enrollees into a defined-contribution program. While Medicare would remain an entitlement, the government's financial commitment would no longer be open-ended but rather subject to hard budget caps. In addition, Republicans proposed to extract $270 billion from Medicare over seven years.[26] Democrats had just lost their House majority for the first time in forty years, partly in reaction to voter backlash to Clinton's health reform proposal. They were overjoyed that Republicans were plunging ahead with a risky health care plan of their own and expressed their fervent wish that the GOP would push the proposal through the House "so hard that they would prompt a public backlash."[27] That is indeed what happened. Public opinion surveys showed that three-quarters of Americans opposed the cuts in the rate of Medicare spending.[28] Clinton vetoed the spending reductions and leveraged his protection of both Medicare and Medicaid as a signature issue in his successful 1996 reelection campaign.

MANAGED CARE

The countermobilization against "managed care" constitutes a third major backlash cluster. Managed care is a broad category that includes both HMOs and a diverse set of organizational strategies that payers use to restrain health care spending and curb the use of low-value medical services, such as conducting utilization reviews and requiring patients to be treated within a limited network of physicians.[29] Managed care plans grew rapidly during the 1990s and covered almost three in four workers with employer-provided health insurance by 1995.[30]

While it would go too far to argue that the federal government created or planned managed care in the commercial sector, it clearly established a policy framework that was conducive to its emergence and growth. During the early 1970s, President Nixon endorsed HMOs as part of his strategy to restrain medical costs and establish "incentives for preventative health care and efficient services and a more competitive health-care market."[31] Congress responded to Nixon's interest by passing the HMO Act of 1973. While the American Medical Association (AMA) never got on board, commercial insurers reversed their initial opposition to the measure "once they recognized that the program would, if nothing else, create a precedent for enhanced insurer authority over physicians."[32] The law "provided start-up funds to encourage the development of HMOs, overrode State anti–managed care laws, and required large firms to offer an HMO choice to their employees."[33] While the 1973 act failed to stimulate the growth of government-subsidized HMOs, it nonetheless encouraged private insurers "to experiment with HMOs" and "embrace tighter provider relationships."[34] The growth of managed care arrangements in the private sector was further encouraged in 1983 when Congress changed the way Medicare compensated hospitals. Instead of reimbursing hospitals for reported costs, Medicare would use a prospective payment system to compensate hospitals according to a fee schedule based on each patient's diagnosis.[35] As a result of these developments, "insurers spread managed care techniques throughout the health care system during the 1980s."[36]

Initially, managed care appeared to be quite successful in slowing the growth of employer premiums. By the mid-1990s, however, both the public and many doctors had soured on the model. As David Mechanic writes, "The chorus of opposition from physicians and other professionals, negative media coverage, repeated atrocity-type anecdotes, and bashing by politicians all contribute[d] to the public's discomfort with new arrangements. . . . But a more fundamental reason for the public perception is that most Americans are discomforted by the idea of having their care rationed and, at some level, they understand that managed care is a mechanism for doing so."[37] In other advanced democracies, like Canada and the United Kingdom, providers can ration the care that patients receive because government policymakers impose upstream limits on the overall quantity of medical services that are available downstream. In the United States, however, policymakers do not set limits on the supply of medical services. As health economist Uwe E. Reinhardt observed, "Rationing health care explicitly, with appeal solely to money budgets and within sight of excess physical capacity, is much more irritating than seems to be the implicit rationing with appeal to limited physical capacity that is commonly practiced abroad."[38]

Managed care began to generate a backlash in the 1990s in large part because it was perceived to impose concentrated costs on patients, such as prior authorization requirements, which required them to get permission before they could receive a particular treatment or see a specialist. Additionally, managed care plans began to mobilize opposition because their own operations produced self-undermining feedback effects. Initially, most patients signed up for HMOs on a voluntary basis. HMOs were attractive for low-risk, healthy people who did not object to restrictions on utilization or physician choice because they assumed they would not need to use medical services. But many employers—observing the apparent success of the plans in restraining premium growth—began switching their entire workforce to managed care plans.[39] As a result, higher-risk patients with expensive medical conditions were forced to join the plans. These patients naturally began incensed when they discovered they were not getting the kind of coverage to which they had been accustomed in comprehensive indemnity plans. In sum, the very success of the low-cost, highly restrictive managed care model changed the enrolled population, and in so doing, it disrupted health insurance arrangements to which people had been strongly attached. According to health economist Alain Enthoven,

> Large numbers of consumers were converted—often involuntarily—from the freedom of FFS [fee-for-service] coverage to the limitations of HMOs, often without much explanation of the limitations or their relationship to cost-containment. Neither the employers nor the managed care organizations wanted to emphasize the limitations on choice of doctor. So people approached managed care with the expectations they had acquired under FFS. Suddenly people found themselves under limitations they had not experienced before. In many cases, people were forced to change doctors, not permitted to go to the doctor they wanted, or were denied proposed medical procedures. Because they experienced no direct visible financial benefit, these differences between

FFS and managed care coverage were perceived as a pure "takeaway." Employers waited too long to respond to rising costs and then were in too much of a hurry and they were too reluctant to offer employees a choice and expose them to premium differences.

The backlash was made worse by the fact that large numbers of people were offered no choice of health insurance plan. A survey done by the Harvard School of Public Health found that 42% of Americans with employer-based health insurance had no choice of plan. Even of those with choices, 20% complained that they did not have enough variety of choice, and 31% of the total sample said their employer forced them to change health plans in the past five years. This and other surveys found that dissatisfaction levels among those without choice are typically twice as high as among those with choices.[40]

Executives of U.S. managed care organizations found themselves the object of public scorn. Characters in popular movies, such as the single-mom of an ill child (played by Helen Hunt) in the 1998 hit *As Good as It Gets*, won cheers from audiences around the country for cursing out HMO decision making.[41] While defenders of the industry argued that claims of public opposition were overblown, a careful review of public opinion data by Robert J. Blendon and colleagues confirmed that Americans' negative impressions of managed care were driven by two main factors. First, a "significant proportion of Americans were reporting problems with managed care plans," including frustration about waiting times and access to specialists and tests.[42] Second, public awareness of rare, but highly threatening and dramatic, events associated with managed care made the public fearful that "regardless of how well their plans perform today, care might not be available or paid for when they are very sick."[43]

Questions of how to respond to the managed care backlash dominated the health policy debate for nearly a decade. According to one count, more than one thousand bills responding to the backlash were introduced in Congress and state legislatures.[44] At the national level, President Clinton signed the Newborns' and Mothers' Health Protection Act of 1996 to require insurance plans to pay for at least a forty-eight-hour hospital stay following childbirth.[45] States adopted "'patients' bills of rights' that limited the ability of managed care firms to restrict care and shape the incentives of medical practitioners," such as regulations ensuring that maternity patients could see their gynecologist without a referral.[46] These responses had a material impact on health care spending. According to a careful study in the *RAND Journal of Economics*, restrictions on managed care led to a large and significant increase in hospital spending in counties with high levels of managed care.[47]

Finally, the public health arena has long been subject to backlash forces. One of the most important manifestations of public health backlash is "vaccine hesitancy." Even before the COVID-19 pandemic, U.S. states were experiencing significant declines in the percentage of parents vaccinating their children for diseases like measles, mumps, and rubella.[48] Research suggests that vaccine hesitancy has increased due to declining trust in the pharmaceutical industry, internet-circulated allegations that vaccines cause autism, declining deference to medical authority, and, ironically, the decrease in the prevalence of many diseases (showing that vaccination can be the victim of its own success).[49] Some state legislatures have attempted to increase childhood vaccination rates by curbing nonmedical exemptions, only to provoke furious public backlashes.[50]

The COVID-19 pandemic created perfect conditions for backlashes against public health policies. Virtually every decision that officials made threatened some constituency's social identity or imposed costs on organizations or individuals. If policymakers shut down the economy, they threatened the livelihood of small business owners. If they allowed businesses to remain open, they threatened people who feared contracting the disease. Closing public schools imposed massive learning and socialization costs on children, but policymakers in many states struggled to keep the schools open without triggering countermobilizations from both teachers' unions and parents who were anxious about their kids returning to the classroom. The polarization of COVID-related issues like mask use, capacity restrictions on houses of worship, and even what the virus should be labeled (President Trump called it the "Chinese virus") encouraged actors to "pick a side" in these conflicts consistent with their partisan identity.[51] While the overwhelming majority of the protests against COVID-related policies were law-abiding, some were not. In California, antivaccine protesters temporarily shut down a mass vaccination site at Dodger Stadium.[52] And in Michigan, the Federal Bureau of Investigation thwarted a plot by right-wing extremists to kidnap Governor Gretchen Whitmer, who had "become a focal point of antigovernment views and anger over coronavirus control measures."[53] The conservative backlash to the perceived overreach of COVID-related health orders will constrain the response to future pandemics. Since 2020, many states have curtailed the authority of public health officials to close businesses and schools, issue mask mandates, and impose other restrictions without the approval of elected officials.[54]

Backlash against Landmark Health Policy Enactments

Another way to explore backlash dynamics in the health care sector is by tracking the histories of major health policy laws. Table 3.2 uses Mayhew's list of "landmark laws" to identify major health laws enacted by Congress between 1960 and 2019.[55] There are twenty-five laws in all, beginning with the Kerr-Mills Act of 1960 and ending with the opioid crisis response legislation

TABLE 3.2. Landmark Health Laws, 1960–2019

Law	Final Roll Call Votes	Congress, President, Party Control of House and Senate	Backlash Indicators and Comments
Kerr-Mills aid for the medically needy aged	H: 369–17 S: 74–11	1959–1960, Eisenhower, D Congress	Many states declined to participate.
Drug regulation	H: 347–0 S: 78–0	1961–1962, Kennedy, D Congress	This strengthened FDA regulation and capacity.
Aid for the mentally ill	H: 335–18 S: 72–1	1963–1964, Kennedy, D Congress	Only about half the planned community-based mental health centers were built due to budget constraints and bureaucratic tensions, but there was no public backlash.
Aid to medical schools	H: 288–122 S: 71–9	1963–1964, Kennedy, D Congress	This was expanded several years later.
Medical Care for the Aged (Medicare)	H: 307–116 S: 70–24	1965–1966, Johnson, D Congress	AMA cooperation was secured through major concessions, and no public backlash occurred postenactment.
Regional medical centers for heart disease, cancer, and stroke	Passed by voice votes in both House and Senate	1965–1966, Johnson, D Congress	The final bill reflected accommodations to the AMA; it expired in 1974 and was replaced by the National Health Planning and Resources Development Act.
Ban on cigarette advertising on radio and TV	H: voice vote S: 75–9	1969–1970 Nixon, D Congress	Tobacco firms sued but the Supreme Court declined to review the lower court decision upholding the dvertising ban.
National Cancer Act	H: 350–5 S: 85–0	1971–1972, Nixon, D Congress	There was modest pushback from scientists, who argued that the "war on cancer" distorted research priorities.
Aid for development of health maintenance organizations	H: 369–40 S: 83–1	1973–1974, Nixon, D Congress	This encouraged the emergence of managed care, which sparked intense backlash in the 1990s.

TABLE 3.2. (*continued*)

National Health Planning and Resources Development Act of 1974	H: 236–79 S: 65–18	1973–1974, Ford, D Congress	This was a failed effort to promote national health planning; the Reagan administration ended federal certificate-of-need requirements in 1986.
Catastrophic health insurance for the aged	H: 328–72 S: 86–11	1987–1988, Reagan, D Congress	This triggered a ferocious backlash, leading to repeal.
Health insurance portability act	H: 421–2 S: 98–0	1995–1996, Clinton, R Congress	Some states did not comply, forcing the federal government to enforce the law directly.
Overhaul of Food and Drug Administration	H: voice vote S: 98–2	1997–1998, Clinton, R Congress	This built on prior reforms; there was smooth implementation.
Medicare Reform (Medicare Modernization Act)	H: 220–215 S: 54–44	2003–2004, G. W. Bush, R Congress	This was enacted with a contentious partisan vote; the law did not trigger a sharp public backlash, though initial public approval was low.
Guarantee of mental illness insurance	H: 263–171 S: 74–25	2007–2008, G. W. Bush, D Congress	The ACA built on this framework to expand the reach of federal requirements for mental health parity.
Expansion of State Children's Health Insurance Program	H: 290–135 S: 66–32	2009–2010, Obama, D Congress	This was a Democratic expansion of a program that once had bipartisan support. George W. Bush twice vetoed its reauthorization.
Tobacco regulation	H: 307–97 S: 79–17	2009–2010, Obama, D Congress	Many tobacco companies opposed the measure, but Phillip Morris, seeing advantage in tighter regulation, came out in support.
Affordable Care Act	H: 220–207 S: 56–43	2009–2010, Obama, D Congress	This sparked public, electoral, and organizational backlash.
Permanent fix to Medicare's sustainable growth rate formula	H: 392–37 S: 92–8	2015–2016, Obama, R Congress	This was a successful phase-out of the previous physician payment mechanism.
Opioids policy	H: 407–5 S: 92–2	2015–2016, Obama, R Congress	This was a bipartisan effort.
21st Century Cures Act	H: 392–26 S: 94–5	2015–2016, Obama, R Congress	This was embraced by industry and patient groups.
Repeal of Affordable Care Act's individual mandate (included in tax cut legislation)	H: 224–201 S: 51–48	2017–2018, Trump, R Congress	This was the GOP's major policy accomplishment in the ACA repeal drive.

(continues)

TABLE 3.2. (continued)

Law	Final Roll Call Votes	Congress, President, Party Control of House and Senate	Backlash Indicators and Comments
Veterans Affairs Whistleblower Protection	H: 368–55 S: voice vote	2017–2018, Trump, R Congress	This law protected whistleblowers and made it easier for the VA to fire bad employees.
Veterans Affairs Mission Act	H: 347–70 S: 92–5	2017–2018, Trump, R Congress	This expanded veterans' access to private care and created a commission (which triggered backlash) to make recommendations for facility closures.
Opioid Crisis Response Act of 2018	H: 393–8 S: 99–1	2017–2018, Trump, R Congress	This was a bipartisan effort.

Sources: The list of health policy enactments is from David R. Mayhew's updated list of landmark laws, https://works.bepress.com/david-mayhew/?q=landmark+laws. Roll call votes from the Mayhew list through 2012 are from Curry and Lee 2020 and from Congress.gov for subsequent years. Sources for implementation histories include Starr 1982, 2017; Oliver 2011; Oberlander 2003; Mueller 1988; Gritter 2019; Kronenfeld 1997; and Rein 2022.

of 2018. For each, I examined standard secondary sources to assess whether there was evidence of backlash during or after their passage. Laws that Mayhew identifies as especially significant are in italics. The twenty-five laws can be categorized as follows:

- Two of the laws sparked backlash and were terminated: the MCCA and the National Health Planning and Resources Development Act of 1974. The latter was a broadly unsuccessful attempt to constrain health care spending through federal planning, whereby states were required to adopt "certificate-of-need" (CON) laws before approving new health facilities or services. Congress scrapped the CON mandate and associated federal funding in 1986 due to opposition from the Reagan administration, the AMA, and the American Hospital Association.[56]
- Many states declined to participate in the Kerr-Mills Act, and by 1963, less than 1 percent of seniors were covered by the program.[57]
- The ACA survived an intense, decade-long countermobilization. Another of the laws on the list (the repeal of the individual mandate) was the result of the backlash.
- One law (the HMO Act of 1973) expressed federal support for an alternative to traditional health insurance models.[58] While this law's early effects were modest, it facilitated the growth of managed care, which sparked a ferocious public backlash in the 1990s.

- The health insurance portability act, adopted on a bipartisan basis in the wake of the backlash to Clinton's comprehensive health reform proposal, provided only marginal benefits to people who already had insurance. Some states failed to implement the law's regulations, forcing the federal government to assume direct enforcement responsibilities.[59]

- The 2018 overhaul of the Veterans Administration (VA) sparked backlash on Capitol Hill. The act established a commission (similar to the Defense Base Closure and Realignment Commission) to approve or modify recommendations from the department to close or reduce the services of underused VA hospitals and clinics. The goal was to allow members of Congress to avoid blame for imposing concentrated costs on geographic communities, but the strategy failed. When lawmakers were briefed on possible service reductions in their districts, they "went on the offensive, some holding rallies in opposition, others issuing defiant statements that previewed the battle to stave off reductions."[60] A bipartisan group of senators then killed the commission.

- Of the remaining seventeen laws on Mayhew's list, two (the MMA and the children's health insurance program) sparked significant opposition during or after their enactments. The reactions to the fifteen other laws were relatively consensual.

In sum, nearly one-third of the landmark health laws enacted between 1960 and 2019 sparked (or were the casualty of) backlash politics in one fashion or another. The mobilization of opposition forces in response to shifts in the health policy status quo is clearly not an atypical pattern. Rather, it happens regularly.

The ACA and the Politics of Backlash

By far the most intense backlash in the health policy arena since 1960 was the ten-year war over the ACA ("Obamacare").[61] The ACA is not the first major health law to be enacted after a highly contentious debate. Supporters of Medicare had to overcome the AMA's strenuous opposition in order to win its adoption in 1965.[62] But the backlash against the ACA has nonetheless been distinctive. Once Medicare was enacted, both voters and key stakeholders embraced the law. In contrast, the ACA's partisan enactment (not a single Republican voted for it) and rocky rollout stimulated voter backlash against the Democrats in the 2010 elections and contributed to the party's loss of its House majority.[63] Beyond the ballot box, the law sparked grassroots protests by Tea Party activists and countermobilizations by businesses, unions, and providers.[64] Scholars debate just how close Republicans came to killing Obamacare. Some argue that the GOP's ideological divisions on health care made it extremely unlikely that the party would ever coalesce in favor of a repeal-and-replace bill.[65] Others emphasize that Republicans came very close to success, noting that a repeal bill fell just three votes short in the Senate in 2017.[66] Either way, the ACA backlash was remarkable.

CONSEQUENCES OF THE BACKLASH

The backlash against the ACA had significant policy consequences. First, it clipped the Obama administration's wings, making its health reform project less ambitious than it might have been.[67] The interest-group countermobilization against the ACA began during the preenactment phrase. Health reform legislation posed a financial risk to the drug industry, which feared that the law would authorize the federal government to negotiate drug prices under Medicare (a power finally granted on a limited basis in 2022) and permit the importation of cheap prescription drugs from Canada. The Pharmaceutical Research Manufacturers Association—the lobbying organization for the drug industry—threatened to withhold its support for the bill unless these provisions were excluded. Fearing that the drug industry could run a massive negative media campaign—similar to the way in which the insurance industry had tarnished Clinton's health care bill through its famous "Harry and Louise" ads—the administration accepted these demands.[68] Other key provisions that were excluded from the law included a national exchange that would not be dependent on the cooperation of state government, tough "pay-or-play" requirements for small businesses, and—to the great dismay of progressives, who felt it was important—a government-sponsored insurance program or "public option" for the uninsured. While many factors contributed to these omissions, including the GOP's unrelenting opposition, the countermobilization of interest groups was instrumental. Health industry firms and their employees gave almost $1.5 million in campaign contributions to Senate Finance Committee chair Max Baucus (D-MT) between 2007 and 2008.[69]

In addition to limiting what was included in the law, the backlash created new geographic inequalities in the U.S. health care system by widening differences among the states in how the Medicaid program is administered.[70] While the ACA was intended to broaden access to health care services for low-income people, for a period of time, access to Medicaid services ironically became *more* restrictive in a number of states than it was before the ACA was enacted.

How did this happen? In an insightful article, Richard C. Fording and Dana Patton demonstrate that some GOP governors had reservations about accepting funding under the ACA to expand Medicaid coverage for most low-income adults to 138 percent of the federal poverty level but recognized that taking the federal money would bring financial benefits to their state and help protect rural hospitals.[71] As a result, Republican governors in states such as Arizona, Ohio, and Indiana made the pragmatic decision to embrace Medicaid expansion even though it created electoral problems for them with their conservative bases. In some conservative states, concerns were raised about whether people eligible for Medicaid expansion were truly "deserving."[72] To manage the potential for a backlash from conservative voters, many red-state governors requested permission from the federal government to limit Medicaid eligibility in their programs. A popular move was to impose work requirements for able-bodied, nonelderly Medicaid recipients. Work requirements and similar proposals allowed GOP governors in participating states to argue that Medicaid expansion was not welfare and distinct from the traditional Medicaid program. Once the forces of backlash were unleashed, however, they took on a life of their own. Fording and Patton show that work requirements then diffused to states that did *not* participate in the Medicaid expansions.[73] In these states, services became harder for lower-income people to get than before the ACA was enacted. To be sure, the courts blocked Medicaid work requirements from going into effect in many states and the Biden administration subsequently withdrew the Trump-era policy. But research shows that Medicaid work requirements led to coverage losses during the brief period in which they were implemented.[74]

While the backlash against the ACA undercut the law's ability to achieve the goals of its architects, the law survived.[75] Indeed, the GOP's attempt to repeal the ACA *itself* sparked voter backlash against Republicans in the 2018 midterms, helping the Democrats retake the House. In sum, backlash to the ACA cost the Democrats congressional seats and likely majority status in the House for eight years. And yet, defending the ACA proved to be a winning issue for the Democrats in 2018. Moreover, some of the ACA's benefits, such as regulatory protections for people with preexisting conditions, now appear to be entrenched.

Two factors explain these patterns. The first is partisan polarization, which has given elected officials of both parties an incentive to make the perceived and actual losses associated with the ACA focal points for countermobilizations.[76] The second factor is the policy design of the law itself, which has produced a mix of negative (self-undermining) and positive (self-reinforcing) feedbacks.[77] Next I examine how policy feedbacks and partisan forces fueled the backlash against the ACA as well as the subsequent backlash against the GOP's repeal drive.[78]

POLARIZATION AND THE ACA BACKLASH

In the past, conservative officeholders have often bitterly contested the enactment of major new programs but supported, or at least resigned themselves to, the policies once they won adoption. For example, the GOP's 1936 presidential nominee, Alf Landon, called for the repeal of Social Security and conservatives in Congress attacked the program on financial, ideological, and legal grounds. Yet by the early 1950s, strong bipartisan majorities in Congress supported increasing Social Security benefits.[79] The response was broadly similar for Medicare. There were no efforts to repeal Medicare or challenge its constitutionality following its enactment.[80]

In contrast, the ACA had to survive a ten-year partisan battle marked by constant conflict, widespread challenges to its implementation, and serious threats to its existence.[81] The policy backlash played out in many institutional venues. At the federal level, congressional Republicans voted to repeal the ACA over *seventy* times during 2010–2017.[82] Republican-led states joined a suit against the law that challenged the constitutionality of the individual mandate requiring most Americans to obtain insurance coverage or pay a penalty to the federal government. In 2012, the Supreme Court narrowly upheld the mandate as a tax but surprisingly ruled that the ACA's provision for Medicaid expansion was unconstitutional because it unduly coerced the states. That ruling effectively made Medicaid expansion optional for the states, thus forcing Republicans policymakers to decide whether to accept ACA funding or use their power to undercut a central pillar of the law's insurance expansion. Despite the lure of federal funding, the political influence of hospital lobbies that wanted more insured patients, the support in many states of business associations, and the potentially sizable benefits to state economies and budgets, eleven states had not implemented Medicaid expansion as of January 2023.[83] Medicaid rejectionism has reflected the growing influence of right-wing networks that are active in state politics, such as the Koch brothers–funded Americans for Prosperity and the American Legislative Exchange Council (ALEC). In some GOP-led states, the strong opposition of such conservative networks to Medicaid expansion served as an effective counter to support for liberalizing the program from Republican governors and groups such as hospital associations and chambers of commerce.[84]

Conservative opposition to the ACA emerged on another important front in the states. Health insurance exchanges, the purchasing pools where the uninsured can shop for coverage, became a major flashpoint in the ACA's implementation.[85] The controversy arose despite the fact that Republicans had previously proposed such purchasing pools in their own reform plans. Virtually all Republican-governed states refused to create exchanges, leaving the federal government responsible for their establishment and operation. Many of these states have played no role in nor devoted any resources to promoting ACA enrollment, and some have adopted policies that make signing up for coverage more difficult, such as imposing stringent requirements on the navigators who assist in the enrollment process.[86]

Why was the conservative backlash to the ACA so intense and long-lived? In her important book *Policymaking for Social Security*, Martha Derthick drew a sharp distinction between conflicts over "boundary" issues and those over "distributive" issues. She claimed that boundary issues, which entail enlarging the scope of the public sector, produce much more partisan and ideological conflict than distributive issues.[87] Derthick's argument is broadly persuasive for the 1935–1980 period, and it helps explain why conservative backlash to Social Security faded by the early 1950s and why political contestation over Medicare dissipated soon after its enactment. However, in the current era of polarization, the dichotomy between the politics of boundary issues and those of distributive issues has collapsed. Boundary and distributive issues are frequently contested at the same time, resulting in conflict over how to divide the public from the private spheres and the degree to which government should combat economic inequality.

The conservative backlash to the ACA also reflected the radicalization of the Republican Party.[88] In the 1950s and 1960s, many conservatives acquiesced to an expansion of safety-net programs for "deserving" groups like the elderly and the poor. It was during this relatively consensual period that Social Security matured and Medicare and Medicaid emerged as central pillars of the welfare state. Such tranquility has long since disappeared, however. The emergence of the hard-right House Freedom Caucus in the aftermath of the ACA debate symbolizes the GOP's rightward turn. As moderates within the Republican Party lost power to conservatives over the past half century as a result of the civil rights movement, the growing agitation of party base voters, and the emergence of the Koch network connecting big-money funders and issue advocates, conservatives' political and policy goals, as well as their strategies, have become more radical.[89] By linking "newly energized associations and networks to partisan politics," an invigorated conservatism now pursues increasingly bold objectives, aiming to circumscribe and redirect big government.[90] Whatever the ACA's substantive merits, the conservatives' backlash to health reform is explicable given the incentives for radicalism created by the primary system, conservative media, and donor-funded organizations.

The conservative backlash to the ACA was also powered by the considerable institutional resources available to Republicans. Throughout most of the tranquil postwar era, Republicans were in the political minority in Congress. Their inability to control the agenda encouraged congressional Republicans to accept half a policy loaf and move on. Now, as Lee argues, majority control is up for grabs in almost every election. That competitiveness encourages both parties to heighten their campaign messaging and discouraged the GOP from beating a hasty retreat on ACA repeal.[91]

Moreover, the ACA was hardly pleasing to Republicans on substantive grounds. Whatever its conservative design elements, the ACA nonetheless entails a vast expansion in the role of activist government. Moreover, as data analyzed by Brookings Institution economists Henry J. Aaron and Gary Burtless show, the ACA is highly redistributive.[92] Indeed, the ACA is arguably "the federal government's biggest attack on economic inequality" since inequality began climbing in the 1970s.[93] The ACA funds insurance coverage for low-income Americans largely through higher taxes on wealthier Americans. That's quite different from programs such as Social Security and Medicare, which rely on "contributory" financing. Given the GOP's rightward shift, increasing hostility to progressive taxation and other redistributive policies, and electoral incentives, it is ultimately not surprising that conservatives have used all available weapons to oppose and weaken the ACA.

In sum, the ACA was caught up in a perfect backlash storm. Its embedding process occurred at a moment when conservatives had become radicalized and gained control of the levers of power in both Washington and many states. At the same time, the ACA's redistributive goals and financing collided with Republicans' growing antitax ideology and commitment to lowering taxes on wealthy Americans.

SELF-UNDERMINING FEEDBACKS

Beyond the hyperpolarized context in which the ACA was enacted, two other factors contributed to the backlash. The first was a botched rollout. In contrast to the smooth launch of Medicare, the ACA had a rocky start. Problems with implementation, including the crash of the healthcare.gov website, created a highly negative first impression that took years for the program to overcome.[94]

The second key factor was that the ACA's policy design initially failed to produce uniformly strong positive-feedback effects.[95] The ACA lacks many of the programmatic arrangements of programs like Social Security and Medicare, which helped make those programs popular and durable. Additionally, the ACA's primary beneficiaries—low-income Americans, including many childless adults—are not as sympathetic, politically influential, or organized a group as senior citizens. The ACA's political image is confusing. It provides different benefits to different groups of Americans, making it less of a single, coherent program than an admixture of subsidies, regulations, and mandates targeted at different populations.[96] That fragmentation made it more difficult to build a constituency for the ACA, which has never come close to reaching the heights

TABLE 3.3. Self-Undermining Policy Feedback and the ACA

Mechanism	Examples from ACA (repealed items in italics)
Visible losses	• *Individual mandate*
	• New requirements for covered benefits and services, leading to the cancelation of "noncompliant" insurance plans on the individual and small group markets
	• Taxes on the wealthy: 3.8 percent tax on investment income; 0.9 percent increase in the Medicare Part A payroll tax paid by individuals earning more than $200,000 and couples making more than $250,000
	• Fee on branded prescription drug manufacturers
	• *"Cadillac" tax on high-cost employer-sponsored insurance*
	• *Health insurance industry fee*
	• *Medical device excise tax*
	• *Independent Payment Advisory Board*
Threats to social identities	• Expansion of Medicaid to groups outside traditional demographic categories
Challenges to the power of groups highly reliant on, or attached to, existing arrangements	• Medicare reimbursement changes
Failures to represent the preferences and priorities of average voters	• Focus on expanding coverage for the uninsured rather than lowering out-of-pocket costs for the already insured

Source: Patashnik and Oberlander 2018a.

of public support that Medicare or Social Security achieved. To be sure, many of its individual provisions quickly became popular. However, most Americans, and especially Republicans, initially viewed the law as a whole unfavorably.[97]

The architects of the ACA were aware of the disastrous MCCA experience and tried to avoid it by frontloading some benefits, such as allowing young adults to be included on their parents' policies.[98] Nonetheless, the ACA contained a number of elements that generated self-undermining policy feedbacks. These included unpopular cost-control measures, which were much less aggressive than the system-wide cost controls that helped doom Clinton's health reform proposal in the early 1990s but were nonetheless seen as a threat to the incomes of providers and the benefits of other groups (table 3.3).[99] Some of these elements (which are italicized in the table) were subsequently repealed on a bipartisan basis.

Several elements of the ACA imposed highly visible losses on voters and organized constituencies. No provision generated greater public backlash than the individual mandate—the requirement that people obtain health insurance or pay a penalty. Making people purchase health insurance may not be analogous to requiring them to eat broccoli (as the Supreme Court famously debated in *National Federation of Independent Business v. Sebelius*), but the mandate struck many ordinary Americans as coercive and an infringement on liberty.[100] The individual mandate was the least accepted element of the ACA during its early rollout: 43 percent of Americans had a "very unfavorable" opinion of it, according to a November 2011 survey.[101] Congress effectively repealed the individual mandate by zeroing out the penalty through tax legislation enacted in 2017.

The architects of the ACA understood that the withdrawal of existing benefits can generate backlash. In his sales pitch for the act, President Obama therefore promised Americans, "If you like your health-care plan, you'll be able to keep your health-care plan, period. No one will take it away, no matter what."[102] What Obama failed to explain is that while the ACA did minimize the disruption of the employer-sponsored health insurance market, it required most nongroup health insurance plans to offer a minimal set of benefits, such as coverage for prescription drugs and mental health services.[103] The implementation of these new regulatory standards led to the cancelation of millions of noncompliant plans in 2014. The blowback was intense, and the Obama administration was forced to apologize and allow the substandard plans to stand for another year.[104]

The ACA also imposed visible losses on some constituencies by levying taxes on better-off Americans. The revenue produced by the taxes was used to defray the expense of providing marketplace subsidies to lower-income citizens and keep the cost of the law within bounds. For example, the ACA imposed a 0.9 percent Medicare tax on earnings and a 3.8 percent tax on net investment income on high-income individuals. In addition, the law imposed a 40 percent excise tax on high-cost, employer-sponsored health insurance plans. The so-called Cadillac tax was designed to encourage employers to offer less lavish insurance plans and curtail excessive utilization by forcing workers to spend more of their own money on medical services.[105] Many experts viewed this tax as the ACA's most important cost-control mechanism, but surveys show that most Americans opposed the Cadillac tax, especially once they learned that it would compel some people pay more out of pocket.[106] Moreover, unions viewed the tax as a direct threat to their hard-earned health benefits, which they had won at the bargaining table. Recognizing that the Cadillac tax was poison politics, Congress repeatedly delayed its implementation. In 2019, lawmakers permanently repealed the tax on a bipartisan basis, along with taxes on insurers and medical device companies, at a cost of $373 billion in lost revenue over ten years.[107]

Many Americans who benefited from the ACA's regulatory protections nonetheless opposed the law during its first decade.[108] Some middle-class

Americans perceived the law's allocation of benefits as disrespectful of their belief that government should only provide special assistance to those who cannot help themselves. Some citizens were resentful of the provision of comprehensive Medicaid benefits (often without premiums or deductibles) to citizens with incomes up to 138 percent of the federal poverty level. Under the traditional Medicaid program, recipients generally had to fit into a certain demographic category, such as pregnant women, children, or disabled persons. These groups are widely seen as weak and vulnerable, and even conservatives generally accept that it is appropriate for government to provide health care to these populations. But many struggling workers earned too much to be eligible for Medicaid yet were burdened by high medical bills. Some were aware that other people were getting free or nearly free coverage through Medicaid and resented the fact that they were not receiving the same help.[109]

Partisan and racial identities heavily influenced public backlash to the ACA. Surveys consistently found stark partisan differences in the public's views, not only on the ACA overall, but also on its Medicaid component. Republicans were significantly less likely than Democrats to view Medicaid as important, and uninsured Republicans were less likely than uninsured Democrats to favor increases in Medicaid spending.[110] Research suggests that the backlash to Medicaid expansion was also influenced by racial resentment.[111] Colleen M. Grogan and Sunggeun (Ethan) Park show not only that white people were much less supportive of Medicaid expansion than Black people, but also that states were significantly less likely to approve the expansions if white support was low and the size of the Black population was relatively large.[112]

Some older Americans also reacted negatively to the ACA because they believed it threatened Medicare, an institution on which they relied for their financial security. While the ACA did *not* cut Medicare benefits directly—in fact, Obamacare provided Medicare recipients with some early benefits, such as rebates on prescription drug costs that fell into the "donut hole"—it did reduce payments to doctors, hospitals, and Medicare Advantage plans by a total of $716 billion over ten years to offset the cost of the expansion of the law's coverage.[113] The Obama administration insisted that this cut would not reduce Medicare beneficiaries' access to services, but many seniors were unconvinced. Cues from political elites raised concerns among Medicare beneficiaries about the law's impact. As Vanessa Williamson, Theda Skocpol, and John Coggin argue, "Health care reform was portrayed by GOP leaders as a threat to Medicare and an expensive new entitlement that would force hardworking and hard-pressed citizens and businesses to pay higher taxes to provide health insurance to younger, less well-to-do, and often 'undeserving' people—including illegal immigrants, it was claimed."[114]

Yet another reason why the ACA sparked backlash is because it failed to respond effectively to what many citizens most wanted: lower personal health care costs, including for those who already had insurance, rather than expanded coverage for the uninsured.[115] In a 2009 *USA Today* / Gallup survey, about four in ten Americans (38 percent) cited cost or affordability as the nation's biggest health care problem. Only 15 percent said the number of uninsured people was the largest problem facing the country at that time.[116] Many Americans who have middle-class incomes and decent coverage struggle with covering their health care costs. Under the ACA, persons who are not in the very low-income group receive only limited financial assistance to purchase insurance on the marketplace and often face high costs for premiums, deductibles, and copayments. Meanwhile, out-of-pocket costs continue to rise for Americans with employer-sponsored insurance, a trend predating the ACA that the law has not reversed. According to a Kaiser Family Foundation survey, premiums have increased 55 percent since 2010, more than double the rise in wages or inflation.[117] To be sure, some economists hoped the Cadillac tax, Accountable Care Organizations (groups of doctors, hospitals, and other providers that coordinate care), bundled payments, and other delivery reforms contained in the ACA would do more to make health care affordable for all Americans, including those with private health insurance. However, a deep commitment among the ACA's designers to making coverage expansion the law's major objective, together with their unwillingness (influenced by a fear of interest-group backlash) to create a public option or employ more direct tools like provider rate–setting for controlling costs, arguably resulted in insufficient attention to addressing the public's top reform priority.[118]

Ironically, some of the watered-down cost-control mechanisms that made their way into the ACA triggered backlashes. An example is the Independent Payment Advisory Board (IPAB), a technocratic panel set up to make recommendations for restraining the growth of Medicare spending. Congress was required to consider IPAB's recommendations under special rules on an expedited basis; if it failed to act, IPAB's recommendations would take effect automatically. As it turned out, IPAB never launched because Medicare costs grew at a rate below the triggers contained in the law during the ACA's first decade of operation. Yet physicians, hospitals, pharmaceutical firms, and disease advocacy groups viewed the board as a grave financial threat.[119] While most of the countermobilization against IPAB was elite-driven, the entity also generated populist backlash. Some conservatives, including 2008 vice presidential candidate Sarah Palin, claimed that IPAB was a notorious "death panel," even though it had no legal authority to recommend restrictions on Medicare benefits.[120] Ultimately, IPAB failed to consolidate a base of support, and Congress terminated the agency on a bipartisan basis in 2018.[121] Like the Cadillac tax, the IPAB would never have passed Congress as a standalone bill in 2010. These cost-control elements were obscure parts of the ACA, which were protected by their initial invisibility, but they fizzled out once their implementation approached and the losses they would impose on constituency groups became more visible.[122]

THE COUNTERBACKLASH AGAINST ACA REPEAL

The remarkable backlash triggered by Obamacare, along with the radicalization of the GOP, kept alive conservatives' hopes that it could be repealed. So long as Obama was president, the Republicans had to focus their counter-mobilization efforts in venues such as courts and the statehouses. But after the 2016 election, which saw Trump's victory over Hillary Clinton and Republicans retaining control of Congress, the GOP at last appeared to have secured the political conditions necessary to make good on its pledge to repeal Obamacare. The president and Republican congressional leaders made repeal and replace a legislative priority during the administration's first year. While the House of Representatives did succeed in passing such a bill, Republicans initially could not get similar legislation through the Senate. They failed largely because the GOP had a slim majority (52–48) in the Senate and majority leader Mitch McConnell could not keep a few Republican senators (John McCain [AZ], Lisa Murkowski [AK], and Susan Collins [ME]) from joining with all the Democrats in opposition to repeal-and-replace legislation. Republicans' difficulties in dismantling the ACA also reflected conservatives' inability to fashion a credible alternative. The Congressional Budget Office forecast that GOP bills would have increased the uninsured population by thirty-two million over a decade.[123] Moreover, the GOP repeal plans went beyond the ACA in proposing to cap federal funding for Medicaid, a radical change in the program's financing arrangements that was projected to produce a $800 billion cut in Medicaid funding over ten years.

During the ACA's early years, the law's self-undermining feedback left it vulnerable to repeal efforts but Republicans lacked the institutional resources to capitalize on them. Not until Trump was elected in 2016 and the GOP gained unified control of government were conservatives in a position to follow through on their promises to repeal the ACA. By the time this political window of opportunity opened, however, the ACA's marketplace subsidies and insurance benefits were fully in effect and the law had begun to generate significant positive feedback. The law's revenue flows to hospitals and providers stimulated vested interests, and virtually every major health care organization lobbied against its repeal.[124] The ACA also began to generate positive feedback among the mass public. Lawrence R. Jacobs, Suzanne Mettler, and Ling Zhu surveyed the same Americans every two years about their views toward the ACA and found that between 2010 and 2018, Americans became significantly more appreciative of the law's impact on their lives and were coalescing into a constituency that could be mobilized.[125]

The positive feedback generated by the ACA eight years into its implementation helps explain why public opinion surveys found that the GOP repeal bill was "the most unpopular piece of major legislation with a real chance of passage in the past quarter century."[126] Republican health care plans illuminated the political risks associated with withdrawing insurance benefits without providing an adequate replacement. While Democrats ran away from the ACA during the first several election cycles following its enactment, the party's challengers went on offense in the 2018 election cycle, attacking GOP incumbents who had voted to strip Americans of their health insurance and protections for preexisting conditions.[127] According to the Wesleyan Media Project, health care was mentioned in a majority (54.5 percent) of Democratic campaign ads.[128] The threat to the ACA from the GOP's repeal drive made the law's benefits much more salient to voters, including to low-income Americans and others who had not previously paid close attention to the issue. In so doing, it mobilized Democrats to make health care a key consideration in their voting decisions while dampening such behavior among Republicans.[129] As a result, the GOP's attack on the ACA "had the ironic effect of generating consistent majority support for the program for the first time since its enactment in 2010."[130]

The election of Biden and a Democratic Senate in 2020 finally gave the party the opportunity to repair some of the law's weaknesses. The American Rescue Plan Act expanded subsidies for buying insurance on the exchanges and extended subsidies to those who previously earned too much to receive assistance. In addition, the legislation boosted financial incentives for states to expand their Medicaid programs.[131] These enhancements were temporary, however, and some conservative states continue to resist Medicaid expansion. Moreover, there was no attempt to repair the ACA's mechanisms for reducing medical spending in the private sector, where most Americans obtain their coverage.

Despite campaigning on a bold health care agenda, Biden scaled back his reform ambitions after the 2020 election. With slim majorities in Congress and the painful memory of the ACA backlash, Biden trimmed his sails. He struggled to repeal the Trump-era policy allowing the purchase of "skinny" insurance plans that do not have to comply with the ACA's ban on discrimination against people with preexisting conditions—which he dismissed as "junk" plans during the campaign. Biden had learned from the ACA experience that throwing people off their existing insurance plans will provoke strong opposition.[132]

The ACA backlash thus not only left a permanent imprint on the law's design but also established legacies that constrained subsequent health policymaking. Still, after surviving a decade of opposition, the ACA is much closer to becoming an entrenched feature of the U.S. health policy landscape.

Discussion

Three key factors—policy attributes, the participatory and organizational capacities of stakeholder groups, and partisan polarization—have combined to make health policymaking highly susceptible to the politics of backlash. First, American health care is enormously expensive. The need to keep health spending from destabilizing the federal budget can lead policymakers to impose concentered costs to offset rising expenditures, such as tax increases on the affluent, budget cuts in existing programs, and regulatory changes that lower payments to providers. Even when health care proposals offer new benefits to some stakeholders, they often impose perceptible costs on others, inviting blowback.

Second, the health care sector is awash with vested interests, including physicians and hospitals that receive substantial public money under programs like Medicare; employers and unions that structure their insurance plans based on government tax preferences; and well-insured patients, who enjoy relatively unfettered access to expensive medical technologies. These constituencies have developed strong reliance interests in existing ways of doing things in health care, and they possess the capacity to mobilize when proposals threaten to alter or disrupt the arrangements to which they are attached.

Finally, health policymaking is highly polarized. To be sure, health politics has long been contentious. The AMA and conservatives blocked Medicare's passage until the Democrats' 1964 election landslide made the program's enactment inevitable. But backlash forces in the health care arena have grown much stronger as partisan politization has accelerated since the 1980s. The original Medicare act received the support of a majority of House Republicans and almost half the GOP senators on final passage, which contributed to its smooth rollout.[133] In contrast, the ACA failed to win a single Republican vote even though the law contained provisions that conservatives had once found acceptable, such as insurance purchasing pools. In a hyperpolarized context, the GOP had an incentive to withhold its support for Obamacare and keep the battle over the law's implementation going for ten years.[134]

While health policy changes carry significant risks of backlash, policymakers find it hard to resist the call of reform. The glaring weaknesses of the U.S. health care system—including its jaw-dropping costs, inconsistent quality, and failure to guarantee universal access—weaken the base of support for existing arrangements, which motivates policymakers to search for more efficient and equitable alternatives. Advancing policy solutions without instigating backlash has been a decades-long challenge of governance, leading to alternating cycles of reform and countermobilization.[135]

Appendix 3.1

Table A3.1 reports the results of a negative binomial regression model of the annual count of *NYT* articles about health policy backlash (shown in figure 3.1). The independent variables in the model include partisan polarization; a dummy variable for years of Democratic presidencies; the "health policy mood," a measure of the public's liberalism on health policy issues; the percentage of Americans who name health care as the most important problem facing the country in a given year; and the annual change in total national health care expenditures.

The results show positive, statistically significant relationships between media-identified health policy backlash and partisan polarization, Democratic presidencies, and the public's belief that health care is the nation's most important problem. The other variables are not significant.

TABLE A3.1. Factors Influencing Count of *New York Times* Articles Mentioning Health Policy Backlash, 1961–2018

Partisan polarization	8.468**
	(2.597)
Democratic president	0.739*
	(0.322)
Annual percentage change in national health expenditures	0.094
	(0.081)
Percentage of Americans naming health care as most important problem facing the country	4.278*
	(2.058)
Health policy mood	0.015
	(0.022)
Lagged dependent variable	−0.006
	(0.036)
Constant	−7.741
	(2.994)
Pseudo R^2	0.152
N	58

Sources: Data for health policy mood and health as most important problem are from the Comparative Agendas Project, accessed December 8, 2020, https://www.comparativeagendas.net/; data for health care spending are from the Organisation for Economic Co-operation and Development, accessed November 17, 2020, https://www.cms.gov/Research-Statistics-Data-and-Systems/Statistics-Trends-and-Reports/National HealthExpendData/NationalHealthAccountsHistorical.

Note: The model is a negative binomial regression with standard errors in parentheses.

#$p < .10$; *$p < .05$; **$p < .01$; ***$p < .001$.

Trade, Immigration, and
the Antiglobalization Backlash

Backlash against free trade agreements and immigration reached a fever pitch during the 2016 presidential campaign. In his speech accepting the Republican Party's nomination, Trump contended that Americans had been "crushed" by "horrible and unfair trade deals."[1] He promised to crack down on China's trade violations and renegotiate NAFTA. He also pledged to build a "beautiful" wall along the Mexican border to deter illegal immigration. Trump's positions on trade and immigration challenged a central tenet of neoliberalism: the belief that the free movement of products, money, and people across international borders generates enormous benefits for the United States and its citizens.[2] To be sure, Trump failed to deliver on many of his immigration reform promises. He did not defund sanctuary cities, triple the number of Immigration and Customs Enforcement (ICE) deportation officers, or persuade Congress to pass a law to restrict legal immigration.[3]

But Trump's anti-immigration rhetoric was not just bluster. The Trump administration introduced a "zero tolerance" immigration control policy that required the Department of Justice to prosecute all undocumented persons who crossed the border illegally, which resulted in the separation of migrant families.[4] The administration also cut the level of legal immigration, lowered the cap on refugees, and made it more difficult for people to seek asylum in the United States.[5] And even though Trump did not compel Mexico to pay for the building of a full-scale border wall, his administration could take credit for the construction of 458 miles of a "border wall system."[6]

Trump also shifted the trajectory of U.S. trade policy. He withdrew the United States from the Trans-Pacific Partnership, imposed tariffs on steel and aluminum imports, undercut the World Trade Organization (WTO), and bullied Canada and Mexico into renegotiating the North American Free Trade

Agreement. These moves failed to boost U.S. exports or reduce trade deficits.[7] Yet the Trump administration clearly reversed the decades-old U.S. commitment to multilateralism. As Michael Mastanduno writes, "It has orchestrated what could fairly be called a revolution in American trade policy. The Trump team has transformed both the substance of trade policy and the traditional postwar role the US has played in its global management."[8]

In breaking with long-standing patterns of U.S. trade and immigration policymaking, Trump amplified an antiglobalization backlash that already had support among a segment of the public. As Kenneth F. Scheve and Matthew J. Slaughter argue, "The backlash against globalization goes far beyond Trump himself. In fact, his presidency is more a symptom of it than its cause. Even as they may decry Trump's particular methods, many voters and politicians in both parties approve of his objectives."[9] Indeed, Biden's positions on immigration and trade during his first two years in office displayed far more continuity with those of his predecessor than many people had expected. For example, he delayed lifting Trump's tariffs on China-made goods.[10] While he ended workplace raids by ICE and raised the cap on refugee admissions, he continued many of Trump's restrictionist policies at the southern border, including using the federal government's public health authority under Title 42 to expel unauthorized migrants during the COVID-19 pandemic.[11] Some accounts suggest that Biden moved cautiously to reverse Trump's nationalist policies to signal that he sympathizes with the economic plight of less-educated, blue-collar voters.[12]

How did the United States arrive at this point? The liberal trade and immigration policy regime had been supported by presidents of both parties since the 1980s. Why did it unravel? What forms has the antiglobalization backlash taken, and what have been its consequences? These are among the questions this chapter addresses.

The Origins of the Free Trade Regime

While Trump's attack on free trade departed from the GOP's core position since the 1940s, there is a long history of U.S. trade policies generating adverse reactions.[13] For example, the McKinley Tariff (which boosted import duties to protect domestic industries) contributed to a voter blowback in the 1890 midterm elections, allowing Democrats to flip control of the House.[14] The Smoot-Hawley Tariff of 1930 is another instance.[15] A GOP initiative, Smoot-Hawley pushed "the average tariff on dutiable imports to near-record levels" just as the American economy was cratering.[16] Farmers, some business leaders, and the automobile industry all opposed the measure.[17] Economists and newspaper editors also railed against it. While most economists now believe that Smoot-Hawley did not cause the Great Depression, Canada and many other nations did retaliate by imposing new duties on American goods. With the U.S. economy in a state of collapse, the Democrats won back the House in 1930. They then gained unified control of government in 1932 on a platform that condemned Smoot-Hawley for harming farmers and producers.[18]

USING INSTITUTIONAL DESIGN TO BLUNT PROTECTIONIST BACKLASHES

How can a relatively open trading system with low tariffs prevent protectionist backlashes? As political scientist E. E. Schattschneider observed, the benefits of higher tariffs "are concentrated while costs are distributed."[19] As a result, special interests possess a stronger incentive to lobby for higher duties than ordinary citizens have to press for tariff reductions. New Deal Democrats who favored free trade recognized that their preferred economic policies could trigger countermobilizations. Accordingly, they crafted a set of institutional arrangements to lock in trade liberalization by making it harder for a pro-protectionist coalition to gain power.[20] There were three key features:

- First, Congress delegated authority over trade policy to the president. The Reciprocal Trade Agreement Act of 1934 (RTAA) authorized the president to lower U.S. tariff rates by up to 50 percent if he received a reciprocal reduction in a trading partner's tariff—without a subsequent congressional vote. Congress continued to pass both general trade laws and measures to renew the president's negotiating authority. Lawmakers could defend producer interests, "secure in the knowledge that most actual decisions would be made elsewhere."[21] Allowing the president to "bundle" domestic and international tariff reductions further promoted the regime's durability.[22]
- Second, the General Agreement on Tariffs and Trade (GATT) was adopted in 1947 to entrench the liberal trade regime. The GATT held eight rounds of global talks between the United States and its trading partners over the following decades.[23] The WTO was established in 1995 to replace the GATT and provide a stronger process for dispute resolution.[24] By the time of the Kennedy administration, U.S. trade politics was an entirely bipartisan affair.[25]
- Finally, Congress reasserted its power to approve final trade deals, but it took steps to insulate members from the pressure from narrow special interests.[26] In particular, in 1974 Congress established a legislative procedure called "fast track" that allowed for the expedited consideration of trade agreements. The fast-track process gave U.S. trading partners confidence that trade deals would

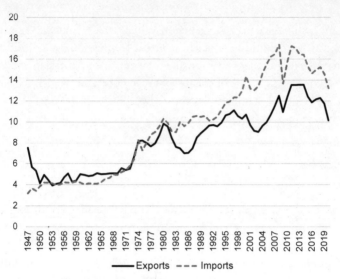

FIGURE 4.1. Exports and Imports as a Share of GDP, 1947–2019
Sources: U.S. Bureau of Economic Analysis, Federal Reserve Bank of St. Louis, accessed February 4, 2023,
https://fred.stlouisfed.org/series/B020RE1Q156NBEA; https://fred.stlouisfed.org/series/B021RE1Q156NBEA.

stick once presidents negotiated them and that Congress would not destroy
them through particularistic amendments.[27]

Reinforced by an ideational commitment to international cooperation, the
postwar trade regime saw tariffs fall to their lowest levels in American history.[28] As figure 4.1 shows, U.S. exports and imports of goods and services increased significantly as a share of GDP between 1947 and the mid-2000s. The
liberal trade regime produced increasing returns that helped endow it with
political durability. Many U.S. firms made long-term investments and developed reliance interests in the export business, including those in the financial
services, telecommunications, and entertainment sectors. As David Vogel argues, "For these firms, an increase in American trade barriers would be extremely costly, since it would make their access to foreign markets vulnerable
to retaliation by other countries. These firms have formed the backbone of
domestic support for trade liberalization."[29]

Backlash in the Trade Policy Arena since 1960

While the liberal trade regime was built on solid institutional foundations,
trade policies had the potential to generate losses for firms and workers un-

der unfavorable economic conditions. To be sure, the United States enjoyed a position of absolute and relative economic strength following World War II. Domestic constituencies received massive benefits from this dominance. Even when the nation's economic position began to decline in the 1960s and 1970s, the United States maintained its commitment to freer trade and multilateralism.

Yet this commitment did generate counterreactions among some constituencies. Figure 4.2 displays the annual count of *New York Times* articles mentioning "backlash" in the trade policy arena since 1960. I coded the main focus of each article—whether the backlashes are in opposition to trade liberalization, in opposition to efforts to restrict or condition trade, both, or neither. The figure shows that the count of trade backlashes began to rise in the 1980s. Most of the articles included in the database are about organizational resistance to trade liberalization. However, the direction of the backlashes shifted after 2016, when the Trump administration's trade wars began to engender opposition from exporters and other constituencies.

Backlashes against free trade policies have come in three major waves. The first occurred during the 1980s, when businesses mobilized against the liberal trade regime, pressing for protections against "unfair" foreign competition. The second wave took place during the 1990s and 2000s, when labor unions, environmentalists, and other antiglobalization groups mobilized against NAFTA and the WTO. Most recently, there has been a populist backlash among Americans who believe that trade deals harm workers and undercut national sovereignty. I discuss each of these three waves next, focusing on their organizational bases of support and political consequences.

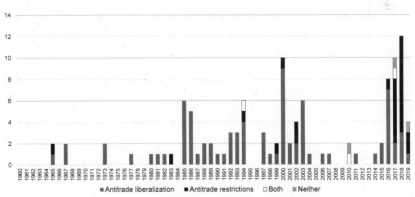

FIGURE 4.2. Annual Count of *New York Times* Articles about Trade Policy Mentioning Backlash, 1960–2019
Source: Author's compilation of *New York Times* articles.

PROTECTIONIST BACKLASH BY BUSINESS

The perception that the trade practices of nations like Japan were harmful to U.S. interests provoked a protectionist backlash in the 1980s.[30] This perception was grounded in changes in economic conditions that caused the benefits of existing U.S. liberal trade policies to become much less clear to many domestic businesses in industries like steel, apparel, and automobiles. U.S. imports increased dramatically, allowing domestic consumers to gain access to Japanese cars and other high-quality goods. However, exports stagnated and the U.S. trade deficit climbed rapidly. While short-term economic factors—including a steep recession, high interest rates, and the rising value of the dollar—were the proximate causes of growing trade imbalances, the problem also stemmed from a relative decline in the nation's position in the global economy.

In confronting emergent losses due to the new economic landscape, U.S. firms that had supported open trade reevaluated their positions. As Pietro S. Nivola wrote in 1986, "Leading industries with long histories of support for free trade—the automakers, for instance, which had once been one of a handful of big business to oppose Smoot-Hawley—had switched sides. Even competitive and profitable companies in high-technology growth areas such as medical equipment and electronics chimed in."[31] U.S. policymakers came under pressure from domestic industries to restrict imports. The number of congressional hearings on foreign trade increased from thirty-four in 1976 to eighty-six in 1987 (figure 4.3). Lawmakers introduced a growing number of trade bills

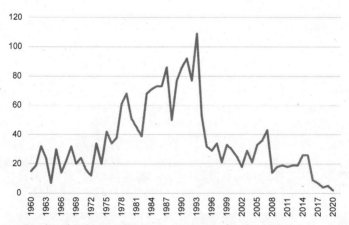

FIGURE 4.3. Number of Congressional Hearings on Foreign Trade, 1960–2020
Source: Comparative Agendas Project, 2015, https://www.comparativeagendas.net/.

with protectionist provisions, such as steel quotas.[32] There was a sharp congressional backlash in 1985 against the allegedly predatory trade practices of Japan.[33] Both chambers passed resolutions urging the Reagan administration to retaliate.[34] Moderate Democrats, including representatives Dan Rostenkowski of Illinois (Ways and Means chair) and Richard Gephardt of Missouri and Senator Lloyd Bentsen of Texas, called for the imposition of a duty on exports from Japan and other nations that were found to have erected trade barriers.[35]

Yet the 1980s protectionist backlash produced only a marginal erosion of the liberal trade regime. Despite the economic distress of many domestic producers, Congress did not resurrect the high tariff policy of Smoot-Hawley. The thrust of the 1988 omnibus trade bill was to reinforce the U.S. commitment to trade liberalization. As Irving M. Destler wrote, "The dikes constructed over the decades to protect liberal trade policies did spring some leaks, but in general they held."[36]

Three factors help explain why the 1980s protectionist backlash produced only a modest impact. First, the macroeconomic conditions that caused domestic firms to experience unanticipated losses receded. For example, the trade-weighted value of the dollar fell by almost 30 percent in real terms between 1985 and 1988, which enabled export growth to accelerate.[37] Once economic conditions improved, the demand for protectionism declined. Second, the protectionist backlash received mixed support from policymakers. The consensus on free trade among political elites did not collapse. There were some exceptions, however. For example, Congressman Gephardt called for a tougher American stance on unfair foreign trade practices. But many Democratic lawmakers were hesitant to abandon the party's long-standing positions on free trade.[38] Most importantly, President Reagan believed in the principle of free trade. As Douglas A. Irwin observes, the president blunted the momentum for protectionist legislation by making strategic accommodations to domestic constituencies that were demanding relief.[39] For example, in 1985 Reagan ordered his chief trade negotiator, Clayton K. Yeutter, to start proceedings against several foreign nations that were engaging in "unfair trade practices." "While we will use our powers as a lever to open closed doors abroad, we will continue to resist protectionist measures that would raise prices, lock out trade, and destroy the jobs and prosperity trade bring to all," Reagan said.[40] The Reagan administration employed a strategy of "trade management" to get trading partners to "voluntarily" agree to cut back their exports of particular goods. For example, Japan agreed to reduce its exports of automobiles for several years.[41] In sum, a business-led protectionist backlash occurred during the 1980s, but the political opportunity structure was unfavorable, and the backlash received little amplification from policymakers.

LABOR AND ENVIRONMENTAL BACKLASH

The next important milestone was the debate over NAFTA. The congressional debate over whether to grant President George H. W. Bush "fast-track"
authority to negotiate the trade deal with Mexico and Canada and the subsequent debate during Clinton's presidency over legislative approval of the package itself sparked notable backlashes. Unlike the battles over trade liberalization during the Reagan years, the countermobilization against NAFTA was not
driven by business firms seeking protection from foreign competition. Rather,
labor unions and environmental organizations were the key backlashers.[42]

By the time of the trade debates of the 1990s, the business community was
no longer a key backlashing actor. In an era of increased foreign investment,
major domestic corporations were less interested in gaining protection through
trade barriers than in obtaining greater access to global markets. A key sign
that coalitional alignments had shifted from the 1980s is that business demand
for protectionism did not return even during the Great Recession. As Irwin
explains, "The largest firms in the United States, Europe, and Asia were multi-
national in their production operations and supply chains so that they no
longer had a vested interest in pushing for higher trade barriers."[43] These firms
had made hard-to-reverse investments in global business operations that would
yield continuing financial benefits. In sum, global trade has become self-
reinforcing, generating positive feedbacks that created a new politics.

While the business community had developed a vested interest in the maintenance of free trade, labor unions and environmentalists believed that trade
deals were harmful. Prior to the NAFTA debate, environmental groups had
never participated in a backlash against a trade agreement, but organizations
like the National Wildlife Federation viewed NAFTA as a policy threat.[44] Their
fear was that the trade tribunals could strike down U.S. environmental laws as
illegitimate restrictions on trade. They also worried that Mexican free trade
zones ("maquiladoras") would become major sources of pollution. At the same
time, some environmentalists viewed the NAFTA debate as an opportunity to
establish a precedent that all future trade agreements should include strong
environmental enforcement mechanisms.[45]

In his 1998 book *Interpreting NAFTA*, Frederick W. Mayer observes that
during the NAFTA debate most mainstream economic analysts projected that
the trade deal would cause little dislocation for workers.[46] Nearly three hundred leading economists—including Nobel prize winners Milton Friedman
on the right and James Tobin on the left—published a statement endorsing the
agreement.[47] Mayer thus frames his inquiry around the puzzle of why NAFTA
generated such strong adverse reactions from labor unions and political fig-

ures as diverse as Ralph Nader and Pat Buchanan. He leans on a nonmaterial explanation for the backlash. "A symbolic lens applied to the domestic politics of NAFTA can explain why NAFTA evoked such a disproportionate response. . . . Opposition to NAFTA wasn't a calculated choice to maximize one's interests, it was a matter of honor, a matter of moral imperative, and an affirmation of identity," he writes.[48]

The NAFTA debate clearly had a deep cultural resonance. Many blue-collar workers construed the treaty as a threat to their political identity and way of life. Yet material interests were also at stake. One of NAFTA's key provisions was to remove tariffs and other trade barriers between Mexico and the United States over a period of fifteen years. Labor unions insisted that NAFTA would shrink American wages and prompt U.S. firms to move their production lines to Mexico to exploit the cheaper labor force. Foreshadowing Trump, independent presidential candidate Ross Perot famously warned during his 1992 campaign of a "giant sucking sound" caused by U.S. jobs moving south of the border.[49] Top economists dismissed these concerns, arguing that the trade deal would be "a net positive" for the U.S. economy and that "the assertions that NAFTA will spur an exodus of U.S. jobs to Mexico are without basis."[50]

This assessment would prove mistaken, however. Projections of NAFTA's economic impact relied on labor market data from the 1980s and early 1990s showing little evidence that free trade was depressing U.S. wages.[51] However, newer economic studies suggest that labor unions were correct to fear that increased trade with Mexico, a low-wage country, would harm affected American workers.[52] Using an event-study analysis, Jiwon Choi and colleagues show that NAFTA significantly reduced employment in U.S. counties that were exposed to Mexican import competition.[53] Counties whose labor forces were reliant on manufacturing and other industries impacted by the trade deal lost a large number of jobs relative to counties that were less affected by NAFTA. Choi and colleagues further demonstrate that NAFTA generated significant political feedback effects, causing exposed counties to shift their partisan identification from Democratic to Republican in House elections following the law's passage in 1993.

Viewing NAFTA as a clear and present danger, union leaders had little trouble mobilizing their memberships against the deal. As Steve Beckman, the lead strategist on NAFTA for the United Auto Workers, recalls: "From the very beginning of the fast-track debate, this was a visceral issue with members. NAFTA was very much a gut issue. Members understood that it was a direct threat to their jobs. If we had wanted to make a deal [trading union support for NAFTA for better worker adjustment assistance] we couldn't have."[54]

By the 1990s, the political environment was becoming more receptive to a backlash against free trade deals. Union leaders received critical support from key liberals in their political networks, including House Majority Leader Richard Gephardt (D-MO), House Whip David Bonior (D-MI), civil rights leader Jesse Jackson, and consumer advocate Ralph Nader. In addition, Ross Perot and conservative presidential candidate Pat Buchanan attacked the deal. With opposition spanning the ideological spectrum, NAFTA's prospects in Congress initially looked dim.

But the most important player in trade politics is the president, and Clinton decided to make ratification of the agreement one of his administration's priorities. As historian Gary Gerstle argues, just as Dwight D. Eisenhower "acquiesced to the core principles of the New Deal order in the 1950s," so Clinton "accepted the central principles of the neoliberal order in the 1990s."[55] Clinton attempted to minimize backlash by signing side agreements with Mexico to protect workers' rights and the environment. The environmental pact won over some moderate environmental groups, but labor unions dismissed the labor side deal as toothless and inadequate.[56] "We certainly believe that the rights of workers were shortchanged in this agreement, and it is clear that even the imperfect environmental accord is stronger," said Mark A. Anderson, the director of the American Federation of Labor and Congress of Industrial Organizations (AFL-CIO) Task Force on Trade.[57] In September 1993, Gephardt announced that he would vote against NAFTA.[58] In the end, Clinton relied on Republicans to win the trade deal's adoption. House Republicans voted for the agreement by 132–43, while House Democrats opposed it by 156–102. The Senate approved NAFTA by 61–38, with Republicans voting 34–10 in favor of the deal and Democrats voting 28–27 against it.[59]

While labor unions and their anti-NAFTA allies suffered a major defeat, their countermobilization generated momentum. Under strong labor union pressure, in 1997 House Democrats blocked the renewal of fast-track authority, handing President Clinton a notable loss on a key agenda item. Unions organized a national letter-writing and phone-call campaign against fast track, and the AFL-CIO ran ads against the measure in key congressional districts.[60] Changes in the geographical base of the Democratic Party's congressional delegation helped amplify this countermobilization. By the 1990s, southern Democrats, who had long supported freer trade (as long as the textile and apparel industry received special protections), had been almost entirely replaced by Republicans. As a result, prounion northern Democrats came to "dominate the party and determine its position on trade issues."[61]

The labor movement participated in the mass protests that occurred at the 1999 Seattle meeting of the WTO (the so-called Battle of Seattle). Tens of thousands protested against the negative effects of globalization on workers' rights and the environment.[62] As C. Donald Johnson writes, "The local Seattle Machinists Union at Boeing—the nation's largest exporter, deriving nearly half its revenues from foreign sales—supplied 900 marshals for the Seattle protest. An estimated 9,600 dockworkers from the International Longshore and Warehouse Union took part in the protest by temporarily shutting down not only the Seattle port but dozens of others all along the West Coast, including Los Angeles and Long Beach, California."[63] President Clinton responded to the protests by signaling his support for sanctions against nations that violated labor standards, but the meeting concluded without action.[64]

POPULIST BACKLASH

While the organizational countermobilizations by labor unions and environmental groups generated political energy, they did not reverse the U.S. commitment to trade liberalization. During the 2008 campaign, Obama made critical comments about multilateral trade deals. These comments were largely tactical, however. Once in the White House, he failed to break with the free trade policies of his predecessors. Obama even championed the Trans-Pacific Partnership (TPP) and other new trade agreements during his second term.[65]

A major shift occurred during the 2016 presidential campaign, when both major party nominees declined to give a full-throated defense of trade liberalization for the first time. Hillary Clinton argued that she favored fair trade deals and said she no longer supported the TPP, which she had previously called the "gold standard" of trade agreements.[66] Trump was less nuanced. He stoked a nationalist backlash against trade agreements, arguing that the United States was "being ripped off" by other countries.[67]

There is little evidence that Trump's incendiary rhetoric by itself shifted public opinion on international trade. A majority of Americans continued to see trade as an opportunity for economic growth.[68] Yet the enduring popularity of trade among the public as a whole masks important ways in which public views on trade were becoming more tightly linked to partisan and social identities.[69] Economist David Autor and colleagues found that counties that were exposed to rising import competition from China experienced increasing consumption of *Fox News*, and trade-exposed white-majority counties became more likely to support a conservative Republican for Congress.[70] In a study of individual-level political behavior, Dani Rodrik found that both opposition to trade agreements and belief in the claim that immigrants "steal jobs" had a statistically significant influence on the decision to switch to Trump in 2016 among those who had voted for Obama four years earlier, after controlling for voters' level of racial resentment, economic anxieties, social class, and party identification.[71] In sum, there is evidence that antiglobalization attitudes contributed to Trump's electoral success.

In stoking a populist backlash against trade deals, Trump had a good hand to play. While consumers were benefiting from the availability of more goods and lower prices, some American workers were bearing significant losses from foreign competition. Research has found an association between import competition with low-wage nations like China and a host of negative outcomes in the United States, including rising unemployment, falling wages, declining labor-force participation, and growing reliance on disability insurance.[72]

Trump's ability to leverage a populist backlash against global trade had roots in the self-undermining feedbacks of the liberal trade regime itself. In the aftermath of the Smoot-Hawley debacle, U.S. policymakers had recognized that the benefits of free trade are diffuse and opaque. As a result, they crafted trade institutions that shielded politicians from the influence of voters who were experiencing pain and seeking redress. As Judith Goldstein and Robert Gulotty argue, these institutions succeeded in locking in the path of trade liberalization during the postwar era. Yet they also contained a structural weakness that left them potentially vulnerable to erosion.[73] In particular, by making policymakers less democratically responsive to loss-bearing constituencies, the institutions undermined incentives for politicians to develop redistributive policies and other necessary correctives as the costs to less-educated workers mounted in an era of inequality. In short, the institutions had a built-in potential to produce self-undermining feedbacks.[74] As Goldstein and Gulotty write:

> Instead of responding to short-term dislocations that occurred over the ensuing 75 years, central decision makers crafted policy in the absence of pressures from those who were hurt by the policy. The result was that instead of developing tools to help in the adjustment to market forces, the institutions became increasingly dissociated with the costs of the policy they advocated. As global forces led to increasingly more dislocating, there was no institutional facility to respond to the growing number of "losers" from trade. Although unintentional, the lack of mediating policies eventually encouraged collective action targeted at the trade regime, leading to support for politicians who criticized the underlying policy.[75]

The limitations of the Trade Adjustment Assistance (TAA) program illustrate this governance failure. The program provides federal assistance to workers who lose their jobs or suffer lower wages or hours as a result of increased imports or outsourcing. Groups of workers are required to petition the Department of Labor (DOL) to recognize the role of global trade in their losses. Once the DOL certifies the petition, individual workers can apply for benefits, including training, reemployment services, and income support. Originally proposed by President Kennedy in 1962 to win AFL-CIO support for the Trade Adjustment Act, the TAA program had a difficult launch.[76] During its first seven years, the Tariff Commission did not approve a single TAA petition.[77] In response to union complaints, Congress revised the program in 1974 to make it easier for workers to obtain relief. Spending for the program increased from $79 million in fiscal year (FY) 1976 to $1.6 billion in FY 1980 ($4.7 billion in 2021 dollars), and the number of new recipients per year climbed from 62,000 to 532,000 over this period.[78]

But the Reagan administration believed the TAA program was failing to help workers in declining domestic industries transition to other jobs, and in the Omnibus Reconciliation Act of 1981 it targeted the program for large cuts.[79] The program survived the attack and Congress even passed some new forms of adjustment assistance in response to NAFTA. However, the program remains tiny, having served just 23,436 workers in FY 2020.[80] Evaluation studies have concluded that the TAA program is underused and broadly ineffective.[81] According to a Brookings Institution report, there are many reasons for the program's poor performance. For one thing, the process for applying for benefits is administratively cumbersome.[82] To minimize "wasteful" spending, the federal government incurs significant costs policing whether a given worker was directly affected by trade—even though trade-related displacement can affect many workers who do not themselves experience layoffs.[83]

When viewed as a political mechanism to shore up support for the liberal trade regime by allocating resources to losers, the limitations of the TAA program become apparent. To be sure, a case could be made that backlash forces would have been even *more* intense without the program. One empirical study found that electoral support for Trump in both the 2016 GOP primary and the general elections was moderately lower in counties where more workers benefited from the TAA program.[84] As Goldstein and Gulotty argue, trade adjustment assistance has served as a "pressure valve for exactly the groups that have the motivation and capacity to potentially target Congress."[85] This pressure valve has promoted the durability of the liberal trade regime by incentivizing displaced workers to work within the system to obtain compensation.

Yet the TAA program is a meager one. It suffered large budget cuts during the Reagan years and lacked the resources to respond to the economic dislocations created by growing import competition from developing nations. As

Jeffry Frieden argues, the TAA program's most basic flaw is that it is "targeted at individuals, who must show direct harm from imports. This means that the program cannot address the broader effects of globalization on *communities* rather than specific workers—the main channel for transmission of globalization discontent to the political system."[86] About nine in ten of the U.S. regions most affected by trade (mainly in the South and Midwest) voted for Trump in 2016, while only about seven in ten of the least affected communities did so.[87] Policymakers during the 1990s and early 2000s could have potentially blunted the incipient backlash against free trade by updating the TAA program and making it larger and more generous. When they failed to do so, they created space for a political entrepreneur to run on an antiglobalization platform and Trump seized the opportunity.

Backlash in the Immigration Policy Arena

In his 2016 campaign, Trump argued that Americans were being devastated not only by unfair trade deals but also by out-of-control immigration.[88] In stoking a populist backlash, Trump was tapping into a long-standing belief that immigrants constitute a threat to the American way of life. As Peter H. Schuck observes, while the United States may be a nation of immigrants, it is not the case that Americans are "wholly enthusiastic about immigration. Quite the contrary; they are not—and never have been."[89]

The door to immigrants has opened and closed repeatedly throughout American history. During the late nineteenth and early twentieth centuries, the influx of large numbers of immigrants from southern and eastern Europe provoked a nativist backlash among progressive elites.[90] Organizations like the Immigration Restriction League, a Boston-based entity whose members included descendants of the *Mayflower*, mobilized to prevent the "dilution" of the older-stock American population.[91] Congress responded by enacting policies that were intended, in the words of Harvard president A. Lawrence Lowell, to protect "the need for homogeneity in a democracy."[92] In 1917, Congress imposed a literacy test for immigration admission and barred nearly all Asians from entry. Seven years later, it enacted a landmark immigration law (the Reed-Johnson Act) that established permanent national origins quotas (set at 2 percent of the number of persons of each nationality group living in the United States as of the 1890 census) to prioritize northern and western Europeans.[93] The effects of this policy backlash were long-lasting, and only about five million immigrants entered the United States between 1931 and 1965.[94]

The enactment of the Immigration and Nationality Act of 1965 (also known as the Hart-Celler Act) ended national origins quotas. In their place, the law

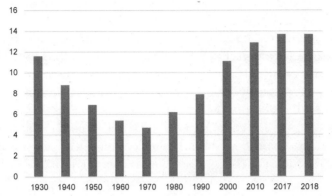

FIGURE 4.4. Foreign-Born Share of the U.S. Population, 1930–2018

Source: William H. Frey, 2019, "US Foreign-Born Gains Are Smallest in a Decade, Except in Trump States," analysis of decennial censuses and 2010 to 2018 American Community Surveys, Brookings Institution, October 2, https://www.brookings.edu/blog/the-avenue/2019/10/01/us-foreign-born-gains-are-smallest-in-a-decade-except-in-trump-states/.

established a new preference system that prioritized family reunifications while reserving some visa slots for professionals, workers who filled labor shortage needs, and refugees. While Americans welcomed the bipartisan 1965 law, the measure had a much larger downstream impact than many had anticipated.[95] Millions of newcomers began arriving from Latin American, Asian, and Caribbean nations.[96] Most came legally. However, the 1965 law's ceiling on legal immigration from the Western Hemisphere, together with Congress's termination in 1964 of the Bracero guest worker program, unintentionally encouraged illegal immigration.[97] During the 1990s, about one in four immigrants living in the United States had entered illegally.[98] As historian Jane Hong observes, "Whole groups of migrants from Mexico and Latin America whose entrance to the U.S. would have been considered legal before 1965 suddenly became illegal."[99] The total number of immigrants who entered the United States between 1970 and 2000 has been estimated at twenty-eight million.[100] Moreover, birth rates among native-born Americans fell during this period. As a result, the foreign-born share of the population climbed, increasing from 4.7 percent in 1970 to 11.1 percent in 2000 (figure 4.4).

In the politics of immigration backlash, perceptions can matter more than realities. Natives may blame immigrants for the relative decline in their economic status, even if other factors like the weakening of unions or technological change are much more important. Nonetheless, it useful to review the available evidence.

Many experts agree that the net economic effects of immigration on the American economy are positive, leading to "more innovation, a better educated workforce, greater occupational specialization, better matching of skills with jobs, and higher overall economic productivity."[101] There is little evidence to support the claim that the surge in immigration has depressed the wages of the typical native-born worker.[102] Yet not all native-born workers have benefited equally from immigration. A 2017 National Academies of Sciences, Engineering, and Medicine study concluded that "natives who own more capital" will gain more of the economic benefits that immigrants generate than natives who own less capital.[103] The affluent enjoy lower prices for goods and services and higher returns on their investments than they would in the absence of immigration. The biggest losers from mass immigration among native-born workers are high school dropouts, who may well suffer lower wages due to the increased competition for jobs, although there is no consensus among experts on the magnitude of the wage loss.[104]

Many people believe that immigrants impose costs on native taxpayers. This claim has some basis, although the fiscal impact of immigrants varies according to the generosity of social benefits offered by state and local governments, the socioeconomic composition of the immigrant population, and many other factors. Immigrants are clearly not a drain on the federal budget; on the contrary, they are net contributors. Most immigrant adults are relatively young, pay income and payroll taxes, and do not consume significant benefits from programs like Social Security and Medicare. The situation is different at the state and local levels. First-generation immigrants—many of whom have larger families with children who attend public schools—impose net costs on many state and local governments, which are mainly responsible for K–12 education funding. The report from the National Academies found that the average net cost to state and local budgets of first-generation adults (including the costs generated by their dependent children) was sixteen hundred dollars for 2011–2013.[105] To be sure, the descendants of immigrants pay more in state and local taxes than they consume in public benefits, which more than offsets the fiscal impact of the first generation.[106] But immigrants do burden taxpayers in some states and localities over the short run.

The political reactions to immigration have never stemmed from immigrants' economic effects alone. Fears of cultural displacement along with threats to the status of the native born are another driver of antagonism toward immigration. While some natives who oppose immigration may worry about losing their job, others appear to "associate unskilled immigrants with crime, undocumented immigration, public goods congestion, and deterioration of compositional amenities," such as the racial and ethnic composition of neighborhoods.[107]

In his excellent book *Dividing Lines*, Daniel J. Tichenor argues that debates over U.S. immigration policy have occurred along two main dimensions:

(1) whether actors believe immigrant admissions should be maintained, expanded, or restricted and (2) whether actors favor expanded or restrictive immigrant rights in areas such as public benefits and naturalization.[108] Using these dimensions, I distinguish among four types of backlashes that have occurred in the immigration arena: a backlash against expanded immigration (a *restrictionist admissions* backlash); a backlash against expanded immigration rights (a *restrictive rights* backlash); a backlash against restricted admissions (an *expansionary admissions* backlash); and a backlash against restrictive immigrant rights (an *expansive rights* backlash). In practice, there is a relationship between backlashes (whether restrictive or expansionary) over immigrant admissions and rights. For example, some actors may seek to make it harder for immigrants to become citizens or to receive government benefits in order to deter immigration.[109] Nonetheless, it is useful to identify the main, near-term goals of backlashers and to investigate how the target of backlashes in this sector have shifted over time.

Figure 4.5 displays the annual count of *NYT* articles about the four types of backlashes since 1960. I discuss each type separately next. Three trends are prominent. First, the landmark 1965 act did not trigger an immediate backlash.

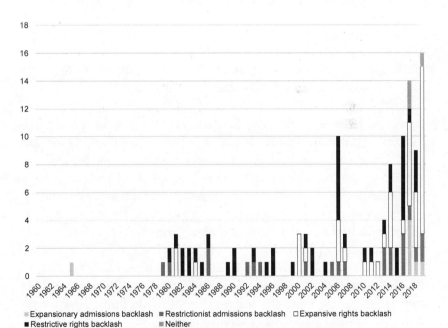

FIGURE 4.5. Annual Count of *New York Times* Articles about Immigration Mentioning Backlash, 1960–2019
Source: Author's compilation of *New York Times* articles.

Backlash forces did not occasion coverage in the *New York Times* until the 1980s, by which time the foreign-born share of the population had grown and the federal government's inability to curb unauthorized immigration had become clear to ordinary citizens. Second, a large proportion of the backlashes over the past few decades have focused on issues related to the rights of immigrants under federal and state law. How immigrants should be treated once they enter the country has been as contentious an issue as that of how many immigrants should be permitted to gain admission in the first place. Finally, the character and direction of immigration-related backlashes have shifted markedly over the past several decades. The period of 1980–2000 was dominated by backlashes by groups that favored restricted immigration levels as well as a narrow definition of immigrant rights. More recently, Trump's anti-immigrant rhetoric and policy moves spurred countermobilization by civil liberties groups and immigrant rights advocates. In appendix 4.1, I show that the trend in immigration backlash is positively associated with partisan polarization, the percentage of Americans who name immigration as the nation's most important problem, election years, and the Trump presidency. It is negatively associated with the policy mood (immigration backlash declines when public opinion becomes more liberal) and Democratic presidencies.

RESTRICTIONIST ADMISSIONS BACKLASH

Some policies generate increasing returns, causing the public to demand increasing amounts of what it is already receiving. For example, the public has long expressed support for higher spending on Social Security, even as spending on the program climbed.[110] But other policies generate negative (equilibrating) feedback. The 1965 immigration act is an example of the latter. The significant increase in immigration admissions did not generate a public demand for even higher levels of immigration. As figure 4.6 shows, the percentage of Americans who said they believe immigration levels should be decreased exceeded the percentage of Americans who said it should be increased in every Gallup survey between 1965 and 2019. Public demand for increased immigration did climb during the 2000s, but more Americans still favored keeping immigration at the present level. In 2020, for the first time more Americans (34 percent) said they preferred to see immigration increased rather than decreased (28 percent). President Trump's harsh anti-immigrant rhetoric policy moves triggered a thermostatic backlash.[111] However, the upwelling of support ended shortly after the start of the Biden presidency. In 2022, 35 percent of Americans preferred that immigration be decreased, up 7 percentage points from two years earlier.

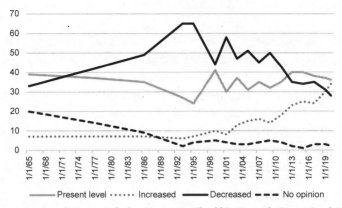

FIGURE 4.6. Americans' Views on Whether Immigration Should Be Kept at the Present Level, Increased, or Decreased, 1965–2020

Sources: Jim Norman, "Solid Majority Still Opposes New Construction on Border Wall," 2019, Gallup, February 4, https://news.gallup.com/poll/246455/solid-majority-opposes-new-construction-border-wall.aspx; Mohamed Younis, "Americans Want More, Not Less, Immigration for the First Time," 2020, Gallup, July 1, https://news.gallup.com/poll/313106/americans-not-less-immigration-first-time.aspx.

To be sure, public support for more restrictive immigration does not automatically generate a policy response. As Gary P. Freeman argues, the concentrated benefits of immigration for higher-income elites (such as businesses that employ low-wage labor) typically prevail over the more diffuse costs of immigration for the general public. While the workers who compete directly with immigrants for jobs experience concentrated losses, they usually lack political resources and are not a potent constituency.[112] As a result of this imbalance of forces, anti-immigration backlashes may require perceptions of a crisis and the intervention of political entrepreneurs who can open windows of opportunity and find ways to make immigration a salient issue.[113]

The influx of a large number of refugees in the late 1970s served as a "focusing event" that helped backlash forces coalesce.[114] The arrival of hundreds of thousands of refugees, primarily from Asia, including tens of thousands of "boat people" who had escaped Vietnam on small vessels, deeply unsettled the public.[115] An even more notable public backlash occurred in 1980 when a quarter of a million Cuban refugees—many of whom were the victims of Fidel Castro's mass expulsions—fled to Florida. Fear that the Cuban refugees would be willing to work for low wages, along with cultural discomfort, generated resistance among both Anglo and Black working-class people in Miami.[116] A 1986 survey found that about half (49 percent) of Americans believed that immigration should be decreased. There was a significant split in support for immigration along educational lines. While 55 percent of people with less than a high school degree favored decreased immigration, only 35 percent of college graduates did.[117] This survey also found that 69 percent of Americans believed that employers who hire unauthored immigrants should be penalized.

In addition to negative opinion feedback, the backlash spurred the mobilization of new restrictionist organizations. The most visible group has been the Federation for American Immigration Reform (FAIR). It was founded in 1979 by John Tanton, a former Sierra Club leader, and others who shared a neo-Malthusian belief that the population growth caused by immigration would deplete the nation's natural resources.[118] FAIR called for a significant reduction in immigration levels and the total elimination of illegal immigration. During its early years, FAIR built a professional lobbying operation and attempted to forge alliances with national policymakers and other groups to shape the immigration policy agenda. Tanton also formed offshoot organizations, including NumbersUSA and the Center for Immigration Studies, a think tank that produced media-friendly reports on the negative impacts of immigration. FAIR gained influence during the 1970s and 1980s by framing immigration as a threat to the white political majority without using explicitly racist language. As historian Carly Goodman writes, "The public embraced the label 'nation of immigrants' and, historically, immigration exclusion was shot through with racism and bigotry. Since the civil rights movement, excluding immigrants based on race or national origin was understood to be chauvinistic and backward. Tanton wanted to make sure FAIR was seen as 'middle of the road'—not racist—and worked continuously to set it apart from the more emotional, hate-driven white nationalists who shared his goals."[119]

By the Reagan era, policymakers anticipated a public rebuke should they fail to take steps to stem unauthorized immigration. After several years of debate, in 1986 Congress passed the Immigration Reform and Control Act (IRCA).[120] The law reflected a bargain between advocates of expanded immigration and immigrant rights and supporters of a restrictionist immigration policy. It granted amnesty to undocumented immigrants who had been living in the country, and it also barred employers from discriminating on the basis of a worker's national origins or citizenship status. At the same time, IRCA sought to curb illegal immigration through border control and employer sanctions. The amnesty program was successfully implemented—nearly three million undocumented persons gained legal status.

Once IRCA was done, Congress felt comfortable expanding legal immigration in the Immigration Act of 1990.[121] Yet IRCA's attempt to seal the border did not succeed. As John D. Skrentny argues, its enforcement mechanisms "not only miserably failed to control illegal immigration, but also had a series of deleterious consequences."[122] The employer sanctions were toothless and poorly enforced.[123] The government only penalized employers if they know-

ingly hired an unauthorized immigrant. Without an effective employee veri-
fication system, that rarely happened. Undocumented immigrants from Mexico easily obtained fake identification documents and continued to enter the
United States in massive numbers.

The failure of IRCA to curb unauthorized immigration created negative
policy feedbacks, which convinced restrictionists that it was foolish to pursue
"grand bargains" in immigration reform.[124] As Harold L. Wilensky wrote, "Sympathetic critics of comprehensive reform argue that the failure to implement
the 1986 reforms, especially employer sanctions, and the failure to reduce the
flow of illegals, gave comprehensive reform a bad name. Implementation failures increased cynicism among voters and lawmakers and therefore made subsequent reform attempts more difficult."[125] Notably, George W. Bush's push for
comprehensive immigration reform—which was motivated by a desire to court
Latino voters and provide the labor demanded by the business community—
provoked fierce opposition from Republican base voters, who considered Bush's
proposal of a pathway to legal status for undocumented immigrations tanta-
mount to amnesty.[126]

The restrictionist backlash was evident in both public opinion and electoral
politics beginning in the early 1990s.[127] According to a 1993 survey, 90 percent of
Americans favored beefing up border controls to curb illegal immigration.[128]
In late 1994, seven in ten Americans saw immigration as a "critical threat" to
the country's "vital interests."[129] Republican presidential candidate Pat Buchanan, who challenged the incumbent, George H. W. Bush, and won the New
Hampshire primary, called for building a wall on the Mexican border to deter
illegal immigration.[130] In 1996, Congress responded by enacting the Illegal Immigration Reform and Immigrant Responsibility Act, which one analyst described as the "most radical reform of immigration law in decades."[131] The
measure sought to curb illegal immigration by increasing funding for the border patrol, expediting deportation procedures, tightening the process of claiming asylum, and imposing new penalties for smuggling people across the
border.[132] But these measures only had a limited impact, and the number of
unauthorized immigrants in the country nearly doubled, from 5.7 million in
1995 to 11.1 million in 2014.[133] While the 1996 reform incorporated the demands of restrictionist backlashers, it disheartened FAIR, which favored cuts
in legal immigration and tougher employer sanctions.[134]

RESTRICTIVE RIGHTS BACKLASH

The most important policy consequence of the restrictionist backlash has
been the limitation of the immigrants' access to government services and

legal protections once they crossed the border. As historian Sarah R. Coleman observes, U.S. immigrants "entered the twenty-first century with few of the governmental benefits they had enjoyed thirty years earlier."[135] While curbing the influx of immigration has proved to be a formidable political, legal, and technical challenge for federal policymakers, the backlash against the right of immigrants to access social services and other public benefits has gained significant traction.

An early response of states and localities to the mounting fiscal burden of immigrants was to seek compensation from the federal government. In 1982, the National Association of Counties warned that its members could not support the legalization of undocumented immigrants if the federal government failed to reimburse the costs incurred by state and local governments.[136] When this attempt by state and local actors to leverage the public backlash against immigration into federal money failed, they began pushing anti-immigrant measures of their own. In 1994, California governor Pete Wilson (R) won re-election by blaming the state's poor economy, budget deficit, and crime wave on the influx of undocumented immigrants.

The centerpiece of Wilson's campaign was his strong support for Proposition 187, a ballot initiative that denied undocumented immigrants access to most state benefits, including nonemergency health care and primary and secondary public education. California voters approved the measure by 59–41 percent.[137] Many liberal groups, including the American Civil Liberties Union (ACLU) and the Mexican American Legal Defense and Education Fund, challenged the measure. The policy threat posed by Proposition 187, together with the Wilson administration's executive orders and anti-immigrant rhetoric, stimulated a counteraction among newly naturalized Latinos in California, who responded by substantially increasing their voter participation.[138] After several years of litigation, in 1997 a federal court found the measure's major provisions unconstitutional.[139]

Yet the anti-immigration backlash stoked by Governor Wilson did not dissipate. In subsequent years, other states followed California's example and passed punitive immigration laws of their own. The most controversial was Arizona's SB 1070, which requires police officers to check the immigration status of anyone they arrest or stop if they suspect the person might be an unauthorized immigrant. The ACLU and other rights groups challenged the law, but the Supreme Court upheld its central provisions.[140] The federal government also responded to the anti-immigration backlash, retrenching many of the "legal protections and social entitlements that legal and undocumented aliens could claim."[141] In 1996, a Republican-controlled Congress enacted an immigration reform law that eliminated the judicial review of key Immigration and Naturalization Service enforcement actions, tightened asylum procedures, and limited the rights of certain immigrants to reenter the country. As Peter H. Schuck writes, "The 1996 reforms should be viewed as a kind of counterrevolution in immigration law. Congress decisively . . . repudiated the liberalization and 'proceduralization' of immigration law that the courts had nourished since the early 1980s."[142] In addition, in 1996 Congress passed welfare reform legislation that barred millions of noncitizens who were legal immigrants from receiving a range of federal benefits, including welfare (Aid to Families with Dependent Children), food stamps, and cash assistance for poor people who are aged, blind or disabled (Supplemental Security Income).[143]

The backlash against immigrants' access to benefits and legal rights also led to a widening partisan divide. While leaders of the two parties once held broadly similar views on immigration, they had diverged by the early 2000s. Anti-immigrant measures have generally been introduced by Republicans and opposed by Democrats at both the state and national levels, creating an incentive for voters who have economic or cultural fears about immigrants to support the GOP. In their excellent book *White Backlash*, Marisa Abrajano and Zoltan L. Hajnal use survey data to demonstrate that "whites who live in states with more Latinos are more punitive, less supportive of welfare and other public services, and generally more conservative than whites in other states. Whites in those same states are also significantly more likely to support the Republican party."[144] In sum, Republican leaders moved right on immigration during the 1990s and 2000s, partly in response to grassroots pressure but also as the result of their own opportunistic reading of the changing electoral landscape. The effect was to rebrand the GOP as an anti-immigration party, which altered the meaning of Republican partisan identity for many rank-and-file voters.

EXPANSIVE RIGHTS BACKLASH

In response to both the Republicans' rightward lurch on immigration and their own internal coalitional dynamics, Democrats have moved significantly left on immigration-related issues since the early to mid-2000s.[145] The party had long been divided on immigration due to a conflict between two core constituencies: ethnic groups (which supported immigration and immigrant rights) and labor unions (which viewed immigrants as a threat to the jobs of native workers). As recently as 2010, nearly half (46 percent) of Democrats supported building a wall or security fence on the Mexican border to stop illegal immigration.[146] In 2000, however, the AFL-CIO reversed its position, calling for amnesty for undocumented workers and the repeal of employer sanctions. The AFL-CIO's dramatic shift reflected pressure from service worker unions with significant Latino memberships.[147]

Over time, the views of rank-and-file Democrats have moved left in tandem with the change in position of the party elites.[148] The repositioning of the Democratic Party was reinforced by the massive immigrant rights protests that were held in spring 2006. According to a University of Washington estimate, about six million people participated in more than four hundred protests across the nation.[149] One proimmigrant rally in downtown Dallas attracted a crowd of five hundred thousand people. The major policy target of the protests was a restrictionist immigration bill that had narrowly passed the Republican-controlled House the previous winter. The bill would have made it a felony to enter the United States without authorization and a crime for a person to give assistance to undocumented immigrants.[150]

During his eight-year presidency, Obama struggled to balance the growing demand from restrictionists for tougher action to curb illegal immigration and pressure from the immigration rights countermovement that was ascendant in the Democratic Party.[151] With little prospect for getting a comprehensive immigration reform bill through a polarized Congress, Obama resorted to executive actions, but nearly every unilateral step he took triggered backlash from some constituency. For example, Latinos and immigration rights activists denounced Obama as "deporter-in-chief" for deporting more than 2.8 million unauthorized immigrants.[152] Facing growing political pressure to shield people who had been brought to the United States illegally as children (known as the "Dreamers") from deportation, Obama launched the Deferred Action for Childhood Arrivals (DACA) program in 2012.

The immigrant rights countermobilization intensified during the Trump administration. Trump's announcement in 2017 that he would terminate DACA triggered a national backlash that enlisted the participation not only of Democrats, but also of Republicans, the business community, and large numbers of ordinary citizens.[153] As *Politico* reported, "Within hours after Attorney General Jeff Sessions broke the news on September 5 that President Trump was canceling the program known as DACA, protesters were blocking traffic in streets near the White House. In New York, at least 34 demonstrators were arrested for sitting down across Fifth Avenue in front of Trump Tower. Students walked out of high schools in Denver, Fort Worth, Phoenix and Albuquerque, among many places."[154] While Trump's core preferences were restrictionist, he had an instinct for self-preservation. He searched for a political escape but soon discovered that any effort to manage backlash pressures by finding a middle ground risked provoking a counteraction. When rumors circulated that he might be willing to strike a deal with Democratic congressional leaders that would involve giving the Dreamers a pathway to citizenship, Trump faced a swift backlash from conservatives. Representative Steve King (R-IA) said that if the deal were true, the "Trump base [would be] blown up, destroyed, irreparable and disillusioned beyond repair. No promise is credible."[155]

EXPANSIONARY ADMISSIONS BACKLASH

Few recent backlashes have been more furious than the public and elite countermobilization against Trump's effort to reduce the number and type of immigrants who enter the United States. Just days into his administration, he announced that he was indefinitely ending the admission of Syrian refugees and barring entry into the country from seven predominately Muslim nations (Libya, Iran, Iraq, Somalia, Sudan, Syria, and Yemen) for three months.[156] The so-called Muslim ban led to mass protests at airports and other locations for weeks.[157]

A second and even more politically explosive move was the administration's implementation of a "zero tolerance" policy for people caught crossing the border illegally, which led to the separation of more than five thousand families.[158] Under this policy, every unauthorized adult migrant who was apprehended faced criminal prosecution and was sent to federal jail.[159] The policy was far out of synch with the preferences of Americans, as even those who wanted to see immigration restrictions tightened found it inhumane, and the political backlash was ferocious. Countermobilization activities included mass protests across the country, statements by civic leaders and the business community, and rebukes by Democratic politicians.[160] Negative media coverage of the policy played a key role in inciting opposition. As one reporter wrote, "The news media's pictures and footage of the family separation policy in action, quickly disseminated via Facebook and Twitter, became ubiquitous around the world. Images of young children in cages covered with foil sheets for blankets shaped a narrative that the Trump administration is cruel and indifferent to the suffering of innocent victims. That narrative was publicly restated by prominent leaders at home and abroad, including individuals who might otherwise be seen as typical Trump supporters."[161] Most Republican officeholders initially declined to criticize the administration. In June 2018, however, twelve of Trump's key GOP allies in the Senate signed a letter asking him to pause the policy.[162] Trump signed an executive order ending the controversial policy shortly thereafter.[163]

Despite the defeat on family separations, Trump achieved a number of his immigration reform goals, including a significant reduction in the level of legal immigration. According to a Cato Institute analysis, "Trump cut the average number of monthly green cards issued by 18.2 percent relative to Obama's second term."[164] Still, Trump's most visible policy moves triggered strong resistance among both mass publics and political elites. Like the backlash against global trade, the immigration backlash signaled the political exhaustion of existing policy approaches rather than the emergence of a strong consensus on a new way forward.

Discussion

The central claim of this chapter is that the economic and demographic shifts engendered by globalization created the potential for a robust policy backlash by imposing perceived costs on segments of the American population. This backlash potential remained largely unexploited for many years because the political opportunity structure provided only weak external incentives for countermobilization. U.S. political elites, across party lines, were mostly united on the benefits of free trade. While antiglobalization social movements gained strength in the 1990s, they lacked influential political allies. Moreover, the legislative debate over immigration reform was bogged down in conflicts among rival constituencies. Trump's singular insight—intuition may be a better word—was that the neoliberal regime was more fragile than it appeared and that U.S. immigration and free trade policies were imposing perceived costs (both economic and cultural) on a mobilizable constituency. None of this is to suggest that the backlash against globalization was the primary cause of Trump's surprising 2016 election victory.[165] But the antiglobalization backlash strengthened Trump's appeal among key groups, enabling him to capitalize on a perception that Washington politicians were leaving some communities behind.

Economists have long argued that the benefits of foreign trade and immigration—including lower consumer prices and higher economic productivity—more than offset their costs. But the political reactions to globalization are shaped by how losses and gains are *distributed*. Since the 1980s, the economic shocks generated by globalization have imposed concentrated costs on workers living in regions that are exposed to rising import competition, high school dropouts who compete for the same jobs as immigrants, and taxpayers in states and localities with large numbers of low-income immigrants whose families use public services like education.[166] These losses have been exacerbated by exogenous factors such as automation, as well as by factors endogenously shaped by politics, such as the decline of unions.[167] During the neoliberal era, politicians of both parties did little to mitigate the distributional costs of the commitment to globalization, despite the increase in economic inequality. They did not upgrade trade adjustment assistance, take meaningful steps to contain illegal immigration, or manage the fiscal burdens that immigrants were placing on some states and localities.[168]

In addition, there was a growing gap between the consensus of the business community and political elites on the benefits of immigration and skepticism at the grassroots level. In 2016 Republican presidential candidates like Jeb Bush and John Kasich held positions on immigration that were far more liberal than the views of Republican voters.[169] As the primary election season approached, surveys showed that "majorities of Republicans supported building a fence along the Mexican border, said that 'immigrants are a burden because they take jobs, housing and health care,' and wanted tougher restrictions on immigration in general."[170] In sum, there was an opportunity for a 2016 presidential candidate to amplify the antiglobalization backlash, and Trump seized it.[171]

Appendix 4.1

Appendix table A4.1 uses a binomial regression to examine the correlates of the count of articles about immigration-related backlashes (all four types combined). The results indicate that polarization, the percentage of Americans who name immigration as the nation's most important problem, election years, and the Trump presidency are positively associated with the yearly count of articles. A liberal policy mood and a Democratic presidency are negatively associated with the count.

TABLE A4.1. Factors Influencing Count of *New York Times* Articles Mentioning Immigration Backlash, 1961–2018

Partisan Polarization	6.571**
	(2.271)
Percentage of the public naming immigration as most important problem facing the nation	28.943***
	(6.850)
Policy mood	−0.141**
	(0.046)
Election year	0.502*
	(0.216)
Democratic presidency	−0.835*
	(0.345)
Trump presidency (2017–2018)	1.623**
	(0.527)
Unemployment rate	0.024
	(0.783)

(continues)

Lagged dependent variable	−0.081
	(0.053)
Constant	3.671
	(2.388)
Pseudo R^2	0.276
N	58

Sources: Data on policy mood and immigration as the most important national problem are from the Policy Agendas Project, https://www.comparativeagendas.net/us.

Note: The model is a negative binomial regression with standard errors in parentheses.

#$p < .10$; *$p < .05$; **$p < .01$; ***$p < .001$.

Backlash at the Grassroots: Segregated Private Schools, Gun Control, and Transgender Rights

As chapter 2 showed, the ideological direction of policy backlash in the United States between the 1960s and 2010s was disproportionately conservative. Much of this backlash was driven by a perception among many working-class whites, evangelical Christians, residents of rural communities, and other groups of Americans that efforts to use government to promote equality, address injustices experienced by historically marginalized groups, and solve collective problems constituted a threat to their interests, values, and the civil society institutions they organized their lives around.[1] In this chapter, I examine three instances in which liberal reform efforts generated negative reactions at the grassroots level.

First, I examine the backlash of fundamentalist Christians and other conservative religious groups during the late 1970s against an Internal Revenue Service (IRS) rule denying tax-exempt status to private schools deemed to be racially discriminatory. Promulgated during the Carter administration, the IRS rule played a critical role in forging the powerful alliance between the religious right and the GOP. Next, I examine the countermobilization of gun rights advocates following the election of progressive Democrats who sought to pass gun control regulations. In states like Virginia, the backlash took the form of "Second Amendment sanctuary" declarations. Viewing restrictions on gun ownership and use as a threat to their citizens' liberties and lifestyles, counties and towns passed resolutions avowing they would not enforce federal or state gun control measures. Finally, I examine the conservative backlash in North Carolina to the adoption in 2016 of a nondiscrimination ordinance by the city of Charlotte that allowed transgender people to use bathrooms matching their gender identity. In response to an outcry from religious and social conservatives, the North Carolina General Assembly passed a state law (HB2) mandating that transgender people use bathrooms that correspond with the sex listed on their birth certificate.

I selected the three cases for study based on several factors.[2] First, they capture the key late 1970s period, when the two political parties were beginning to diverge on a host of social issues, as well as the contemporary era of hyperpolarization. Second, the cases involve policymaking at both the national and state levels. Finally, in some of the cases financial incentives and the desire to defend traditional cultural values were mutually reinforcing (the threatened loss of tax exemptions for segregated schools), while in others they were in tension (the bathroom bill case).

By examining the details of these three cases, we see how policy attributes, the participatory capacities of groups, and political opportunity structures converge to construct conservative countermobilizations. Overall, my analysis suggests it is a mistake to construe right-wing populist backlashes as either wholly organic, spontaneous public reactions to liberal reforms or as events manufactured and controlled by powerful elites. Rather, similar to Theda Skocpol and Vanessa Williamson's analysis of the Tea Party, I argue that the backlashes considered here resulted from a combination of bottom-up *and* top-down forces.[3] They linked grassroots activism to the electoral strategies of political elites, activated citizens' social identities, and shaped the structure of coalitional alignments.

Evangelicals and the Tax-Exempt Status of Private Schools

In many accounts of the rise of the religious right, the backlash against the Supreme Court's 1973 *Roe v. Wade* decision plays a starring role. However, the historical record suggests a more nuanced story. Catholic opposition to abortion predated the 1973 decision. But while many fundamentalist and evangelical Protestants also held conservative views on abortion before *Roe*, the leaders of evangelical organizations did not join the prolife movement until much later.[4] For example, the Southern Baptist Convention "did not adopt a strong antiabortion stance until 1980."[5]

The issue that triggered the countermobilization of white evangelicals—and the forging of their electoral alliance with the GOP—was race and the federal effort to desegregate private schools.[6] In states like Virginia, the backlash to the 1954 *Brown v. Board of Education* decision initially took the form of "massive resistance." Localities closed their public schools rather than integrate. When massive resistance failed to prevent the issuing of integration orders for public schools, many white families began sending their children to white-only private schools. According to one estimate, four hundred thousand children in southern states attended so-called segregation ("seg") academies in 1970.[7] The number of church-affiliated private schools also exploded in the aftermath of public school integration.[8] Scholars debate whether segregation academies and church schools were the same phenomenon.[9] There were many commonalities. Both types of schools served an overwhelmingly white clientele, and some seg academies even met in church facilities. Yet segregation academies taught the same secular curriculum as local public schools, while church schools provided a religious education.[10] Advocates insisted that church schools were not racist, but rather were a response to alienation from the dominant secular culture.[11] The Baptist minister and educator Robert J. Billings, who cofounded the Moral Majority, said that the schools were a reaction to the Supreme Court's school prayer decision and to "the decline of academic standards in the public school, the rise of permissiveness, [and] the lack of discipline in the public school."[12] Many found this claim unconvincing. Whatever the motivations behind them, church schools emerged as the leading private school model in the South by the mid-1970s.[13]

ROOTS OF THE IRS CONFLICT

The federal government initially did little to discourage the growth of segregated private schools. In 1967, the IRS issued a narrow rule denying tax-exempt status to segregated schools that received taxpayer money, but most all-white private schools did not have access to public funding, and were left untouched.[14] The Nixon administration was torn about whether to crack down on white private schools. Nixon was pursuing a "Southern Strategy" to build GOP support among southern white voters opposed to the civil rights movement. At the same time, he hoped to maintain support from moderate voters who were uncomfortable with George Wallace.[15] Nixon ultimately decided he had more to gain politically by aligning himself with moderates, and he ordered the IRS to develop a new policy for racially discriminatory schools.[16] In 1971, the IRS ruled that the denial of tax exemptions applied to segregated, independent private schools that did not receive state assistance, but it did not resolve the status of tax exemptions for religious schools.[17] Four years later, the agency announced that it would begin denying tax-exempt status to church schools that discriminated against minority students. The initial enforcement of the policy was weak.[18] To maintain their tax exemptions, all the church schools had to do was adopt and advertise a nondiscrimination policy.[19]

But in 1978, the federal government got serious. In response to pressure from the civil rights community, the IRS issued rules to hold racially discriminatory private schools accountable.[20] The rules featured an array of legal tests

that shifted the burden of proof onto private schools—including those spon-
sored by churches—that had been established or expanded at the time of local
school desegregation. Rather than being permitted to assert that they did not
discriminate, the schools were required to demonstrate that they were non-
discriminatory and were attempting to recruit minority students.[21] If the IRS
leadership in Washington, DC, concluded that a school had a "student body
whose percentage of minority students was less than 20 percent of the minority school age population in the community served by the school"[22] and was
not taking affirmative steps to demonstrate nondiscrimination (e.g., providing scholarships to minority students), it would lose its tax-exempt status.[23] In
short, *church schools would have to prove to the federal government that they
were not racist.*

The rule constituted both a material and a cultural threat to fundamentalist Christians. Lacking large endowments, few church schools could afford to incur substantial legal fees to defend themselves against the federal
government.[24] At the same time, the rule reinforced religious conservatives'
belief that the bureaucratic state was hostile to their religious liberty.[25] They
signaled that even private, religious institutions were not beyond the federal government's reach, threatening the ability of evangelicals to "raise their
families and teach their children in their own way."[26] The IRS controversy was
thus the key issue in "politicizing a broad range of conservative Christians."[27]
According to Paul Weyrich, a conservative activist, it convinced the religious
right that "unless they got active in the political process . . . they were going to
have regulations forced upon them that they found unacceptable."[28]

The schools responded by arguing that the IRS policy was *itself* discriminatory. They argued that the rules would impose arbitrary racial quotas and
that their minority enrollment could easily fall below the 20 percent threshold for any number of reasons having no connection to discrimination. As
Daniel Schlozman argues in his excellent account of the alliance between the
Christian right and the Republican Party, the proposed regulations "would
have invited lawsuits from schools denied their tax exemptions. Federal district judges would have served as the final arbiters of tax-exempt status for
reviewable schools, and consent decrees [as] the modus operandi for resolving disputes."[29]

A FURIOUS BACKLASH

The IRS rule triggered a furious backlash. As historian Joseph Crespino argues, the reaction of the conservative Christian community "bordered on the
apoplectic."[30] The IRS received 150,000 letters from opponents of the rules,

and Congress received 60,000 more.[31] The IRS also received pushback from citizens who testified at public hearings on the proposed role held by the agency.[32] The IRS responded to this uproar by softening the rule. The new proposal scrapped "mechanical" formulas for determining whether a school was discriminating. Instead, the agency would evaluate schools on a case-by-case basis and consider special circumstances that could make it hard for a school to enroll minority students. In effect, the revised version shifted the burden of proof to prove discrimination back to the government.[33] But these modifications failed to assuage the fears of conservative Christians that the government was interfering with the right of parents to decide how to educate their children.[34]

While the proposed IRS rule was the trigger, religious conservatives used the backlash as a vehicle to communicate a broad sense of grievance about their changing place in American society. At a 1979 hearing of the Senate Finance Committee's Subcommittee on Taxation and Debt Management, Christian conservative leaders characterized the IRS regulations not just as heavy-handed or misguided, but as a government attack on their way of life. Rev. Jim Nicholls of the International Council of Christian Churches lamented that to avoid offending people, Christians had to say "winter vacation" instead of "Christmas vacation." "We lost prayer in our school," he said, "We lost Bible reading in our schools. We have lost Christian morality in our schools. . . . There was a pastor from Denver, Colo., who addressed [the federal government] and says we want you to know we have dug our trenches. We are not losing anything more."[35]

Many Christian conservatives were at pains to emphasize that they supported racial equality.[36] Nonetheless, some speakers at the subcommittee hearing expressed resentment that minority groups were, in their view, receiving more favorable treatment than Christians. For example, Nicholls pointed out that schools "have special days set aside" for Black History Month, and asked, "If this is recognized as a thing to do for blacks, why then cannot Christian culture [be] in our schools."[37] Significantly, the main target of the populist backlash was the *federal government*, not minorities. As Crespino puts it, "Disaffected conservative groups focused their animus not against African Americans or other historically disadvantaged groups but rather against 'liberal elites' and 'unelected bureaucrats.'"[38] Targeting backlash against unelected officials was a potent countermobilization strategy in a nation where many people lack trust in government.

White religious parents in the South lived in the same communities, belonged to the same churches, and sent their children to the same schools. The strong social networks among these groups facilitated their participatory

capacity and democratic engagement. Elite leadership also played an important role in promoting the populist backlash. Political entrepreneurs within
the New Right served as "instigators," helping religious parents grasp the magnitude of the policy threat they were facing from the IRS.[39] Billings founded a
new national lobbying organization, Christian School Action, and launched
a newsletter, *Christian School Alert*, to bring attention to the issue, which received extensive media attention on Christian television shows such as Pat
Robertson's *700 Club* and Jim Baker's *PTL Club*.[40]

Not only did religious conservatives possess the internal capacity for democratic participation, they also received external support from elected officials.
Virtually all Republican lawmakers, together with some Catholic Democrats—
including Senator Joe Biden (D-DE)—rallied to their side.[41] Congress stayed
enforcement of the IRS regulations by passing an amendment to the Treasury
Department appropriations act.[42] The House passed the rider by an overwhelming margin with the support of all but one Republican.[43] In the Senate,
Jesse Helms (R-SC) proposed an even more sweeping measure that would have
prevented the IRS from enforcing the new guidelines altogether.[44] During a
Senate Finance Committee subcommittee hearing, Helms defended the "good
faith" of the people who ran Christian schools in his state and argued that it
was wrong that they had to "live under the threat of going to enormous expense to prove themselves innocent."[45] Congress passed similar riders in the
following two years.

During the 1980 presidential election, the GOP elevated the IRS dispute to
a campaign issue. The GOP's platform pledged to "halt the unconstitutional
regulatory vendetta launched by Mr. Carter's IRS Commissioner against independent schools."[46] Ronald Reagan attacked the IRS rules during a January
1980 speech at Bob Jones University, a fundamentalist school that had lost its
tax-exempt status for banning interracial dating.[47] After Reagan soundly defeated Carter in the fall campaign, he signaled a willingness—under pressure
from Senator Trent Lott (R-MS)—to reinstate Bob Jones University's tax-exempt
status and reverse the long-standing IRS ban on tax exemptions for discriminatory schools. While this posture thrilled the Christian right, it elicited a
counterbacklash from the civil rights community and Democratic lawmakers, as well as from centrist Republicans and staffers of the Justice Department.
Seeking to calm the waters, the Reagan administration proposed legislation
to deny tax exemptions for discriminatory schools, but the measure never
gained support in Congress.[48] The Supreme Court settled the legal issue in
1983 by ruling, 8–1, that racially discriminatory schools are not entitled to tax
exemptions.[49]

BACKLASH CONSEQUENCES

While the backlash did not succeed in reversing the federal bar on discrimination, it had significant policy consequences. Most importantly, it staved off more aggressive federal efforts to root out lingering racial discrimination in private schools.[50] While private schools were required to post their non-discrimination policies in order to retain their tax-exempt status, the federal government had stripped only 111 schools (out of a total of around 3,500) of their tax exemptions by 1983.[51] In 1984, the Supreme Court dismissed a class action suit brought by Black parents who argued that IRS enforcement of the tax-exemption policy was too lenient and was undermining the desegregation of public schools by making it too easy for whites to exit the system.[52] The majority opinion, written by Justice Sandra Day O'Connor, argued that that plaintiffs lacked standing and had failed to show a clear linkage between lax administration of the IRS policy and public school quality.[53] Many private schools that began as segregation academies in states like Mississippi remain open today and enroll virtually no minority students.[54]

The backlash also had significant political ramifications. It reinforced a belief among religious conservatives that the national bureaucratic state was antagonistic to their interests and institutions. Moreover, it stimulated the evangelical community to become far more engaged politically. In the 1976 presidential election, fundamentalists supported Carter over Gerald Ford by 56–44 percent. In 1980, six in ten white, born-again voters supported Ronald Reagan.[55] As Thomas Byrne Edsall and Mary D. Edsall write, "The activation of the organized Christian right was the culmination of one current of conservative reaction to the events of the post-*Brown* civil rights era, a mobilization that began to achieve organizational coherence in the 1970s, reflecting the complex interweaving of race, taxes, rights, and broader social and cultural conflicts as they contributed to the growing national strength of the Republican party."[56]

Second Amendment Sanctuaries

The establishment of Second Amendment sanctuaries is a fascinating instance of a right-wing populist backlash to the threat of liberal policy change. Borrowing the term *sanctuaries* that progressive cities used to describe their refusal to cooperate with federal immigration agents, local jurisdictions—mostly rural counties and towns—passed resolutions declaring that they would not enforce any gun control laws that they "deem to be an unconstitutional restriction of their Second Amendment rights."[57] Some of the resolutions merely express opposition to proposals for tighter gun regulations while others endorse noncooperation with enforcement agencies. As legal scholar Shawn E. Fields argues, the declarations represent an attempt to "claim immunity from superior government enactments, reopening debates about the proper balance of power between state and local governments, the ability of superior governments to compel compliance from sanctuary judications, and the substantive contours of the Second Amendment itself."[58]

GUN OWNERS AS A CONSERVATIVE IDENTITY GROUP

Gun owners are one of the most active constituencies in American politics. They are more likely than gun control advocates to vote, donate money, and join organizations based on the issue.[59] What is less widely recognized is that the social identity of gun owners did not emerge of its own accord. According to a study by Matthew J. Lacombe, the self-understanding of American gun owners as members of a distinct group, whose way of life is under threat, was strategically constructed by the National Rifle Association (NRA) over many decades. Based on a meticulous review of editorials published between 1930 and 2008 in *American Rifleman*, the NRA's house organ, Lacombe shows that the organization "cultivated a distinct, politicized gun owner social identity over many years," describing gun owners as "patriotic," "law-abiding," "honest," and "peaceable" average citizens who love their country.[60] Opponents of gun rights were described in highly negative terms. For example, the media was described as "liar(s), coward(ly), elitist, phony, cynical, devious, shameless, and propaganda/propagandists."[61] Lacombe finds that the majority (66 percent) of the NRA editorials portray gun rights as threatened and over one-third (36 percent) contained calls to action, such as encouraging members to contact politicians and tell them to leave their guns alone.[62] Finally, Lacombe shows that this identity language has diffused widely among gun supporters, who use it when they write letters to newspapers. In sum, gun owners have been stimulated to think of themselves as "good Americans" in a battle with enemies who are opposed to the values they hold most dear.

THE RISE OF SECOND AMENDMENT SANCTUARIES

The rights of gun owners in the United States have expanded significantly in recent decades, especially following the Supreme Court's landmark 2008 decision in *District of Columbia v. Heller*, which asserted an individual's right to bear arms outside service in militias. The policy status quo has clearly moved to the right, yet gun owners have perceived a looming threat to their freedom from the public's anger and frustration about gun violence. They have recognized that public support for stricter gun laws and attention from policymakers to gun control issues climb following high-profile mass shootings, at least temporarily.[63] While gun control legislation did not gain traction in Congress during the 2010s, some rural constituencies feared the federal government could impose new gun control measures in the future. The *New York Times* reported that after twenty children and six educators died at the Sandy Hook Elementary School shooting in 2012, fifteen states considered bills to "nullify any new efforts to further restrict access to guns," with some measures calling for the arrest and prosecution of any federal agents "who dare to enforce new firearm regulations."[64]

The creation of Second Amendment sanctuaries formalized this idea. In the "blue wave" election of 2018, Democrats took back the U.S. House of Representatives, gained seven governorships, and flipped six state legislative chambers.[65] For rural conservative voters, the ascendancy of progressive majorities symbolized a society that was undergoing an unwelcome change. Gun rights activists increased their countermobilization activities, winning the support of local government officials and sheriffs for sanctuary declarations. There were no gun sanctuaries before 2018.[66] Yet by January 2020, more than four hundred gun sanctuary jurisdictions existed around the country, "including [in] a majority of counties in Colorado, Illinois, Nevada, New Mexico, and Virginia."[67]

Ground zero for the Second Amendment sanctuary movement has been Virginia, a state that has been transformed from a solid red state to a purple (or even blue-leaning) state in recent decades as the state's population center and economic base shifted toward the affluent and highly educated suburbs near Washington, DC.[68] Until Glenn Youngkin was elected governor in 2021, no Republican had been elected to statewide office since 2009.[69] While traditional southern conservative voters and politicians had long dominated Virginia state government, the growth of a liberal electorate in Northern Virginia "wrested statewide control from the once-powerful western and southern regions of the state."[70]

In the 2019 elections, Democrats gained unified control of Virginia state government for the first time in more than a quarter century. Gun control was a major election issue. Many Democratic legislators had "run for office on a platform of gun violence prevention, backed by funding from national gun control groups."[71] For rural Virginians, who had assumed that pro–gun rights officials would always govern their state, the 2019 election was a "wake-up call." "The biggest reaction I have seen has just been shock, just kind of a disbelief that it's gone from zero to 60, as it were," said Chris Murphy, a gun safety instructor.[72]

Virginia's political realignment on gun rights triggered a fierce backlash.[73] Between the November election and mid-January, some 125 Virginia counties and towns passed a law or resolution stating that they would not enforce gun control regulations.[74] The passion and intensity of the backlash against gun control drew frequent comparisons to the Tea Party, except that the sanctuary movement was focused on a single issue.[75] "I think [the Democrats] will come in and try and confiscate my guns," said a female resident of Pulaski, Virginia, who had attended a meeting of her board of supervisors to register her support for the creation of a local Second Amendment Sanctuary. "I'm very worried because you have a lot of Northern or state people that are very leftie and they don't care if we can defend ourselves or that we go out and kill our meals," another female meeting attendee said.[76] After a mass shooting at the Virginia Beach municipal building in 2019, the state's newly elected Democratic governor, Ralph Northam, called a special legislative session to consider gun restrictions, including universal background checks, an assault rifle ban, and "red flag" laws, which would permit authorities to temporarily confiscate guns from people who had been determined to be dangerous. Public opinion surveys showed that Virginians overwhelmingly favored these reforms.[77] However, the Republican-controlled general assembly refused even to debate the proposals, instead ending the special session less than two hours after it began.[78]

VIRGINIA CITIZENS DEFENSE LEAGUE

The organizational engine behind Virginia's Second Amendment sanctuary movement is the Virginia Citizens Defense League (VCDL), a pro–gun rights grassroots group with a reputation for being more ideologically extreme and uncompromising than the NRA. Originally known as the Northern Virginia Citizens Defense League (the organization's founder, Paul Moog, hailed from Northern Virginia), the group was established in 1994 in response to Congress's passage of a ten-year assault weapons ban. The group's first major accomplishment was to neuter Virginia's "concealed carry" permit law, which had given state officials the authority to determine whether applicants had provided an acceptable reason for needing such a permit. In response to pressure from the group, the law was modified to say the state "shall issue" a concealed permit to anyone eligible to own a gun in Virginia.[79]

The rural Virginia backlash to the Democrats' resounding victory in the 2019 election catapulted the VCDL to prominence, and its membership tripled from eight thousand to twenty-four thousand following the election.[80] The group organized a gun rights rally on "Lobby Day," an annual event (which happen to fall on Martin Luther King Day in 2020) when citizens' groups gather in Richmond, the state capital, to convey their concerns to lawmakers. Some twenty-two thousand gun rights activists showed up for the rally. Despite fears that the presence of white nationalists would result in violent confrontationism as had occurred in 2017 in nearby Charlottesville, Virginia, the rally was peaceful.[81]

I interviewed Philip Van Cleave, VCDL's president, about the organization's membership, goals, and values.[82] Van Cleave told me that while people from all walks of life have joined his group in recent years—including a growing number of women and minorities—white Christian men constitute a majority of his membership. He described most of his members as "prolife" but said the organization focuses narrowly on gun rights; it purposely does not engage with the abortion debate or other issues. Van Cleave believes that his members are primarily motivated to participate by their ideological commitment to gun rights. However, he said that a secondary motivation is fellowship. "Our members have a great time when we get together—it's nice being around people who like guns," he said.[83] Shortly before the Richmond rally, Van Cleave released a public statement welcoming the attendance of "our militia brothers and sisters," although he declined the offers of some militias to provide security for the event.[84] He acknowledged that his membership includes people who participate in militias but said that this was "irrelevant" and that there were no formal ties between the VCDL and militias. At a minimum, however, it's fair to conclude that groups like the VCDL have helped collapse the "boundaries between the mainstream and the fringe" within the gun rights movement.[85]

Van Cleave views the Second Amendment as guaranteeing an absolute right to keep and bear arms: the state can no more regulate the kind or quantity of guns citizens purchase and own than it can regulate the number of times a person attends church every month. Van Cleave stated that he believes that gun control advocates will never be satisfied with modest gun regulations. "There is no doubt they want to take away all guns," he said. Indeed, Van Cleave expressed his belief that gun control proponents secretly do not even think police officers should carry guns: "They would prefer a bobby system."[86]

The political opportunity structure has provided external incentives for the VCDL's mobilization. The organization has forged a tight alliance with local law enforcement officials in the more rural parts of the state, particularly county sheriffs. As Robert J. Spitzer points out, county sheriffs in forty-six states gain office through elections rather than by appointment or competitive exams. Many sheriffs "represent the most politically conservative (and gun friendly) election districts in the country," and they support Second Amendment sanctuaries because they "see political and electoral benefit in embracing that position."[87] In Culpepper County, Virginia, Sheriff Scott Jenkins gained national attention when he vowed at a public meeting of his board of supervisors (where many attendees wore bright orange "guns save lives" stickers) that he would deputize his citizens—giving them expanded rights to possess guns as law enforcement officers—if the state legislature passed new gun control laws. "My statement was simply that I would choose to swear in hundreds or even thousands of our citizens as deputy sheriffs if need be, to allow them to possess weapons and push back on that overreach by our government," he told a reporter after the meeting.[88] On his Facebook page, Jenkins declared that as a sheriff he has the authority and duty to resist policies that he regards as unconstitutional overreaches:

> An elected Sheriff answers only to the citizenry. He or she is not beholden to any government unit, no supervisory body, and no legislature. My promise, my sacred oath to God, is to use my best abilities to support the Constitutions of the United States and of the Commonwealth of Virginia.
>
> My devotion to our Constitution is non-negotiable, especially whenever and wherever I see our freedoms threatened. I will always respect the rule of law but don't need to wait for a court to interpret my duty for me. My actions will always be in service of liberty and to the hard-working, freedom-loving people I am privileged to serve, so help me God.[89]

As University of Virginia law professor Rich Schragger, a strong critic of the VCDL, writes, "These kinds of claims reveal the increasingly frightening confluence of gun rights advocacy, Christian nationalism, and—to be frank— white supremacy. An advocacy group that does not recognize or does not acknowledge the rhetorical links between interposition, the Civil War, and Massive Resistance is playing a dangerous game, one that barely conceals its discredited provenance."[90] In early 2021, Facebook permanently removed the VCDL's page without explaining the basis for its decision.[91]

Virginia's attorney general at the time, Democrat Mark Herring, pushed back on Second Amendment sanctuaries, arguing that the "resolutions have no legal force, and they're just part of an effort by the gun lobby to stoke fear."[92] In an advisory opinion, he argued that "local constitutional officers"—such as sheriffs—are "obligated to follow duly enacted state laws" and lack the authority to "declare state statutes unconstitutional or decline to follow them on that basis."[93]

IMPACT OF THE BACKLASH

Did the Second Amendment sanctuary movement shape policy outcomes in Virginia? Or was it merely symbolic? The VCDL failed to achieve its ambitious goal of preventing Virginia governor Ralph Northam from signing into law a package of gun control measures, including mandatory background checks on gun sales, a limit on handgun sales to one a month, and a "red flag" law that allows law enforcement officials to take guns away (temporarily) from people deemed to be a risk to themselves or others.[94] The VCDL nonetheless declared victory because several provisions in the legislative package were significantly watered down.[95] In addition, a proposed ban on sales of assault weapons—the provision most unacceptable to gun rights activists—was defeated in the Virginia Senate.[96] It is difficult to tease out the causal impact of the sanctuary movement. As Schragger points out, however, the "expressive impact of [the] sanctuary declarations, and the 'show of force' by gun rights advocates in Richmond during the debate on the bill" may well have shaped the political environment in which the 2020 law was considered.[97] Some gun control proponents attributed the removal of the assault weapons ban to the backlash. "The sanctuary nonsense kind of got people spooked," lamented Senator Mamie E. Locke (D-Hampton).[98]

Besides narrowing the scope of the legislation, the Virginia Second Amendment sanctuary movement could have also shaped policy outcomes by reducing the intensity of local enforcement of the new gun control laws. Law enforcement officials possess considerable discretion in deciding what potential threats to investigate. For example, under Virginia's red flag law, authorities are required to go through multiple procedural steps before they can get a court order to seize a dangerous person's firearms, which provides many opportunities to slow the process. Subjects have the right to a full hearing on the merits of their case.[99] Law enforcement officers who are committed to the sanctuary idea could presumably find a way during this process to resist or slow-walk enforcement. The experience thus far suggests that this is not the case, however. Court records show that some sanctuary declaration counties are actively using the red flag law to confiscate guns from people—a development that Van Cleave considers surprising and disappointing.[100]

In sum, the main effect of the Second Amendment sanctuary movement, at least in Virginia, has been to reinforce the geographical dimension of polarization by sharpening the divide between rural and urban communities. It also resurrected old ideas about local defiance and "interposition," and it radicalized the gun control movement by creating at least some overlap between the memberships of radical gun rights groups and militias. Backlashes against perceived policy threats can be highly consequential even when they do not leave an immediate imprint on public policy.

The North Carolina Bathroom Bill and Transgender Rights

The rules governing access to public bathrooms might seem to be an improbable issue to generate a right-wing populist backlash. Yet, as Neil J. Young writes, bathrooms have long "been a political flash point. For generations, Americans have imparted bathrooms with their deepest anxieties about changing social norms and practices. From the Industrial Revolution to Jim Crow to women's lib to today, restrooms have been a proxy for political fights on almost every major issue in American life—race, class, gender, crime, sexuality, you name it."[101] In recent years, the question of which bathroom transgender persons should be allowed to use has polarized public opinion. A 2016 survey found that the Americans most supportive of requiring transgender people to use the bathrooms that reflect the gender they were born into include white evangelicals, those who attend religious services frequently, older people, and Republicans. Democrats, younger people, and those who know someone who is transgender were more likely to say that transgender people should use the bathroom corresponding to the gender they currently identify with.[102]

CHARLOTTE NONDISCRIMINATION ORDINANCE

Transgender rights emerged as a salient civil rights issue during Obama's second term. In 2014, the Education Department's Office for Civil Rights (OCR) issued guidance stating that transgender students enjoy protections under Title IX, which bars sex-based discrimination in federally funded education programs.[103] Two years later, the OCR and the Department of Justice issued a letter requiring states to respect the rights of transgender students, including the right to use bathrooms that match their gender identity.[104] In a backlash to the federal government's policies, conservative policymakers in South Dakota and other states began introducing proposals requiring students to use bathrooms corresponding to their biological sex at birth.[105] Proponents argued that these measures were necessary to ensure safety and privacy and to prevent male sexual predators (falsely claiming to be transsexual women) from entering girls' bathrooms. LGBTQ advocates argued that there was no evidence to support such fears, while transgender people have been the victims of verbal harassment and even physical violence.[106]

Charlotte, North Carolina, galvanized the national debate over transgender rights when, on February 22, 2016, its city council voted, by 7–4, to add sexual orientation, gender expression, and gender identity to the list of protected categories in its existing nondiscrimination ordinance.[107] A majority of the 140 citizens who made public comments at the council meeting in which the ordinance was enacted "voiced concerns over allowing transgender people to use the bathrooms and locker rooms consistent with their identity, claiming it would put women and girls at risk." Many speakers "evoked God, Jesus and the Bible," imploring the city's mayor and council members "that they need to 'turn away from sin' and accept Jesus Christ."[108]

Support from Republican policymakers amplified the backlash. North Carolina governor Pat McCrory pledged that the Charlotte ordinance would be reversed. "This action of allowing a person with male anatomy, for example, to use a female restroom or locker room will most likely cause immediate State legislative intervention which I would support as governor," he wrote in the email to two council members.[109] McCrory, who had previously served as mayor of Charlotte, had been elected governor as a moderate but was facing a difficult reelection campaign. By all accounts, he feared that his legislative agenda would stall if he failed to align himself with conservatives in his party on the issue of bathroom access.[110]

HB2 PASSAGE

McCrory argued that state lawmakers should address the Charlotte bill during the next regular legislative session. However, House Speaker Tim Moore and other conservative Republicans in the general assembly demanded expedited action, and they gathered the support from lawmakers required to convene a special session. After a single day of debate, on March 23, 2017, the general assembly passed a sweeping bill, House Bill (HB) 2, which McCrory signed that evening.[111] Republicans in both chambers of the legislature unanimously supported the bill. In the Senate, Democrats walked out in protest and refused to cast their votes.[112]

HB2 not only prohibited transgender people from using bathrooms located in public buildings that do not correspond to their biological sex. It also created a new statewide discrimination policy that *excluded* gay and transgender people as protected groups. In addition, HB2 barred cities from passing their own local LGBTQ nondiscrimination ordinances like Charlotte's—and from adopting local minimum-wage and leave policies, too.[113] Senate Democratic leader Dan Blue called HB2 "a direct affront to equality, civil rights, and local autonomy."[114]

This was not the first time North Carolina's legislature had overridden a liberal policy emanating from one of its local judications. As David A. Graham observes in his *Atlantic* essay, "Red State, Blue City," "previously, it had banned sanctuary cities, prohibited towns from destroying guns confiscated by the police, and blocked local fracking regulations."[115] The tension between a conservative state legislature and progressive cities is particularly strong in North Carolina, but it exists in many other red states as well, where Republican-controlled state legislatures have been overruling Democratic cities and blocking them from passing measures that go beyond state policy on issues such as civil rights, paid leave, and business regulation.[116] As the rural-urban political divide grows, preemption laws and similar efforts by state lawmakers to cabin the legal authority of cities has become a growing trend in subnational politics.[117]

THE LIBERAL COUNTERBACKLASH

What makes the HB2 case fascinating is that North Carolina's action generated a liberal counterbacklash "as swift as backlash to the policy it nullified."[118] The two reactions were a study in contrasts. The most striking difference is that the Charlotte ordinance primarily countermobilized local actors, including religious conservatives and Republicans in the state's general assembly, while the coalition against HB2 featured many of the nation's most powerful corporations. Among the more than eighty major firms that pledged or signaled they would not do business in North Carolina unless HB2 was repealed were Google, Apple, Facebook, Microsoft, American Airlines, United Airlines, and Deutsche Bank (which halted a plan to bring 250 new jobs to the Raleigh area because of the law).[119]

The participation of major firms in the counterbacklash against HB2 reflected a transformation in corporate governance. Over the past several decades, well-educated professionals who hold culturally liberal values and progressive views on issues of social identity have risen to leadership positions in many business corporations. As Grossmann and Hopkins observe, "This trend has profoundly influenced corporate America, where increasing deference to the worldview of the educated classes not only reflects the sincere beliefs of rising generations of top executives but also represents a strategic response to the prevailing sensibilities of key actors both inside and outside the organization itself: managers, legal advisors, consultants, media figures, business partners, potential employees, and customers."[120] During the 2010s, corporate America was under growing pressure from stakeholders to become more activist and "enlightened" on social issues.

Democratic mayors and governors also supported the counterbacklash against HB2. Some banned taxpayer-funded governmental travel to the state.[121] Even Great Britain injected itself into the conflict, issuing a travel advisory warning that North Carolina and Mississippi (which had passed a law allowing businesses to refuse to serve gay couples based on religious objections) were unwelcoming states for the LGBTQ community.[122] The counterbacklash against HB2 also featured public protests organized by groups such as the Campaign for Southern Equality.[123] But the most important backlashers were elite actors, who used their political power and economic clout to send the message that North Carolina had to decide "which side of history" it wanted to be on.

The financial impact of the counterbacklash was substantial. The Associated Press projected that North Carolina stood to lose $3.76 billion in economic activity over twelve years from the boycotts, cancelations, and abandoned investments.[124] PayPal, the online payment company, stated that it was canceling a $3.6 million investment to establish a global operations center in Charlotte.[125] The National Collegiate Athletic Association (NCAA) announced it was relocating a number of marquee sports events scheduled to be held in North Carolina, including the first two rounds of "March Madness," the national collegiate basketball championship. In July, the National Basketball Association (NBA) further tarnished North Carolina's brand in the world of big-time sports when it pulled the all-star game from Charlotte. The NBA's decision came on the heels of the cancelation of a number of concerts in North Carolina by famous musicians, including Bruce Springsteen, Ringo Starr, and Itzhak Perlman. McCrory bitterly complained that the "the sports and entertainment elite" had "maligned the people of North Carolina simply because most people believe boys and girls should be able to use school bathrooms, locker rooms and showers without the opposite sex present."[126]

The conflict over HB2 also played out in the courts. The U.S. Justice Department sued North Carolina for violating the civil rights of transgender persons. "[North Carolina] created state-sponsored discrimination against transgender individuals who simply seek to engage in the most private of functions in a place of safety and security," said Attorney General Lorretta Lynch at a news conference in Washington, DC. "None of us can stand by when a state enters the business of legislating identity and insists that a person pretend to be something or someone that they are not." North Carolina Governor McCrory countersued, accusing the federal government of a "baseless and blatant overreach."[127] The issue eventually went to the U.S. Supreme Court, which declined to review a federal appeals court decision upholding the rights of transgender students to use bathrooms that match their self-identified gender.[128]

Conservative GOP legislators in North Carolina attempted to sustain HB2 in the face of national opposition. Representative Phil Shepard, a Baptist minister, dismissed the mobilization against HB2 as "a dishonest, media-fueled carpet-bombing."[129] But the economic pressure on North Carolina continued to intensify, and surveys showed that six in ten North Carolina voters believed that HB2 had hurt the state's national image.[130] After McCrory lost his reelection bid by a razor-thin margin—an outcome many observers attributed to the controversy over the bathroom bill—he called for a special session of the general assembly to vote on a repeal of HB2. In exchange, Charlotte agreed to repeal its nondiscrimination ordinance. However, the special session adjourned without a resolution amid mutual accusations of bad faith by actors on all sides. The following March, the newly elected governor, Democrat Roy Cooper—who had refused to defend HB2's constitutionality in his previous role as North Carolina's attorney general—worked out a truce that fully satisfied neither HB2's supporters or its opponents. Under the terms of the deal, HB2 was nominally repealed. However, the new law (HB 142) also reversed local protections for gays and transgender people and banned local governments in North Carolina from enacting nondiscrimination ordinances for three and a half years.[131] LGBTQ rights advocates denounced the measure as a betrayal.[132] When the moratorium on the passage of local nondiscrimination ordinances expired in December 2020, the two sides resumed their battle, and within months, several progressive North Carolina cities had moved to enact new protections for their LGBTQ communities.[133]

Yet the conservative backlash to the transgender rights movement continues to gain momentum. By 2023, nine states had enacted bills barring transgender people from using bathrooms that match their gender identity.[134] In addition, GOP state legislators have introduced a surge of bills to block female transgender students from participating in girls' sports teams and prevent minors from accessing gender-transition medical care.[135] There is some evidence that the public is becoming more conservative on transgender issues. For example, in a 2023 survey, 69 percent of Americans said that transgender athletes should only be allowed to play on sports teams that match their birth gender, up from 62 percent in 2021.[136] Public attitudes are not yet settled, however, and it is too soon to know how these debates will be resolved. Until a clear political consensus emerges, efforts to expand the rights of transgender people are likely to provoke backlashes from the right while anti-trans bills may trigger countermobilizations from the left.

Discussion

Conservative populist backlash first emerged in the post-1960s era as anticipated electoral blowback to the civil rights movement and civil rights legislation. The 1964 presidential election pitted Lyndon Johnson, the signer of the 1964 Civil Rights Act, against Barry Goldwater, who opposed the law as an unconstitutional intrusion on states' rights. Goldwater was the first GOP presidential nominee since Reconstruction to win five states in the Deep South.[137] Over time, right-wing populism continued to manifest itself as voter backlash to the Democratic Party's racial liberalism, but it also energized grassroots protests, stimulated the emergence of social movements, and fostered conservative organization-building on a host of other social issues.

Despite their similarities, the three conservative backlash episodes considered here varied in their dynamics. The backlash of religious conservatives against the IRS nondiscrimination rule mobilized the Christian right and forged its long-term alliance with the GOP. The Second Amendment sanctuary movement built grassroots support for the radical idea that gun control laws and regulations are not just onerous to gun owners but illegitimate.[138] Finally, the countermobilization against the Charlotte nondiscrimination ordinance established transgender rights as a new cleavage in American politics. While many factors help explain these patterns, several are especially important.

First, the affected constituencies varied in the amount of electoral leverage they could exert.[139] In Virginia, voters who supported gun rights were a major electoral constituency for county sheriffs, who had a strong incentive to support sanctuary declarations. Similarly, the GOP's need to broaden its electoral coalition gave southern conservatives and evangelicals considerable leverage over the party during the 1970s. In the North Carolina transgender case, in contrast, religious conservatives who opposed the Charlotte ordinance were able to win the initial support of the governor and GOP legislators, but when the boycotts began harming the state's economy, key politicians began searching for an escape.

Second, the relationship of external actors to the threatened constituencies varied across the cases. When do third parties possess an incentive to join a backlash conflict, and why do they provide assistance to one adversary rather than the other? Donald Black's theory of partisanship offers insights into these questions.[140] Emphasizing the role of social distance, Black argues that a third party is more likely to get involved in a conflict when it is socially and culturally close to one adversary and remote from the other. When third parties are equally proximate to both adversaries, the safest course is to stay neutral (as anyone who is close friends with both partners in a divorcing couple knows). Further, Black argues that third parties will choose the side of the disputant with whom they share cultural or social characteristics, such as religion or ethnicity.[141] Black's theory helps explain the involvement of third parties in each of the three cases. The white parents involved in the tax-exemption

battle received support from other white Christians in their local communities. These actors were relationally and culturally much closer to the private
school parents than to civil rights advocates. The members of the VCDL received support not only from sheriffs but also from some militia members, who
shared a basic mistrust of the government.

What was most interesting from this perspective was the decision of tech
firms and other major national corporations and Hollywood celebrities to join
the side of transgender people in the conflict over the North Carolina bathroom bill. These actors would appear to have a financial incentive to remain
on the sidelines. Why would actors who seek to maximize their brand appeal
take a risk of alienating consumers who happen to be conservatives? The safest course for business executives is usually to steer clear of the culture wars.
Yet shareholders, employees, and other stakeholders sometimes drag companies into battles over contentious social issues. In today's hyperpolarized era,
knowledge industry and entertainment figures are culturally much closer to
historically marginalized groups than to religious conservatives, who are less
likely to have attended the same elite universities and who believe in traditional gender norms and values. To use Black's terminology, the cultural
proximity of these firms to the LGBTQ community—combined with their
cultural distance from social conservatives—generated a "gravitational field"
that pulled them into the conflict on the side of the liberals in the mobilization
against North Carolina's bathroom bill.[142] Polarization today has both a partisan and a cultural dimension, which encourages third parties who have no
geographic or community-based connection to the combatants in a backlash
dispute to "pick a side" and join conflicts that they might well have skipped
during a less tribal era.

Where's the Backlash? The Air Traffic Controllers, the S&L Crisis, and Benefits for Drug Felons

To gain insight into the conditions under which policy backlashes occur, it is useful to examine cases in which policymakers took actions that *could* have triggered strong negative reactions yet the responses were relatively muted. In this chapter, I examine three such instances. The first is President Ronald Reagan's firing of eleven thousand members of the Professional Air Traffic Controllers Organization (PATCO) for carrying out an illegal strike in 1981. Reagan's advisers warned him that a "major air disaster might result from the wholesale replacement of striking controllers."[1] The airlines lost billions of dollars due to flight reductions, and businesses in related industries experienced negative spillovers.[2] In sum, Reagan's action imposed concentrated costs on the strikers and general costs on the U.S. economy, and it threatened air passenger safety. Yet the blowback was minimal.

The second case is the failure of the nation's savings and loan (S&L) industry, and its subsequent resolution by Congress. Policymakers imposed significant costs on taxpayers to clean up "the greatest collapse of U.S. financial institutions since the Great Depression."[3] By 1999, U.S. taxpayers had paid $211 billion (in 2022 dollars) to resolve the thrift crisis.[4] The S&L industry's downfall—which received extensive media attention—was due in no small part to the federal government's own regulatory decisions and oversight lapses. While lawmakers feared that enacting an expensive package to resolve the mess would trigger a voter backlash, only a handful of incumbents lost their seats. Ultimately, the public's reaction was modest relative to the magnitude of the fiasco.

In the last case, I examine the lack of backlash to state-level decisions to remove or modify an existing lifetime ban on the provision of food stamps and cash welfare to people with prior felony drug convictions, which was established in 1996 under the federal welfare reform law. Drug felons are not

an especially powerful or sympathetic constituency. Indeed, as Michael Leo
Owens and Adrienne R. Smith observe, drug felons not only lack the political
resources to influence policymaking, they also "have a negative social construction as undeserving or scorned citizens, resulting from their master status as a criminal."[5] The combination of low power resources and an association with negative stereotypes places drug felons in the "deviant" category of
Anne L. Schneider and Helen M. Ingram's framework for classifying target
populations.[6] One might expect policymakers to leave intact a policy status
quo that denies social benefits to this marginalized constituency. Yet many
states have passed laws to remove or modify the ban on public benefits, and
they have provoked little or no opposition in doing so.

It could not be known with certainty in advance that backlashes would
fail to materialize in these cases. Some ingredients were clearly present. A few
differences at the start might have unleashed backlash forces in at least some
of the cases. But policy motives, participatory means, and political opportunities never fully combined to fuel robust countermobilizations. The lack of
alignment reflects both contingent factors and strategic actors' purposive use
of backlash management tactics.

Ronald Reagan's Firing of the Air Traffic Controllers

Ronald Reagan's victory in his showdown with the air traffic controllers created a negative legacy that labor unions have struggled to overcome to this
day.[7] As historian Jefferson Cowie writes, PATCO's fall has become "the pivotal event—both symbolically and substantively—in almost everyone's understanding of the massive realignment of class power in the United States
in the last few decades."[8] Understanding how Reagan busted the controllers'
union and threatened the air transportation system without unleashing a backlash requires paying attention to the context of the labor dispute, public perceptions of who was to blame for the conflict, and the reactions of other actors within PATCO's institutional network.

PATCO'S PRE-1981 HISTORY

When the air traffic controllers went on strike in August 1981, their primary
aim was to win a ten-thousand-dollar across-the-board raise, better retirement
benefits, and a shorter workweek, of thirty-two hours.[9] As federal employees,
the controllers' salaries and benefits were set by Congress. Many controllers
believed that the intense pressure of their work, together with the importance
of the aviation system to the economy, entitled them to better compensation

than other federal workers. As Michael Barone writes, "The controllers were mostly young men without college educations who believed they possessed a unique skill which the mass of air travelers—mostly college-educated, affluent businessmen—could not do without and who believed they were overworked in their stressful positions."[10]

PATCO had successfully used aggressive bargaining tactics to win concessions in the past. Between 1968 and 1981, "PATCO was involved in no fewer than six serious disruptions of air transport services," including a twenty-day "sick-out" in 1970 in which twenty-two hundred controllers around the country failed to show up to work, nearly bringing commercial air travel to a standstill.[11] While the federal government imposed penalties against controllers who participated in these illegal job actions, it had never sent an unmistakable signal that the actions would *not* be tolerated. As a result, PATCO believed that the federal government would respond to the 1981 strike as it had to past labor disputes. As Joseph A. McCartin writes in *Collision Course*, the definitive account of the 1981 controllers' strike, "They anticipated that known leaders might indeed lose their jobs—at least for a while. They did not understand that the Reagan administration was finalizing a decision to break dramatically with precedent in handling a walkout by issuing blanket and permanent terminations."[12]

PATCO's president, Robert E. Poli, believed that the legal prohibition on strikes by federal workers was "outdated" and was confident the Reagan administration would negotiate.[13] This was not an unreasonable assumption. In 1970, federal postal workers conducted a wildcat strike to obtain better wages. President Nixon vowed not to negotiate and, declaring the strike a national emergency, he enlisted military reservists to keep the mail moving. But the government's effort to replace the striking postal workers proved "futile."[14] "Letters, bills and checks to pay those bills, birthday cards, passports, legal documents, and even draft notices piled up in mail sacks on post office floors across the nation."[15] Surveys showed that the public overwhelmingly supported the postal workers.[16] Nixon and the Congress had little choice but to return to the negotiating table. In the end, the mail carriers won a large salary increase and none of the strikers were disciplined.

HOW THE AIR TRAFFIC CONTROLLERS LOST

Unlike the postal workers eleven years earlier, however, the air traffic controllers failed to obtain more favorable contractual terms. They lost their jobs, and their union was decertified. PATCO badly miscalculated its bargaining strength. It had a weak hand, given the context of the strike, and it played it poorly. By contrast, the Reagan administration "played a strong hand superbly well."[17]

To be sure, PATCO had reasons to believe that Reagan would be sympathetic to the demands. Reagan had led a strike as head of the Screen Actors Guild during his career as a Hollywood actor. In addition, PATCO had endorsed Reagan for president, one of only a few unions in the country to have done so. In exchange, Poli, PATCO's president, had asked Reagan to commit to the right for the union to strike. Reagan's letter of reply was vague on this point, but PATCO leaders believed he had given a "wink and a nod" to their demands.[18] In June 1981, the federal government offered PATCO a new contract featuring a substantial raise, of about four thousand dollars. Poli initially agreed to the offer but was forced to withdraw his acceptance under pressure from union membership.[19] PATCO broke off negotiations, and Reagan stated that there would be "no amnesty" for strikers who did not return to work within forty-eight hours.[20]

PATCO believed its ability to shut down the commercial aviation system gave it bargaining leverage. But the federal government had a much greater capacity than the union realized to adjust air traffic flow by using computer programs and recruiting replacement workers who had the ability to operate the system.[21] The Federal Aviation Administration (FAA) moved quickly to supplement the more than five thousand existing controllers who did not join the strike with FAA managers, air traffic controllers from the military, retired controllers, and new graduates of its flight control training centers.[22] To be sure, the strike did impose significant costs on the economy, as the number of daily commercial flights initially plummeted by more than 40 percent.[23] Some carriers suffered major losses. Braniff Airways laid off 15 percent of its domestic workforce, and eventually ceased flight operations altogether.[24] Pan Am's departures in 1982 were almost one-third below its prestrike level.[25] Commercial air traffic remained below the prestrike level for more than a year. Taxi companies, hotels, and other air travel–related businesses also suffered losses.[26]

The economic impact of the strike never became large enough to force the Reagan administration back to the negotiating table, however. While the commercial aviation system was tested, it did not collapse. The Federal Labor Relations Authority decertified PATCO in October 1981. By late November of that year, "local PATCO offices were closed, picket lines had dwindled, and fired controllers who had not yet done so began searching for work."[27]

WHERE WAS THE BACKLASH?

The lack of a robust backlash deserves scrutiny. Once Reagan fired the strikers, why was PATCO unable to countermobilize effectively? Why were

PATCO's grievances not amplified by other actors in its political network? What would have been needed in the early days for a backlash to have generated momentum?

Part of the answer to these questions lies with the inability of PATCO to sustain its day-to-day operations. As Matthew J. Lacombe persuasively argues, some policy losses are empowering for constituencies. They build a sense of shared identity and linked fate among targeted groups. However, losses will fail to build solidarity when they undercut the resources and mechanisms vital to a membership-based organization's ability to maintain itself.[28] This is precisely what happened in the case of the air traffic controllers' strike. The federal government decertified PATCO, eliminating its ability to recruit and retain members. In addition, it fined the union for conducting an illegal strike, forcing it to pay $28.8 million (an amount much larger than its assets) to the airlines. The Department of Justice also took steps to demoralize union members, arresting some seventy-eight strikers. Many of those who were arrested struck deals, but some were convicted and had to pay fines or serve jail time.[29] In sum, the union no longer possessed the human capital or political resources required for countermobilization.

By spring 1982, PATCO was broke and had no paid employees left on its staff.[30] The volunteerism of union members enabled PATCO to operate, but only as a shell operation. The union needed the public's backing in the dispute, but a Gallup poll taken shortly after the strike found that 59 percent of the public approved of how Reagan had handled the conflict. Just 30 percent disapproved and 11 percent had no opinion. Moreover, 68 percent of respondents in this survey agreed that the controllers should not be permitted to strike.[31] The Reagan administration managed the public relations battle skillfully, arguing that the strikers had broken a solemn pledge not to strike and that their wage demands were excessive.

Another part of the explanation is that the general public failed to react negatively to the controllers' firing. To be sure, PATCO, tried to convince the public that the replacement controllers were unqualified and thus a danger to public safety, but this argument was ill-timed. As McCartin argues, "Even had the union tried to court public opinion it could not have chosen a less auspicious moment to undertake that task."[32] In 1981, the American economy was sputtering. With unemployment and inflation both at high levels, many citizens were feeling financially pinched and believed it was a time for shared sacrifices. In contrast to the coverage of the postal workers' strike in 1970, media coverage painted the air traffic controllers in an unflattering light, noting that that they enjoyed high salaries and had achieved middle-class status. One *New York Times* headline described them as "young, affluent, and angry."[33] An

Associated Press article pointed out that "many people probably would consider [the controllers] well paid" and noted that a "journeyman controller at centers with much traffic earns from $38,000 to $50,000 a year not counting overtime. With average overtime some controllers at O'Hare International Airport near Chicago earn more than the governor of Illinois."[34] (In 2022 dollars, those amounts were equivalent to $122,000–$161,000.)

A third part of the explanation is that the strikers lacked influential external allies. Republican officeholders strongly backed President Reagan's action, and many tried to stoke public backlash against PATCO by characterizing the strikers as dishonorable and selfish.[35] Newt Gingrich (R-GA) denounced the strikers as "terrorists."[36] More importantly, few congressional Democrats were willing to expend political capital to defend PATCO's actions. The strike occurred at the beginning of the neoliberal era, as policymakers of both parties were abandoning the assumptions of the New Deal order—a shift that Democratic president Carter had contributed to by supporting the deregulation of the airline industry.[37] As a result, Reagan's breaking of the union, although anathema to many liberals, never became a major partisan issue. One Democratic who did speak out forcefully on PATCO's behalf was Representative John Conyers of Michigan, who argued that federal employees should have the same collective bargaining rights to strike as private-sector workers.[38] However, few of Conyers's Democratic colleagues endorsed this position.

Further, many Democrats were irritated that PATCO had backed Reagan in the 1980 presidential campaign. And even Democrats who might overlook the endorsement found it untenable to support a union that was engaged in an illegal strike.[39] Many voters took their cue from President Reagan and decided that the controllers had broken faith with the country. As PATCO president Poli would later reflect, "I don't know how many times I was told, 'Mr. Poli, I understand all the things that you say forced you to strike, but you broke your oath!' In the battle for the hearts and minds of middle America, the administration won uncontested when they raised the oath issue. No matter how often we explained why we had to strike, the people of this country place a high value on oaths—and properly so."[40] Democratic lawmakers who might have been inclined to support the union were further dissuaded by the climb in Reagan's poll numbers in August.[41]

A potential ally in PATCO's institutional network was organized labor. For Democratic politicians to feel pressure to defend the striking controllers, PATCO's brother unions needed to provide significant assistance, sharing resources to compensate for its losses. Some labor organizations, especially the flight attendants' union, did provide material support. However, most national union leaders kept their distance from PATCO, not wishing to embrace a union that they believed had "embarked on a doomed course."[42] The AFL-CIO condemned the Reagan administration's position but stopped short of taking meaningful actions like mass walkouts to support the strike.[43] In view of the bad economy, many union members were anxious about the security of their own jobs and felt the air traffic controllers' demands were excessive. The AFL-CIO's leaders feared that taking bold steps to defend PATCO would only serve to divide a weakened labor movement.[44] As Robert Reich observes, by the time Reagan busted PATCO, organized labor had already lost significant clout. Union membership had fallen significantly from its peak in the mid-1950s, and employers were increasingly contesting union elections to curb union power.[45]

The Air Line Pilots Association (ALPA) was the single most important potential ally.[46] If the pilots' union had declared the air traffic control system to be unsafe when managed by replacements, the strikers might have won their jobs back. Instead, the pilots went out of their way to tell the media that the air traffic system remained safe. "ALPA went down and below the call of duty attempting to hurt us," Poli lamented.[47] Many pilots had no sympathy for PATCO's grievances, and they were "furious that the controllers' strike cut back flights during the peak summer travel season, giving the airlines an excuse to demand concessions from them."[48] John J. O'Donnell, the president of the pilots' union, said that his membership would expel him from office if he insisted that pilots respect PATCO's picket lines.[49]

The presidents of the major airlines were a key source of opposition. All "pledged total support" for Reagan's position.[50] While many so-called legacy airlines—carriers that were flying before deregulation—suffered losses from the reduction in flights and passenger traffic, the strike ironically served their long-term interests. The industry was coming off several unprofitable years due to high fuel costs and the transition to the lifting of government regulatory controls. Being forced to scale back operations provided these carriers with a welcome opportunity to shed redundant employees and aircraft, which helped them become more competitive in the new business environment.[51]

In sum, multiple factors explain the absence of a public or corporate backlash to Reagan's firing of the striking controllers. First, PATCO lost the resources necessary to maintain itself, and it received only modest compensatory support from nominal allies. Most congressional Democrats who were weighing what stance to take on the strike looked to public opinion, and most Americans were unsympathetic to the strikers' demands. Moreover, organized labor was experiencing a secular decline in its power when the air traffic controllers' strike occurred, and many union workers were focused on saving their own jobs.

Yet it is possible to imagine a counterfactual history under which Reagan's action would have triggered public blowback. If a major air disaster had occurred in the first few days after the controllers walked off the job, the public might have linked the disaster to Reagan's intransigence.[52] In fact, a major air disaster *did* occur on January 13, 1982, when Air Florida Flight 90 plunged into Potomac River in Washington, DC, killing seventy-four passengers. The air traffic controller who cleared the flight for takeoff was a replacement supervisor. After investigation, the FAA and the National Transportation Safety Board concluded that the controller's action was not a factor in the crash. Moreover, coming as it did more than five months after Reagan had fired the striking controllers, the event had no impact on the public's reaction to the strike. It was too distant in time for voters to trace it back to Reagan's action.[53]

The Savings and Loan Bailout

The S&L bailout of the late 1980s is a second instance of subdued backlash.[54] It was the largest federal bailout on record at the time, "eclipsing the combined bailouts of Lockheed, Chrysler, Penn Central and New York City."[55] As I discuss next, policymakers recognized that the bailout could cause voters to lash back and took many steps to reduce this risk. They were broadly successful in this blame-avoidance project, although a few legislators were tarnished by the scandal and lost their seats in the 1990 midterms.

HOW THE S&L INDUSTRY WENT BUST

The first American savings and loans (also known as S&Ls or "thrifts") were established in the early nineteenth century to provide financing for home mortgages. The postwar housing boom encouraged the industry's growth.[56] By 1980, nearly four thousand thrifts were in operation across the United States.[57] S&Ls occupied a "specialized niche" in the financial industry.[58] The federal government tightly regulated the rate S&Ls could pay on deposits, and most thrifts made long-term fixed-rate mortgages. These arrangements worked tolerably well under favorable economic conditions, but when interest rates climbed steeply in the 1970s, "thrifts were forced to pay higher rates on their deposits than they could earn on their assets. The resulting mismatch in the maturities of thrifts' assets and liabilities almost wiped out the market value of the industry's net worth."[59]

The federal government responded to the industry's financial troubles by deregulating it. Through the Depository Institution Deregulation and Monetary Control Act of 1980, the Garn–St. Germain Act of 1982, and other measures, S&Ls were freed to charge higher interest rates, offer adjustable-rate mortgages, and make a wider range of investments. Policymakers hoped the industry would grow itself back to health.

Unfortunately, however, deregulation created perverse incentives. Thrifts were given more latitude to chase profits, yet they retained access to federal deposit insurance.[60] In other words, the federal government continued to backstop insured S&L accounts with the "full faith and credit" of the United States, even as it removed or relaxed regulations that "fostered safety and soundness in thrifts' operations."[61] Undercapitalized thrifts now possessed an incentive to "gamble for resurrection" by making risky investments. If the high-risk investments did well, the S&Ls would win; and if the investments went south, taxpayers would lose.[62] Some S&Ls used their now-expanded investment authority to turn initial profits, but steep losses soon followed. By late 1988, almost a quarter of the industry's assets were held by so-called zombie institutions, which were either in or headed toward insolvency.[63]

CONGRESS HELPED CAUSE THE S&L CRISIS— BUT MOST LAWMAKERS ESCAPED A BACKLASH

While economic factors like rising interest rates, falling oil prices, and the collapse of real estate markets in Texas and other states contributed to the S&L industry's troubles, Congress's policy of "regulatory forbearance" was also a major culprit. As Thomas Romer and Barry W. Weingast argue, members of Congress failed to beef up the staffs of the financial-regulatory agencies, increase capital requirements, or take other prudent steps to keep the crisis from spiraling out of control.[64] Congressional behavior reflected political incentives. Thrift owners were located in every congressional district in the nation, and they were a prime source of campaign donations for members of key committees. Industry leaders were adept at avoiding blame for their own mistakes. Congress largely accepted the industry's claim that "they were the victim of external events," such as rising interest rates.[65] While powerful, concentrated business interests pushed for continued regulatory forbearance, "there was no significant constituency in favor of confronting the full magnitude of the S&L problem when it was still relatively small."[66] The constituency that would have gained from timely reform was too diffuse to exert counterpressure. Further, the costs of regulatory forbearance to taxpayers were not concentrated in time. As Jacobs and Weaver argue, policies are less likely to generate strong negative feedback when the costs they produce occur as a series of small drops.[67]

To be sure, the "Keating Five" scandal—a major national news item—did educate the public about the adverse consequences of Congress's solicitude to the S&L industry. In 1987, five U.S. senators—four Democrats along with future GOP presidential nominee Senator John McCain (AZ)—intervened with federal regulators to convey that the government was coming down too hard on Charles Keating, a major donor and the head of an insolvent thrift who would ultimately be convicted on charges of fraud and racketeering. The Senate Ethics Committee conducted a multiyear investigation of the senators' conduct, examining whether there was evidence of corruption. The ethics panel recommended varying penalties and reprimands for each of the lawmakers, but all five survived the scandal.[68]

The Keating Five episode raised the salience of the crisis to average voters, focusing public attention on the lengths to which lawmakers had gone to shield powerful S&L owners from accountability. But ordinary Americans struggled to connect the S&L industry's mounting losses to policy decisions. In one national opinion survey, just 14 percent of the public said that lax government regulation was a primary reason for the S&L crisis. The most frequently cited reason in the survey was industry fraud and mismanagement (48 percent).[69] The linkage between regulatory forbearance and taxpayer liabilities was not direct enough to trigger backlash.[70]

While the government's failure to resolve the S&L crisis was not at the top of voters' minds, incumbent politicians nonetheless worried that challengers or other actors could rouse the public and that Congress's role in the crisis was an electoral liability. Accordingly, they took steps to avoid blame and insulate themselves from voter accountability.[71] While the need for additional funding to resolve the S&L crisis was known by mid-1988, both Democratic and Republican incumbents agreed to delay action until after the November elections. Not only were members of both parties eager to avoid having to pass legislation authorizing a bailout before the election, but each had particular reasons to be concerned about the risk of voter backlash. Democrats feared that they might be held responsible because some of their leaders, such as House Speaker Jim Wright (TX), had been accused of protecting their political allies in the industry.[72] Congressional Democrats cautioned the party's presidential nominee, Michael Dukakis, not to raise the S&L issue during the campaign.[73] For their part, Republican incumbents knew the crisis had started on the Reagan administration's watch. With both sides seeking to avoid blame, the two parties agreed to let the next Congress deal with the mess.[74] "In a period of divided government, with a Republican president and a Democratic Congress, incumbent protection was valuable all around," write Nolan McCarty, Keith T. Poole, and Howard Rosenthal.[75]

THE BAILOUT

Just weeks after his inauguration, President George H. W. Bush introduced a comprehensive plan to resolve the S&L crisis. As signed into law on August 9, the Financial Institutions Reform, Recovery, and Enforcement Act of 1989 (PL 101-73) established two new entities to carry out the S&L rescue.[76] The first was the Resolution Trust Corporation (RTC), a government corporation that was charged with disposing of the assets of insolvent thrifts.[77] The second was the Resolution Funding Corporation (REFCORP), a government-sponsored enterprise whose job was to raise the money required to liquidate troubled thrifts by selling long-term bonds. The interest on the debt would be repaid by industry premiums and federal appropriations.[78]

A NARROW VOTER BACKLASH

The public's initial reaction to the S&L bailout was quite negative. In a survey taken shortly after Bush announced his rescue plan, 69 percent of respondents expressed opposition and only 20 percent said they were in favor of it.[79] Public support increased as Congress debated and reworked the proposal, but even right before the legislation's passage, a plurality of those surveyed still opposed it (46 against to 36 percent for, with the rest unsure).[80]

Public anger about the S&L scandal provided the raw materials for a populist backlash. The *Washington Post* reported that members of Congress received thousands of letters about the crisis from angry voters. Many of the letters expressed disgust at the "executives who got rich, at the prosecutors for not prosecuting harder, at Congress for deregulating the industry in the first place, at the prospect of paying billions of dollars to clean up the mess."[81] Still, congressional staffers reported that the volume of mail on the S&L crisis was lower than on several other recent hot-button issues, such as the Medicare Catastrophic Coverage Act (MCCA) and the federal pay raise.[82]

Several factors explain why the backlash to the S&L situation was relatively muted. First, the timing mattered. The S&L legislation was enacted early in the election cycle, meaning it was over a year before lawmakers who voted for the act had to face the voters in the 1990 midterms. In contrast, when the U.S. House of Representatives voted down the initial version of the Troubled Assets Relief Program (TARP) out of fear of a populist backlash at the polls, the vote occurred just weeks before the 2008 election. As Representative Paul Ryan (R-WI) acknowledged after the House rejected the bill, "We're all worried about losing our jobs."[83] To be sure, a handful of lawmakers who

were implicated in the S&L crisis were defeated in the 1990 midterms, including Representatives Douglas Bosco (D-CA), Charles Pashayan Jr. (R-CA),
and Denny Smith (R-OR).[84] But many more incumbents survived campaign
attacks on their ties to the industry, including Representatives Frank Annu-
zuio (D-IL), Doug Barnard Jr. (D-GA), Bill Lowery (R-CA), and David E.
Price (D-NC).[85]

Second, the S&L rescue reduced backlash motives by minimizing visible
losses. The legislation imposed no new taxes, instead relying mainly on debt
financing.[86] In fact, a proposal to avoid government borrowing by raising taxes
made by Sam M. Gibbons (D-FL) during the Ways and Means Committee
markup was soundly rejected by a strong bipartisan majority.[87]

Third, policymakers crafted the governing structure of the S&L bailout
to weaken the traceability of policy costs and reduce the likelihood of voter
retribution.[88] The legislation created a complex oversight board and director-
ship whose members included two cabinet secretaries, the chairman of the
Federal Reserve, two private citizens, and leaders from the Federal Home Loan
Bank and Federal Deposit Insurance Corporation. While this oversight structure was an administrative nightmare, it insulated politicians from any problems that might arise during the implementation of the rescue measure. As
Donald F. Kettl writes, "The alphabet soup of overseers distanced both the
president and the Congress from the oversight . . . so it helped minimize the
electoral fallout from the bailout."[89]

Fourth, the economic shock from the S&L crisis was much smaller than
the economic shock from the 2008 financial crisis that launched the Tea Party.[90]
The S&L rescue was a significant expense for taxpayers, but the bursting of the
S&L bubble did not lead to mass unemployment or crash the stock market.

Finally, Congress's role in the S&L crisis never became a partisan issue,
which undercut its potential to mobilize an opposition coalition. In a 1990
exit poll, 41 percent of respondents blamed both parties equally for the mess,
16 percent blamed Democrats, and 25 percent blamed Republicans.[91] To be
sure, House Democrats opposed President Bush's initial proposal for fixing
the mess. But the main point of contention was arcane—whether the cost of
the S&L bailout should be "off-budget" (as Bush wanted) or "on-budget" (as
many Democrats preferred). The conflict was less about fomenting a populist
backlash than a proxy battle in the 1980s partisan war over the federal budget.[92] Both Democrats and Republicans were concerned about how the prec-
edents established by the massive rescue measure would affect the prospects
for tax increases and spending cuts in the future.[93] In the end, a compromise
was reached in which most of the spending was placed off-budget.[94]

Social Benefits for Ex-Drug Felons

Finally, I take a brief look at the lack of backlash to the decisions of many states to opt out of a lifetime federal ban on the receipt of food stamps through the Supplemental Nutrition Assistance Program (SNAP) and cash assistance through Temporary Assistance for Needy Families (TANF) for individuals with felony drug convictions. This case merits scrutiny because it involves the provision of benefits to a marginalized and unsympathetic constituency, creating a situation that can trigger a backlash. As noted in chapter 3, one reason why some Americans were initially opposed to the Affordable Care Act (ACA) was resentment that unemployed people could often obtain more comprehensive and affordable health care benefits through Medicaid than was available to working-class families.[95] Perceptions of the deservedness of target populations are shaped by many factors, including whether the social constructions of groups activate negative stereotypes, such as a belief that the recipients of government assistance are not striving to be self-reliant.[96] When policymakers stigmatize or otherwise impose costs on groups cast as "deviants" (e.g., criminals), they often receive little pushback. "In fact, legislators will anticipate that most other people will applaud the 'toughness' of policy directed at groups considered 'undeserving,' and this too will help solidify support for the policymakers," write Schneider and Ingram.[97]

WELFARE REFORM IMPOSES A LIFETIME BAN ON BENEFITS FOR EX-DRUG FELONS

It was thus not terribly surprising when, in 1996, a newly ascendant Republican congressional majority imposed a lifetime ban on cash assistance and food stamps for people convicted of selling, possessing, or using drugs as part of the welfare reform bill signed into law by Clinton. In addition to abolishing the Aid to Families with Dependent Children program, the measure imposed work requirements and limited the length of time for which people could receive cash assistance.[98]

The ban on means-tested benefits for drug felons was inserted as an amendment to the welfare reform bill, which was proposed by Senator Phil Gramm (R-TX). The amendment received only a few minutes of floor debate and passed by a voice vote.[99] Gramm framed the amendment as a crime control measure, stating that "if we are serious about our drug laws, we ought not to give people welfare benefits who are violating the Nation's drug laws."[100] Senator Ted Kennedy (D-MA) spoke against the proposal. He noted that the

Conference of Mayors and the National League of Cities both strongly opposed the measure, arguing that it would undermine access to drug treatment.[101]

But the political context of the 1990s thwarted countermobilization against a punitive policy targeted at drug felons. This was an era "when the war on drugs was raging, welfare use was heavily stigmatized through racialized attacks linking assistance to sloth and criminality, and policies that inflicted punishment on people with histories of drug activity were popular across the aisle."[102] This political orthodoxy was not confined to Washington; it also influenced state-level policymaking. In 1997, the California legislature debated whether to allow the federal ban to stand. A conference committee initially decided to exempt welfare mothers convicted of the possession (but not the sale) of drugs, but moderate Democrats insisted on maintaining the strict federal ban. "I felt that a person shouldn't be in a position of using drugs and receiving public money," said Assemblyman Michael Machado (D-Linden). "We cannot continue to hand out money if people are not going to make an attempt to use it to better their lives."[103]

The implementation of the Gramm Amendment had a massive impact on the target population. According to one estimate, states removed around 92,000 adults with felony drug convictions from the welfare rolls between 1997 and 2002.[104] The policy also had a disparate impact on women and minority communities. According to a study by the Sentencing Project, 180,000 women were affected by the welfare ban between 1996 and 2011, including 66,000 women in Texas alone.[105] While whites, African Americans, and Latinos use drugs at similar rates, minorities were much more likely to be convicted for drug offenses and lose their benefit eligibility.[106] The policy was not only harsh, but arbitrary—people who committed other felonies, including rape and murder, were not subject to the ban. Yet drug felons were never likely to countermobilize. Not only did this group lack political resources and interest-group support, but the diversity and complexity of the rules governing welfare programs across states made it "unlikely any welfare recipient knows or fully understands them unless or until she finds herself subject to them."[107]

STATE MODIFICATIONS OF THE BAN

In 1996 proponents could assume that few states would use their discretion under the welfare reform law to opt out of the ban. As one member of a progressive advocacy group would later reflect, "The architects of the federal law were very smart in pushing the responsibility for opt-out down to the states. Anytime you have something involving both drugs and welfare, it'll be very controversial."[108]

Yet in a remarkable liberalization of social benefits for a marginalized constituency, many states have voted to lift or modify the bans over the past two decades. By the end of 2004, nineteen states retained a full ban on drug felons receiving TANF, while seventeen still completely banned drug felons from receiving SNAP.[109] By 2022, however, only seven states maintained a full ban on TANF benefits, and just one (South Carolina) had not lifted or modified the lifetime ban on SNAP.[110]

The lifting or relaxation of these bans generated pushback in only a few states. In Texas, for example, supporters of lifting the ban on SNAP ran into some opposition within the legislature.[111] They were forced to agree to a compromise that reinstated the ban for any individual who committed a second offense while receiving assistance. Pennsylvania lifted the ban on both TANF and SNAP in 2003 but later reversed course. In 2018, Democratic governor Tom Wolf signed a GOP-sponsored bill reinstating a ten-year TANF ban.[112] But resistance to the liberalization of social benefits for drug felons has been notable for its relative absence. Three factors help explain the lack of strong backlashes.

First, proposals to lift or modify the bans received relatively little media attention. In some cases, the measures were buried in larger bills or overshadowed by more controversial ideas, such as an unsuccessful Texas proposal to require state residents to pass a drug test before receiving food stamps.[113] As Alison L. Gash argues, low-visibility advocacy can be an effective way to promote egalitarian policies without triggering a strong public backlash.[114]

Second, proposals to lift or modify the bans have been framed as criminal justice reforms to reduce recidivism and mass incarceration rather than as expansions of the welfare state.[115] As David Dagan and Steven Teles argue in their book *Prison Break*, many conservatives in red states have embraced the goal of curbing prison growth, thus moving away from the tough-on-crime policies of the 1990s. "In no other cases during the era of polarization has one of our political parties changed so thoroughly, and so suddenly, as Republicans have on criminal justice," they write.[116] Many policymakers found the criminal justice reform case for removing the bans compelling. One careful study found that people who were eligible for welfare and food stamps at the time of their release from prison were up to 10 percent less likely to return to prison in the following year.[117]

Most importantly, and relatedly, proposals to lift or modify the bans have drawn bipartisan support among policy elites. The fact that prominent Republicans like then-governor of Georgia Nathan Deal supported relaxing the food stamp ban was critical in dampening public backlash.[118] If state-level GOP politicians had maintained their party's prior commitments to both the

War on Drugs and a paternalistic welfare policy, proposals from progressive advocacy groups or Democratic lawmakers to provide public assistance to drug felons might well have provoked grassroots resistance. But without divisions among elites, the political context provided weak external incentives for a conservative countermobilization.[119]

Discussion

In this chapter, I have briefly examined three cases where policy moves could have plausibly generated backlash reactions but negative responses were comparatively subdued. Why didn't motives, means, and political opportunities align themselves in these cases to generate the type of counterreactions depicted in previous chapters? Several factors were critical to each of these outcomes.

The first has to do with the timing and sequencing of events. Backlashes only happen if people decide to resist a shift in the status quo through their participatory acts. What occurs soon after a loss or threat becomes clear thus influences whether a potential backlash will actualize and build momentum— or peter out. As Pierson argues, "Because early parts of a sequence matter much more than later parts, an event that happens 'too late' may have no effect, although it might have been of great consequence if the timing had been different."[120] In the cases examined here, loss-imposing actors displayed an awareness of the importance of these temporal factors. For example, the decision to delay the S&L bailout until after the 1988 elections was clearly intended to blunt backlash motives. Together with the convoluted design of the oversight structure, this step made it much harder for ordinary voters to connect the costs of the rescue measure to specific legislative actions. Similarly, the public would have been far more likely to blame Reagan for endangering public safety if Air Florida Flight 90 had crashed five days after the striking controllers were fired rather than five months later.

Second, some of the loss-bearing groups lacked the means to mount an effective countermobilization. In the S&L case, taxpayers comprised a diffuse constituency that could not overcome the cost of collective action. In contrast, PATCO was a concentrated interest, but the Reagan administration used aggressive steps—including imposing fines and decertifying the union— to undercut PATCO's capacity to maintain itself, which led to the organization's collapse.

Finally, the political opportunity structures were not conducive to backlash politics. Significantly, partisan forces were absent or weak in all three cases. In the case of the air traffic controllers, President Reagan's command of public opinion simply overwhelmed any partisan opposition from Democrats. In contrast, in the S&L case, Democratic and Republican lawmakers conspired to keep the mounting cost of the financial crisis from becoming a major partisan issue in federal elections in order to promote their shared objective of incumbent protection. Finally, partisan factors were missing with respect to benefits to drug felons because there was a bipartisan consensus on the direction of the policy change. This was the case both when bans on TANF and SNAP for drug felons were imposed during the 1990s and when the bans were lifted or eased in many states during the most recent period. These dramatic swings in social policymaking had enormous consequences for the lives of marginalized citizens, yet they generated little pushback in either direction. Partisanship is the major cleavage in American democracy, and policy backlashes are much less likely to gain momentum when that cleavage is not present.

Conclusion

The backlashes against the Affordable Care Act (ACA), the No Child Left Behind (NCLB) Act, and the North American Free Trade Agreement (NAFTA), just three of the many cases explored in this book, were noteworthy events in recent American political history. It is valuable for scholars, advocates, and citizens to understand why the hard-won enactment battles to expand health insurance coverage, improve educational outcomes through school accountability reforms, and remove barriers to global trade mobilized opposition among mass publics and organized interests. We also need to understand why other policy moves like the breaking of the air traffic controllers' union *failed* to unleash backlash forces, even though the targeted constituencies suffered heavy losses.

But the main reason I wrote this book was not to explore particular cases, fascinating as they may be. Rather, I wrote the book to illuminate the dynamics of the contemporary policy state. Without taking backlash forces into account, we cannot understand why some policies are kept off the domestic agenda, why other policies face mounting resistance following their enactment, or how partisan polarization has transformed U.S. governance. Without studying the mobilization of opposition to policy change, we cannot understand the mobilization of support.

In this conclusion, I reflect on the broader implications of my analysis. I focus on how attention to backlash politics can advance the study of policy feedback. I then take stock of the consequences of backlash politics for America's polarized policy state, discuss the relationship between backlash politics and policy learning, and draw out some practical implications of my findings for navigating backlash risks. Finally, I discuss whether backlash is an inherently racialized phenomenon and whether we will see a liberal backlash against the rising conservative threat to previously won social rights and policy gains.

Backlash and the Study of Policy Feedback

Backlash can be understood as a feedback process in which policies construct, fortify, or mobilize opposition forces rather than build supportive coalitions. Negative feedbacks have received only limited attention from historical institutionalists who study U.S. politics. There are several reasons for this lacuna. First, historical institutionalists have focused on the feedback from social policies like Social Security and the GI Bill and have devoted less attention to the feedback generated by other types of programs, such as the provision of governance assistance to rural constituencies.[1] Second, the feedback literature has mainly focused on policymaking during the postwar era, a period in which American politics was less polarized and the intensity of partisan combat was much lower than today.[2]

Nothing in policy feedback theory suggests, however, that actors' reactions to policy moves should invariably point in a single direction.[3] Indeed, Theda Skocpol's 1992 book on the origins of U.S. public social provision, *Protecting Soldiers and Mothers*, argued that the perceived corruption of the patronage associated with Civil War pensions provoked *negative* reactions among elite reformers, which constrained the opportunities for expanding the welfare state for decades thereafter.[4] Yet with the important exception of Jacobs and Weaver's illuminating article on self-undermining feedback, "When Policies Undo Themselves," most recent historical institutionalist research has instead explored the conditions under which programs produce increasing returns and become entrenched rather than the conditions under which programs mobilize opposition forces.[5]

My analysis suggests seven broad conclusions about backlash politics for the study of policy feedback. First, *policy attributes significantly influence the risk and potency of a backlash.* Backlash is not only a product of what opponents or partisan media outlets claim about a policy's effects, although cues from elites can, of course, be extremely important. The *substance* of policy also has a large, and sometimes decisive, influence on the reactions of individuals and groups. Specifically, other things being equal, the probability of backlash politics increases when policies impose concentrated costs on groups or geographic communities or salient general costs on the public; flout voters' clear preferences and priorities; deliver valuable benefits to groups that many people see as "undeserving"; or threaten the stability of existing economic or social arrangements to which people are strongly attached. These policy attributes do not guarantee that policies will mobilize an opposition coalition; contingency also plays a role. But they make adverse reactions much more likely to happen.

Constituency reactions are driven by the *perceptions* of policy effects, not the actual incidence of costs and benefits. If, for example, in 1974 most Americans had viewed the Department of Transportation's seatbelt interlock system (which required seatbelts to be fastened before cars could be started) as a friendly reminder from a caring government about the importance of auto safety rather than a major nuisance, as many people actually did, it would not have triggered a public backlash. Backlash potential thus cannot be simply "read" from policy design features. Rather, certain policy characteristics increase the *probability* that policies will trigger backlash, given citizens' expectations of government, the preexisting arrangements on which they rely, and how targeted constituency groups define their identities and interests. These factors can change over time due to cultural or political shifts, but they are typically sticky in the medium run.

A second broad conclusion is that *backlash is not an automatic or inevitable response to constituency losses.* A countermobilization requires political resources, including money, recognition, and legitimacy. These resources may be in greater or lesser supply, and a resource-starved group may well be unable to mobilize effectively even if suffers a colossal defeat. *Patterns of policy backlash typically reflect rather than mitigate existing inequalities in mobilization capacity.*

My analysis suggests that the capacity of a loss-bearing group to countermobilize hinges on two key factors. The first is how the loss influences the group's potential for collective action. I have mentioned Matthew Lacombe's study of how the NRA recovered from legislative defeats (e.g., the Gun Control Act of 1968). Lacombe shows that some policy losses can ironically build an organization's power by reinforcing a sense of shared social identity among its followers.[6] Yet, as Lacombe acknowledges, policy defeats can also be *disempowering* if they undercut a group's capacity to perform the tasks necessary for its organizational maintenance. The case of the air traffic controllers (discussed in chapter 6) illustrates this dynamic. After Ronald Reagan terminated the striking controllers, their capacity for collective action virtually ended. Facing heavy fines for violating the law, PATCO had to fire its professional staff. Some of the union's members were arrested, and its organizational resistance collapsed.

The second key factor is whether a loss-bearing group receives political sustenance from allies in its institutional network. PATCO received surprisingly little support from its brother unions. Yet in other cases, key allies bolstered the political capacity of backlashing groups. For example, county sheriffs pledged that they would support Second Amendment sanctuary movements even though this stance raised questions about their fidelity to the law. Many Democratic officeholders supported the teachers' union countermobilization against school accountability reforms and high-stakes testing. And legislators of both parties passed patient bills of rights to amplify the countermobilization of patient advocacy groups against managed care restrictions. In sum, the ability of loss-bearing groups to countermobilize reflects not only their own internal participatory capacities but also the support they receive from other actors in their institutional networks, who make decisions about whether to join coalitions based on their own incentives.[7]

A third general conclusion is that *political opportunity structures shape the strength of backlash forces.* As my analysis has showed throughout, partisan polarization is the major contextual factor driving backlash politics in American democracy today. In chapter 2, I described the association I found between the count of *NYT* articles about backlash and the degree of polarization in Congress over the 1960–2019 period. In a polarized era, party elites have a strong incentive to use backlash politics as a tool to rouse base supporters and maintain the unity of their partisan teams. Backlashes are less likely to occur and gain momentum when issues are not polarized. For example, the lack of public backlash to the removal of bans on food stamps and cash welfare for drug felons can be explained by the decision of many GOP leaders to embrace a bipartisan agenda of criminal justice reform.[8] In contrast, when policy issues remain sharply polarized, the external incentives for countermobilization are much stronger. As my discussion of the North Carolina bathroom bill case showed, tech firms and other major national corporations, together with Hollywood actors and musicians, mobilized against HB2, even though they risked alienating socially conservative Americans who attend movies and concerts and buy consumer products. The social proximity of corporate leaders and entertainment elites to the LGBTQ community—and their cultural remoteness from social conservatives—pulled them into the conflict on the side of the advocates of transgender bathroom access. It was untenable for these cosmopolitan actors to remain bystanders in an era in which "red" and "blue" stand not just for two parties but increasingly for two distinct ways of life.

Fourth, *the growth of the policy state has abetted backlash politics.* As Orren and Skowronek argue, "Policy has expanded its role in American government and society by eroding the boundaries and dissolving the distinctions that once constrained policy's reach."[9] Due to the dramatic expansion of federal government activity in areas like civil rights, consumer affairs, health care, and the environment and the resulting nationalization of American politics, the "cushion for consensus once provided by decentralization" has been displaced.[10] The broadening of the federal government's role has transformed the interest-group system, stimulating a countermobilization among loss-bearing groups, including powerful business actors.[11] At the same time, the dynamics of federalism have changed. As Jacob M. Grumbach argues, state policymaking increasingly reflects conflicts between the Democratic and Republican partisan coalitions at the national level.[12]

Fifth, *most, but not all, backlashes happen during or shortly after policy enactment*. The backlashes against the ACA, the cap-and-trade bill, and the MCCA, for example, were all fast-moving events. Yet it is also possible for the onset of backlashes to occur years or even decades after policy adoption. Lags in backlash processes can occur due to backloaded costs, administrative problems that show up late in the implementation process, or significant changes in how people experience a policy's impact due to a shift in the interaction between policy characteristics, program enrollments, and the external environment. Further, it can take time for people to recognize a loss or emerging threat and take steps to countermobilize against it. But once that happens, backlashes may build momentum.

For example, the managed care backlash did not emerge as a major force until two decades after the federal government created a policy framework conducive to the growth of HMOs. Initially, managed care provoked little opposition. As discussed in chapter 3, one reason for the absence of an early blowback was that the first HMOs mainly enrolled healthy patients who joined the plans voluntarily. These low-risk patients were not particularly bothered by prior authorization requirements since they did not expect to consume many medical services. By the 1990s, however, managed care's perceived success in slowing the growth of employer premiums caused a growing number of firms to shift their workforces into the plans. As a result, some patients with serious medical conditions were involuntarily pushed into managed care. These patients were strongly attached to the relatively unrestricted coverage of their previous fee-for-service plans, and they bristled at prior authorization requirements and other managed care restrictions. In sum, a government decision at time t (encourage HMOs to tame the growth of health care costs) generated private-sector reactions (expanding, and changing the composition of, managed care enrollments) at time $t+1$ that helped build an opposing constituency. While the managed care backlash was driven by many factors, including media coverage of medical service denials, self-undermining feedbacks were critical.

A sixth conclusion is that *countermobilizations do not necessary fade away after the threats that prompted their emergence subside.* For example, the business community's expansion of its political capacity in response to the dramatic growth of consumer and social regulation during the 1970s continued even after the political climate became more conservative in the 1980s and 1990s. Similarly, while the Tea Party initially mobilized grassroots conservatives in response to Obama's election and the ACA, it eventually matured into the dominant faction within the GOP and laid the foundation for Trump's rise to power.[13] In many instances, backlash forces outlast the shocks that caused them to be unleashed in the first place.

Finally, *while structural factors shape adverse reactions, individual leaders can play an important role in either amplifying backlashes or dampening them.* The organizational backlash against globalization first emerged among labor unions and environmentalists in the 1990s, and President Clinton chose to resist rather than amplify it. When he signed NAFTA, Clinton argued, "We cannot stop global change. We cannot repeal the economic competition that is everywhere."[14] In contrast, Trump leaned into the antiglobalization backlash, helping to make opposition to free trade and immigration a factor in the choices of some voters in the 2016 presidential election.[15] On issues ranging from immigration and education reform to health care, many Americans have signaled that they do not wish to buy the policies on offer from political elites. Yet even when backlashes have genuine grassroots support, few countermobilizations are created entirely from the bottom up. Leaders play a crucial role in backlash politics. They give political direction to backlash movements, translating public dissatisfaction, frustration, and resentment into concrete proposals, advocacy strategies, and policy decisions.

Consequences of Backlash Politics

What have been the consequences of policy backlashes in recent American politics? In the end, how much difference does backlash politics make for governance and democracy? My analysis suggests that backlash politics has produced notable effects along three dimensions: the political sustainability of policy changes; democratic engagement and coalitional alignments; and the shaping of future governing possibilities.

POLITICAL SUSTAINABILITY

The political sustainability of policies cannot be taken for granted. Agendas can change rapidly, and the political commitment to tackle a problem may dissipate long before the problem is solved. The coalition of politicians who voted to adopt a policy will not remain in office forever, and their successors may have different priorities or ideological commitments. If politicians unravel a policy before it accomplishes its core objectives, the time, resources, and political capital that went into its adoption will have been for naught.[16]

Backlash politics can undercut the embedding and expansion of policy accomplishments. The case studies examined here suggest that backlashes pose a range of threats, from outright repeal (e.g., the MCCA, the individual mandate under the ACA, the Independent Payment Advisory Board, and the Cadillac tax on expensive health plans) to legislative or judicial erosion (e.g., Medicaid expansion; Section 2 of the Voting Rights Act), weakened implementation (e.g., anemic IRS enforcement of antidiscrimination rules for private schools), or the use of executive discretion to reconfigure policy (e.g., reduced legal immigration flows and the disregarding of the WTO's authority under President Trump).

To be sure, many backlashes leave only a faint imprint on governance. Backlash coalitions vary in their breadth, intensity, and duration and in the external support they receive from other actors. Adverse reactions to changes in the status quo often fade once a new policy is consolidated. Yet it would be a grave mistake to view most backlash politics as "sound and fury, signifying nothing." For policy advocates who wish to build power and protect their victories, backlashes are rarely good news.

In the end, whether policies last or are subject to one or more types of unraveling depends largely on the evolving balance of *sustainability-enhancing factors*, such as the provision of concentrated benefits (which mobilize supporters) and *sustainability-undermining factors*, such as the imposition of concentrated costs (which mobilize opponents). In sum, when a backlash does *not* produce a policy's erosion or repeal, the reason may be either because the backlash itself was weak or because its impact was offset by other policy attributes that generated political support. It is only by examining the *net* impact of the positive and negative feedbacks put in motion by a policy that the prospects for political sustainability can be assessed.[17] For example, the combination of the ACA's frontloading of costs (e.g., the botched rollout of the healthcare.gov site and the cancelation of noncompliant insurance plans) and delayed benefits (the major insurance benefits did not go into effect until four years after the law's passage) both aroused opponents *and* delayed constituency building. It takes time for new policies to generate the social expectations required for their embedding, and they can be vulnerable to repeal or erosion if backlash forces are not tamed before the consolidation process is successfully underway.[18]

DEMOCRATIC ENGAGEMENT
AND COALITIONAL ALIGNMENTS

The ability of citizens and groups to signal their distress over government actions through ballots, petitions, protests, social movement activity, issue advocacy, and other types of countermobilization—provided such activities are
nonviolent and respectful of the rights of other citizens—is at the heart of a
pluralist democracy. This is so even when the preferences of backlashers are
dubious or misguided.

An important distinction can be drawn between backlashes that tap into
existing cleavages and cases where policy discussions stimulate the emergence
of new opposition coalitions. The first type of backlash is the more common.
For example, proposals to raise corporate taxes tend to simulate business countermobilization, proposals to use Medicare savings to fund other programs
predictably trigger backlash from senior citizens, and so forth. There is little
uncertainty about who will react negatively to the proposals—the only questions are how intense the opposition will be, how third parties will respond,
and which side will win. This is backlash politics at its most quotidian.

But backlash politics can also be a disruptive, creative force in politics, stimulating new coalitional patterns. For example, the backlash against school accountability reforms ushered in a strange bedfellow coalition among teachers'
unions, conservatives, and parents who believed their children were being over-
tested. The most potent backlashes contribute to *durable* shifts in coalitional patterns. For example, the growing power of industrial labor unions
following the Wagner Act of 1935 elicited a conservative backlash in which
southern Democrats and Republicans joined together to roll back labor protections and provide more support for employer interests, which was a contrib-
utor to the weakening of the New Deal political order.[19]

Since the 1960s, the Republican Party has used backlash politics to mobilize its base supporters and expand its electoral coalition.[20] This is not to suggest that backlash against liberal policies is primarily responsible for the existence of right-wing attitudes—or that reactionary politics would not exist in
the United States if major laws like Medicare and the Civil Rights Act of 1964
had not been enacted. Many people opposed activist government prior to
the Great Broadening era of the 1960s and 1970s. Moreover, anti-Black racism
obviously existed long before the passage of civil rights measures.[21] But policy
backlash, conservative social movement activity, and the electoral success of
the GOP in midterm elections like those of 1966, 1994, and 2010 have been
mutually reinforcing, giving opponents of an expanded federal role specific

policy targets around which to mobilize. It is one thing to make the case against activist government in the abstract, and quite another to highlight how specific policies are imposing costs or threatening the values or status of targeted constituency groups.

Whether motivated by individualism, a lack of trust in government, a desire to preserve a rural lifestyle, unease with egalitarian gender roles, racial resentment, nativism, or opposition to secular culture, citizens who have opposed the liberal reform thrust of the U.S. policy state have comprised the popular base of conservative backlash. This is not to deny the strategic role that leaders from Vice President Spiro Agnew to Florida governor Ron DeSantis have played in fomenting populist backlashes against cultural elites to advance their own projects, including promoting conservative economic policies.[22] Without such top-down influence, the conservative countermobilization would have been far less potent.[23] But the right-wing backlash against egalitarianism and progressive cultural values clearly has grassroots support, as seen in the political engagement of evangelicals, the rise of the Tea Party, and the growth of the Second Amendment sanctuary movement. Until recently, the countermobilization against liberal reform has helped the GOP to unify its two main factions (social conservatives and the business community). Regardless of their disagreements over economic and social priorities, the two factions could agree that liberal government is a menace. In recent years, however, national corporations—under pressure from employees, consumers, and activists—have begun to adopt culturally liberal positions on social issues that are anathema to evangelicals and social conservatives.[24] This development has provided an opening for strategic politicians, such as DeSantis in his 2022 fight with Disney World over the company's opposition to a measure banning the teaching of gender-related issues to young children, to push back against "woke" businesses to gain credibility with the conservative base and national visibility.[25] In sum, new divisions among elites have emerged on the right, which represents a potentially significant change in the political opportunity structure. Whether the tensions between corporate America and social conservatives are a fleeting development or a more enduring shift that will force the GOP to alter its alliance management strategies remains to be seen.[26]

SHAPING FUTURE GOVERNING POSSIBILITIES

Backlash politics can create political legacies that shape governing possibilities for the future.[27] For example, the countermobilization of business-friendly organizations like the American Legislative Exchange Council (ALEC) following the expansion of the regulatory and administrative state in the 1960s and early 1970s has had a significant impact on state policymaking by playing a key role in the diffusion of state preemption laws that prevent blue cities from passing policies that go beyond state law in areas like the minimum wage, paid family leave, and environmental standards.[28] Further, the Supreme Court's unexpected decision to uphold the ACA's individual mandate as a constitutional exercise of Congress's taxing power rather than as a proper use of the Commerce Clause may well constrain the scope of federal regulatory activity in the future. Moreover, the *failure* of backlashes to emerge can also create significant political and policy legacies. For example, the lack of a public backlash to Reagan's firing of the air traffic controllers encouraged employers to adopt a harder line in labor disputes.[29]

At the national level, backlash politics has mediated and constrained government action on issues like climate change, health care, and education. As I discuss next, the backlash against the cap-and-trade bill altered the menu of options for tackling climate change but ultimately did not foreclose progress, but in other sectors, the legacies of backlashes have been more challenging to overcome. Policymakers who seek to make health care more affordable in the United States are well aware of the countermobilizations against the Cadillac tax and the Independent Payment Advisory Board. If such relatively modest reforms sparked backlashes, how can the country ever hope to implement global budgets, broad-based price regulations, and similar approaches that other nations use to control health care spending? Likewise, future efforts to improve the education of students who are trapped in low-performing urban schools must reckon with the countermobilization of teachers' unions and middle-class parents against accountability reforms like the No Child Left Behind Act. To be sure, none of these policies were without flaws. There may well have been better alternatives for promoting student learning and controlling medical inflation. Yet whatever their defects, these policies represented good-faith efforts to tackle serious national problems. Their unraveling highlights the fact that backlash politics can have long-lasting consequences for governance.

Backlashes and Political Learning

When backlash events occur, they offer lessons that policymakers can draw on to manage backlash risks in the future.[30] When political learning operates smoothly, it functions like an equilibrating feedback process. As John D. Sterman writes, policymakers ideally would "compare information about the state of the real world to various goals, perceive discrepancies between desired and actual states, and take actions that (they believe) will cause the real world to move towards the desired state."[31] The detection of gaps between policy goals and real-world outcomes would be continuous, allowing policymakers to close them before they became too large. Backlash-infused policy learning sometimes occurs. For example, the backlash to the Medicare Catastrophic Coverage Act (MCCA) "taught" policymakers that senior citizens resent being forced to pay for coverage they believe they don't need. Accordingly, the Medicare Prescription Drug and Improvement Act of 2003 made drug coverage voluntary.[32]

Policy learning can even cause policymakers and advocates to alter their strategy for attacking a complex problem. Consider the change in how Democrats are addressing climate change.[33] While the Obama administration's cap-and-trade program was an efficient, market-based solution, it mobilized strong opposition from both the fossil fuel industry and ordinary Americans, who worried it would lead to higher electricity bills. Raising prices on consumers today to save the planet for future generations is not a politically viable solution. The "ignominious failure" of the cap-and-trade bill helped to stymie legislative progress on climate change for more than a decade. It fractured the environmental policy community, leading to bitter recriminations.[34]

Yet over time, political learning took place. By 2020, a broad consensus had formed "around a climate policy platform that is both ambitious enough to address the problem and politically potent enough to unite all the left's various interest groups."[35] Rather than seeking to penalize carbon emissions, the new strategy is to make green energy more plentiful and affordable. This approach informs the landmark climate package contained in the Inflation Reduction Act (IRA), which was signed into law by President Biden in 2022. The IRA measure provides incentives for industry to increase the production of renewable energy. In addition, it gives consumers tax credits to purchase electric vehicles, install heat pumps and solar panels, and adopt other low-emission technologies. Consumers could save up to $1,840 annually on their energy bills if they take advantage of all these subsidies.[36] In sum, the law uses carrots rather than sticks to promote reductions in carbon emissions.[37] To be sure, the bill was not pristine. To win the support of Senator Joe Manchin (D-WV), Democratic leaders had to promise to support new oil and gas leasing, thus helping to reduce the initial level of opposition to the bill from the fossil fuel industry. Unlike the cap-and-trade bill in 2010, however, the IRA generated no public backlash. The lack of countermobilization against the most ambitious climate law ever enacted in the United States may have contributed to the Democrats' better-than-expected performance in the 2022 midterms, and it highlights the importance of policy design in shaping public reactions.[38]

Unfortunately, the American political system's capacity for policy learning is less than perfect, and large policy errors can persist for long periods of time. As Bryan D. Jones and Frank R. Baumgartner argue, the cognitive constraints of decision makers and institutional frictions that narrow attention to particular problems can cause the gaps between goals and outcomes to accumulate over time until they become so large that they can no longer be ignored. "Disproportionate information-processing leads to a pattern of extreme stability and occasional punctuations, rather than either smooth adjustment processes or endless gridlock," they write.[39]

Inherited policy designs can inadvertently discourage policymakers from recognizing a problem while it is still small enough to be manageable. As discussed in chapter 4, during the 1990s and 2000s, many policymakers failed to see that workers in import-sensitive sectors were losing economic ground due to growing competition with low-wage nations. Public policy played a role in this lack of error correction. As Goldstein and Gulotty argue, the trade adjustment assistance program provided just enough assistance to eligible workers to undermine "the incentive of those hurt by trade to organize."[40] At the same time, the program's narrow scope (which only provided benefits to individual workers who were directly harmed by imports rather than to affected communities) failed to prevent an antiglobalization backlash from building momentum. Trump's blunt responses to this backlash—which did little to improve the material well-being of American workers—signal the type of episodic disruption the U.S. political system may generate when routine policy learning is attenuated.

Strategic Approaches to Backlash Risks

Because political learning is not automatic, policy designers need to make a conscious effort to identify and manage backlash risks. To be sure, the aim of politics is *not* to eliminate the possibility of backlash but to serve the public good. There are always trade-offs in governing, and the advancement of important goals may require leaders to impose losses or override the preferences of voters and organized constituencies. Further, just because a policy does not trigger a backlash does not mean it is efficient, effective, or socially just. A "bad" policy might never provoke a backlash (e.g., environmentally harmful subsidies to large agribusinesses). What should actors do when they determine that a "good" policy they support seems likely to create or mobilize opposition forces?[41]

There are four generic strategic options. First, actors can *lower their sights* by deciding not to pursue the policy. This is a common response. It avoids squandering political capital on a losing cause and preserves the option to advance the policy later, after a window of opportunity opens. The downside is that it gives opponents (who may be acting in bad faith) a veto over the reform process.

Second, actors can *ignore* backlash risks and rush headfirst to advance the policies they think are best regardless of the blowback.[42] Policy stances here are governed by moral commitments and ultimate ends. This posture greatly simplifies decision making: the actors do not need to assess the political feasibility of their options or whether they will be punished by voters for enacting unpopular policies; they simply pursue the course of action they consider to be ethically correct. The downside risk is that by focusing on the ideal, actors may advance their agendas less effectively than if they considered alternative policies that were less likely to mobilize countercoalitions and thus more likely to expand and endure after their enactment.

The third approach is to *lean in* to backlash risks. The aim is not to forestall opposition forces, but to provoke them. When viewed in this light, the failure to anger targeted constituencies becomes an indicator that the policy is insufficiently ambitious. This posture is attractive to proponents of radical social change who seek to intensify conflicts. As Anne Applebaum summarizes this position, "If lots of people object to what you are doing, then it must be right. The contradictions deepen as the ultimate crisis draws closer, as the old Bolsheviks used to say."[43] It is an aggressive stance favored by actors who consider their opponents to be not just wrong but illegitimate.

Finally, actors can *manage* backlash risks by using policy design to neutralize or undercut opposition forces, at least to some extent. The objective is to move the policy forward while reducing the risk of a damaging countermobilization. On the positive side, this strategy has a better chance of achieving tangible policy results. As Aaron Wildavsky argued, "Popularity in a democracy is no mean recommendation; a policy that is marginally preferable has much to commend it compared to one that is perfectly impossible."[44] The downside risk is policy timidity. One way to navigate backlash risks without sacrificing long-run ambitions is through policy sequencing in which each policy move builds momentum for more ambitious policy in the next round. This is not simply a matter of starting small. Instead, policies are designed strategically to produce positive feedbacks that generate pressure for increasingly larger changes over time.[45]

No strategic choice will be suitable for all actors or under all circumstances. The decision of how best to respond to backlash forces hinges on many factors, including an actor's tolerance for risk, time horizons, a projection of whether the political landscape is likely to become more or less favorable in the future, and most importantly, an assessment of whether the anticipated blowback justifies the gains. The more substantively important, politically urgent, and socially beneficial the proposed policy is, the more likely it is that the generation of a backlash will be a risk worth taking. For example, President Johnson signed the Civil Rights Act of 1964 even though he predicted that it would "deliver the South to the Republican party for a long time to come."[46] To his great credit, the advancement of civil rights mattered more to Johnson than partisan power. Yet he did not ignore backlash risks entirely. For example, Johnson sought to maximize Republican votes for the landmark law, believing that bipartisan support was essential to its political sustainability in the face of likely southern resistance and possible violence.[47]

The strategic choices that actors make depends not only on the policy involved and their personal values but also on the role they play in the political process. As political theorist Andrew Sabl argues, there are many different "offices" in a pluralist democracy, each of which performs necessary and distinct functions. He focuses on three ideal types—the "senator," the "moral activist," and the "organizer."[48] The senator contributes "deliberation and interest mediation" to the polity.[49] The moral activist "seeks to achieve social reform primarily by making public appeals (spoken, written, or both) to widely shared public values."[50] And the organizer seeks to "exert pressure on the political process . . . in order to promote the interests and civic activity of a class, neighborhood, or social group."[51] Sabl's sensitive analysis suggests that there are good reasons why each of these actors would respond in a distinctive way to information that a policy they support is provoking a backlash, *even when they share the same normative commitments and have the same assessment of the reactions that policy move will generate.* For instance, moral activists might ask whether witnessing the backlash will help educate the public and elevate public preferences. In contrast, organizers might ask whether the backlash fight will empower or disempower their group. (Indeed, strategic organizers might even deliberately provoke a backlash from external actors to signal their willingness to bear costs to advance their group's objectives.)[52]

Senators will pose a different set of questions, reflecting their unique status as holders of formal office who, unlike the activists and the organizers, have "special obligations of governance."[53] The questions might include: Does the backlash articulate the legitimate concerns and fears of my constituents about the proposal—or is the backlash indulging their "most ill-advised passions"?[54] And is there a way to reconcile the concerns of my constituents with both the objective, long-term interests of my state or district and the concerns of people in other parts of the nation? Representatives who pose such questions will be interested in ways to manage backlash risks while still responding to their constituents and advancing progress on collective problems. They will adhere to Weber's "ethic of responsibility," willingly embracing the duties of governance even though performing such duties may require compromises and moral sacrifices.[55]

Tactics for Managing Backlash Risks

Many factors predict backlash, and only some are under some control on the part of policy designers, especially in a polarized age. Some of the policy designers' control involves deciding whether to pursue something in the face of inevitable backlash rather than developing a way to prevent it. Nonetheless, they may find themselves in a situation where they wish to move forward with a project while doing what they can to lower foreseeable backlash risks and safeguard their policy accomplishments from attacks.

The best tactical approach depends on the sources of opposition, and what works in one context may not work in another. As a result, the most important step is to ensure that backlash risks receive attention during the design process. Policymakers should project how different constituencies may react to a policy, whether the policy has the potential to provoke negative feedback, and how opponents might be neutralized or divided.[56]

Yet politicians sometimes fail to take feasible steps to tame backlash risks, even when the warning lights are flashing. The backlash against the MCCA offers a cautionary lesson. As Mark A. Peterson observes, the MCCA imposed costs that were "concentrated, immediate and obvious, while too many of the benefits were diffuse, delayed, obscure, and not yet in hand when the opposition that began to mobilize proved disastrous."[57] In comparison to the MCCA, the ACA was much better designed, yet it still produced a number of self-undermining feedbacks that undermined its embedding.[58] These negative feedbacks were foreseeable to some degree. They might have been avoided (or better managed), but they received too little attention during the bill's drafting. Political scientist Eileen Burgin interviewed key Democratic congressional staffs who were involved in drafting the ACA about this failure. The interviews took place in 2014, when policy design decisions were still fresh in respondents' minds. Burgin's conclusions are worth stating at length:

> During the deliberation over health care reform, congressional actors were not focused on a plan's self-reinforcing and self-undermining feedback potential, macro-level coalitional factors, and deck stacking. Interviewees expressed a lack of concern about implementation and policy embedding generally, the impact of the partisan milieu and intense polarization surrounding reform, the possibility that the opposition would continue the misinformation campaign, the delegated governance model for key coverage expansion components, and

a new law's ability to cultivate supportive constituencies. Only on the matter of implementation timing—the roll-out of benefits—were most of the respondents aware of downstream political effects.[59]

Burgin attributes the limited attention to the backlash potential of the ACA to several specific factors, including institutional obstacles, process constraints, and the actors' psychological avoidance of potential threats to the durability of their accomplishment.[60]

While there is no guaranteed way to reduce backlash risks and much remains outside the policy designers' control, it is helpful to make the costs of a policy change as "small, invisible, and untraceable as possible."[61] In his classic book *The Logic of Congressional Action*, Arnold offers suggestions for how policymakers can make it harder for citizens to notice policy costs or connect them to identifiable government actions, such as by dispersing costs widely rather than concentrating them on an organized constituency.[62] Another way to reduce backlash risks is to gain bipartisan support for policy changes.[63] To be sure, this is easier said than done. It can be very difficult for Democrats to find Republican allies nowadays on issues like health care, the environment, assistance for the poor, and transgender rights. Yet the Biden administration's ability to score several bipartisan wins during its first two years—including a major infrastructure package and the first significant gun safety legislation since the 1990s—provides an important reminder that bipartisan lawmaking still happens even in a polarized age.

In addition, the following five tactics can be used to target the policy characteristics that are particularly likely to generate negative feedback among both interest groups and mass publics (see table 7.1). By using these tactics—while simultaneously using policy design to build supportive coalitions—policymakers can manage backlash risks and increase the odds that their accomplishments will survive and expand.[64]

UPROOT INSTITUTIONAL BASES OF SUPPORT

Organized interests can often recover from policy defeats if they retain control over the strings of power. One effective strategy to reduce the risk of countermobilization is to uproot the institutional bases of support of these groups. For example, before the airline deregulation of 1978, the airline industry had largely captured the Civilian Aeronautics Board (CAB), the federal agency that regulated aviation fares and routes. Given the agency's close ties with the industry and its narrow mission, the CAB issued regulations in line with carriers' preferences, protecting them from fair market competition. One way the

TABLE 7.1. Backlash Mechanisms and Strategic Responses

Backlashing Actors	Mechanism	Strategic Responses
Interest groups	• Countermobilization to recoup lost benefits or rents	• Undercut institutional bases of support • Fragment opponents and split off potential losers
Mass publics and voters	• Voter backlash to overreach • Resentment of "undeserving" beneficiaries • Challenges to the identities and status of people strongly attached to preexisting arrangements	• Balance responsiveness to party bases and marginal supporters • Increase progressivity of benefits after policy embedding • Recognize that policy expansion can threaten existing stakeholders, even when their own benefits are left untouched

airline deregulation act prevented the industry from countermobilizing to recoup its lost economic rents is by terminating the CAB. Federal aviation policymaking now shifted to the Department of Transportation (DOT), which has a diverse set of stakeholders, making it much less responsive to the narrow preferences of the airline industry.[65]

FRAGMENT OPPONENTS AND SPLIT OFF POTENTIAL LOSERS

A second, related reason why the airline industry has been unable to countermobilize is that deregulation vastly increased the fluidity and heterogeneity of sector interests as new discount airlines entered the market (and old carriers that were unable to compete went bankrupt, merged with other airlines, or otherwise disappeared). The effect has been to shake up the industry's roster of players and decrease its political cohesion, making it far more difficult for the industry's trade association to achieve a consensus position and engage in effective lobbying efforts.[66] The broader lesson is that fragmenting and dividing opponents can be an effective strategy for reducing the potency of backlash. On many issues, divisions are ready to be exploited through smart policy design.

The IRA takes an important step in this direction by imposing a tax on methane emissions above a set threshold. Oil and gas producers vary enormously in the amount of methane emissions they generate.[67] While some of the largest industry players oppose the methane tax, others companies have signaled that they can live with the proposal, in part because they have already taken steps to reduce their emissions.[68] The more policymakers can target methane-intensive firms, the harder they can make it for industrywide trade groups to reach a consensus among their members, which makes sectoral countermobilization less likely.

A related tactic for narrowing the opposition is to split off potential losers.[69] This can be accomplished in various ways, including through *category exemptions* (e.g., subject only gun owners below the age of twenty-one to enhanced background checks; exclude most prescription drugs from Medicare's authority to negotiate prices), *exit options* (e.g., allow parents who are displeased with the constraints of traditional public schools to set up charter schools), *transition schemes* (e.g., apply a new pollution control requirement only to newly built factories), *geographic devolution* (e.g., permit states to regulate abortion rather than imposing a national ban), and *compensation mechanisms* (e.g., provide financial assistance to small businesses for making their facilities more accessible for customers with disabilities). These tactics undercut the policy impact but may increase the political feasibility of policy adoption.

BALANCE RESPONSIVENESS TO PARTY BASES AND MARGINAL SUPPORTERS

It is not easy to be a politician in the current era of polarization and close party control. Officeholders who fail to energize, satisfy, and solidify their party base will not be nominated, but if officeholders (except for those elected from completely safe districts) completely ignore the views, values, and priorities of their marginal supporters, they risk being defeated in the general election. Bases and marginal supporters not only have different policy preferences, they also have different outlooks on politics. As Mayhew observes, bases are "astute" and "in it for the long run," while ordinary voters want near term payoffs like "a good economy right now [and] a government check in the mail."[70] In other words, bases typically have more ambitious expectations of government than do ordinary voters, but ordinary voters have more insistent ones. No precise formula dictates how to balance support from the base and marginal supporters, but managing backlash risks from both constituencies is essential.

INCREASE THE PROGRESSIVITY OF PROGRAMS AFTER POLICY EMBEDDING

As discussed in chapter 3, one reason why the ACA initially generated backlash is that many Americans earned too much to be eligible for Medicaid (if they even resided in an expansion state) or to receive subsidies on the exchanges. Yet some of these working- and middle-class citizens faced rising health care costs at a time when their wages were stagnant, and they were resentful of Medicaid recipients, who received more generous coverage under the law than they did. In an era of growing inequality, there is an understandable desire to make social policies as redistributive as possible as quickly as possible, but sometimes redistributive goals can be achieved more durably by increasing the progressivity of programs *after* policy embedding.

The political development of Social Security illustrates this tactic. When Social Security was established in 1935, there was a linkage between the amount of benefits retired workers received and the cumulative wages on which they had paid taxes over their careers. As Derthick observed, this arrangement served the "strategic purpose of preserving the public's perception of the program as insurance."[71] As Social Security expanded over the 1950s, however, the program's emphasis shifted from allocating benefits in proportion to individual tax payments to allocating them on the basis of need. By then, Social Security was so popular that the higher benefits that affluent people received triggered little resentment. While the current political context is different from that of the postwar era, a case can be made that building a protective constituency among the middle class should at times be an early priority in expansions of the welfare state. After the program is consolidated, the progressivity of benefit flows can be increased.

The lapsing of the expanded child tax credit in 2022 illustrates this lesson.[72] The American Rescue Plan provided monthly payments to families with children up to age seventeen. The tax credit was fully refundable and made available to families with low or no earnings in a year. While studies show that the expanded child tax credit was enormously successful in lifting children out of poverty, Congress was unable to build a coalition for the program's renewal and it expired after only one year. The pivotal vote in the Senate again belonged to Joe Manchin (D-WV), who believed the program gave excessive assistance to the poor and encouraged unemployment. While many policy experts disputed this view, Manchin was in a position to insist on the addition of a work requirement for parents. A case can be made that proponents of the expanded child care tax credit should have accepted the deal, even though work requirements have significant costs. (Research shows work requirements do little to promote work, but make it harder for eligible people to obtain benefits.) Once the program was deeply embedded in the social fabric, it might have been possible to broaden its eligibility rules to provide benefits to some or all of the nonworking poor.[73]

RECOGNIZE THAT POLICY EXPANSIONS CAN
THREATEN EXISTING BENEFICIARIES

At the same time, advocates should recognize that policy expansions can sometimes stimulate backlash among existing program beneficiaries, who may regard the incorporation of the formerly disadvantaged into their programs as a threat to their status and social identity, even if their own benefits are left untouched. As Starr points out, "Medicare for All" proposals could generate backlash among seniors who regard Medicare as their program and who "fear—or can be made to fear—that extending the program to others will jeopardize their coverage. They also see Medicare as an earned benefit, and many of them resist extending it to people who they believe haven't earned it."[74] Starr argues that a senior citizen backlash can be minimized by opening Medicare to people ages fifty to sixty-four. Existing Medicare recipients are likely to accept this modest expansion because the younger enrollees have already paid substantial Medicare taxes over their working lives, thereby maintaining the program's contributory design. The broader lesson is that policy designers should recognize that program building not only can cultivate new constituencies but also can unsettle old ones. Program expansions can be accomplished, but their timing and implementation must be carefully managed to avoid jarring existing stakeholders.

Policy Backlash as an Inherently Racialized Phenomenon?

In the introduction, I noted that the literature on backlash has two major strands. One defines backlash as a conservative reaction to a liberal advance while the second adopts a nonideological definition of backlash as an adverse reaction to any change or attempted change in the status quo.[75] I have built primarily on the second approach in the belief that a neutral definition of backlash accommodates examining a wider set of cases and promotes the integration of the backlash concept into policy feedback theory. Yet it is worth reflecting on whether backlash is an inherently racialized phenomenon in the United States. In the end, is most backlash simply white backlash?[76]

It would be impossible to account for the backlash phenomenon in modern American politics without acknowledging the past and current role of white backlash. My analysis of the *New York Times* data shows that there was a concentration of backlash articles during the civil rights era of the 1960s and during the Obama and Trump administrations. These were moments when racial identity and the progress of American democracy were in the foreground.

Since the 1960s, white backlash has been integral to the conservative counter-mobilization, not only against civil rights laws but also against race-neutral expansions of the welfare state, such as the ACA. As discussed in chapter 1, a prime motive for policy backlash is the belief that the government is providing benefits to an "undeserving" constituency. Negative racial stereotypes have played a key role in shaping perceptions of deservedness.[77] As Williamson, Skocpol, and Coggin argue, "The Republican Party and popular conservative mobilization have expressed opposition to strong federal government interventions in social and economic life, often viewing such interventions as intended to force racial integration and provide special help to people of color."[78]

Yet to reduce all backlash politics to white backlash would be to oversimplify the causes of a great deal of countermobilization activity. There have been many prominent instances of backlash that cannot be coded as white backlash without strain, such as the patient backlash against managed care, the union and environmentalist backlash against free trade deals, the backlash of the business sector against consumer regulations, and even the backlash of social conservatives against abortion and gay marriage. Conservative backlash often manifests itself as white backlash in the United States for deep historical reasons, but this relationship is politically contingent and varies both over time and across issues. Further, broadening the concept of white backlash to encompass all manifestations of right-wing backlash downplays the influence of partisanship, public trust in government, reliance interests, religious beliefs, and perceptions of material self-interest in mediating constituent reactions to policy proposals. Finally, it implies that the resistance to progressive reform proposals is restricted to white voters, yet this assumption is clearly not always correct.[79]

The Coming Liberal Backlash?

The most important reason why it is a mistake to reduce backlash politics to reactionary white backlash is that an increasing share of policy backlash is emanating from the left. As I discussed in chapter 2, liberal backlash activity increased during the 1980s, when Republicans increased their hold on national power, and reached a peak during the Trump administration. The Women's March that took place the day after Trump's inauguration drew 4.2 million people. Many of the participants "became involved in new groups formed to resist Trump and his agenda, they began citizen lobbying and mounted protests and events, and many ran for office."[80] Voter backlash against Trump drove the 2018 "Blue Wave" election. While they seek to be the party of "hope and change," Democrats have recently had more success in tapping into public fears about what could be lost under GOP control. The relatively greater ability of conservatives to mobilize their supporters than that of liberals over the past several decades may stem less from inherent organizational or financial advantages and more from the direction of public policy itself. As threats to the policy status quo increasingly emanate from the right, the incentives for liberal countermobilization will likely strengthen.

With the recent emergence of a conservative supermajority on the Supreme Court, the overturning of *Roe v. Wade*, and growing policy activism by red states, liberals see a widening array of threats. In addition to the loss of reproductive rights, they now face the erosion of voting rights in some states, a chipping away at the boundary between church and state, the overturning of long-standing municipal and state-level gun regulations, and many other threats to the policy status quo ante. Liberals are increasingly playing defense, fighting to preserve their previous gains. "Though generally forward moving, policy is also known for turning back and biting its most ardent advocates," write Orren and Skowronek.[81]

Some observers predict a coming liberal backlash that will rival the intensity of the conservative backlash of the past few decades. "Indeed, the angry demand for a reversion to the prior order—what we can call the politics of backlash—has been the basis of Republican electoral success for decades. . . . But right now we're seeing something extraordinary: a *liberal* backlash, potentially equal in potency to what we're used to seeing from the right. The left is already mad because of their own sense of loss, and it's about to get much worse," predicted Paul Waldman in 2018.[82]

The strength of the liberal backlash will be influenced not only by the political opportunity structure, the intensity of partisan polarization, and the energy level of the advocacy community. It will also be determined by where conservatives direct their attacks and whether targeted groups possess both a motive for and a means of countermobilization. Will conservatives seek to impose costs only on people in the knowledge and entertainment industries, such as journalists, public school teachers, and college professors? Or will they focus their attacks on more vulnerable, harder-to-defend targets, such as the independence of the federal civil service and the capacity of the Environmental Protection Agency (EPA) and other bureaucracies to regulate business and respond to changing conditions? In light of the victories for abortion rights in the 2022 midterm elections—including the defeat of an antiabortion amendment in Kentucky—will prolife conservatives concede that the public will reject efforts to make abortion illegal nationwide? Or will abortion opponents overreach by seeking to impose a national abortion ban or even to constitutionalize fetal personhood when Republicans capture unified control of government?[83] Will conservatives focus their attacks on social issues where the views of the public (and political elites) are not yet consolidated, such as gender-affirming medical care for minors, or will they try to dismantle deeply embedded programs like Social Security?

The most important questions concern the rules of the political game itself. Will conservatives find ways to weaken the mechanisms for political accountability, such as through gerrymandering or by restricting the ability of citizens to bypass state legislatures through ballot measures? How far will Republicans go to discourage voting by younger citizens, minorities, and residents of urban areas, and what countermeasures will liberals take? Answers to these questions will provide insight into the prospects for liberal backlash in the coming decades.

✳

Backlash politics has become an endemic feature of American's disunited policy state. The broadening of government's role over the past half century has built supportive clienteles, but it has also mobilized opposing coalitions. While the participants in backlash politics are a diverse bunch, they share a desire to defend their interests, institutions, and values against unwelcomed policy changes.

The adverse reactions provoked by policies can have significant repercussions for democracy, equality, and governance. Backlashes can affect election outcomes, singling out for punishment members of the president's party who supported unpopular initiatives. In an era of tight partisan competition, voter backlashes can sometimes contribute to a party's loss of its governing majority—and disrupt the embedding of its hard-won policy accomplishments. Backlashes can influence interest-group activities, coalitional alignments, and partisan strategies for rallying supporters. Moreover, a fear of triggering backlashes can constrain the menu of policy options—and even determine which problems are put on the agenda in the first place.

None of this is to suggest that policies cannot mobilize support or become deeply rooted in people's expectations. The risks and potency of backlash can be tamed through policy design, at least to some degree. Further, backlashes often fade over time, and their impact can sometimes be offset by the support engendered by processes of positive feedback and increasing returns—which strategically oriented policy designers can help create. The study of backlash politics thus expands and refines our understanding of the multiple ways in which "new policies create a new politics," and it offers lessons into how we can make government work better in an age of disunity and polarization.

Acknowledgments

This book originated with an invitation from Jacob Hacker and Paul Pierson to participate in a project that brought together scholars to consider how policy feedback research should be updated to account for America's changing politics and, in particular, increasing partisan polarization. Much of the policy feedback literature has focused on how policies mobilize supportive constituencies and become self-reinforcing, and there has been much less attention paid to the conditions under which policies provoke countermobilization and undermine their own entrenchment and expansion. I was pleased to publish an essay on strategies for backlash prevention in a 2019 special issue of the *ANNALS of the American Academy of Political and Social Science* that Jacob and Paul coedited. I am grateful to them for giving me an opportunity to present my initial thoughts about policy backlash within the framework of such a timely and important collaborative project.

I wish to acknowledge my debt to several colleagues and friends who took the time to read portions of various drafts of this manuscript and offer me the benefit of their suggestions and criticisms. The feedback of Matt Grossmann, Jacob Hacker, Suzanne Mettler, Jon Oberlander, Jill Rutter, Steve Teles, Daniel Tichenor, Julian Zelizer, and reviewers for the University of Chicago Press made this a much better book than I could have written without their assistance. An extended email exchange with David Mayhew was very helpful to my thinking about backlash as a core pattern in American politics. I am grateful to Jon Oberlander and Kent Weaver for collaborating with me on articles related to this project, and to Sarah Binder and Frances Lee for sharing data. Needless to say, I alone deserve backlash for any errors of fact or interpretation in the final product.

Sara Doskow shepherded the manuscript for the University of Chicago Press. I am grateful for her enthusiastic support and sound advice. Thanks to Nicole Balant for copyediting the manuscript, to Elizabeth Ellingboe for overseeing the copyediting, and to Tobiah Waldron for preparing the index.

Brown University generously provided a sabbatical during the 2020–2021 academic year, which enabled me to begin working on the book. I appreciate the support of my colleagues Rick Locke, Wendy Schiller, and Ed Steinfeld.

My work was supported by three talented undergraduate research assistants at Brown University: Emma Ashwin-Rinaldi, Maya Dayan, and Marin Furuyama. Marin worked with me for the most time, and I'm very grateful for the creativity and energy she brought to every research task.

My family has sustained me throughout this project, and I dedicate the book to them with love. I am not certain my son Josh realizes how much I learned from our conversations about American politics or how much he inspired me to bring out the full potential of this project. My son Michael provided humor, encouragement, and support. My wife, Debbie Gordon, offered many valuable suggestions and provided insightful comments on chapter drafts. And I am deeply grateful for the support of my parents, Anne and Bernie Patashnik.

Notes

Introduction

1. Broder 2009; M. Jacobs 2018.
2. Skocpol 2013.
3. See Pooley 2010.
4. Quoted in Reis 2021.
5. Turner and Isenberg 2018.
6. Ansolabehere and Konisky 2014, 185.
7. Brady, Fiorina, and Wilkins 2011.
8. Quoted in A. Jenkins 2018.
9. Yoon-Hendricks and Greenberg 2018.
10. Sides 2018.
11. Parks, Detrow, and Snell 2018.
12. Mayhew 2000, 6.
13. McGeehan 2005.
14. On threshold effects, see Pierson 2004, 83–87.
15. Schickler 2016, 257.
16. On the politics of policy drift, see Galvin and Hacker 2020.
17. See Torriero 2008.
18. See Slaughter 1986.
19. Bradburn 2008; Sharp 1993; Mettler and Lieberman 2020.
20. Quoted in Lepore 2018, 159.
21. Bradburn 2008, 594.
22. Mettler and Lieberman 2020, 99–100.
23. Valelly 2016, 460.
24. Hacker and Pierson 2019.
25. Green 2022.
26. Kruse and Zelizer 2019. In 2002, the Congressional Progressive Caucus sparked a backlash among Democrats after it issued a letter calling for the Biden administration to change its strategy in the Ukraine war and pursue a diplomatic solution with Russia. See Sotomayor and Abutaleb 2022.
27. Abrajano and Hajnal 2015.

28. Baldassarri and Park 2020.

29. Norris and Inglehart 2019. At the same time, some argue that the rising level of secularism and religious disaffiliation in the United States is itself a backlash to the politicization of religion and the rise of the religious right. See D. Campbell 2020.

30. Hochschild 2016.

31. Cramer 2016.

32. B. Jones, Theriault, and Whyman 2019; see also Vogel 1989.

33. See A. Campbell 2003a.

34. Leech et al. 2005, 28.

35. Ragusa and Birkhead 2020, 111.

36. Pierson 1994.

37. Grossmann and Hopkins 2016, 264.

38. Orren and Skowronek 2017, 5–6.

39. Some backlashes advance key values like equality and democracy while others undermine them. Similarly to Alter and Zürn (2020b), I believe it is best to analyze these normative implications separately rather than to fold normative assessments into the definition of backlash itself. As they argue, "To be sure, something fundamental is challenged by backlash politics. But it is neither necessary nor desirable to include a normative position of this challenge into the definition of backlash movements. Said differently, backlash should not be considered inherently regressive. Instead, the normative analysis of both the objectives of backlash movements and their opponents, and the outcomes of backlash politics must be done separately, drawing on normative theories that are independent of the definition of backlash politics" (742).

40. Lipset and Raab 1970, 29.

41. Glickman 2020; see also Glickman 2023.

42. Glickman (2020, 2023) offers an analysis of how white backlashers portray themselves as victims, using preemptive arguments about looming catastrophes to frame social reforms as a threat to their liberty. On the rhetoric of reactionary backlash, see Hirschman 1991.

43. V. Weaver 2007.

44. Ibid., 237.

45. Ibid., 238.

46. Ibid.

47. Ibid., 230. Interestingly, politicians and journalists in the 1960s employed a different meaning of the term "frontlash," referring to public *support* for civil rights.

48. Ibid.

49. Prasad 2018, 224.

50. On vested interests, see Moe 2015.

51. Mansbridge and Shames 2008, 623, 626. My definition is even closer to that of Sanbonmatsu (2008), who defines backlash as "resistance to attempts to change the status quo" (634), and it permits backlash to occur before, during, or after enactment.

52. Alter and Zürn 2020a, 564. See also Alter and Zürn 2020b.

53. Shao and Friedman 2023, A13.

54. Snyder 2020.

55. Alter and Zurn 2020b, 742.

56. Bishin et al. 2021, 188.

57. Through survey experiments and observational studies, Atkinson (2017) demonstrates that exposure to portrayals of policymaking as partisan brawls depresses public support for bills

that would otherwise be popular. She also shows that the media gives much more attention to important laws enacted by slim majorities than to those enacted by large bipartisan coalitions.

58. Mayhew 2000, x.

59. Pierson 2004, 2.

60. On venue shopping, see Baumgartner and Jones 1993.

61. Atkinson et al. (2021) distinguish among three types of issues: partisan (issues such as the role of government in the economy, which correspond to the thermostatic model of opinion change), nonpartisan (consensual issues such as maintaining the national parks), and cultural shift (issues, such as gay marriage, where public opinion has been moving in a more liberal, egalitarian direction over time). On thermostatic opinion, see Wlezien 1995.

62. Lacombe 2022.

63. My analysis of political opportunity structures draws heavily on Tarrow 2011.

64. This is one reason why gerrymandered legislatures are problematic: lawmakers can pass unpopular policies without fear of voter punishment.

65. On the strategy change, see C. Davenport and Friedman 2022.

Chapter One

1. Social Security n.d.

2. Arnold 2022, 121.

3. Scattschneider 1935, 288.

4. The generation of positive feedback is not automatic but contingent on policy design, institutional, and temporal factors. See Patashnik and Zelizer 2013.

5. On self-undermining feedback, see A. Jacobs and Weaver 2015; see also Oberlander and Weaver 2015.

6. Key sources for my conceptual framework include A. Jacobs and Weaver 2015; Wilson 1973; Arnold 1990; Pierson 1994; Lacombe 2022; Moe 2015; Tarrow 2011.

7. Willsher 2018.

8. Castle 2017.

9. "Merkel at Her Limit" 2015.

10. On the distinctive features of the U.S. polity, see Hacker et al. 2022, 14–17.

11. Lee 2022, 112.

12. Kagan 2019.

13. Moe 2019, 17.

14. Wlezien 1995. See also Erikson, MacKuen, and Stimson 2002. Thermostatic opinion is an example of a homeostatic process or self-correcting feedback. Self-correcting feedback is emphasized in equilibrium models of politics in which disruptions generate offsetting reactions, returning the system to an equilibrium outcome. For a discussion of self-correcting mechanisms in politics, see Baumgartner and Jones (2002, 8–13). As Pierson (2000, 85) notes, historical institutionalist research on backlashes and countermobilizations typically does not assume equilibration. Rather, reactions may neither reinforce nor dampen the initial move but rather move the system in an entirely new direction (see Jervis 1997, 128). For a discussion of the distinctions between punctuated equilibrium models and historical institutionalist research on negative feedback, see Jacobs and Weaver 2015. For a typology of feedback effects, see Busemeyer et al. 2020.

15. Atkinson et al. 2021, 6. In contrast to Wlezien (1995), Atkinson et al.'s modified version of the thermostatic model assumes that voters who lack knowledge of the actual direction of

policy change are aware of which party controls the White House and thus can make a reasonable inference.

16. Grossmann and Wlezien 2023, 26.

17. Using experiments, Bishin et al. (2021) find no evidence of a large, enduring mass opinion backlash against the expansion of gay rights. In contrast, Wheaton (2022) marshals evidence that enduring mass opinion backlashes occur on many social issues. In his central study, Wheaton examines the staggered introduction of state equal rights amendments using a difference-in-differences design. He finds that the adoption of a state ERA led to a decline in attitudes toward women's equality among men and that fathers pass on the opinion backlash to their sons, though with declining intensity.

18. Wlezien and Soroka (2012) demonstrate that the thermostatic model of public opinion works across many countries.

19. King 1997. To be sure, voter participation in nonpresidential elections is often quite low, which enhances the influence of organized groups that can bring their members to the polls. See Anzia 2013.

20. Mayhew 2016, 433.

21. C. Cook 2021.

22. Lee 2022, 109.

23. On the influence of the abortion issue in the 2022 midterms, see Schneider and Otterbein 2022.

24. Yglesias 2022.

25. Jacobson and Carson 2020, 199–204.

26. Mayhew 2016, 433. Nyhan et al. (2012) provide evidence that support for the Affordable Care Act damaged Democratic incumbents in the 2010 midterms.

27. Brady, Fiorina, and Wilkis 2011. See also Nyhan et al. 2012.

28. Mansbridge and Shames (2008, 629n4) make a similar point.

29. Burgin 2018, 293.

30. Eyal 1998, 212.

31. Quoted in ibid., 192.

32. Ibid., 193.

33. On the role of contingency in politics, see Einstein and Hochschild 2016.

34. Milwood 2022.

35. This analysis builds on Patashnik and Weaver 2021.

36. Patashnik 2019b. For a related categorization, see A. Jacobs and Weaver 2015. In contrast to Jacobs and Weaver's framework, I do not require losses to be unanticipated.

37. Arnold 1990, 31.

38. Ibid., 21–22.

39. As Gerber et al. (2017) argue, one reason why public opinion studies often fail to demonstrate self-interest effects is because they discount citizens' perceptions of how policies affect them.

40. Oberlander and Weaver 2015, 58.

41. My analysis here follows Wilson 1973 and Arnold 1990.

42. A. Jacobs and Weaver 2015, 448.

43. Ibid.

44. Stokes 2016.

45. A. Jacobs and Weaver 2015.

46. On the traceabilty of policy effects, see Arnold 1990, 47.

47. Tversky and Kahneman 1981.

48. Arnold 1990, 26.

49. Ibid., 142. Arnold (1990) further argued that "the relative magnitude of a specific cost or benefit appears to be more important than its absolute magnitude" in determining whether a citizen will notice it and acquire an intense preference on the matter (28). Gerber, Patashnik and Tucker 2022 provide experimental support for this claim.

50. Wawro and Schickler 2007, 147.

51. See Arnold 1990, 30–31.

52. Garwin and Fay 1973, 42.

53. Moe 2015.

54. Robertson 2020, 114.

55. Ibid., 128.

56. Patashnik, Gerber, and Dowling 2017.

57. On the social construction of constituencies, see A. Schneider and Ingram 1993.

58. Skocpol 1992, 149.

59. Jeene, van Oorschot, and Uunk 2013. See also F. Cook and Barrett 1992.

60. Gollust and Lynch 2011, 1064.

61. Gilens 1995.

62. Kuziemko et al. 2014, 106.

63. See Kliff 2017.

64. Fiorina 2017.

65. Pew Research Center 2009.

66. Thrush 2009.

67. Grossmann 2018.

68. Abramowitz 2001.

69. D. A. Hopkins 2022.

70. A. Campbell 2012, 336.

71. On the absence of positive feedback, see Patashnik and Zelizer 2013.

72. Soss 1999.

73. Reese 2005, 129.

74. Lacombe 2022, 508.

75. Ibid.

76. Wilson 1973.

77. This paragraph draws on Patashnik 2008.

78. Tarrow 2011, 163. See also Kitschelt 1986. The concept of political opportunity structure has been used to explain the emergence of social movements and protests. For a review of the literature, see Meyer 2004.

79. Tarrow 2011, 163–67.

80. Even when entrepreneurial elites are seeking to "sell" backlashes to the public (e.g., the conservative backlash against the teaching of critical race theory), they have to find willing "buyers." Polarization incentivizes leaders to gin up backlashes as a tool for mobilizing supporters, but it does not explain why certain issues resonate with ordinary citizens more than others. For a similar argument, see Zelizer 2022, 126.

81. Hacker and Pierson 2019, 23.

82. Mettler, Jacobs, and Zhu, 2022. On the "calcification" of the American electorate, see Sides, Tausanovitch, and Vavreck 2022.

83. See Carmines and Woods 2002.

84. American Presidency Project 1976b.

85. American Presidency Project 1976a.

86. Greenhouse and Siegel 2011, 2083.

87. Ibid.

88. O'Brian 2022.

89. Black 1998, 126.

90. Ibid.

91. Grossmann and Hopkins 2022.

92. Moe 2014, 140.

93. Rhodes 2012.

94. Teles 2008, 3.

95. Ibid.

96. Ibid., 5.

97. Quoted in McGraw 2021.

98. McCarthy 2022.

99. Quoted in Thomson-DeVeaux 2017.

100. Blazina and Baronavski 2022. On public support for anti-trans policies in red states, see Radcliffe and Rogers 2023.

101. Atkinson et al. 2021, 2. The authors point out (201, 54–55) that Americans support equality of opportunity, not outcomes. As a result, specific proequality policies (such as affirmative action) enjoy less support than equality as an abstract value.

102. On the limits of postloss power-building when groups face collective action problems, see Lacombe 2022.

103. Franklin 1982, A1.

104. Dewar 1981.

105. As Pierson (2000) argues, "Note the claim is not that of equilibrium analysis, where 'negative feedback' means that disruptions to the status quo induce off-setting responses, returning the system to its prior equilibrium. Rather, action and reaction shift the system in a new direction, but not one that reinforces the first move" (85).

106. Fording and Patton 2020, 133.

107. Jervis 1998. As Jervis points out, the claim that "policy makes politics" is illustrative of sideways feedback (128). Policy moves neither forward nor backward, but rather in a new direction. This type of feedback—which is central to the understanding of feedbacks in historical institutionalist research—is excluded from leading theories of system dynamics (see, e.g., G. Richardson 1991), which focus on amplifying and stabilizing feedbacks along a single dimension.

108. Falleti and Mahoney 2015, 220. Included in the authors' framework, but not displayed here, are continuous sequences (in which an early event is stably reproduced over time) and self-amplifying processes (in which early events causes a process to increase or strengthen). Falleti and Mahoney do not identify oscillating processes as a distinct sequence, but I believe they warrant separate attention.

109. Ibid.

110. Aiken 2019.

111. Falleti and Mahoney 2015, 222.

112. Bardach 2006, 341–45; see also Sterman 2000, 114–16.

113. Tucker 2016; Hess and Eden 2017.

114. Falleti and Mahoney 2015, 222.

115. V. Weaver 2007.

Chapter Two

1. Excluding these cases did not change any core findings reported in this chapter.

2. A total of 5.3 percent of the bylines appeared seven or more times: Carl Hulse (47 articles), Tom Wicker (24), Ben A. Franklin (22), Paul Krugman (22), Robin Toner (18), Donald Janson (17), Alan Rappeport (17), Sheryl Gay Stolhberg (17), Richard W. Stevenson (14), Milt Freudenheim (12), Austin C. Wehrwein (12), Steven Greenhouse (11), Fred M. Hechinger (11), Jonathan Martin (11), Robert Pear (11), Richard L. Berke (10), John D. Pomfret (10), Steven V. Roberts (10), Ross Douthat (9), John Herbers (9), Eric Schmitt (9), Hedrick Smith (9), Ronald Sullivan (9), Jackie Calmes (8), Robert D. Hershey Jr. (8), Gladwin Hill (8), Stephen Labaton (8), Anthony Lewis (8), Claude Sitton (8), Peter Baker (7), Jonathan Martin and Alexander Burns (7), Lawrence E. Davies (7), Julie Hirschfeld Davis (7), Clyde H. Farnsworth (7), Joseph Kahn (7), Alison Mitchell (7), Charles Mohr (7), Adam Nagourney (7), Jeremy W. Peters (7), Howell Raines (7), David E. Sanger (7), and Keith Schneider (7).

3. Childs 1950.

4. Glickman 2020.

5. If the Ngrams language search is narrowed to specific types of backlashes, the correspondence between the two data sources moves closer. For example, the correlation between the count of *NYT* articles about backlashes in the civil rights arena and the trend for the term *white backlash* in Ngrams over the 1960–1979 period is $r = .63$.

6. A total of 94 percent of the articles (1,817) are coded in a single policy area; the remainder (115) are coded in two or more areas.

7. Lawmakers of both parties have long viewed the agriculture and infrastructure bills as vehicles for credit-claiming. In addition, the beneficiaries of these bills have traditionally enjoyed positive social constructions. Whether these sectors will remain isolated from backlash forces in an age of polarization remains to be seen. Sheingate (2020) shows that the political foundations of the agricultural policy regime are beginning to decay.

8. I use negative binomial regression because there is evidence of overdispersion. The results are substantively similar when using Poisson and ordinary least squares (OLS) regressions.

9. See, for example, Binder 2003; McCarty, Poole, and Rosenthal 2016.

10. McCarty 2014.

11. Lee 2016. To measure the divergence from partisan parity, Lee first calculates an index of two-party competition at the national level for every Congress, which is the average of the Democratic Party's share of the two-party presidential vote, House seats, and Senate seats. She then calculates the index's divergence from a 50-50 balance. I coded both years of each congressional biennium with the same measure of divergence from partisan parity. I thank Frances Lee for generously sharing the data.

12. Lee 2014.

13. Ibid.

14. Stimson 1991. Data are from James Stimson's site, accessed August 20, 2020, http://stimson.web.unc.edu/data/.

15. A large body of literature has examined whether divided partisan control of Congress and the presidency makes a difference for governance. While this research is diverse, there is

evidence that divided government affects the production of laws and congressional investiga-
tive activities under some conditions. See, for example, Mayhew 1991; Binder 2003; Kriner and
Schickler 2016.

16. Federal nondefense spending rose from $369 billion in 1962 to $3.16 trillion in 2019 in
constant 2012 dollars. Calculated from Office of Management and Budget n.d.

17. My preferred specifications use a lagged dependent variable because the time trend and
the polarization variable are highly correlated.

18. As a placebo test, I ran a model in which the dependent variable is Ngrams of the term
backlash (three-year moving average) and the independent variables were polarization, policy
mood, unemployment, divided government, election year, budget outlays, and time. None of the
independent variables approached statistical significance.

19. B. Jones, Theriault, and Whyman 2019, 208.

20. As Jones et al. point out, government growth over the past several decades has consisted
primarily of a "thickening" of government's role in sectors in which it is already active, such as
education and health. Ibid.

21. On the interplay between partisan and social polarization, see Mettler and Lieberman
2020, chap. 8.

22. Mayhew 2012a, 263.

23. Pew Research Center 2016.

24. Mason 2018, 6.

25. Lee 2016. The polarization variable is dropped from this model because it is highly correlated ($r = -.72$) with divergence from partisan parity.

26. Erikson, MacKuen, and Stimson 2002; Grossmann 2014.

27. Grossmann 2014, 52.

28. Ibid., 5.

29. The data are based on Mayhew's (1991) list of important legislation. Erikson, MacKuen,
and Stimson (2008) coded the ideological orientation laws in the Mayhew data set through 2006.
Grossmann (2014; 2018) extended the data set through 2018. I thank Matt Grossmann for sharing
data and for helpful correspondence.

30. Relatedly, Grossmann (2018) shows that there is a negative correlation (−0.47) between
the net number of major liberal laws passed by each Congress and the change in the Democrats'
share of the popular vote in the House from the previous election.

31. Perlstein 2020, 244.

32. Ibid., 245–46.

33. Culpepper 2011.

34. Rhodes 2017, 5.

35. Smith 2000.

36. Vogel 1983, 26.

37. Vogel 1996, 5–6.

38. Hertel-Fernandez 2016, 4.

39. Stokes 2020, 5.

40. Gerstle 2022, 147.

41. A. Klein 2015.

42. Rhodes 2012, 163–64.

43. Ibid., 165.

44. Davis 2015, A22.

45. Moe 2014.

46. Mayhew 2000, 106–14.

47. On the second phase of power, see Bachrach and Baratz 1962. For a discussion of the study of anticipated reactions in power relations, see Pierson 2015b.

48. Arnold 1990.

49. In a negative binomial regression, I find that the anticipated backlash in year t-1 predicts materialized backlash in year t ($p < .05$), when controlling for polarization, the policy mood, and time.

50. Rugaber 1974.

51. On the structural power of business, see Lindblom 1983. For a recent treatment, see Culpepper 2015.

52. Elder 1986.

53. Greenhouse 1987.

54. Holmes 1990.

55. Quoted in DeParle 1994, B6.

56. On the role of policy design and delivery in promoting citizen engagement, see Mettler 2018.

57. On the linkage between the rise of the activist state and conservative countermobilization, see the excellent essays in Pierson and Skocpol 2007.

58. B. Jones, Theriault, and Whyman 2019.

59. I thank Suzanne Mettler for helpful correspondence on this point.

60. Mayhew 1991, 177.

Chapter Three

1. Leading works on the politics of U.S. health care policymaking include Starr 1982, 2011; Hacker 2002; Oberlander 2003. For data on the performance of the U.S. health care system in cross-national perspective, see Tikkanen and Abrams 2020.

2. For an excellent analysis, see Hacker 1998.

3. My discussion of the MCCA draws on Himmelfarb 1995; see also Patashnik 2008.

4. On policy updating, see Mettler 2016.

5. Himelfarb 1995, 73.

6. Ibid., 24.

7. Rovner 1995, 165–66.

8. Dahl 1989.

9. Oberlander 2003, 69.

10. Himmelfarb 1995.

11. Starr 2011.

12. On policy learning in health policymaking, see M. Peterson 1997; Hacker 2001.

13. On the design of Medicare Part D, see Oliver, Lee, and Lipton 2004.

14. For an excellent analysis of Congress's performance in health care cost control, see Oberlander 2016a.

15. Organisation for Economic Co-operation and Development n.d.

16. See Oberlander 2016; Hacker 1998; Hacker 2002; Marmor et al. 2009; Bagley 2012; Patashnik, Gerber, and Dowling 2017.

17. Starr 2011.

18. Oberlander 2016a, 219.

19. Ibid.

20. See Lyons 1970; Oberlander 2016a.

21. Foote 2002.

22. Gusmano 2014, 220.

23. Oberlander 2003, 109.

24. Starr 1982, 375.

25. Specifically, Medicare would reimburse doctors retrospectively on a fee-for-service basis based on "reasonable charges" and would reimburse hospitals retrospectively according to "reasonable costs" (Oberlander 2003, 33).

26. M. Peterson 1998.

27. Toner 1995, A26.

28. M. Peterson 1998, 207.

29. Mechanic 2001.

30. Starr 2011.

31. Ibid., 54.

32. Chapin 2015, 241.

33. Glied 2000, 718.

34. Chapin 2015, 241.

35. Ibid., 242.

36. Ibid.

37. Mechanic 2001, 37.

38. Reinhardt 1999, 904.

39. Starr 2011, 144.

40. Enthoven 1999; see also Pauly and Nicholson 1999.

41. Hilzenrath 1998.

42. Blendon et al. 1998, 90.

43. Ibid., 91.

44. Ibid.

45. Rubin 1996. Congress also debated patients' rights legislation but Republicans blocked its passage.

46. Pinkovskiy 2020, 60.

47. Ibid.

48. Hoffman 2019.

49. Salmon et al. 2015.

50. Rabin 2019.

51. On partisan polarization and the pandemic, see Sides, Tausanovitch, and Vavreck 2020.

52. Stanley-Becker 2021.

53. Bogel-Burroughs, Dewan, and Gray 2020, A1.

54. Weber and Achenbach 2023.

55. I focus on laws regulating heath care delivery and financing, medical education, and disease prevention. Excluded from the list are broader social insurance reforms (e.g., Social Security disability insurance and the Family and Medical Leave Act) and the many health related laws enacted as part of omnibus budget legislation.

56. Mueller 1988.

57. Gritter 2019.

58. For an excellent analysis of the role of Washington policymakers in the rise of HMOs, see Brown 1983.

59. On the portability act, see Haeder and Weimer 2013; Starr 2011, 138–40.

60. Rein 2022.

61. This section draws on Patashnik and Oberlander 2018a, 2018b.

62. Oberlander 2003.

63. Brady, Fiorina, and Wilkins 2011; Nyhan et al. 2012.

64. On the Tea Party's opposition to the ACA, see Williamson, Skocpol, and Coggin 2011.

65. Ragusa and Birkhead 2020.

66. Hacker and Pierson 2018.

67. I thank Jacob Hacker for correspondence on this point.

68. Starr 2011, 204–5.

69. Hacker 2010, 868.

70. Oberlander 2020, 474.

71. Fording and Patton 2020.

72. Grogan, Singer, and Jones 2017.

73. Fording and Patton 2020. On the politics of policy diffusion, see Shipan and Volden 2008.

74. Wagner and Schubel 2020.

75. For an insightful comparison of the ACA and MCCA, see M. Peterson 2018.

76. Hacker and Pierson 2019.

77. Oberlander and Weaver 2015.

78. I do not discuss all the feedbacks that the ACA has produced among mass publics and policy elites. See Oberlander and Weaver 2015; Lerman and McCabe 2017; Clinton and Sances 2018; Chattopadhyay 2018; Hacker and Pierson 2018; D. J. Hopkins and Parish 2019; L. Jacobs and Mettler 2018; Béland, Rocco, and Waddan 2019; Fording and Patton 2020; A. Campbell 2020.

79. Derthick 1979.

80. Marmor 1973.

81. Oberlander 2020.

82. Riotta 2017.

83. KFF 2022b.

84. Hertel-Fernandez, Skocpol, and Lynch 2016.

85. Béland, Rocco, and Waddan 2016.

86. D. Jones 2017.

87. Derthick 1979, 370–71.

88. Hacker and Pierson 2018.

89. Hacker and Pierson 2016; Skocpol and Hertel-Fernandez 2016.

90. Pierson and Skocpol 2007, 4.

91. Lee 2016.

92. Aaron and Burtless 2014.

93. Leonhardt 2010.

94. A. Goldstein 2016.

95. See Patashnik and Zelizer 2013; Oberlander and Weaver 2015; Hacker and Pierson 2018.

96. Oberlander 2012.

97. For Kaiser Family Foundation survey data on the public's views on the ACA, see KFF 2022a. As of May 2021, only 15 percent of Republicans expressed a generally favorable opinion of the law as a whole.

98. M. Peterson 2018; Patashnik and Weaver 2021.

99. For a similar categorization, see Oberlander and Weaver 2015.

100. Stewart 2012.

101. M. Peterson 2018, 640.

102. Quoted in Kessler 2013.

103. Clemens-Cope and Anderson 2015.

104. Patashnik and Zelizer 2013.

105. Goodnough 2019.

106. Kliff 2015.

107. Keith 2019.

108. As noted later in the chapter, Congress attempted to address many of these shortcomings in the recovery legislation that was passed after Biden became president.

109. Kliff 2017; Gawande 2017; Tolbert and Antonisse 2017.

110. Grogan and Park 2017a.

111. Michener 2020.

112. Grogan and Park 2017b.

113. Edsall 2015.

114. Williamson, Skocpol, and Coggin 2011, 34.

115. White 2020.

116. Saad 2009.

117. Abelson 2020.

118. On the ACA and the public option, see Hacker 2010.

119. Oberlander and Spivack 2018.

120. Kessler 2012.

121. Sanger-Katz 2018.

122. I thank Jon Oberlander for this point.

123. A. Goldstein 2017; Oberlander 2017.

124. Cancryn, Karlin-Smith, and Demko 2017.

125. L. Jacobs and Mettler 2018; L. Jacobs, Mettler, and Zhu 2019.

126. Hacker and Pierson 2018, 557.

127. G. Jacobsen 2019.

128. Wesleyan Media Project 2018.

129. Mettler, Jacobs, and Zhu 2022.

130. G. Jacobson 2019, 28.

131. Kliff and Sanger-Katz 2021.

132. Roubein 2022.

133. On the origins of Medicare, see Zelizer 2015a.

134. Patashnik and Oberlander 2018a, 2018b.

135. For an excellent analysis of these cycles, see Starr 2011.

Chapter Four

1. Quoted in ABC News 2016.

2. For an excellent overview of the neoliberal order, see Gerstle 2022. On the backlash against globalization, see Scheve and Slaughter 2018.

3. On Trump's immigration record, see Valverde 2020.

4. Kandel 2019.

5. Herrera 2021; Kanno-Youngs and Shear 2020; Narea 2019; Nowrasteh 2021.

6. Hansen 2022.

7. Krueger 2020a, 2020b, 2020c.

8. Mastanduno 2020, 523–24.

9. Scheve and Slaughter 2018, 98.

10. Lobosco 2021.

11. Gass 2022; Shear and Kanno-Youngs 2021. The Biden administration lifted Title 42 in May 2023.

12. Beauchamp 2021.

13. The literature on U.S. trade policy is voluminous. The modern classic is Irwin 2017; see also Destler 2005; Johnson 2018.

14. Johnson 2018, 122–24.

15. Ibid., 202–3.

16. Ibid., 371.

17. Rauchway 2008, 28–29.

18. Irwin 2017, 414.

19. Schattschneider 1935, 127–28.

20. On the institutional foundations of the liberal trade regime, see Bailey, Goldstein, and Weingast 1997; see also J. Goldstein and Gulotty 2019.

21. J. Goldstein 2014, 206; Destler 2005, 12.

22. Bailey, Goldstein, and Weingast 1997; see also Irwin 2017, 495; Destler 2005, 22.

23. Irwin 2017.

24. On the creation of the WTO, see Destler 2005.

25. J. Goldstein 2014, 206.

26. Ibid., 207–9. On the creation of fast track, see Destler 2005, 71–77.

27. J, Goldstein 2014, 209.

28. Vogel 2001, 313.

29. Ibid., 327.

30. On the protectionist backlash in the 1980s, see Nivola 1986; Irwin 2017; Destler 2005; Vogel 1999.

31. Nivola 1986, 583.

32. Yoffie 1989, 113.

33. Destler 2005, 88.

34. Nivola 1986, 578.

35. Salmans 1985.

36. Destler 1991, 252.

37. Irwin 2017, 619.

38. Destler 2005, 174.

39. Irwin 2017, 606–10.

40. Quoted in Weinraub 1985b, D1.

41. On voluntary export restraints, see J. Richardson, Olmer, and Stern 1994; Irwin 2017; Destler 1991.

42. Vogel 2001, 330.

43. Irwin 2017, 683.

44. Mayer 1998, 74–75.

45. Ibid., 98.

46. Ibid., 5.

47. Lauter 1993.

48. Mayer 1998, 272.

49. Quoted in Porter 2019, A13.

50. Quoted in Lauter 1993.

51. Mishel and Bivens 2021, 32.

52. These studies confirm that trade with low-wage countries puts significant downward pressure on the wages of U.S. workers, especially those without a college education. Ibid.

53. Choi et al. 2021.

54. Quoted in Mayer 1998, 73.

55. Gerstle 2022, 2–3.

56. The labor side pact included a nonbinding commitment by Mexico that its wages would rise with increases in the productivity of the Mexican economy. See Lichtenstein 2018.

57. Quoted in Bradsher 1993, 1.

58. Rosenbaum 1993.

59. See "Congress OKs North American Trade Pact" 1994, 171–79.

60. Abramson and Greenhouse 1997.

61. Irwin 2017, 659.

62. Olson 1999.

63. Johnson 2018, 4.

64. Irwin 2017, 662.

65. Ibid., 681–85.

66. Quoted in Bradner 2016.

67. Quoted in Calmes 2016, A14.

68. Younis 2021.

69. On the polarization of public opinion on trade, see J. Goldstein and Gulotty 2019.

70. Autor et al. 2020. In contrast, exposure to rising import competition caused majority-minority counties to become more likely to support liberal Democrats.

71. Rodrik 2021.

72. Autor, Dorn, and Hanson 2013.

73. J, Goldstein and Gulotty 2019.

74. For a similar argument that the cosmopolitan bias (such as support for open borders) of nonmajoritarian institutions like central banks and international organizations (such as the WTO) has generated an authoritarian-populist counteraction, see Zürn 2021.

75. J. Goldstein and Gulotty 2019, 59–60.

76. On the program's origins, see Irwin 2017, 523.

77. Wilensky 2002, 106.

78. House Ways and Means Committee 2012.

79. Destler 2005, 150.

80. United States Department of Labor 2021.

81. Goger 2019.

82. On administrative burdens, see Herd and Moynihan 2019.

83. Goger 2019.

84. Ritchie and You 2021.

85. J. Goldstein and Gulotty 2019, 73.

86. Frieden 2019, 189–90.

87. Parilla and Muro 2016.

88. A third issue (not discussed here) is financial globalization. For an excellent analysis of congressional backlash against Chinese direct investment, see Canes-Wrone, Mattoli, and Meunier 2020.

89. Schuck 2008, 349. Schuck observes that public opinion surveys have consistently shown that Americans tend to give low marks to newer immigrant groups and higher marks to groups that arrived in the more distant past.

90. See Higham 1985.

91. On the Immigration Restriction League, see Swidey 2017.

92. Quoted in Tichenor 2002, 120.

93. Tichenor 2002, 145–46.

94. Patterson 2005, 293.

95. Scholars debate whether this demographic transformation was anticipated or was an unintended consequence of the 1965 law. See Schuck 2008, 351.

96. Patterson 1996, 577–78.

97. The Bracero program had, since the 1940s, authorized millions of Mexicans to harvest crops in the United States on a seasonal basis. It generated opposition from the AFL-CIO and other groups. After 1965, employers in the Southwest and West continued to hire low-wage immigrant workers illegally.

98. Huntington 2004, 179.

99. Hong 2015.

100. Patterson 2005, 293.

101. Penn Wharton Budget Model 2016, 1.

102. New immigrants mainly compete for jobs with immigrants who arrived earlier.

103. National Academies of Science, Engineering, and Medicine 2017, 172.

104. Ibid., 5. Economists have not reached a consensus on the magnitude of the wage loss suffered by native-born high school dropouts due to immigration. Estimates range from 0 to around 3 percent over the long run. See Edsall 2016.

105. National Academies of Science, Engineering, and Medicine 2017, 12.

106. Penn Wharton Budget Model 2016, 7. The net costs to state governments are influenced by both state variables (e.g., the level of state expenditures on programs like education) and the socioeconomic composition of the immigrant community (e.g., the proportion of the immigrant community that is well-educated and high-income).

107. Alesina and Tabellini 2022, 19.

108. Tichenor (2002) notes that interests and ideologies can be sorted into four groups based on their positions on these two dimensions: *cosmopolitans* (who favor both expanded or maintained immigration admissions and expansive immigrant rights); *nationalist egalitarians* (who support expansive immigrant rights but believe immigration admissions should be restricted); *free market expansionists* (who believe that immigration admissions should be expanded or maintained and that immigrant rights should be restrictive); and *classic exclusionists* (who believe that both immigration admissions and immigrant rights should be limited).

109. Ibid., 35.

110. On public support for higher spending on Social Security, see Shapiro and Smith 1985.

111. Younis 2020.

112. Freeman 1995, 885.

113. On rising public dissatisfaction with immigration during the first two years of the Biden administration, see Brenan 2022.

114. On focusing events, see Kingdon 1984.

115. Quoted in I. Peterson 1979, A14.

116. Raines 1980. See also Tichenor 2002, 246–49.

117. Pear 1986.

118. On the creation of FAIR, see Coleman 2021, 70–72; Tichenor 2002, 237.

119. Goodman 2019.

120. On the 1986 immigration reform law, see Tichenor 2002, chap. 9.

121. On the 1990 act, see ibid., 270–75.

122. Skrentny 2011, 278.

123. Schuck 2008, 352.

124. Ibid., 286. See also Tichenor 2002, 282, 216, 255.

125. Wilensky 2012, 255.

126. Tichenor 2012, 104.

127. Sontag 1992.

128. Cable News Network (CNN) / *USA Today*, Gallup / CNN / *USA Today* 1993.

129. Tichenor 2002, 277.

130. Bell 1992.

131. Schuck 2001, 121.

132. "White House Calls the Shots, as Illegal Alien Bill Clears" 1997.

133. National Academies of Sciences, Engineering, and Medicine 2017, 19.

134. Tichenor 2012.

135. Coleman 2021, 12.

136. *New York Times* 1982.

137. Martinez 2010.

138. Pantoja, Ramirez, and Segura 2001.

139. Terry 1997.

140. Liptak 2012.

141. Tichenor 2002, 284.

142. Schuck 2001, 122.

143. See Kolker 2016 for a review of noncitizens' eligibility for federal benefits.

144. Abrajano and Hajnal 2015, 19–20.

145. Samuels 2021.

146. Enten 2017.

147. Gonyea 2013.

148. By September 2015—sixteen months before Trump took office—only 29 percent of Democrats supported building a wall on the Mexican border. See Enten 2017.

149. Bada, Fox, and Guskin n.d.

150. McFadden 2006.

151. See Tichenor 2021.

152. Lind 2014; Sakuma 2017.

153. Sheth 2017. The Supreme Court, by a vote of 5–4, blocked the Trump administration from carrying out its termination of DACA in 2020.

154. Preston 2017.

155. Quoted in Everett et al. 2017.

156. Shear and Cooper 2017.

157. Kruse and Zelizer 2019, 353; Huetteman 2017. Lower courts struck down Trump's initial travel ban, but the Supreme Court, by a vote of 5–4, upheld a modified version of Trump's travel ban in 2021.

158. Narea 2021.

159. Lind 2018.

160. Smith and Phillips 2018; Yoon-Hendricks and Greenberg 2018.

161. Esparza 2018.

162. Landers 2018.

163. Parks, Detrow, and Snell 2018.

164. Nowrasteh 2021.

165. For an excellent analysis of the 2016 presidential election that emphasizes the role of identity politics, see Sides, Tesler, and Vavreck 2019.

166. On the distributional cost of immigration, see Card 2009; Edsall 2016. On the distributional impact of trade, see Mishel and Bivens 2021.

167. See Rosenbluth and Weir 2021.

168. On the need for policy upkeep and maintenance, see Mettler 2016.

169. Sides, Tesler, and Vavreck 2019, 82.

170. Ibid., 83.

171. Why the main response to the backlash, both in the United States and in many European countries, has been cultural populism rather than economic redistribution is a fascinating question beyond the scope of this chapter. Some scholars emphasize the demand side of the equation. For example, Gennaioli and Tabellini (2019) argue that adverse economic shocks can make cultural identities more salient to ordinary citizens, causing the losers from globalization to lower their demands for redistributive policies. In contrast, Hacker and Pierson (2020) focus on the supply side, arguing that conservative political elites have primed cultural identities in order to distract voters and deflect attention from rising inequality. Rodrik (2021) emphasizes the importance of both demand- and supply-side factors.

Chapter Five

1. For an early analysis that places conservative backlash in a broader political frame, see Edsall and Edsall 1991; for ethnographic analyses of populist resentment in the 2010s, see Cramer 2016 and Hochschild 2016.

2. The stories in this chapter are more specific than those covered in the previous two chapters, and they illustrate the limitations of the *New York Times* measure for the purposes of investigating specific events rather than broad patterns of countermobilization over time. The *NYT* measure includes nineteen articles about the conflict over bathroom access for transgender persons. My discussion of the gun control case focuses on the Second Amendment sanctuary movement in Virginia, which gained prominence in 2020 (my main *NYT* database ends in 2019). I searched the *NYT* for subsequent years and found that the newspaper published three articles in 2020–2021 discussing this case as a backlash event. The event was also discussed as a backlash by both the *Washington Post* and *Wall Street Journal*. While the *NYT* covered the furor over the IRS's proposed withdrawal of tax benefits from segregated schools, it did not use the term *backlash* with reference to this case during 1978–1979. One editorial (*New York Times* 1978) stated that the IRS's proposed rule "provoked a reaction—115,000 protest letters and an outcry in public

hearings" (A28). A subsequent editorial (*New York Times* 1983) described Ronald Reagan's support for tax exemptions to segregated private schools as one of the ways he was "appealing to the white backlash" (20). This case is included here because it was identified in one of the historical sources (Patterson 2005) cited in table 2.1.

3. Skocpol and Williamson 2016, 12.

4. O'Brian 2022.

5. Hacker and Pierson 2020, 83.

6. Edsall and Edsall 1991, 131–34; Schlozman 2015, 90–101; Perlstein 2020, 354.

7. Crespino 2008, 93.

8. Perlstein 2020, 348.

9. For an argument that seg academies and church schools had few differences in practice, see Nevin and Bills 1976.

10. Perlstein 2020, 348–49.

11. See Skerry 1980.

12. Quoted in PBS 1978.

13. Nevin and Bills 1976.

14. F. Graham 1970.

15. Crespino 2008.

16. Ibid.

17. Neuberger and Crumplar 1979; Shanahan 1975.

18. Crespino 2008, 98.

19. Perlstein 2020, 348.

20. On litigation challenging the tax-exempt status of discriminatory schools, see Drake 1978.

21. Ibid., 209; see also Crespino 2008, 99; Schlozman 2015, 94–95.

22. Quoted in Drake 1978, 463n2.

23. Sulzberger 1978.

24. Crespino 2008.

25. Ibid.

26. Freedman 2005, 235.

27. Crespino 2008, 90.

28. Quoted in Freedman 2005, 236.

29. Schlozman 2015, 95.

30. Crespino 2008, 100.

31. Perlstein 2020, 473.

32. Sulzberger 1978.

33. Pine 1979.

34. Crespino 2008, 102.

35. Senate Finance Committee 1979, 126.

36. Senator Paul Laxalt (R-NV) introduced the "Family Protection Act," which would have given parents higher tax exemptions for adopting a mixed-race child. The act would also have given parents the right to review public school textbooks. See Freedman 2005, 249.

37. Senate Finance Committee, 127.

38. Crespino 2008, 92.

39. On the role of instigators in helping mass publics understand policy costs and benefits, see Arnold 1990.

40. Milkis and Tichenor 2019, 209–10.

41. Biden voted for the rider to bar funding for enforcement of the IRS rule. See Perlstein 2020, 473.

42. Devins 1984, 407.

43. Schlozman 2015, 98–99.

44. Crespino 2008, 103.

45. Quoted in Senate Finance Committee 1979, 61.

46. American Presidency Project 1980.

47. Crespino 2008, 104.

48. Ibid. See also Milkis and Tichenor 2019, 248–54; Schlozman 2015, 99–100.

49. *Bob Jones University v. United States* 461 US 574 (1983).

50. S. Taylor 1983, B16.

51. S. Cohen 1983.

52. *Allen v. Wright* 468 US 737 (1984).

53. *New York Times* 1984.

54. Carr 2012.

55. Edsall and Edsall 1991, 134.

56. Ibid., 131.

57. Toscano 2019. For an analysis of key differences between the Second Amendment sanctuary movement and the immigrant sanctuary movement, see Spitzer 2022, 93.

58. Fields 2020, 440.

59. See Grossmann 2012; Goss 2010; Aronow and Miller 2016; Joslyn et al. 2017.

60. Lacombe 2019, 1342, 1347.

61. Ibid., 1348.

62. Ibid., 1353.

63. Brenan 2021.

64. Healy 2013, A16.

65. The Democrats also took functional control of the New York Senate. See Kousser 2018; see also Milligan 2018.

66. Fields 2020, 446. The author provides a normative analysis of the legal viability of Second Amendment sanctuaries, arguing that there is "limited path forward for localities to resist state action" (444) in the area of gun regulation based on "home rule" considerations, the unsettled constitutional status of Second Amendment rights, and other factors. Not all legal scholars agree, however. While acknowledging that there may be "some contested space in the interstices of state constitutional law for forms of local resistance," Schragger (2020) cautions against "domesticating" the claims of Second Amendment Sanctuary advocates by "treating them seriously within a legal and institutional framework that is supposed to resolve disputes by law."

67. Fields 2020, 456.

68. Ibid.

69. G. Schneider and Scherer 2019.

70. Fields 2020, 459.

71. Beckett 2020.

72. Murphy was interviewed in PBS 2020.

73. See, for example, Witt 2020.

74. Beckett 2020.

75. Ibid.

76. The quotes are from a television news report. See WSLS10 2019.

77. G. Schneider, Vozzella, and Clement 2019.

78. G. Schneider, Vozzella, and Olivo 2019.

79. M. Cohen 2020.

80. M. Miller 2020. The figure of twenty-four thousand is from a phone interview with Philip Van Cleave conducted on January 28, 2021.

81. Williams et al. 2020.

82. All quotes are from my phone interview with Van Cleave. For a profile of Van Cleave, see Dodd and MacFarquhar 2020. Van Cleave became the object of national media attention after he appeared alongside comedic actor Sacha Baron Cohen (who was disguised as an Israeli antiterror expert) in a fake gun-training video for children. Van Cleave maintains that he knew the video was a con and played along to learn who was behind it.

83. On solidary benefits, see Clark and Wilson 1961.

84. Van Cleave stated, "Various militia groups from Virginia and nearby states have graciously volunteered to provide security. With a large Capitol, Richmond, and State police presence, not to mention enough citizens armed with handguns to take over a modern mid-sized country, we have the security base covered nicely. That said, we welcome our militia brothers and sisters to be part of making the day a success!" See Van Cleave 2019.

85. Homans 2021.

86. Van Cleave is here making a "slippery slope" argument that is a staple of conservative rhetoric. For a classic analysis of the "jeopardy thesis," see Hirschman 1991.

87. Spitzer 2022, 103–4.

88. Quoted in Gunter 2020.

89. Scott Jenkins, January 11, 2020, "Culpeper County Sheriff's Office," Facebook, https://bit.ly/2N0gxGC.

90. Schragger 2020.

91. Shiver 2021.

92. Quoted in G. Schneider 2019.

93. Mark R. Herring, December 20, 2019, letter to Jerrauld C. Jones, https://www.oag.state.va.us/files/Opinions/2019/19-059-Jones-issued.pdf.

94. R. Miller 2020.

95. Interview with Van Cleave.

96. Suderman 2020.

97. Personal correspondence with Richard Schragger, February 15, 2021.

98. Quoted in Vozzella 2020.

99. Bowes 2020.

100. Moomaw 2020.

101. Young 2016.

102. Lipka 2016.

103. See Department of Justice 2016.

104. Melnick 2018, 12.

105. Leff 2016; Rogers 2016.

106. Steinmetz 2016; see also James et al. 2016.

107. For local television news coverage of the decision, see Crump 2016.

108. Quoted in J. Taylor 2016.

109. Quoted in Banchiri 2016.

110. Katz and Eckholm 2016.

111. Philipps 2016.

112. Ibid.

113. The text of HB2 can be found at General Assembly of North Carolina 2016.

114. Quoted in Reilley 2016.

115. D. Graham 2017.

116. See Tobias 2017.

117. A major organizational force behind the state preemption wave has been the American Legislative Exchange Council (ALEC), a conservative network of state legislators, donors, and business groups that drafts "model legislation" for statehouses across the nation. However, the North Carolina bathroom bill was not one of the ALEC's model bills. On the ALEC, see Hertel-Fernandez 2019.

118. Hubert 2020, 26.

119. Winkler 2016; see also Human Rights Campaign and Equality North Carolina n.d.

120. Grossmann and Hopkins 2022, 4–5.

121. Katz and Eckholm 2016.

122. Holley 2016.

123. On the protests, see Blinder 2016b.

124. Associated Press 2017.

125. Katz and Eckholm 2016.

126. Quoted in Cacciola and Blinder 2016.

127. Quotes are from Blinder, Pérez-Peña, and Lichtblau 2016.

128. See Quilantan 2020.

129. Quoted in Blinder 2016b.

130. Thirty-eight percent of respondents said they supported HB2, and 50 percent were opposed. Support was greatest among very conservative voters (61 percent). Opposition was greatest among very liberal voters (72 percent) and among people who almost never attend religious services (80 percent). See WRAL-TV (Raleigh) 2016.

131. Avery 2020.

132. Berman and Phillips 2017.

133. Yurcaba 2021. In 2019, a federal judge approved a consent degree in which North Carolina agreed to allow transgender people to use bathrooms in certain public buildings controlled by the state government (such as state offices, highway rest stops, and state parks) that match their gender identities. See Levin 2019.

134. See Paris 2023.

135. See Price, Yawn, and Clark 2021.

136. Jones 2023. For other recent public opinion surveys on transgender issues, see Block 2022 and Meckler and Clement 2023.

137. Edsall and Edsall 1991, 41.

138. Spitzer 2022, 93.

139. For a similar argument about the political leverage of social movements, see Milkis and Tichenor 2019.

140. Black 1998, 126–27. Black further argues that a third party is more likely to participate in a conflict when one side has a higher status than the other and also more likely to take the side of the higher-status adversary.

141. Ibid. See also B. Campbell and Manning 2014, 700.

142. Black 1998, 127.

Chapter Six

1. McCartin 2011b, A25.

2. McCartin 2011a, 332.

3. Curry and Shibut 2000, 33.

4. Ibid.

5. Owens and Smith 2012, 533–34.

6. A. Schneider and Ingram 1993.

7. My discussion of the PATCO case draws heavily on McCartin 2011a; Northrop 1984; Morgan 1984; and Hurd and Kriesky 1986.

8. Cowie 2017, 203.

9. Witkin 1981.

10. Barone 1990, 617.

11. Northrop 1984, 169.

12. McCartin 2011a, 285.

13. Morgan 1984, 167.

14. Rubio 2016, 575.

15. Smithsonian National Postal Museum 2010.

16. Rubio 2016, 574.

17. Morgan 1984, 182.

18. McCartin 2011a, 247.

19. Quoted in UPI 1981, A15.

20. Witkin 1981, A1.

21. McMartin 2011a, 281–82.

22. Ibid.

23. Treaster 1981.

24. Purnick 1981.

25. McMartin 2011a, 305.

26. Purnick 1981.

27. McMartin 2011a, 319.

28. Lacombe 2022.

29. McCartin 2011a, 306.

30. Ibid., 331.

31. Rosentiel 2011.

32. McCartin 2011a, 304.

33. Serrin 1981b, D10.

34. Associated Press 1981.

35. There was one minor break in GOP support for Reagan's position. Representative Guy Molinari (R-NY), who had supported the firing of the strikers, feared that the lack of adequate staffing was jeopardizing the safety of the air traffic system. In 1985, Molinari introduced a bill that would permit the rehiring of a limited number of top controllers who could demonstrate that they had not played a central role in the strike. The Reagan administration opposed the proposal and blocked its passage. Until his final day in office, Reagan rebuffed calls to permit fired controllers to apply for their old jobs, even with a loss of pay and seniority perks. Moderate Republicans like Molinari found themselves marginalized in the GOP, and uncompromising opposition to the strikers' rehiring became a defining element of the party's brand. One of the most

important policy feedbacks of the PATCO case was thus a hardening of the Republican Party's positions on union issues. See McCartin 2011a, 337–38.

36. Quoted in Morgan 1984, 168.

37. Gerstle 2022, 121.

38. Conyers 1981, A22.

39. Morgan 1984, 175.

40. Poli 1982, 2.

41. McCartin 2011a, 307.

42. Northrup 1984, 179.

43. Serrin 1981.

44. McCartin 2011a, 317.

45. Reich 2007, 80–81.

46. Another potential source of support for U.S. air traffic controllers was from their counterparts abroad. The Canadian Air Traffic Controllers Association (CATCA) initially refused to clear flights into or out of U.S. airspace. Under pressure from U.S. authorities, however, the Canadian government threatened the CATCA with legal action and the union swiftly backed down. See Northrup 1984, 181.

47. Poli 1982.

48. McCartin 1981a, 307.

49. Raskin 1981.

50. Poli 1982, 2.

51. Morgan 1984, 176.

52. See McMartin 2011a, 326–27. On traceability, see Arnold 1990.

53. In his 1982 State of the Union (SOTU) address, Reagan saluted Lenny Skutnik, a federal worker who had jumped into the Potomac River to save a drowning passenger from the flight, thus beginning a new presidential tradition in which presidents use the SOTU address to highlight the heroism or good works of an ordinary citizen.

54. My discussion of the S&L case draws heavily on Congressional Budget Office 1993; Romer and Weingast 1991; McCarty, Poole, and Rosenthal 2013; and Kettl 1991.

55. Hershey 1989, A1.

56. Mason 2004, 4–5.

57. Robinson 2013.

58. McCarty et al. 2010, 62.

59. Congressional Budget Office 1993, xi.

60. Romer and Weingast 1991.

61. Congressional Budget Office 1993, xi.

62. McCarty et al. 2010.

63. Ibid.

64. Romer and Weingast 1991.

65. England 1991, 7.

66. McCarty et al. 2010, 62–63.

67. A. Jacobs and Weaver 2015, 448.

68. D. F. Thompson 1993.

69. Cambridge Reports / Research International 1989.

70. On the lack of legislative accountability for indirect policy effects, see Arnold 1990.

71. On the politics of blame avoidance, see R. Weaver 1986.

72. Kilborn 1988, A1.

73. Bode 1990.

74. Weaver 1986.

75. McCarty, Poole, and Rosenthal 2013, 182.

76. Kettl 1991.

77. Congressional Budget Office 1993.

78. Webel et al. 2020.

79. *Time Magazine* / Cable News Network 1989.

80. Cambridge Reports / Research International 1989.

81. Quoted in Knight 1990.

82. Ibid.

83. Quoted in Temple-Raston 2008.

84. Apple 1990.

85. "Voters React More to Local Issues" 1991.

86. On the design of the rescue measure, see Hershey 1989.

87. "Voters React More to Local Issues" 1991.

88. On weakening traceability chains, see Arnold 1990, 100–104.

89. Kettl 1991, 444.

90. McCarty et al. 2010.

91. ABC News / CBS News / NBC News / CNN 1990.

92. Day 1989.

93. Ibid.

94. The conference report passed 201–175 in the House. The conference report passed in the Senate by a division vote. See "Sweeping Thrift Bailout Bill Cleared" 1990.

95. See Kliff 2017.

96. Gollust and Lynch 2011.

97. A. Schneider and Ingram 2019, 209.

98. On the politics of welfare reform, see R. Weaver 2000.

99. Mauer and McCalmont 2013.

100. Congressional Record, July 23, 1996 (142 Cong. Rec. S8498–S8499).

101. Ibid.

102. Osgood 2021.

103. Quoted in Ellis 1997, A3.

104. Gustafson 2009, 672.

105. Mauer and McCalmont 2013.

106. Ibid.

107. Gustafson 2009, 673.

108. Quoted in Rosenthal 2015.

109. Owens and Smith 2012, 548.

110. D. Thompson and Burnside 2022. As the authors note, the fact that TANF is a cash benefit partly funded by the states while SNAP is an in-kind benefit paid entirely by the federal government may help explain this pattern.

111. Rosenthal 2015.

112. Quinn 2019.

113. Rosenthal 2015.

114. Gash 2015.

115. Quinn 2019.

116. Dagan and Teles 2016, xiii.

117. Yang 2017.

118. Walker 2016.

119. On the role of divided elites in incentivizing grassroots mobilization, see Tarrow 2011.

120. Pierson 2004, 44.

Conclusion

1. In an important study, Anzia, Jares, and Malhotra (2022) show that farm aid programs that serve mainly a conservative rural population do not produce more positive views of government.

2. See Hacker and Pierson 2019. For an excellent synthesis of the historical institutionalist feedback literature, see Beland, Campbell, and Weaver 2022.

3. In contrast to historical institutionalists, scholars working in the punctuated equilibrium tradition have focused on the self-correcting type of negative feedback. See, for example, Baumgartner and Jones 2002.

4. Skocpol 1992.

5. A. Jacobs and Weaver 2015.

6. Lacombe 2018, 2022.

7. For an insightful analysis of the politics of organizational coalition building, see Weir 2006.

8. Dagan and Teles 2016.

9. Orren and Skowronek 2017, 6.

10. Ibid., 178.

11. B. Jones, Theriault, and Whyman 2019.

12. Grumbach 2022.

13. Blum 2020.

14. Quoted in Gerstle 2022, 157.

15. Rodrik 2021.

16. This section draws on Patashnik and Weaver 2020; see also Patashnik 2008.

17. This paragraph benefited from correspondence with Jacob Hacker.

18. In a careful empirical study of repeal legislation, Ragusa and Birkhead (2020) show that a "significant law's likelihood of repeal increases from the moment it is signed by the president until about ten years after passage." After a decade passes, "the risk of repeal drops dramatically" (46).

19. On the Wagner Act, see Plotke 1989. Drawing on public opinion data from the 1930s and 1940s, Schickler and Caughey (2011, 163) show that "a perceived growth in the power and radicalism of labor unions was accompanied by a broad-based anti-labor reaction in the mass public. The reaction was particularly consequential in the solidly Democratic South . . . [but] Northern voters also evinced a dramatic anti-labor turn, providing Republican leaders with a potent wedge issue among Northern Democrats as a well as a basis for a coalition with conservative Southerners."

20. Edsall and Edsall 1991.

21. Martin Luther King Jr. stated, "The white backlash has existed since the founding of the nation because of the American ambivalence on the subject of race. Any action here could not lead to a greater backlash than already exists." Quoted in Robinson 1967, 30.

22. On Agnew, see Holsden, Messette, and Podair 2019; on DeSantis, see Bouie 2023.

23. Hacker and Pierson 2020.

24. For an insightful analysis of this development, see Grossmann and Hopkins 2022.

25. Heyward 2022.

26. Grossmann and Hopkins 2022.

27. Skocpol 1992; Orloff and Skocpol 1984.

28. Hertel-Fernandez 2016.

29. McCartin 2011a.

30. Lesson-drawing from political events is anything but straightforward, however. See Hacker 2001.

31. Sterman 2000, 15.

32. Patashnik 2008, 90.

33. C. Davenport and Friedman 2022.

34. D. Roberts 2020.

35. Ibid.

36. Stein, Joselow, and Roubein 2022.

37. Krugman 2022.

38. On the role of policy design in the lack of climate backlash, see Meyer 2022.

39. B. Jones and Baumgartner 2005, 5.

40. J. Goldstein and Gulotty 2019, 73.

41. How can backlash risks be systematically identified? One technique that R. Kent Weaver and I (Patashnik and Weaver 2021) recommend is developing a "checklist" of factors that signal potential trouble with political sustainability. For each of those factors, we identify warning signs that actors can watch for to assess whether a proposed or already implemented policy may be vulnerable, develop a set of tools to assess the likely degree of threat, and offer a set of strategies that advocates can use to influence the policy's sustainability going forward.

42. Some people who recommend this course argue that backlash forces are not influenced by policy designs in a polarized age. Opponents will criticize policies irrespective of their substantive content, they argue, so policymakers might as well pursue the course of action they think is best. While it may be true that the *rhetoric* of opponents (and of pundits on media outlets like Fox News) has only a tangential relationship to policy realities, I see little evidence that policy attributes have no bearing on the manifestation and intensity of backlash politics in recent decades. A fair reading of the history of health care reform, for example, suggests that the backlash to the ACA from insurance companies and drug companies, as well as ordinary citizens, would have been *dramatically* stronger if Obama had supported a single-payer system and the elimination of private insurance.

43. Applebaum 2021.

44. Wildavsky 1989, 406.

45. Hacker 2019.

46. Quoted in Zelizer 2015b, 129.

47. Ibid., 123.

48. Sabl 2002.

49. Ibid., 12.

50. Ibid.

51. Ibid., 13.

52. I borrow this argument from Matush (2023), who develops it in the context of leaders who deliberately antagonize foreign actors to win domestic support.

53. Sabl 2002, 11.

54. Ibid., 12.

55. Ibid., 168. See also Weber 1987; Yglesias 2016.

56. Patashnik 2019b; Patashnik and Weaver 2021.

57. M. Peterson 2018, 637.

58. Oberlander and Weaver 2015.

59. Burgin 2018, 306.

60. Hacker and Pierson (2018) argue that many of the features of the ACA that produced self-undermining feedbacks and intense opposition among some constituency groups were "forced on, rather than pursued by, the designers of the law" (563).

61. Arnold 2022, 31.

62. See Arnold 1990, 100–104.

63. Research suggests that bipartisan enactment lowers the odds that a law will be repealed by a future Congress, all else being equal. See Ragusa and Birkhead 2020, 94.

64. My focus here is on steps to reduce *sustainability-undermining* factors. For a more complete discussion of political sustainability risks that also examines sustainability-enhancing factors (e.g., providing front-loaded concentrated benefits, subsidizing transition costs, etc.), see Patashnik and Weaver 2021.

65. Levine 2006.

66. Ibid.; see also Patashnik 2008.

67. Gordon 2021.

68. Ferek and Morenne 2022.

69. Thanks to David Mayhew for sharing his thoughts on this tactic.

70. Mayhew 2012b, 373.

71. Derthick 1979, 216.

72. On the policy's success in cutting child poverty, see E. Klein 2022.

73. To be sure, Congress should not have designed the program as a one-year extension in the first place. There was no backlash when the program expired. The recipients lacked both organizational resources and a clear social identity, and the program was not in place long enough to build a constituency. It was a mistake to assume the expanded child tax credit would prove so popular that its extension would be guaranteed. Policy entrenchment does not happen automatically. It can take years for programs to shape public expectations and become deeply embedded. See Patashnik 2008.

74. Starr 2017a.

75. See Mansbridge and Shames 2008.

76. White backlash among the electorate is a major theme of Edsall and Edsall 1992. In V. Weaver's (2007) account of the rise of punitive crime policy, elite opponents of the civil rights movement are the prime movers.

77. Gilens 1999.

78. Williamson, Skocpol, and Coggin 2011, 35.

79. Consider the backlash against the proposal to "defund the police." In Minneapolis, a 2021 ballot initiative to dismantle the police department and replace it with a public health–oriented department of public safety—which lost by 56–44 percent—won support in neighborhoods where large numbers of white liberals reside yet lost in the precincts with the heaviest concentration of Black voters. Many Black voters favored police reform but were reported to be concerned about the measure's potential harm to public safety. To be sure, some analysts would

frame the defeat of the defund initiative as white backlash. This interpretation provides certain insights into the structural power of the police, but it directs attention away from the agency of Black voters, their perceptions of the likely effects of the proposal, and the tensions between different factions within the Democratic Party. See Armstrong 2021; Edsall 2022.

80. Fried and Harris 2021, 182.
81. Orren and Skowronek 2017, 5.
82. Waldman 2018.
83. See Starr 2022.

References

Aaron, Henry J., and Gary Burtless. 2014. "Potential Effects of the Affordable Care Act on Income Inequality." Preliminary working paper, Brookings Institution, January 24. https://www.brookings.edu/wp-content/uploads/2016/06/potential-effects-affordable-care-act-income-inequality-aaron-burtless.pdf.

ABC News. 2016. "Donald Trump's 2016 Republican National Convention Speech." July 22. https://abcnews.go.com/Politics/full-text-donald-trumps-2016-republican-national-convention/story?id=40786529.

ABC News / CBS News / NBC News / CNN. 1990. *Voter Research & Surveys: National Election Day Exit Poll.* Edited by Voter Research & Surveys / CBS News / New York Times, Roper Center for Public Opinion Research.

Abelson, Reed. 2020. "Workers with Health Insurance Face Rising Out-of-Pocket Costs." *New York Times*, October 8. https://www.nytimes.com/2020/10/08/health/health-insurance-premiums-deductibles.html.

Abrajano, Marisa, and Zoltan L. Hajnal. 2015. *White Backlash: Immigration, Race, and American Politics.* Princeton University Press.

Abramowitz, Alan I. 2001. "It's Monica, Stupid: The Impeachment Controversy and the 1998 Midterm Election." *Legislative Studies Quarterly* 26 (2): 211–26.

Abramson, Jill, and Steven Greenhouse. 1997. "Labor Victory on Trade Bill Reveals Power." *New York Times*, November 12. https://www.nytimes.com/1997/11/12/us/the-trade-bill-labor-labor-victory-on-trade-bill-reveals-power.html.

Achen, Christopher H., and Larry M. Bartels. 2017. *Democracy for Realists: Why Elections Do Not Produce Responsive Government.* Princeton University Press.

Aiken, Abigail R. A. 2019. "Erosion of Women's Reproductive Rights in the United States." *BMJ* 366:l4444.

Alesina, Alberto, and Marco Tabellini. 2022. "The Political Effects of Immigration: Culture or Economics?" NBER Working Paper Series 30079, National Bureau of Economic Research. https//doi.org/10.3386/w30079.

Alter, Karen J., and Michael Zürn. 2020a. "Conceptualising Backlash Politics: Introduction to a Special Issue on Backlash Politics in Comparison." *British Journal of Politics and International Relations* 22 (4): 563–84.

———. 2020b. "Theorising Backlash Politics: Conclusion to a Special Issue on Backlash Politics in Comparison." *British Journal of Politics and International Relations* 22 (4): 739–52.

American Presidency Project. 1976a. "1976 Democratic Party Platform." July 12. https://www.presidency.ucsb.edu/documents/1976-democratic-party-platform.

———. 1976b. "Republican Party Platform of 1976." August 18. https://www.presidency.ucsb.edu/documents/republican-party-platform-1976.

———. "Republican Party Platform of 1980." July 15. https://www.presidency.ucsb.edu/documents/republican-party-platform-1980.

Ansolabehere, Stephen, and David M. Konisky. 2014. *Cheap and Clean: How Americans Think about Energy in the Age of Global Warming.* MIT Press.

Anzia, Sarah F. 2013. *Timing and Turnout: How Off-Cycle Elections Favor Organized Groups.* University of Chicago Press.

Anzia, Sarah F., Jake Alton Jares, and Neil Malhotra. 2022. "Does Receiving Government Assistance Shape Political Attitudes? Evidence from Agricultural Producers." *American Political Science Review* 116 (4): 1389–1406.

Apple, R. W., Jr. 1990. "The Big Vote Is for 'No.'" *New York Times*, November 8. https://www.nytimes.com/1990/11/08/us/the-1990-elections-signals-the-message-the-big-vote-is-for-no.html.

Applebaum, Anne. 2021. "The Mypillow Guy Really Could Destroy Democracy." *Atlantic*, July 29. https://www.theatlantic.com/ideas/archive/2021/07/mike-lindells-plot-destroy-america/619593/.

Armstrong, Nekima Levy. 2021. "Black Voters Want Better Policing, Not Posturing by Progressives." Opinion, *New York Times*, November 9. https://www.nytimes.com/2021/11/09/opinion/minneapolis-police-defund.html.

Arnold, R. Douglas. 1990. *The Logic of Congressional Action.* Yale University Press.

———. 2022. *Fixing Social Security: The Politics of Reform in a Polarized Age.* Princeton University Press.

Aronow, Peter M., and Benjamin T. Miller. 2016. "Policy Misperceptions and Support for Gun Control Legislation." *Lancet* 387 (10015): 223.

Associated Press. 1981. "Traffic Cops of the Sky." June 21. https://advance-lexis-com.revproxy.brown.edu/api/document?collection=news&id=urn:contentItem:3SJ4-MK50-0011-4245-00000-00&context=1516831.

———. 1989. "House Panel Leader Jeered by Elderly in Chicago." *New York Times*, August 19. https://www.nytimes.com/1989/08/19/us/house-panel-leader-jeered-by-elderly-in-chicago.html.

———. 2017. "How AP Tallied the Cost of North Carolina's 'Bathroom Bill.'" AP News, March 27. https://apnews.com/article/ec6e9845827f47e89f40f33bb7024f61.

Atkinson, Mary Layton. 2017. *Combative Politics: The Media and Public Perceptions of Lawmaking.* University of Chicago Press.

Atkinson, Mary Layton, K. Elizabeth Coggins, James A. Stimson, and Frank R. Baumgartner. 2021. *The Dynamics of Public Opinion.* Cambridge University Press.

Autor, David, David Dorn, and Gordon H. Hanson. 2013. "The China Syndrome: Local Labor Market Effects of Import Competition in the United States." *American Economic Review* 103 (6): 2121–68.

Autor, David, David Dorn, Gordon Hanson, and Kaveh Majlesi. 2020. "Importing Political Polarization? The Electoral Consequences of Rising Trade Exposure." *American Economic Review* 110 (10): 3139–83.

Avery, Dan. 2020. "LGBTQ Rights Fight Reignited 4 Years after N.C.'s 'Bathroom Bill' Controversy." NBC News, December 8. https://www.nbcnews.com/feature/nbc-out/lgbtq-rights-fight-re ignited-4-years-after-n-c-s-n1250390.

Bachrach, Peter, and Morton S. Baratz. 1962. "Two Faces of Power." *American Political Science Review* 56 (4): 947–52.

Bada, Xóchitl, Jonathan Fox, and Jane Guskin. n.d. "Immigrant Rights Protests—Spring 2006." University of Washington, Civil Rights and Labor History Consortium. Accessed June 16, 2021, https://depts.washington.edu/moves/2006_immigrant_rights.shtml.

Bagley, Nicholas. 2012. "Beside Bureaucrats: Why Medicare Reform Hasn't Worked." *Georgetown Law Journal* 101:519–80.

Bailey, Michael A. 2003. "The Politics of the Difficult: Congress, Public Opinion, and Early Cold War Aid and Trade Policies." *Legislative Studies Quarterly* 28 (2): 147–77.

Bailey, Michael A., Judith Goldstein, and Barry R. Weingast. 1997. "The Institutional Roots of American Trade Policy: Politics, Coalitions, and International Trade." *World Politics* 49 (3): 309–38.

Baldassarri, Delia, and Barum Park. 2020. "Was There a Culture War? Partisan Polarization and Secular Trends in US Public Opinion." *Journal of Politics* 82 (3): 809–27.

Banchiri, Bamzi. 2016. "Charlotte Passes Transgender Rights Law: Will North Carolina Let It Stand?" *Christian Science Monitor*, February 23. https://www.csmonitor.com/USA/Politics /2016/0223/Charlotte-passes-transgender-rights-law-Will-North-Carolina-let-it-stand.

Bardach, Eugene S. 2006. "Policy Dynamics." In *The Oxford Handbook of Political Science*, edited by Michael Moran, Michael Rein, and Robert E. Goodin, 336–66. Oxford University Press.

Bardach, Eugene, and Eric M. Patashnik. 2019. *A Practical Guide for Policy Analysis: The Eight-fold Path to More Effective Problem Solving*. 6th ed. CQ Press.

Barone, Michael. 1990. *Our Country: The Shaping of America from Roosevelt to Reagan*. Free Press.

Baumgartner, Frank R., and Bryan D. Jones. 1993. *Agendas and Instability in American Politics*. University of Chicago Press.

———. 2002. "Positive and Negative Feedback in Politics." In *Policy Dynamics*, edited by Frank R. Baumgartner and Bryan D. Jones, 4–28. University of Chicago Press.

Beauchamp, Zack. 2021. "Biden's America First Hangover." Vox, May 1. https://www.vox.com /policy-and-politics/22408089/biden-trump-america-first-policy-immigration-vaccines.

Beckett, Lois. 2020. "Virginia Democrats Won an Election. Gun Owners Are Talking Civil War." *Guardian*, January 10. http://www.theguardian.com/us-news/2020/jan/09/virginia-gun-control -second-amendment-civil-war.

Bedard, Paul. 2019. "Uprising: 90% of Virginia Counties Become Gun 'Sanctuaries,' Expanding Movement to Nine States." Washington Examiner, December 18. https://www .washingtonexaminer.com/washington-secrets/uprising-90-of-virginia-counties-join-gun -sanctuary-movement-expands-to-9-states.

Béland, Daniel, Andrea Louise Campbell, and R. Kent Weaver. 2022. *Policy Feedback: How Policies Shape Politics*. Cambridge University Press.

Béland, Daniel, Philip Rocco, and Alex Waddan. 2016. *Obamacare Wars: Federalism, State Politics, and the Affordable Care Act*. University Press of Kansas.

———. 2019. "Policy Feedback and the Politics of the Affordable Care Act." *Policy Studies Journal* 47 (2): 395–422.

Bell, Jeffrey. 1992. "The Wrong Man on the Right." *New York Times*, March 3. https://www.nytimes .com/1992/03/03/opinion/the-wrong-man-on-the-right.html.

Berman, Mark, and Amber Phillips. 2017. "North Carolina Governor Signs Bill Repealing and Replacing Transgender Bathroom Law amid Criticism." *Washington Post*, March 30. https://www.washingtonpost.com/news/post-nation/wp/2017/03/30/north-carolina-lawmakers-say-theyve-agreed-on-a-deal-to-repeal-the-bathroom-bill/.

Binder, Sarah. 1996. "The Disappearing Political Center: Congress and the Incredible Shrinking Middle." *Brookings Review* 14 (4): 36–39.

———. 2003. *Stalemate: Causes and Consequences of Legislative Gridlock*. Brookings Institution Press.

Bishin, Benjamin G., Thomas J. Hayes, Matthew B. Incantalupo, and Charles Anthony Smith. 2016. "Opinion Backlash and Public Attitudes: Are Political Advances in Gay Rights Counterproductive?" *American Journal of Political Science* 60 (3): 625–48.

———. 2020. "Elite Mobilization: A Theory Explaining Opposition to Gay Rights." *Law & Society Review* 54 (1): 233–64.

———. 2021. *Elite-Led Mobilization and Gay Rights: Dispelling the Myth of Mass Opinion Backlash*. University of Michigan Press.

Black, Donald. 1998. *The Social Structure of Right and Wrong*. Rev. ed. Emerald Group Publishing.

Blazina, Carrie, and Chris Baronavski. 2022. "How Americans View Policy Proposals on Transgender and Gender Identity Issues, and Where Such Policies Exist." *Pew Research Report*, September 15. https://www.pewresearch.org/fact-tank/2022/09/15/how-americans-view-policy-proposals-on-transgender-and-gender-identity-issues-and-where-such-policies-exist/.

Blendon, Robert J., Mollyann Brodie, John M. Benson, Drew E. Altman, Larry Levitt, Tina Hoff, and Larry Hugick. 1998. "Understanding the Managed Care Backlash." *Health Affairs* 17 (4): 80–94.

Blinder, Alan. 2016a. "As Session Opens, Lawmakers Face Pressure over Bias Law from Competing Sides." *New York Times*, April 26. https://www.nytimes.com/2016/04/26/us/north-carolina-house-bill-2.html?searchResultPosition=1.

———. 2016b. "North Carolina Lawmakers Met with Protests over Bias Law." *New York Times*, April 25. https://www.nytimes.com/2016/04/26/us/north-carolina-house-bill-2.html.

Blinder, Alan, Richard Pérez-Peña, and Eric Lichtblau. 2016. "North Carolina and U.S. Duel on Access Law." *New York Times*, May 10. https://www.nytimes.com/2016/05/10/us/north-carolina-governor-sues-justice-department-over-bias-law.html?searchResultPosition=1.

Block, Melissa. 2022. "Americans Are Deeply Divided on Transgender Rights, a Poll Shows." NPR, June 29. https://www.npr.org/2022/06/29/1107484965/transgender-athletes-trans-rights-gender-transition-poll.

Blum, Rachel M. 2020. *How the Tea Party Captured the GOP: Insurgent Factions in American Politics*. University of Chicago Press.

Bode, Ken. 1990. "As a Political Issue, S. & L.'s Fail Again." Opinion, *New York Times*, August 10. https://www.nytimes.com/1990/08/10/opinion/as-a-political-issue-s-l-s-fail-again.html.

Bogel-Burroughs, Nicholas, Shaila Dewan, and Kathleen Gray. 2020. "F.B.I. Says Michigan Anti-Government Group Plotted to Kidnap Gov. Gretchen Whitmer." *New York Times*, October 8. https://www.nytimes.com/2020/10/08/us/gretchen-whitmer-michigan-militia.html.

Bouie, Jamelle. 2023. "Ron DeSantis Likes His Cultural Wars for a Reason." *New York Times*, January 24. https://www.nytimes.com/2023/01/24/opinion/desantis-florida-culture-w.html.

Bowes, Mark. 2020. "36 Virginians Barred from Possessing Guns since Va.'s New 'Red Flag' Law Began July 1." *Richmond Times-Dispatch*, September 18. https://richmond.com/news/state

-and-regional/crime-and-courts/36-virginians-barred-from-possessing-guns-since-va-s
-new-red-flag-law-began-july/article_1ee0ac33-75d0-58f2-8186-81e674e114de.html.

Bradburn, Douglas. 2008. "A Clamor in the Public Mind: Opposition to the Alien and Sedition Acts." *William and Mary Quarterly* 65 (3): 565–600. https://doi.org/doi:10.2307/250 96814.

Bradner, Eric. 2016. "Clinton's TPP Controversy: What You Need to Know." CNN Politics, July 27. https://www.cnn.com/2016/07/27/politics/tpp-what-you-need-to-know/index.html.

Bradsher, Keith. 1993. "Side Agreements to Trade Accord Vary in Ambition." *New York Times*, September 19. https://www.nytimes.com/1993/09/19/us/side-agreements-to-trade-accord -vary-in-ambition.html.

Brady, David W., Morris P. Fiorina, and Arjun S. Wilkins. 2011. "The 2010 Elections: Why Did Political Science Forecasts Go Awry?" *PS: Political Science and Politics* 44 (2): 247–50. https:// doi.org/10.1017/S1049096511000023.

Brands, Henry William. 2016. *Reagan: The Life*. Anchor.

Brenan, Megan. 2021. "Stricter Gun Laws Less Popular in U.S." Gallup.com, November 17. https://news.gallup.com/poll/357317/stricter-gun-laws-less-popular.aspx.

———. 2022. "Dissatisfaction with U.S. Immigration Level Rises to 58%." Gallup.com, February 14. https://news.gallup.com/poll/389708/dissatisfaction-immigration-level-rises.aspx.

Brinkley, Alan. 2012. *John F. Kennedy: The American Presidents Series: The 35th President, 1961– 1963*. Macmillan.

Broder, John M. 2009. "House Passes Bill to Address Threat of Climate Change." *New York Times*, June 29. https://www.nytimes.com/2009/06/27/us/politics/27climate.html.

Brown, Lawrence. 1983. *Politics and Health Care Organization: HMOs as Federal Policy*. Brookings Institution Press.

Burgin, Ellen. 2018. "Congress, Policy Sustainability, and the Affordable Care Act: Democratic Policy Makers Overlooked Implementation, Post-Enactment Politics, and Policy Feedback Effects." *Congress & the Presidency* 45 (3): 279–314.

Busemeyer, Marius R., Aurélien Abrassart, Spyridoula Nezi, and Roula Nezi. 2020. "Beyond Positive and Negative: New Perspectives on Feedback Effects in Public Opinion on the Welfare State—ERRATUM." *British Journal of Political Science* 50 (2): 807.

Cable News Network (CNN) / *USA Today*, Gallup / CNN / *USA Today*. 1993. "Poll: US Immigrants & Immigration Policy" (data set). Question 51, USGALLUP.422002.R19D, Gallup Organization, Cornell University, Roper Center for Public Opinion Research.

Cacciola, Scott, and Alan Blinder. 2016. "N.B.A. to Move All-Star Game from North Carolina." *New York Times*, July 21. https://www.nytimes.com/2016/07/22/sports/basketball/nba-all -star-game-moves-charlotte-transgender-bathroom-law.html.

Calmes, Jackie. 2016. "Trump Scores Points on Trade in Debate, but Not So Much on Accuracy." *New York Times*, September 27. https://www.nytimes.com/2016/09/28/us/politics/hillary -clinton-donald-trump-trade-tpp-nafta.html.

Cambridge Reports / Research International. 1989. *Cambridge Reports / Research International Poll: July 1989*. Roper Center for Public Opinion Research.

Campbell, Andrea L. 2003a. *How Policies Make Citizens: Senior Political Activism and the American Welfare State*. Princeton University Press.

———. 2003b. "Participatory Reactions to Policy Threats: Senior Citizens and the Defense of Social Security and Medicare." *Political Behavior* 25 (1): 29–49.

———. 2012. "Policy Makes Mass Politics." *Annual Review of Political Science* 15:333–51.

———. 2020. "The Affordable Care Act and Mass Policy Feedbacks." *Journal of Health Politics, Policy and Law* 45 (4): 567–80.

Campbell, Bradley, and Jason Manning. 2014. "Microaggression and Moral Cultures." *Comparative Sociology* 13 (6): 692–726.

Campbell, David. 2020. "The Perils of Politicized Religion." *Daedalus* 149 (3): 87–104.

Cancryn, Adam, Sarah Karlin-Smith, and Paul Demko. 2017. "Deep-Pocketed Health Care Lobbies Line Up against Trump." *Politico*, May 3. https://www.politico.com/story/2017/05/03/obamacare-repeal-health-care-237948.

Canes-Wrone, Brandice, Lauren Mattioli, and Sophie Meunier. 2020. "Foreign Direct Investment Screening and Congressional Backlash Politics in the United States." *British Journal of Politics and International Relations* 22 (4): 666–78.

Card, David. 2009. "Immigration and Inequality." *American Economic Review* 99 (2): 1–21.

Carmines, Edward G., and James Woods. 2002. "The Role of Party Activists in the Evolution of the Abortion Issue." *Political Behavior* 24 (4): 361–77.

Carr, Sarah. 2012. "In Southern Towns, 'Segregation Academies' Are Still Going Strong." *Atlantic*, December 13. https://www.theatlantic.com/national/archive/2012/12/in-southern-towns-segregation-academies-are-still-going-strong/266207/.

Castle, Stephen. 2017. "U.K. Conservatives Retreat after Backlash over 'Dementia Tax.'" *New York Times*, May 22. https://www.nytimes.com/2017/05/22/world/europe/uk-theresa-may-conservatives.html.

"Catastrophic-Coverage Law Is Repealed." 1990. *CQ Almanac 1989*, 101st Congress, 1st Session, 150. CQ Press.

Chait, Jonathan. 2017. *Audacity: How Barack Obama Defied His Critics and Transformed America*. Custom House.

Chapin, Christy Ford. 2015. *Ensuring America's Health: The Public Creation of the Corporate Health Care System*. Cambridge University Press.

Chattopadhyay, Jacqueline. 2018. "Is the Affordable Care Act Cultivating a Cross-Class Constituency? Income, Partisanship, and a Proposal for Tracing the Contingent Nature of Positive Policy Feedback Effects." *Journal of Health Politics, Policy and Law* 43 (1): 19–67.

Childs, Marquis. 1950. "Truman and the Kerr Bill." *Washington Post*, April 20.

Choi, Jiwon, Ilyana Kuziemko, Ebonya Washington, and Gavin Wright. 2021. "Local Economic and Political Effects of Trade Deals: Evidence from NAFTA." *NBER Working Paper Series* 29525. https://www.nber.org/system/files/working_papers/w29525/w29525.pdf.

Clark, Peter B., and James Q. Wilson. 1961. "Incentive Systems: A Theory of Organizations." *Administrative Science Quarterly* 6 (2): 129–66.

Clarke, Charles. 2014. Introduction. In *The "Too Difficult" Box: The Big Issues Politicians Can't Crack*, edited by Charles Clarke, xi–xxii. Biteback Publishing.

Clemens-Cope, Lisa, and Nathaniel Anderson. 2015. "QuickTake: Health Insurance Policy Cancellations Were Uncommon in 2014." *Health Reform Monitoring Survey*, March 12. https://apps.urban.org/features/hrms/quicktakes/Health-Insurance-Policy-Cancellations-Were-Uncommon-in-2014.html.

Clinton, Joshua D., and Michael W. Sances. 2018. "The Politics of Policy: The Initial Mass Political Effects of Medicaid Expansion in the States." *American Political Science Review* 112 (1): 167–85.

CNN Wire. 2016. "Gov. McCrory Calls Special Session for Wednesday to 'Reconsider' HB2." Fox8, December 19. https://myfox8.com/news/gov-mccrory-calls-special-session-for-wednesday-to-reconsider-hb2/.

Cohen, Matt. 2020. "A More Extreme Gun Rights Movement Is Emerging in the NRA's Wake." *Mother Jones*, December 2. https://www.motherjones.com/politics/2020/12/a-more-extreme-gun-rights-movement-is-emerging-in-the-nras-wake/.

Cohen, Stephen. 1983. "Let I.R.S. Now End Joneism." *New York Times*, June 10. https://www.nytimes.com/1983/06/10/opinion/let-irs-now-end-jonesism.html.

Cohn, Jonathan. 2020. "The ACA, Repeal, and the Politics of Backlash." *HealthAffairs*, March 6. https://www.healthaffairs.org/do/10.1377/hblog20200305.771008/full/.

Coleman, Sarah R. 2021. *The Walls Within: The Politics of Immigration in Modern America.* Princeton University Press.

Congressional Budget Office. 1993. *Resolving the Thrift Crisis.* Congress of the U.S., Congressional Budget Office, April.

"Congress OKs North American Trade Pact." 1994. *CQ Almanac 1993*, 103rd Congress, 1st Session, 171–79. CQ Press.

Conyers, John. 1981. "The Air Controllers' Strike Should Be Legalized." Opinion, *New York Times*, August 13. https://www.nytimes.com/1981/08/13/opinion/l-the-air-controllers-strike-should-be-legalized-231470.html.

Cook, Charlie. 2021. "The Four Factors That Matter in Predicting 2022." Cook Political Report, February 16. https://cookpolitical.com/index.php/analysis/national/national-politics/four-factors-matter-predicting-2022.

Cook, Fay Lomax, and Edith J. Barrett. 1992. *Support for the American Welfare State: The Views of Congress and the Public.* Columbia University Press.

Cowie, Jefferson. 2017. *The Great Exception: The New Deal and the Limits of American Politics.* Princeton University Press.

Cramer, Katherine J. 2016. *The Politics of Resentment: Rural Consciousness in Wisconsin and the Rise of Scott Walker.* University of Chicago Press.

Crespino, Joseph. 2008. "Civil Rights and the Religious Right." In *Rightward Bound: Making America Conservative in the 1970s*, edited by Bruce J. Schulman and Julian E. Zelizer, 90–99. Harvard University Press.

Crump, Steve. 2016. "Charlotte Nondiscrimination Ordinance Passes 7-4." WBTV 3, March 23. https://www.wbtv.com/story/31282120/charlotte-non-discrimination-ordinance-passes-7-4/.

Culpepper, Pepper D. 2011. *Quiet Politics and Business Power: Corporate Control in Europe and Japan.* Cambridge University Press.

———. 2015. "Structural Power and Political Science in the Post-Crisis Era." *Business and Politics* 17 (3): 391–409.

Curry, Timothy, and Lynn Shibut. 2000. "The Cost of the Savings and Loan Crisis: Truth and Consequences." *FDIC Banking Review* 13 (2): 10–35.

Dagan, David, and Steven Michael Teles. 2016. *Prison Break: Why Conservatives Turned against Mass Incarceration.* Oxford University Press.

Dahl, David. 1989. "Catastrophic Coverage: Lawmaking Gone Awry." *St. Petersburg Times*, December 17.

Dallek, Robert. 1998. *Flawed Giant: Lyndon Johnson and His Times, 1961–1973.* Oxford University Press.

———. 1999. *Ronald Reagan: The Politics of Symbolism: With a New Preface.* Harvard University Press.

———. 2003. *An Unfinished Life: John F. Kennedy, 1917–1963.* Hachette UK.

Davenport, Coral, and Lisa Friedman. 2022. "Five Decades in the Making: Why It Took Congress So Long to Act on Climate." *New York Times,* August 7. https://www.nytimes.com/2022/08/07/climate/senate-climate-law.html.

Davenport, Tiffany C. 2015. "Policy-Induced Risk and Responsive Participation: The Effect of a Son's Conscription Risk on the Voting Behavior of His Parents." *American Journal of Political Science* 59 (1): 225–41.

Davis, Julie Hirschfeld. 2015. "President Obama Signs into Law a Rewrite of No Child Left Behind." *New York Times,* December 10. https://www.nytimes.com/2015/12/11/us/politics/president-obama-signs-into-law-a-rewrite-of-no-child-left-behind.html.

Day, Kathleen. 1989. "On Budget or Off? The Hot Issues behind the SL Bailout's Funding." *Washington Post,* May 14. https://www.washingtonpost.com/archive/business/1989/05/14/on-budget-or-off-the-hot-issues-behind-the-sl-bailouts-funding/6c7243ed-4742-4874-8b2c-719da3b9a320/.

Dean, Adam, and Jonathan Obert. 2021. "Rewarded by Friends and Punished by Enemies: The CIO and the Taft-Hartley Act." *Labor* 18 (3): 78–113.

DeParle, Jason. 1994. "Clinton Wages a Quiet War against Poverty." *New York Times,* March 30. https://www.nytimes.com/1994/03/30/us/clinton-wages-a-quiet-war-against-poverty.html.

Department of Justice. 2016. "U.S. Departments of Justice and Education Release Joint Guidance to Help Schools Ensure the Civil Rights of Transgender Students." May 13. https://www.justice.gov/opa/pr/us-departments-justice-and-education-release-joint-guidance-help-schools-ensure-civil-rights.

Derthick, Martha. 1979. *Policymaking for Social Security.* Brookings Institution Press.

Destler, Irving M. 1991. "U.S. Trade Policy-Making in the Eighties." In *Politics and Economics in the Eighties,* edited by Alberto Alesina and Geoffrey Carliner, 251–84. University of Chicago Press.

———. 2005. *American Trade Politics.* 4th ed. Columbia University Press.

Devins, Neal. 1984. "Bob Jones University v. United States: A Political Analysis." *Journal of Law & Politics* 1:403–21.

Dewar, Helen. 1981. "Senate Unanimously Rebuffs President on Social Security." *Washington Post,* May 21. https://www.washingtonpost.com/archive/politics/1981/05/21/senate-unanimously-rebuffs-president-on-social-security/d74838bd-550a-412b-9d5c-a2809a6cbdcd/.

Dodd, Scott, and Neil MacFarquhar. 2020. "Who Is the Man behind the Gun Rally That Has Virginia on Edge?" *New York Times,* January 18. https://www.nytimes.com/2020/01/17/us/philip-van-cleave-vcdl-gun-rally.html.

Domingo, Ida. 2019. "Culpeper Sheriff Says He'll Deputize Residents If Gun Laws Pass in Virginia." WSET, December 10. https://wset.com/news/local/culpeper-sheriff-says-hell-deputize-residents-if-gun-laws-pass-in-virginia.

Dorf, Michael C., and Sidney Tarrow. 2014. "Strange Bedfellows: How an Anticipatory Countermovement Brought Same-Sex Marriage into the Public Arena." *Law & Social Inquiry* 39 (2): 449–73.

Douthat, Ross. 2010. "The Great Bailout Backlash." *New York Times,* October 25. https://www.nytimes.com/2010/10/25/opinion/25douthat.html.

Drake, Wilfred F. 1978. "Tax Status of Private Segregated Schools: The New Revenue Procedure."
    William and Mary Law Review 20:463.

Drew, Elizabeth. 2007. *Richard M. Nixon: The 37th President, 1969–1974*. Macmillan.

Dumbrell, John. 1995. *The Carter Presidency: A Re-Evaluation*. Manchester University Press.

Edsall, Thomas B. 2015. "Obamacare, Hands off My Medicare." Opinion, *New York Times*,
    April 22. https://www.nytimes.com/2015/04/22/opinion/obamacare-hands-off-my-medicare
    .html.

———. 2016. "What Does Immigration Actually Cost Us?" Opinion, *New York Times*, September 29.
    https://www.nytimes.com/2016/09/29/opinion/campaign-stops/what-does-immigration
    -actually-cost-us.html.

———. 2021. "'Lean into It. Lean into the Culture War.'" Opinion, *New York Times*, July 14.
    https://www.nytimes.com/2021/07/14/opinion/culture-war-democrats-republicans.html.

———. 2022. "The Law of Unintended Political Consequences Strikes Again." Opinion, *New York
    Times*, January 5. https://www.nytimes.com/2022/01/05/opinion/progressive-philanthropy
    -critics.html.

Edsall, Thomas Bryne, and Mary D. Edsall. 1991. *Chain Reaction: The Impact of Race, Rights, and
    Taxes on American Politics*. W. W. Norton.

Einstein, Katherine Levine, and Jennifer Hochschild. 2016. "Studying Contingency Systemati-
    cally." In *Governing in a Polarized Age: Elections, Parties, and Political Representation in
    America*, edited by Alan S. Gerber and Eric Schickler, 304–27. Cambridge University Press.

Elder, Janet. 1986. "Parental Leave Bill: Its Effects on Men." *New York Times*, August 27. https://
    www.nytimes.com/1986/08/27/garden/parental-leave-bill-its-effect-on-men.html.

Ellis, Ralph, Holly Yan, and Nick Valencia. 2016. "North Carolina Legislature Fails to Repeal
    'Bathroom Bill.'" CNN Politics, December 22. https://www.cnn.com/2016/12/21/politics
    /north-carolina-bathroom-bill-hb2/index.html.

Ellis, Virginia. 1997. "Committee OK's Welfare Reform Plan." *Los Angeles Times*, July 3. https://
    www.latimes.com/archives/la-xpm-1997-jul-03-mn-9319-story.html.

England, Catherine. 1991. "How Regulations Made Thrifts Spendthrifts." *Business and Society
    Review* 10 (76): 4–9.

Enten, Harry. 2017. "Democrats Weren't Always Super Liberal on Immigration." FiveThirtyEight,
    September 20. https://fivethirtyeight.com/features/democrats-werent-always-super-liberal
    -on-immigration/.

Enthoven, Alain. 1999. "Managed Care: What Went Wrong? Can It Be Fixed?" Donald C. Ozmun
    and Donald B. Ozmun and Family Lecture in Management, Mayo Clinic, Rochester, Minn.
    https://www.gsb.stanford.edu/insights/managed-care-what-went-wrong-can-it-be-fixed.

Erikson, Robert S., Michael B. MacKuen, and James A. Stimson. 2002. *The Macro Polity*. Cam-
    bridge University Press.

———. 2008. "The Macro Polity Updated." Paper presented at the Midwest Political Science As-
    sociation, Chicago, April 3–6. http://www.columbia.edu/~rse14/Erikson_MacKuen_Stim
    son_2008_Macro_Polity_Updated_MPSA11.pdf.

Esparza, Gabriel Moreno. 2018. "How the Media Dealt a Major Blow to Donald Trump's Fam-
    ily Separations Policy." The Conversation, June 28. http://theconversation.com/how-the
    -media-dealt-a-major-blow-to-donald-trumps-family-separations-policy-98669.

Everett, Burgess, Josh Dawsey, Rachel Bade, and Heather Caygle. 2017. "Trump Denies Deal on
    DACA after Conservative Backlash." *Politico*, September 14. https://www.politico.eu/article
    /donald-trump-denies-daca-deal-conservative-backlash/.

Eyal, Yonatan. 1998. "With His Eyes Open: Stephen A. Douglas and the Kansas-Nebraska Disaster of 1854." *Illinois Historical Journal* 91 (4): 175–217.

Falleti, Tulia G., and James Mahoney. 2015. "The Comparative Sequential Method." In *Advances in Comparative-Historical Analysis*, edited by James Mahoney and Kathleen Thelen, 211–39. Cambridge University Press.

Ferek, Katy Stech, and Benoit Morenne. 2022. "Methane-Tax Compromise Backed by Democrats Faces Industry Skepticism." *Wall Street Journal*, August 5. https://www.wsj.com/articles /methane-tax-compromise-backed-by-democrats-faces-industry-skepticism-11659691981.

Fields, Shawn E. 2020. "Second Amendment Sanctuaries." *Northwestern University Law Review* 115 (2): 437–502.

Fiorina, Morris. 2017. *Unstable Majorities: Polarization, Party Sorting, and Political Stalemate.* Hoover Institution Press.

Flint, Andrew R., and Joy Porter. 2005. "Jimmy Carter: The Re-Emergence of Faith-Based Politics and the Abortion Rights Issue." *Presidential Studies Quarterly* 35 (1): 28–51.

Foner, Eric. 1988. *Reconstruction: America's Unfinished Revolution 1863–1877.* Harper & Row.

———. 2019. *The Second Founding: How the Civil War and Reconstruction Remade the Constitution.* W. W. Norton.

Foote, Susan Bartlett. 2002. "Why Medicare Cannot Promulgate a National Coverage Rule: A Case of Regula Mortis." *Journal of Health Politics, Policy and Law* 27 (5): 707–30.

Fording, Richard C., and Dana Patton. 2020. "The Affordable Care Act and the Diffusion of Policy Feedback: The Case of Medicaid Work Requirements." *RSF: The Russell Sage Foundation Journal of the Social Sciences* 6 (2): 131–53.

Fox, Cybelle. 2019. "'The Line Must Be Drawn Somewhere': The Rise of Legal Status Restrictions in State Welfare Policy in the 1970s." *Studies in American Political Development* 33 (2): 275–304.

Franklin, Ben A. 1982. "45 Weather Posts Given A Reprieve: Outcry Brings Shift by U.S.—30 Stations Still to Be Shut, 45 Weather Stations Withdrawn from Closing List." *New York Times*, March 8. ProQuest. http://search.proquest.com/docview/121923719/abstract/6CC7181E07 454503PQ/1.

Freedman, Robert. 2005. "The Religious Right and the Carter Administration." *Historical Journal* 48 (1): 231–60.

Freeman, Gary P. 1995. "Modes of Immigration Politics in Liberal Democratic States." *International Migration Review* 29 (4): 881–902.

Fried, Amy, and Douglas B. Harris. 2021. *At War with Government: How Conservatives Weaponized Distrust from Goldwater to Trump.* Columbia University Press.

Frieden, Jeffry. 2019. "The Political Economy of the Globalization Backlash: Sources and Implications." In *Meeting Globalization's Challenges: Policies to Make Trade Work for All*, edited by Luis Catão and Maurice Obstfeldt, 181–96. Princeton University Press.

Galvin, Daniel J., and Jacob S. Hacker. 2020. "The Political Effects of Policy Drift: Policy Stalemate and American Political Development." *Studies in American Political Development* 34 (2): 216–38.

Galvin, Daniel J., and Chloe N. Thurston. 2017. "The Democrats' Misplaced Faith in Policy Feedback." *Forum* 15 (2): 333–43.

Garwin, Richard L., and James A. Fay. 1973. "Letters to the Editor: Don't Delay Emission Control." *New York Times*, March 14. https://www.nytimes.com/1973/03/14/archives/letters-to -the-editor-dont-delay-emission-control-bad-arrests-and.html?searchResultPosition=3.

Gash, Alison L. 2015. *Below the Radar: How Silence Can Save Civil Rights*. Oxford University Press.

Gass, Henry. 2022. "Why Biden's Immigration Policy Looks a Lot like Trump's." *Christian Science Monitor*, February 7. https://www.csmonitor.com/USA/Politics/2022/0207/Why-Biden -s-immigration-policy-looks-a-lot-like-Trump-s.

Gawane, Atul. 2017. "Is Health Care a Right?" *New Yorker*, September 25. https://www.new yorker.com/magazine/2017/10/02/is-health-care-a-right.

General Assembly of North Carolina. 2016. "House Bill 2: Ratified Bill." Second Extra Session 2016, March 23, https://www.ncleg.gov/Sessions/2015E2/Bills/House/PDF/H2v3.pdf.

Gennaioli, Nicola, and Guido Tabellini. 2019. "Identity, Beliefs, and Political Conflict." CESifo Working Paper 7707, 70, CESifo Network.

Gerber, Alan S., Donald P. Green, and Christopher W. Larimer. 2008. "Social Pressure and Voter Turnout: Evidence from a Large-Scale Field Experiment." *American Political Science Review* 102 (1): 33–48.

Gerber, Alan S., Gregory A. Huber, Daniel R. Biggers, and David J. Hendry. 2017. "Self-Interest, Beliefs, and Policy Opinions: Understanding How Economic Beliefs Affect Immigration Policy Preferences." *Political Research Quarterly* 70 (1): 155–71.

Gerber, Alan S., Eric M. Patashnik, and Patrick Tucker. 2022. "How Voters Use Contextual Information to Reward and Punish: Credit Claiming, Legislative Performance, and Democratic Accountability." *Journal of Politics* 84 (3): 1839–42.

Gerstle, Gary. 2022. *The Rise and Fall of the Neoliberal Order: America and the World in the Free Market Era*. Oxford University Press.

Gilens, Martin. 1995. "Racial Attitudes and Opposition to Welfare." *Journal of Politics* 57 (4): 994–1014.

———. 1999. *Why Americans Hate Welfare: Race, Media, and the Politics of Antipoverty Policy*. University of Chicago Press.

Glickman, Lawrence. 2020. "How White Backlash Controls American Progress." *Atlantic*, May 21. https://www.theatlantic.com/ideas/archive/2020/05/white-backlash-nothing-new/611914/.

———. 2023. "White Backlash." In *Myth America: Historians Take on the Biggest Legends and Lies about Our Past*, edited by Kevin M. Kruse and Julian E. Zelizer, 211–24. Basic Books.

Glied, Sherry. 2000. "Managed Care." In *Handbook of Health Economics*, vol. 1, edited by Anthony J. Culyer and Joseph P. Newhouse, 707–53. Elsevier.

Goger, Annelies. 2019. "Displaced Workers Need More Than What Economists Are Suggesting." *Brookings*, November 13. https://www.brookings.edu/blog/the-avenue/2019/11/12/dis placed-workers-need-more-than-what-economists-are-suggesting/.

Goldstein, Amy. 2016. "HHS Failed to Heed Many Warnings That HealthCare.Gov Was in Trouble." *Washington Post*, February 23. https://www.washingtonpost.com/national/health -science/hhs-failed-to-heed-many-warnings-that-healthcaregov-was-in-trouble/2016 /02/22/dd344e7c-d67e-11e5-9823-02b905009f99_story.html.

———. 2017. "Senate's Latest ACA Repeal Strategy Would Leave 10 Million More Uninsured Than Its Last Bill, CBO Says." *Washington Post*, July 19. https://www.washingtonpost.com/national /health-science/senates-latest-aca-repeal-strategy-would-leave-10-million-more-uninsured -than-its-last-bill-cbo-says/2017/07/19/c701bc52-6ccd-11e7-b9e2-2056e768a7e5_story.html.

Goldstein, Judith. 2014. "Trade Politics and Reform." In *The Politics of Major Policy Reform in Postwar America*, edited by Jeffery A. Jenkins and Sidney M. Milkis, 203–26. Cambridge University Press.

Goldstein, Judith, and Robert Gulotty. 2019. "The Globalisation Crisis: Populism and the Rise of an Anti-Trade Coalition." *European Review of International Studies* 6 (3): 57–83.

———. 2021. "America and the Trade Regime: What Went Wrong?" *International Organization* 75 (2): 524–57.

Gollust, Sarah E., and Julia Lynch. 2011. "Who Deserves Health Care? The Effects of Causal Attributions and Group Cues on Public Attitudes about Responsibility for Health Care Costs." *Journal of Health Politics, Policy and Law* 36 (6): 1061–95.

Gonyea, Don. 2013. "How the Labor Movement Did a 180 on Immigration." NPR, February 5. https://www.npr.org/2013/02/05/171175054/how-the-labor-movement-did-a-180-on -immigratiom.

Goodman, Carly. 2019. "John Tanton Has Died. He Made America Less Open to Immigrants— and More Open to Trump." *Washington Post*, July 18. https://www.washingtonpost.com /outlook/2019/07/18/john-tanton-has-died-how-he-made-america-less-open-immigrants -more-open-trump/.

Goodnough, Abby. 2019. "House Votes to Repeal Obamacare Tax Once Seen as Key to Health Law." *New York Times*, July 17. https://www.nytimes.com/2019/07/17/us/politics/obamacare -democrats-cadillac-tax.html.

Gordon, Deborah. 2021. *No Standard Oil*. Oxford University Press.

Gordon, Deborah, Adam Brandt, Joule Bergerson, and Jonathan Koomey. 2015. *Know Your Oil: Creating a Global Oil-Climate Index*. Carnegie Endowment for International Peace.

Goss, Kristin A. 2010. *Disarmed: The Missing Movement for Gun Control in America*. Princeton University Press.

Graham, David A. 2016. "The Business Backlash to North Carolina's LGBT Law." *Atlantic*, March 25. https://www.theatlantic.com/politics/archive/2016/03/the-backlash-to-north -carolinas-lgbt-non-discrimination-ban/475500/.

———. 2017. "Red State, Blue City." *Atlantic*, February 2. https://www.theatlantic.com/magazine /archive/2017/03/red-state-blue-city/513857/.

Graham, Fred P. 1970. "Federal Judges Rule Out Benefit for Segregated Private 'Academies.'" *New York Times*, January 14. https://www.nytimes.com/1970/01/14/archives/federal-judges-rule -out-benefit-for-segregated-private-academies-us.html.

Green, Erica L. 2022. "New Biden Administration Rules for Charter Schools Spur Bipartisan Backlash." *New York Times*, May 13. https://www.nytimes.com/2022/05/13/us/politics/charter -school-rules-biden.html.

Greenhouse, Linda. 1987. "Momentum and 'Family Leave.'" *New York Times*, February 3. https:// www.nytimes.com/1987/02/03/us/washington-talk-momentum-and-family-leave.html.

Greenhouse, Linda, and Reva B. Siegel. 2011. "Before (and after) Roe v. Wade: New Questions about Backlash." *Yale Law Journal* 120:2028.

Gritter, Matthew. 2019. "The Kerr-Mills Act and the Puzzles of Health-Care Reform." *Social Science Quarterly* 100 (6): 2209–22.

Grogan, Colleen M., and Sunggeun (Ethan) Park. 2017a. "The Politics of Medicaid: Most Americans Are Connected to the Program, Support Its Expansion, and Do Not View It as Stigmatizing." *Milbank Quarterly* 95 (4): 749–82.

———. 2017b. "The Racial Divide in State Medicaid Expansions." *Journal of Health Politics, Policy and Law* 42 (3): 539–72.

Grogan, Colleen M., Phillip M. Singer, and David K. Jones. 2017. "Rhetoric and Reform in Waiver States." *Journal of Health Politics, Policy and Law* 42 (2): 247–84.

Grossmann, Matt. 2012. *The Not-So-Special Interests: Interest Groups, Public Representation, and American Governance*. Stanford University Press.

———. 2014. *Artists of the Possible: Governing Networks and American Policy Change since 1945*. Oxford University Press.

———. 2018. "Voters Like a Political Party until It Passes Laws." FiveThirtyEight, October 4. https://fivethirtyeight.com/features/voters-like-a-political-party-until-it-passes-laws/.

———. 2020. "Incremental Liberalism or Prolonged Partisan Warfare?" In *Dynamics of American Democracy: Partisan Polarization, Political Competition and Government Performance*, edited by Eric M. Patashnik and Wendy J. Schiller, 40–62. University Press of Kansas.

Grossmann, Matt, and David A. Hopkins. 2016. *Asymmetric Politics: Ideological Republicans and Group Interest Democrats*. Oxford University Press.

———. 2022. "Still the Party of Business? How the Diploma Divide and the Culture War Have Complicated Republicans' Alliance with Corporate America." Paper presented at the Annual Meeting of the Midwest Political Science Association, Chicago, Illinois. April 7–10.

Grossmann, Matt, and Christopher Wlezien. 2023. "A Thermostatic Model of Congressional Elections." Paper presented at the Southern Political Science Association. https://www.matthewg.org/thermostatic.pdf.

Grumbach, Jacob M. 2022. *Laboratories against Democracy: How National Parties Transformed State Politics*. Princeton.

Gunter, Joel. 2020. "Sanctuary Counties: Inside Virginia's Gun Rights Resistance." *BBC News*, February 13. https://www.bbc.com/news/world-us-canada-51483541.

Gusmano, Michael K. 2014. "Promoting Health Care Quality and Safety (1960s–Present)." In *Guide to U.S. Health and Health Care Policy*, edited by Thomas R. Oliver. CQ Press.

Gustafson, Kaaryn. 2009. "The Criminalization of Poverty." *Journal of Criminal Law and Criminology* 99:643–716.

Hacker, Jacob S. 1997. *The Road to Nowhere: The Genesis of President Clinton's Plan for Health Security*. Princeton University Press.

———. 1998. "The Historical Logic of National Health Insurance: Structure and Sequence in the Development of British, Canadian, and U.S. Medical Policy." *Studies in American Political Development* 12 (1): 57–130.

———. 2001. "Learning from Defeat? Political Analysis and the Failure of Health Care Reform in the United States." *British Journal of Political Science* 31 (1): 61–94.

———. 2002. *The Divided Welfare State: The Battle over Public and Private Social Benefits in the United States*. Cambridge University Press.

———. 2010. "The Road to Somewhere: Why Health Reform Happened: Or Why Political Scientists Who Write about Public Policy Shouldn't Assume They Know How to Shape It." *Perspectives on Politics* 8 (3): 861–76.

———. 2019. "Medicare Expansion as a Path as Well as a Destination: Achieving Universal Insurance through a New Politics of Medicare." *ANNALS of the American Academy of Political and Social Science* 685 (1): 135–53.

Hacker, Jacob S., Alexander Hertel-Fernandez, Paul Pierson, and Kathleen Thelen. 2022. "Introduction: The American Political Economy: A Framework and Agenda for Research." In *The American Political Economy: Politics, Markets, and Power*, edited by Jacob S. Hacker, Alexander Hertel-Fernandez, Paul Pierson, and Kathleen Thelen, 1–48. Cambridge University Press, 2022.

Hacker, Jacob S., and Paul Pierson. 2002. "Business Power and Social Policy: Employers and the Formation of the American Welfare State." *Politics & Society* 30 (2): 277–325.

———. 2005. *Off Center: The Republican Revolution and the Erosion of American Democracy.* Yale University Press.

———. 2018. "The Dog That Almost Barked: What the ACA Repeal Fight Says about the Resilience of the American Welfare State." *Journal of Health Politics, Policy and Law* 43 (4): 551–77.

———. 2019. "Policy Feedback in an Age of Polarization." *ANNALS of the American Academy of Political and Social Science* 685 (1): 8–28.

———. 2020. *Let Them Eat Tweets: How the Right Rules in an Age of Extreme Inequality.* Liveright Publishing.

Hacker, Jacob S., Paul Pierson, and Kathleen Thelen. 2015. "Drift and Conversion: Hidden Faces of Institutional Change." In *Advances in Comparative-Historical Analysis*, edited by Mahoney James and Kathleen Thelen, 180–208. Cambridge University Press.

Haeder, Simon F., and David L. Weimer. 2013. "You Can't Make Me Do It: State Implementation of Insurance Exchanges under the Affordable Care Act." *Public Administration Review* 73 (s1): S34–47.

Hansard, Sara. 2020. "Biden Risks Backlash in Trying to Curb 'Skinny' Health Plans." Bloomberg Law, December 23. https://news.bloomberglaw.com/health-law-and-business/biden-bid-to -curb-skinny-health-plans-to-confront-obstacles.

Hansen, Claire. 2022. "How Much of President Donald Trump's Border Wall Was Built?" *US News & World Report*, February 7. https://www.usnews.com/news/politics/articles/2022-02 -07/how-much-of-president-donald-trumps-border-wall-was-built.

Healy, Jack. 2013. "Some States Push Measures to Repel New U.S. Gun Laws." *New York Times*, February 8. https://www.nytimes.com/2013/02/08/us/some-states-try-to-repel-new-federal -gun-laws.html.

Herd, Pamela, and Donald P. Moynihan. 2019. *Administrative Burden: Policymaking by Other Means.* Russell Sage Foundation.

Herrera, Jack. 2021. "One Way Trump May Have Changed Immigration Forever." *Politico*, March 2. https://www.politico.com/news/magazine/2021/03/02/biden-immigration-trump -legacy-asylum-refugees-472008.

Hershey, Robert D., Jr. 1989. "Bush Signs Savings Legislation; Remaking of Industry Starts Fast." *New York Times*, August 10. https://www.nytimes.com/1989/08/10/business/bush-signs-savings -legislation-remaking-of-industry-starts-fast.html.

Hertel-Fernandez, Alexander. 2016. "Explaining Durable Business Coalitions in U.S. Politics: Conservatives and Corporate Interests across America's Statehouses." *Studies in American Political Development* 30 (1):.1–18.

———. 2019. *State Capture: How Conservative Activists, Big Businesses, and Wealthy Donors Reshaped the American States—and the Nation.* Oxford University Press.

Hertel-Fernandez, Alexander, Theda Skocpol, and Daniel Lynch. 2016. "Business Associations, Conservative Networks, and the Ongoing Republican War over Medicaid Expansion." *Journal of Health Politics, Policy and Law* 41 (2): 239–86.

Hess, Frederick M., and Max Eden. 2017. *The Every Student Succeeds Act (ESSA): What It Means for Schools, Systems, and States.* Harvard Education Press.

Heyward, Giulia. 2022. "What We Know about the DeSantis-Disney Rift." *New York Times*, August 25. https://www.nytimes.com/article/disney-florida-desantis.html.

Higham, John. 1985. *Strangers in the Land: Patterns of American Nativism, 1860–1925.* Atheneum.

Hilzenrath, David S. 1998. "Art Imitates Life When It Comes to Frustration with HMOs." *Washington Post*, February 10. https://www.washingtonpost.com/wp-srv/business/longterm/ethics/hollywood.htm.

Himmelfarb, Richard. 1995. *Catastrophic Politics: The Rise and Fall of the Medicare Catastrophic Coverage Act of 1988*. Pennsylvania State University Press.

Hirschman, Albert O. 1991. *The Rhetoric of Reaction: Perversity, Futility, Jeopardy*. Harvard University Press.

Hochschild, Arlie Russell. 2016. *Strangers in Their Own Land: Anger and Mourning on the American Right*. New Press.

Hoffman, Jan. 2019. "How Anti-Vaccine Sentiment Took Hold in the United States." *New York Times*, September 24. https://www.nytimes.com/2019/09/23/health/anti-vaccination-movement-us.html.

Holden, Charles J., Zach Messitte, and Jerald Podair. 2019. *Republican Populist: Spiro Agnew and the Origins of Donald Trump's America*. University of Virginia Press.

Holley, Peter. 2016. "Britain Issues Warning for LGBT Travelers Visiting North Carolina and Mississippi." *Washington Post*, April 20. https://www.washingtonpost.com/news/worldviews/wp/2016/04/20/britain-issues-warning-for-lgbt-travelers-visiting-north-carolina-and-mississippi/.

Holmes, Steven A. 1990. "Bush Vetoes Bill on Family Leave." *New York Times*, January 30. https://www.nytimes.com/1990/06/30/us/bush-vetoes-bill-on-family-leave.html.

Homans, Charles. 2021. "How Armed Protests Are Creating a New Kind of Politics." *New York Times*, January 26. https://www.nytimes.com/interactive/2021/01/26/magazine/armed-militia-movement-gun-laws.html.

Hong, Jane. 2015. "The Law That Created Illegal Immigration." *Los Angeles Times*, October 3. https://www.latimes.com/opinion/op-ed/la-oe-1002-hong-1965-immigration-act-2015 1002-story.html.

Hopkins, Daniel J., and Kalind Parish. 2019. "The Medicaid Expansion and Attitudes toward the Affordable Care Act: Testing for a Policy Feedback on Mass Opinion." *Public Opinion Quarterly* 83 (1): 123–34.

Hopkins, David A. 2022. "A Backlash to Dobbs Depends on How Much It Affects the Middle Class." Honest Graft: The Promise and Puzzles of American Politics, June 28. http://www.honestgraft.com/2022/06/a-backlash-to-dobbs-depends-on-how-much.html.

House Ways and Means Committee. 2012. "Table 6.2: Total Outlays, Number of New Recipients, and Average Weekly Payments for Trade Readjustment Allowances, Fiscal Years 1975–2011," *Green Book*. https://greenbook-waysandmeans.house.gov/sites/greenbook.waysandmeans.house.gov/files/2012/documents/TAA%20Table%206-2.pdf.

Hubert, Gabrielle. 2020. "'Bathrooms and Boycotts': HB2, LGBT+ Nondiscrimination Protections, and Political Misinformation." *Kennedy School Review* 20:25–29.

Huetteman, Emmarie. 2017. "Senate Democrats Aim Their Limited Firepower at Trump's Nominees." *New York Times*, January 31. https://www.nytimes.com/2017/01/30/us/politics/senate-democrats-trump-nominees.html.

Hulse, Carl, and David M. Herszenhorn. 2010. "Bank Bailout Is Potent Issue for Fall Elections." *New York Times*, July 11. https://www.nytimes.com/2010/07/11/us/politics/11tarp.html.

Human Rights Campaign and Equality North Carolina. n.d. Letter to Governor McCrory. Accessed February 21, 2021. http://assets2.hrc.org/files/assets/resources/NC_CEO_Letter_(3).pdf.

Huntington, Samuel P. 2004. *Who Are We? The Challenges to America's National Identity*. Simon and Schuster.

Hurd, Richard W., and Jill K. Kriesky. 1986. "'The Rise and Demise of PATCO' Reconstructed." *Industrial and Labor Relations Review* 40 (1): 115–22.

"Incumbents Dominate Mid-Term National Elections; Democratic Party Makes Small Gains; Predicted Backlash Fizzles." 1990. *Facts on File World News Digest*, November. https://advance-lexis-com.revproxy.brown.edu/api/document?collection=news&id=urn:contentItem:3SJ4-G190-000Y-N360-00000-00&context=1516831.

Irwin, Douglas A. 2017. *Clashing over Commerce: A History of US Trade Policy*. University of Chicago Press.

Jacobs, Alan M. 2011. *Governing for the Long Term: Democracy and the Politics of Investment*. Cambridge University Press.

Jacobs, Alan M., and R. Kent Weaver. 2015. "When Policies Undo Themselves: Self-Undermining Feedback as a Source of Policy Change." *Governance* 28 (4): 441–57.

Jacobs, Lawrence R., and Suzanne Mettler. 2018. "When and How New Policy Creates New Politics: Examining the Feedback Effects of the Affordable Care Act on Public Opinion." *Perspectives on Politics* 16 (2): 345–63.

———. 2020. "What Health Reform Tells Us about American Politics." *Journal of Health Politics, Policy and Law* 45 (4): 581–93.

Jacobs, Lawrence R., Suzanne Mettler, and Ling Zhu. 2019. "Affordable Care Act Moving to New Stage of Public Acceptance." *Journal of Health Politics, Policy and Law* 44 (6): 911–17.

Jacobs, Meg. 2018. "Obama's Fight against Global Warming." In *The Presidency of Barack Obama*, edited by Julian Zelizer, 62–77. Princeton University Press.

Jacobson, Gary C. 2019. "Extreme Referendum: Donald Trump and the 2018 Midterm Elections." *Political Science Quarterly* 134 (1): 9–38.

Jacobson, Gary C., and Jamie L. Carson. 2020. *The Politics of Congressional Elections*. Rowman & Littlefield.

James, Sandy E., Jody L. Herman, Susan Rankin, Mara Keisling, Lisa Mottet, and Ma'ayan Anafi. 2016. *The Report of the 2015 U.S. Transgender Survey*. National Center for Transgender Equality.

Jeene, Marjolein, Wim van Oorschot, and Wilfred Uunk. 2013. "Popular Criteria for the Welfare Deservingness of Disability Pensioners: The Influence of Structural and Cultural Factors." *Social Indicators Research* 110 (3): 1103–17.

Jenkins, Aric. 2018. "Jeff Sessions: Parents and Children Illegally Crossing the Border Will Be Separated." *Time*, May 7. https://time.com/5268572/jeff-sessions-illegal-border-separated/.

Jenkins, Jeffery A., and Sidney M. Milkis. 2014. *The Politics of Major Policy Reform in Postwar America*. Cambridge University Press.

Jervis, Robert. 1998. *System Effects: Complexity in Political and Social Life*. Princeton University Press.

Johnson, C. Donald. 2018. *The Wealth of a Nation: A History of Trade Politics in America*. Oxford University Press.

Jones, Bryan D., and Frank R. Baumgartner. 2005. *The Politics of Attention: How Government Prioritizes Problems*. University of Chicago Press.

Jones, Bryan D., Sean M. Theriault, and Michelle Whyman. 2019. *The Great Broadening: How the Vast Expansion of the Policymaking Agenda Transformed American Politics*. University of Chicago Press.

Jones, David K. 2017. *Exchange Politics: Opposing Obamacare in Battleground States*. Oxford University Press.

Jones, Jeffrey M. 2017. "Americans Hold Record Liberal Views on Most Moral Issues." Gallup .com, May 11. https://news.gallup.com/poll/210542/americans-hold-record-liberal-views-moral -issues.aspx.

———. 2023. "More Say Birth Gender Should Dictate Sports Participation." Gallup.com, June 12. https://news.gallup.com/poll/507023/say-birth-gender-dictate-sports-participation.aspx.

Joslyn, Mark R., Donald P. Haider-Markel, Michael Baggs, and Andrew Bilbo. 2017. "Emerging Political Identities? Gun Ownership and Voting in Presidential Elections." *Social Science Quarterly* 98 (2): 382–96.

Kagan, Robert A. 2019. *Adversarial Legalism: The American Way of Law*. Harvard University Press.

Kandel, William A. 2019. "The Trump Administration's 'Zero Tolerance' Immigration Enforcement Policy." *CRS Report* R45266. Library of Congress, Congressional Research Service.

Kanno-Youngs, Zolan, and Michael D. Shear. 2020. "Trump Virtually Cuts Off Refugees as He Unleashes a Tirade on Immigrants." *New York Times*, October 1. https://www.nytimes .com/2020/10/01/us/politics/trump-refugees.html.

Karnitschnig, Matthew. 2015. "Backlash Grows against Merkel over Refugees." *Politico*, September 11. https://www.politico.eu/article/backlash-merkel-refugees-migration-germany-coali tion-pressure/.

Katz, Jonathan M., and Erik Eckholm. 2016. "Anti-Gay Laws Bring Backlash in Mississippi and North Carolina." *New York Times*, April 5. https://www.nytimes.com/2016/04/06/us/gay -rights-mississippi-north-carolina.html.

Keith, Katie. 2019. "ACA Provisions in New Budget Bill." *Health Affairs*, December 20. https:// www.healthaffairs.org/do/10.1377/hblog20191220.115975/full/.

Kessler, Glenn. 2012. "Sarah Palin, 'Death Panels' and 'Obamacare.'" *Washington Post*, June 27. https://www.washingtonpost.com/blogs/fact-checker/post/sarah-palin-death-panels-and -obamacare/2012/06/27/gJQAysUP7V_blog.html.

———. 2013. "Obama's Pledge That 'No One Will Take Away' Your Health Plan." *Washington Post*, October 30. https://www.washingtonpost.com/news/fact-checker/wp/2013/10/30 /obamas-pledge-that-no-one-will-take-away-your-health-plan/.

Kettl, Donald F. 1991. "The Savings-and-Loan Bailout: The Mismatch between the Headlines and the Issues." *PS: Political Science and Politics* 24 (3): 441–47.

KFF. 2022a. "KFF Tracking Poll: The Public's Views on the ACA." March 31. https://www .kff.org/interactive/kff-health-tracking-poll-the-publics-views-on-the-aca/#?response =Favorable—Unfavorable&aRange=all&group=Party%2520ID::Democrat::Independent.

———. 2022b. "Status of State Medicaid Expansion Decisions: Interactive Map." November 9. https://www.kff.org/medicaid/issue-brief/status-of-state-medicaid-expansion-decisions -interactive-map/.

Kilborn, Peter T. 1988. "A Savings Rescue Looms as Big Issue to Be Faced in '89." *New York Times*, September 23. https://www.nytimes.com/1988/09/23/business/a-savings-rescue-looms-as -big-issue-to-be-faced-in-89.html.

King, Anthony. 1997. "The Vulnerable American Politician." *British Journal of Political Science* 27 (1): 1–22.

Kingdon, John W. 1984. *Agendas, Alternatives, and Public Policies*. Little, Brown.

Kitschelt, Herbert P. 1986. "Political Opportunity Structures and Political Protest: Anti-Nuclear Movements in Four Democracies." *British Journal of Political Science* 16 (1): 57–85.

Klein, Alyson. 2015. "No Child Left Behind: An Overview." *Education Week*, April 10. https:// www.edweek.org/ew/section/multimedia/no-child-left-behind-overview-definition-sum mary.html.

Klein, Ezra. 2022. "America Has Turned Its Back on Its Poorest Families." Opinion, *New York Times*, April 17. https://www.nytimes.com/2022/04/17/opinion/biden-child-tax-credit.html.

Kliff, Sarah. 2015. "One Poll That Explains Why Obamacare's Cadillac Tax Is Doomed." Vox, September 30. https://www.vox.com/2015/9/30/9423335/cadillac-tax-poll.

———. 2017. "Is Health Care a Right? What Ohio and Kentucky Teach Us." Vox, September 29. https://www.vox.com/policy-and-politics/2017/9/29/16387380/health-care-right-ohio -kentucky-atul-gawande.

Kliff, Sarah, and Margot Sanger-Katz. 2021. "At Last, Democrats Get Chance to Engineer Obama-care 2.0." *New York Times*, February 28. https://www.nytimes.com/2021/02/27/upshot /biden-health-plan-obamacare.html.

Knight, Athelia. 1990. "SL Fury Engulfs Congress." *Washington Post*, October 26. https://www .washingtonpost.com/archive/politics/1990/10/26/sl-fury-engulfs-congress/fbe8349a -ded7-4781-addd-f071b69ff7da/.

Kolker, Abigail F. 2016. *Noncitizen Eligibility for Federal Public Assistance: Policy Overview*. Con-gressional Research Service Report RL33809, December 12, 21. https://crsreports.congress .gov/product/pdf/RL/RL33809.

Kopan, Tal, and Eugene Scott. 2016. "North Carolina Governor Signs Controversial Transgen-der Bill." CNN Politics, CNN, March 24. https://www.cnn.com/2016/03/23/politics/north -carolina-gender-bathrooms-bill/index.html.

Kousser, Thad. 2018. "The Biggest Shift of the Midterms Wasn't in Congress—It Was in the States." *Fortune*, November 12. https://fortune.com/2018/11/12/state-legislatures-blue-wave -2018/.

Kriner, Douglas L., and Eric Schickler. 2016. *Investigating the President: Congressional Checks on Presidential Power*. Princeton University Press.

Kronenfeld, Jennie J. 1997. *The Changing Federal Role in US Health Care Policy*. Greenwood Publishing Group.

Krueger, Anne O. 2020a. "America Must Mend Many Fences on Trade." *Project Syndicate*, No-vember 20. https://www.project-syndicate.org/commentary/restoring-us-trade-leadership -after-trump-by-anne-krueger-2020-11.

———. 2020b. "Trump's Backward March on Trade." *Project Syndicate*, January 20. https:// www.project-syndicate.org/commentary/trump-trade-war-damage-2020-by-anne-krueger -2020-01.

———. 2020c. "Trump's Spectacular Trade Failure." *Project Syndicate*, September 22. https:// www.project-syndicate.org/commentary/trump-trade-policy-is-a-failure-by-anne-krueger -2020-09.

Krugman, Paul. 2022. "Can Inflation Reduction Save the Planet?" Opinion, *New York Times*, August 1. https://www.nytimes.com/2022/08/01/opinion/can-inflation-reduction-save-the -planet.html.

Kruse, Kevin M., and Julian E. Zelizer. 2019. *Fault Lines: A History of the United States since 1974*. W. W. Norton.

Kuziemko, Ilyana, Ryan W. Buell, Taly Reich, and Michael I. Norton. 2014. "'Last-Place Aversion': Evidence and Redistributive Implications." *Quarterly Journal of Economics* 129 (1): 105–50.

Lacombe, Matthew. 2018. "This Is How the NRA 'Politically Weaponized' Its Membership." *Washington Post*, February 23. https://www.washingtonpost.com/news/monkey-cage/wp/2017/10/11/this-is-how-the-nra-politically-weaponized-its-membership/.

———. 2019. "The Political Weaponization of Gun Owners: The National Rifle Association's Cultivation, Dissemination, and Use of a Group Social Identity." *Journal of Politics* 81 (4): 1342–56.

———. 2022. "Post-Loss Power Building: The Feedback Effects of Policy Loss on Group Identity and Collective Action." *Policy Studies Journal* 50:507–26.

Landers, Elizabeth. 2018. "Key Trump Senate Ally Asks for Halt to Family Separations." CNN, June 19. https://www.cnn.com/2018/06/19/politics/orrin-hatch-immigration-plan/index.html.

Lauter, David. 1993. "283 Top Economists Back Trade Pact, Letter Shows." *Los Angeles Times*, September 4. https://www.latimes.com/archives/la-xpm-1993-09-04-mn-31519-story.html.

Lavoie, Denise. 2019. "Second Amendment Sanctuary Push Aims to Defy New Gun Laws." AP News, December 21. https://apnews.com/article/b83c6654e4a618aec1e88a2ca2eea07a.

Lawrence, Robert Z. 2002. "International Trade Policy in the 1990s." In *American Economic Policy in the 1990s*, edited by Jeffrey A. Frankel and Peter R. Orszag, 277–327. MIT Press.

Lee, Frances E. 2009. *Beyond Ideology: Politics, Principles, and Partisanship in the U.S. Senate.* University of Chicago Press.

———. 2014. "American Politics Is More Competitive Than Ever. That's Making Partisanship Worse." *Washington Post*, January 9. https://www.washingtonpost.com/news/monkey-cage/wp/2014/01/09/american-politics-is-more-competitive-than-ever-thats-making-partisanship-worse/.

———. 2016. *Insecure Majorities: Congress and the Perpetual Campaign.* University of Chicago Press.

———. 2022. "Crosscutting Cleavages, Political Institutions, and Democratic Resilience in the United States." In *Democratic Resilience: Can the United States Withstand Rising Polarization?*, edited by Robert C. Lieberman, Suzanne Mettler, and Kenneth M. Roberts, 95–117. Cambridge University Press.

Leech, Beth L., Frank R. Baumgartner, Timothy M. La Pira, and Nicholas A. Semanko. 2005. "Drawing Lobbyists to Washington: Government Activity and the Demand for Advocacy." *Political Research Quarterly* 58 (1): 19–30.

Leff, Lisa. 2016. "The Fight over Transgender Rights in School Restrooms Intensifies." *PBS NewsHour*, February 22. https://www.pbs.org/newshour/nation/the-fight-over-transgender-rights-in-school-restrooms-intensifies.

Leonhardt, David. 2010. "In Health Bill, Obama Attacks Wealth Inequality." *New York Times*, March 24. https://www.nytimes.com/2010/03/24/business/24leonhardt.html.

Leonor, Mel. 2020. "Gun-Rights Rally Draws 22,000 to Virginia Capitol; No Violence, One Arrest Reported." *Richmond Times-Dispatch*, January 20. https://richmond.com/news/gun-rights-rally-draws-22-000-to-virginia-capitol-no-violence-one-arrest-reported/article_d865335d-638c-5d57-945c-51828d43e32d.html.

Lepore, Jill. 2018. *These Truths: A History of the United States.* W. W. Norton.

Lerman, Amy E., and Katherine T. McCabe. 2017. "Personal Experience and Public Opinion: A Theory and Test of Conditional Policy Feedback." *Journal of Politics* 79 (2): 624–41.

Levin, Dan. 2019. "North Carolina Reaches Settlement on 'Bathroom Bill.'" *New York Times*, July 23. https://www.nytimes.com/2019/07/23/us/north-carolina-transgender-bathrooms.html.

Levin, Martin A., Daniel DiSalvo, and Martin M. Shapiro, eds. 2012. *Building Coalitions, Making Policy: The Politics of the Clinton, Bush, and Obama Presidencies.* Johns Hopkins University Press.

Levine, Michael E. 2006. "Why Weren't the Airlines Reregulated?" *Yale Journal on Regulation* 23 (2): 269–97.

Lichtenstein, Nelson. 2018. "A Fabulous Failure: Clinton's 1990s and the Origins of Our Times." *American Prospect*, January 29. https://prospect.org/health/fabulous-failure-clinton-s-1990s-origins-times/.

Lind, Dara. 2014. "Obama Is Deporting More Immigrants Than Any President in History: Explained." Vox, April 9. https://www.vox.com/2014/4/9/5575006/2-million-immigrants-have-been-deported-under-obama.

———. 2018. "The Trump Administration's Separation of Families at the Border, Explained." Vox, August 14. https://www.vox.com/2018/6/11/17443198/children-immigrant-families-separated-parents.

Lindblom, Charles E. 1983. "Politics and Markets: The World's Political-Economics Systems." *Journal of Business Ethics* 2 (2): 166–68.

Lipka, Michael. 2016. "Americans Are Divided over Which Public Bathrooms Transgender People Should Use." Pew Research Center, October 3. https://www.pewresearch.org/fact-tank/2016/10/03/americans-are-divided-over-which-public-bathrooms-transgender-people-should-use/.

Lipset, Seymour Martin, and Earl Raab. 1970. *The Politics of Unreason: Right Wing Extremism in America, 1790–1970.* Harper & Row.

Liptak, Adam. 2012. "Blocking Parts of Arizona Law, Justices Allow Its Centerpiece." *New York Times*, June 25. https://www.nytimes.com/2012/06/26/us/supreme-court-rejects-part-of-arizona-immigration-law.html.

Litan, Robert, William Isaac, and William Taylor. 1994. "Financial Regulation." In *American Economic Policy in the 1980s*, edited by Martin Feldstein, 519–72. University of Chicago Press.

Lobosco, Katie. 2021. "Biden Has Left Trump's China Tariffs in Place. Here's Why." CNN, March 25. https://www.cnn.com/2021/03/24/politics/china-tariffs-biden-policy/index.html.

Lopez, German. 2020. "Virginia's Historic Gun Control Fight, Explained." Vox, January 23. https://www.vox.com/policy-and-politics/2020/1/23/21075335/virginia-gun-control-laws-mass-shootings.

Lucas, Deborah. "Measuring the Cost of Bailouts." 2019. *Annual Review of Financial Economics* 11 (1): 85–108.

Lynch, David J. 2021. "Biden Keeps Many Trump Tariffs in Place, Confounding Businesses Hoping for Reprieve." *Washington Post*, August 17. https://www.washingtonpost.com/us-policy/2021/08/17/biden-china-tariffs-trump/.

Lyons, Richard D. 1970. "Administration Seeks Short-Run Gains in Nation's Medical System." *New York Times*, January 12. https://www.nytimes.com/1970/01/12/archives/administration-seeks-shortrun-gains-in-nations-medical-system.html.

Mann, James. 2015. *George W. Bush: The American Presidents Series: The 43rd President, 2001–2009.* Times Books.

Mansbridge, Jane, and Shauna L. Shames. 2008. "Toward a Theory of Backlash: Dynamic Resistance and the Central Role of Power." *Politics & Gender* 4 (4): 623–34.

Marmor, Theodore R. 1973. *The Politics of Medicare*. Transaction Publishers.

Marmor, Theodore, Jonathan Oberlander, and Joseph White. 2009. "The Obama Administration's Options for Health Care Cost Control: Hope versus Reality." *Annals of Internal Medicine* 150 (7): 485–89.

Martinez, Gebe. 2010. "Learning from Proposition 187: California's Past Is Arizona's Prologue." Center for American Progress, May 5. https://www.americanprogress.org/issues/immigration/news/2010/05/05/7847/learning-from-proposition-187/.

Mason, David L. 2004. *From Buildings and Loans to Bail-Outs: A History of the American Savings and Loan Industry, 1831–1995*. Cambridge University Press.

Mason, Lilliana. 2018. *Uncivil Agreement: How Politics Became Our Identity*. University of Chicago Press.

Mastanduno, Michael. 2020. "Trump's Trade Revolution." *Forum* 17 (4): 523–48.

Mattingly, Justin. 2020. "Northam Signs Five Gun Control Measures, Seeks to Amend Two Others." *Richmond Times-Dispatch*, April 10. https://richmond.com/news/virginia/northam-signs-five-gun-control-measures-seeks-to-amend-two-others/article_daeae239-e028-5073-9181-37438221b64b.html.

Matush, Kelly. 2023. "Harnessing Backlash: How Leaders Can Benefit from Antagonizing Foreign Actors." *British Journal of Political Science*, January 25, 1–17. doi:10.1017/S0007123422000370.

Mauer, Marc, and Virginia McCalmont. 2013. *A Lifetime of Punishment: The Impact of Felony Drug Bans on Welfare Benefits*. Sentencing Project, November 14. https://www.sentencingproject.org/reports/a-lifetime-of-punishment-the-impact-of-the-felony-drug-ban-on-welfare-benefits/.

Mayer, Frederick W. 1998. *Interpreting NAFTA: The Science and Art of Political Analysis*. Columbia University Press.

Mayhew, David R. 1991. *Divided We Govern: Party Control, Lawmaking, and Investigations, 1946–1990*. Yale University Press, 1991.

———. 2000. *America's Congress: Actions in the Public Sphere, James Madison through Newt Gingrich*. Yale University Press.

———. 2011. *Partisan Balance: Why Political Parties Don't Kill the US Constitutional System*. Princeton University Press, 2011.

———. 2012a. "Lawmaking as a Cognitive Enterprise." In *Living Legislation: Durability, Change, and the Politics of American Lawmaking*, edited by Jeffrey Jenkins and Eric Patashnik, 255–64. University of Chicago Press.

———. 2012b. "Politics, Elections, and Policymaking." In *Building Coalitions, Making Policy: The Politics of the Clinton, Bush, and Obama Presidencies*, edited by Martin A. Levin, Daniel DiSalvo, and Martin M. Shapiro, 369–90. Johns Hopkins Press.

———. 2016. "Patterns in American Elections." In *The Oxford Handbook of American Political Development*, edited by Richard Valelly, Suzanne Mettler, and Robert C. Lieberman, 425–44. Oxford University Press.

———. 2017. *The Imprint of Congress*. Yale University Press.

McCarthy, Justin. 2022. "Same-Sex Marriage Support Inches up to New High of 71%." Gallup.com, June 1. https://news.gallup.com/poll/393197/same-sex-marriage-support-inches-new-high.aspx.

McCartin, Joseph A. 2011a. *Collision Course: Ronald Reagan, the Air Traffic Controllers, and the Strike That Changed America*. Oxford University Press.

———. 2011b. "The Strike That Busted Unions." *New York Times*, August 2. https://www.nytimes.com/2011/08/03/opinion/reagan-vs-patco-the-strike-that-busted-unions.html.

McCarty, Nolan. 2014. "What We Know and Don't Know about Our Polarized Politics." *Washington Post*, January 8. https://www.washingtonpost.com/news/monkey-cage/wp/2014/01/08/what-we-know-and-dont-know-about-our-polarized-politics/.

McCarty, Nolan, Keith T. Poole, Thomas Romer, and Howard Rosenthal. 2010. "Political Fortunes: On Finance & Its Regulation." *Daedalus* 139 (4): 61–73.

McCarty, Nolan, Keith T. Poole, and Howard Rosenthal. 2013. *Political Bubbles: Financial Crises and the Failure of American Democracy*. Princeton University Press.

———. 2016. *Polarized America: The Dance of Ideology and Unequal Riches*. MIT Press.

McFadden, Robert D. 2006. "Across the U.S., Growing Rallies for Immigration." *New York Times*, April 10. https://www.nytimes.com/2006/04/10/us/across-the-us-growing-rallies-for-immigration.html.

McGeehan, Patrick. 2005. "After Backlash, Amtrak Delays Fare Increase: Washington Wants a Better Explanation." *New York Times*, September 16. https://www.nytimes.com/2005/09/16/nyregion/after-backlash-amtrak-delays-fare-increase.html.

McGraw, Meridith. 2021. "The GOP Waves White Flag in the Same-Sex Marriage Wars." *Politico*, August 16. https://www.politico.com/news/2021/08/16/republicans-gay-marriage-wars-505041.

Mechanic, David. 2001. "The Managed Care Backlash: Perceptions and Rhetoric in Health Care Policy and the Potential for Health Care Reform." *Milbank Quarterly* 79 (1): 35–54.

Meckler, Laura, and Scott Clement. 2023. "Most Americans Support Anti-Trans Laws Favored by GOP, Poll Shows." *Washington Post*, May 6. https://www.washingtonpost.com/education/2023/05/05/trans-poll-gop-politics-laws/.

Mehta, Dhrumil. 2018. "Separating Families at the Border Is Really Unpopular." FiveThirtyEight, June 19. https://fivethirtyeight.com/features/separating-families-at-the-border-is-really-unpopular/.

Melnick, R. Shep. 2018. *The Transformation of Title IX: Regulating Gender Equality in Education*. Brookings Institution Press.

"Merkel at Her Limit." 2015. *Economist*, October 10. https://www.economist.com/europe/2015/10/10/merkel-at-her-limit.

Mettler, Suzanne. 2005. *Soldiers to Citizens: The GI Bill and the Making of the Greatest Generation*. Oxford University Press.

———. 2016. "The Policyscape and the Challenges of Contemporary Politics to Policy Maintenance." *Perspectives on Politics* 14 (2): 369–90.

———. 2018. *The Government-Citizen Disconnect*. Russell Sage Foundation.

Mettler, Suzanne, Lawrence R. Jacobs, and Ling Zhu. 2022. "Policy Threat, Partisanship, and the Case of the Affordable Care Act." *American Political Science Review*, 1–15. https://doi.org/10.1017/S0003055422000612.

Mettler, Suzanne, and Robert C. Lieberman. 2020. *Four Threats: The Recurring Crises of American Democracy*. St. Martin's Press.

Meyer, David S. 2004. "Protest and Political Opportunities." *Annual Review of Sociology* 30 (1): 125–45.

Meyer, Robinson. 2022. "Wait, Why Wasn't There a Climate Backlash?" *Atlantic Monthly*, November 16. https://www.theatlantic.com/science/archive/2022/11/biden-inflation-reduction

-act-midterms-climate/672136/?utm_source=twitter&utm_campaign=the-atlantic&utm
_content=edit-promo&utm_medium=social&utm_term=2022-11-16T22%3A50%3A08.

Michener, Jamila. 2020. "Race, Politics, and the Affordable Care Act." *Journal of Health Politics, Policy and Law* 45 (4): 547–66.

Milkis, Sidney M., and Daniel J. Tichenor. 2019. *Rivalry and Reform: Presidents, Social Movements, and the Transformation of American Politics.* University of Chicago Press.

Miller, Michael E. 2020. "A Tense Debate over Guns in Virginia Beach, Still Reeling from a Mass Shooting." *Washington Post,* January 19. https://www.washingtonpost.com/local/a-tense-debate
-over-guns-in-virginia-beach-still-reeling-from-a-mass-shooting/2020/01/19/a4f514d6
-3a1d-11ea-bf30-ad313e4ec754_story.html.

Miller, Ryan W. 2020. "Virginia Gov. Northam Signs Host of Gun Control Bills into Law Months after Richmond Rally." *USA Today,* April 10. https://www.usatoday.com/story/news
/nation/2020/04/10/virginia-governor-northam-signs-gun-control-measures-law/512
9936002/.

Milligan, Susan. 2018. "Democrats Win Big in Statehouses." *US News & World Report,* November 7. https://www.usnews.com/news/politics/articles/2018-11-07/democrats-win-big
-in-statehouses.

Milwood, Pete. 2022. "No, Not Only Nixon Could Go to China." *Sources and Methods,* Woodrow Wilson International Center for Scholars, February 21. https://www.wilsoncenter.org
/blog-post/no-not-only-nixon-could-go-china.

Mishel, Lawrence, and Josh Bivens. 2021. *Identifying the Policy Levers Generating Wage Suppression and Wage Inequality.* Economic Policy Institute, May 13. https://www.epi.org
/unequalpower/publications/wage-suppression-inequality/.

Moe, Terry M. 2011. *Special Interest: Teachers Unions and America's Public Schools.* Brookings Institution Press.

———. 2014. "Teachers Unions and the Politics of American Education Reform: The Power of Vested Interests." In *The Politics of Major Policy Reform in Postwar America,* edited by Jeffery A. Jenkins and Sidney M. Milkis, 129–56. Cambridge University Press.

———. 2015. "Vested Interests and Political Institutions." *Political Science Quarterly* 130 (2): 277–318.

———. 2019. *The Politics of Institutional Reform: Katrina, Education, and the Second Face of Power.* Cambridge University Press.

Moomaw, Graham. 2020. "Pro-Gun Localities Accounted for Nearly Half of Virginia's Red Flag Orders in Law's First Months." *Virginia Mercury,* October 6. https://www.virginiamercury
.com/2020/10/06/some-virginia-communities-that-took-pro-gun-rights-stances-are
-already-using-the-states-new-red-flag-law/.

Morgan, David. 1984. "Terminal Flight: The Air Traffic Controllers' Strike of 1981." *Journal of American Studies* 18 (2): 165–83.

Mueller, Keith J. 1988. "Federal Programs to Expire: The Case of Health Planning." *Public Administration Review* 48 (3): 719–25.

Murib, Zein. 2021. "Biden Reversed Trump Ban on Transgender People Serving in Military. Expect Backlash in States." *Washington Post,* February 3. https://www.washingtonpost.com
/politics/2021/02/03/biden-reversed-trump-ban-transgender-people-serving-military
-expect-backlash-states/.

Naftali, Timothy. 2007. *George H. W. Bush: The American Presidents Series: The 41st President, 1989–1993.* Macmillan.

Narea, Nicole. 2019. "The Demise of America's Asylum System under Trump, Explained." Vox, November 5. https://www.vox.com/2019/11/5/20947938/asylum-system-trump-demise-mexico-el-salvador-honduras-guatemala-immigration-court-border-ice-cbp.

———. 2021. "Biden Rescinds Trump's 'Zero-Tolerance' Policy That Enabled Family Separation." Vox, January 27. https://www.vox.com/policy-and-politics/2021/1/27/22252294/biden-zero-tolerance-family-separation-trump.

National Academies of Sciences, Engineering, and Medicine. 2017. *The Economic and Fiscal Consequences of Immigration.* Edited by Francine D. Blau and Christopher Mackie. National Academies Press. https://doi.org/10.17226/23550.

National Commission on Excellence in Education. 1983. "A Nation at Risk: The Imperative for Educational Reform." *Elementary School Journal* 84 (2): 113–30.

Neuberger, Thomas Stephen, and Thomas C. Crumplar. 1979. "Tax Exempt Religious Schools under Attack: Conflicting Goals of Religious Freedom and Racial Integration." *Fordham Law Review* 48:229.

Nevin, David, and Robert E. Bills. 1976. *The Schools That Fear Built: Segregationist Academies in the South.* Acropolis Books.

New York Times. 1978. "No More Winking at 'Seg Academies.'" December 8. https://www.nytimes.com/1978/12/08/archives/no-more-winking-at-seg-academies.html.

———. 1981. "The Air Strike Is Lost. Now What?" August 30. https://www.nytimes.com/1981/08/30/opinion/the-air-strike-is-lost-now-what.html.

———. 1982. "Counties Voice Fear of Cost on Alien Legalization." June 8. https://www.nytimes.com/1982/06/08/us/counties-voice-fear-of-cost-on-alien-legalization.html.

———. 1983. "The March and the Dream." August 27. https://www.nytimes.com/1983/08/27/opinion/no-headline-127776.html?searchResultPosition=1.

———. 1984. "Private Schools Backed on Tax-Exempt Status." July 4. https://www.nytimes.com/1984/07/04/us/private-schools-backed-on-tax-exempt-status.html.

Nivola, Pietro S. 1986. "The New Protectionism: U.S. Trade Policy in Historical Perspective." *Political Science Quarterly* 101 (4): 577–600.

Norris, Pippa, and Ronald Inglehart. 2019. *Cultural Backlash: Trump, Brexit, and Authoritarian Populism.* Cambridge University Press.

Northrup, Herbert R. 1984. "The Rise and Demise of PATCO." *Industrial and Labor Relations Review* 37 (2): 167–84.

Nowrasteh, Alex. 2021. "President Trump Reduced Legal Immigration. He Did Not Reduce Illegal Immigration." *Cato at Liberty,* Cato Institute, January 20. https://www.cato.org/blog/president-trump-reduced-legal-immigration-he-did-not-reduce-illegal-immigration.

Nyhan, Brendan. 2018. "How Trumpism Actually Made Americans More Favorable toward Immigrants." Medium, October 26. https://medium.com/@brendan.nyhan/how-trumpism-actually-made-americans-more-favorable-toward-immigrants-907b5a44fc12.

Nyhan, Brendan, Eric McGhee, John Sides, Seth Masket, and Steven Greene. 2012. "One Vote Out of Step? The Effects of Salient Roll Call Votes in the 2010 Election." *American Politics Research* 40 (5): 844–79.

Oberlander, Jonathan. 2003. *The Political Life of Medicare.* University of Chicago Press.

———. 2012. "The Future of Obamacare." *New England Journal of Medicine* 367 (23): 2165–67.

———. 2016a. "The $40 Trillion Question: Can Congress Control Health Care Spending?" In *Congress and Policy Making in the 21st Century,* edited by Jeffrey A. Jenkins and Eric M. Patashnik, 211–41. Cambridge University Press.

———. 2016b. "Implementing the Affordable Care Act: The Promise and Limits of Health Care Reform." *Journal of Health Politics, Policy and Law* 41 (4): 803–26.

———. 2017. "Repeal, Replace, Repair, Retreat—Republicans' Health Care Quagmire." *New England Journal of Medicine* 377 (11): 1001–3.

———. 2020. "The Ten Years' War: Politics, Partisanship, and the ACA." *Health Affairs* 39 (3): 471–78.

Oberlander, Jonathan, and Steven B. Spivack. 2018. "Technocratic Dreams, Political Realities: The Rise and Demise of Medicare's Independent Payment Advisory Board." *Journal of Health Politics, Policy and Law* 43 (3): 483–510.

Oberlander, Jonathan, and R. Kent Weaver. 2015. "Unraveling from Within? The Affordable Care Act and Self-Undermining Policy Feedbacks." *Forum* 13 (1): 37–62.

O'Brian, Neil. 2022. "Evangelicals Opposed Abortion Long before Their Leaders Caught Up." *Washington Post*, May 18. https://www.washingtonpost.com/politics/2022/05/18/dodds-evangelicals-roe-conservative-opinion/.

Office of Immigration Statistics, Department of Homeland Security. 2020. *2019 Yearbook of Immigration Statistics*, p. 125.

Office of Management and Budget. n.d. "Outlays by Budget Enforcement Act Category in Constant (FY 2012) Dollars: 1962–2027." Historical Tables, table 8.2. https://view.officeapps.live.com/op/view.aspx?src=https%3A%2F%2Fwww.whitehouse.gov%2Fwp-content%2Fuploads%2F2022%2F03%2Fhist08z2_fy2023.xlsx&wdOrigin=BROWSELINK.

Oliver, Thomas R., ed. 2014. *CQ Press Guide to U.S. Health and Health Care Policy*. SAGE Publications.

Oliver, Thomas R., Philip R. Lee, and Helene L. Lipton. 2004. "A Political History of Medicare and Prescription Drug Coverage." *Milbank Quarterly* 82 (2): 283–354.

Olson, Elizabeth. 1999. "World Trade Group Picking Up the Pieces from Seattle." *New York Times*, December 13. https://www.nytimes.com/1999/12/13/business/world-trade-group-picking-up-the-pieces-from-seattle.html.

O'Neil, Eleanor. 2018. "Immigration Issues: Public Opinion on Family Separation, DACA, and a Border Wall." *American Enterprise Institute*, June 21. https://www.aei.org/politics-and-public-opinion/immigration-issues-public-opinion-on-family-separation-daca-and-a-border-wall/.

Organisation for Economic Co-operation and Development. n.d. "Health Expenditure and Financing." OECD.Stat. Accessed November 17, 2020. https://stats.oecd.org/Index.aspx?QueryId=24880https://stats.oecd.org/Index.aspx.

Orloff, Ann Shola, and Theda Skocpol. 1984. "Why Not Equal Protection? Explaining the Politics of Public Social Spending in Britain, 1900–1911, and the United States, 1880s–1920." *American Sociological Review* 49 (6): 726–50.

Orren, Karen, and Stephen Skowronek. 2017. *The Policy State: An American Predicament*. Harvard University Press.

Osgood, Brian. 2021. "'Why Am I Still Being Punished?': How a 1996 Law Makes It Harder for Former Drug Felons to Get Food in the US." *Guardian*, September 13. https://www.theguardian.com/environment/2021/sep/13/welfare-reform-law-food-assistance-ban.

Owens, Michael Leo, and Adrienne R. Smith. 2012. "'Deviants' and Democracy: Punitive Policy Designs and the Social Rights of Felons as Citizens." *American Politics Research* 40 (3): 531–67.

Pantoja, Adrian D., Ricardo Ramirez, and Gary M. Segura. 2001. "Citizens by Choice, Voters by Necessity: Patterns in Political Mobilization by Naturalized Latinos." *Political Research Quarterly* 54 (4): 729–50.

Parilla, Joseph, and Mark Muro. 2016. "Where Global Trade Has the Biggest Impact on Workers." *Brookings*, December 14. https://www.brookings.edu/blog/the-avenue/2016/12/14/where -global-trade-has-the-biggest-impact-on-workers/.

Paris, Francesca. 2023. "See the States That Have Passed Laws Directed at Young Trans People." *New York Times*, June 7. https://www.nytimes.com/2023/06/05/upshot/trans-laws-republi cans-states.html.

Parks, Miles, Scott Detrow, and Kelsey Snell. 2018. "Trump Signs Order to End Family Separa- tions." NPR, June 20. https://www.npr.org/2018/06/20/621798823/speaker-ryan-plans-immi gration-votes-amid-doubts-that-bills-can-pass.

Patashnik, Eric M. 2000. *Putting Trust in the U.S. Budget: Federal Trust Funds and the Politics of Commitment.* Cambridge University Press.

———. 2008. *Reforms at Risk: What Happens after Major Policy Changes Are Enacted.* Princeton University Press.

———. 2019a. "The Clean Air Act's Use of Market Mechanisms." In *Lessons from the Clean Air Act: Building Durability and Adaptability into U.S. Climate and Energy Policy*, edited by Ann Carlson and Dallas Burtraw, 201–24. Cambridge University Press.

———. 2019b. "Limiting Policy Backlash: Strategies for Taming Countercoalitions in an Era of Polarization." *ANNALS of the American Academy of Political and Social Science* 685 (1): 47–63.

Patashnik, Eric M., Alan S. Gerber, and Conor M. Dowling. 2017. *Unhealthy Politics: The Battle over Evidence-Based Medicine.* Princeton University Press.

Patashnik, Eric M., and Jonathan Oberlander. 2018a. "After Defeat: Conservative Postenactment Opposition to the ACA in Historical-Institutional Perspective." *Journal of Health Politics, Policy and Law* 43 (4): 651–82.

———. 2018b. "Republicans Are Still Trying to Repeal Obamacare. Here's Why They Are Not Likely to Succeed." *Washington Post*, June 13. https://www.washingtonpost.com/news/monkey -cage/wp/2018/06/13/republicans-are-still-trying-to-repeal-obamacare-heres-why-they -are-not-likely-to-succeed/.

Patashnik, Eric M., and R. Kent Weaver. 2021. "Policy Analysis and Political Sustainability." *Pol- icy Studies Journal* 49 (4): 1110–34.

Patashnik, Eric M., and Julian E. Zelizer. 2013. "The Struggle to Remake Politics: Liberal Reform and the Limits of Policy Feedback in the Contemporary American State." *Perspectives on Politics* 11 (4): 1071–87.

Patterson, James T. 1996. *Grand Expectations: The United States, 1945–1974.* Oxford University Press.

———. 2005. *Restless Giant: The United States from Watergate to Bush v. Gore.* Oxford University Press.

Pauly, Mark V., and Sean Nicholson. 1999. "Adverse Consequences of Adverse Selection." *Journal of Health Politics, Policy and Law* 24 (5): 921–30.

PBS. 1978. "PBS NewsHour for December 8, 1978." *PBS NewsHour*, December 8. https://advance -lexis-com.revproxy.brown.edu/api/document?collection=news&id=urn:contentItem :5G7R-6X51-JB20-G30H-00000-00&context=1516831.

———. 2020. "Gun-Rights Advocates Turn Out in Huge Numbers to Protest Proposed Virginia Restrictions." *PBS Newshour*, January 20. https://www.pbs.org/newshour/show/gun-rights -advocates-turn-out-in-huge-numbers-to-protest-proposed-virginia-restrictions.

Pear, Robert. 1986. "New Restrictions on Immigration Gain Public Support, Poll Shows." *New York Times*, July 1. https://www.nytimes.com/1986/07/01/us/new-restrictions-on-immigration -gain-public-support-poll-shows.html.

Penn Wharton Budget Model. 2016. *The Effects of Immigration on the United States' Economy.* June 27, 1–9. https://budgetmodel.wharton.upenn.edu/issues/2016/1/27/the-effects-of-im migration-on-the-united-states-economy.

Perlstein, Rick. 2020. *Reaganland: America's Right Turn, 1976–1980.* Simon and Schuster.

Peters, Charles. 2010. *Lyndon B. Johnson: The American Presidents Series: The 36th President, 1963– 1969.* Macmillan.

Peterson, Iver. 1979. "'Boat People' Reach Los Angeles after 3 Months." *New York Times*, January 23. https://www.nytimes.com/1979/01/23/archives/boat-people-reach-los-angeles-after -3-months-186000-now-in-us-ellis.html.

Peterson, Mark A. 1997. "The Limits of Social Learning: Translating Analysis into Action." *Journal of Health Politics, Policy and Law* 22 (4): 1077–114.

———. 1998. "The Politics of Health Care Policy: Overreaching in an Age of Polarization." In *The Social Divide: Political Parties and the Future of Activist Government*, edited by Margaret Weir, 181–229. Brookings Institution Press.

———. 2018. "Reversing Course on Obamacare: Why Not Another Medicare Catastrophic?" *Journal of Health Politics, Policy and Law* 43 (4): 605–50.

Pew Research Center. 2009. "Economy, Jobs Trump All Other Policy Priorities in 2009: Environment, Immigration, Health Care Slip down the List." January 22. https://www.pewresearch .org/politics/2009/01/22/about-the-survey-391/.

———. 2016. "Partisanship and Political Animosity in 2016." June 22. https://www.pewresearch .org/politics/2016/06/22/partisanship-and-political-animosity-in-2016/.

Philipps, Dave. 2016. "North Carolina Bans Local Anti-Discrimination Policies." *New York Times*, March 24. https://www.nytimes.com/2016/03/24/us/north-carolina-to-limit-bathroom-use -by-birth-gender.html.

Pierson, Paul. 1993. "When Effect Becomes Cause: Policy Feedback and Political Change." *World Politics* 45 (4): 595–628.

———. 1994. *Dismantling the Welfare State? Reagan, Thatcher and the Politics of Retrenchment.* Cambridge University Press.

———. 2000. "Not Just What, But When: Timing and Sequence in Political Processes." *Studies in American Political Development* 14 (1): 72–92.

———. 2004. *Politics in Time: History, Institutions, and Social Analysis.* Princeton University Press.

———. 2014. "Conclusion: Madison Upside Down: The Policy Roots of Our Polarized Politics." In *The Politics of Major Policy Reform in Postwar America*, edited by Jeffrey A. Jenkins and Sidney M. Milkis, 282–302. Cambridge University Press.

———. 2015a. Goodbye to Pluralism? Studying Power in Contemporary American Politics. Paper presented at the Wildavsky Forum for Public Policy, Goldman School of Public Policy, April. https://inequality.hks.harvard.edu/files/inequality/files/pierson16.pdf.

———. 2015b. "Power and Path Dependence." In *Advances in Comparative-Historical Analysis*, edited by James Mahoney and Kathleen Thelen, 123–46. Cambridge University Press.

Pierson, Paul, and Eric Schickler. 2020. "Madison's Constitution under Stress: A Developmental Analysis of Political Polarization." *Annual Review of Political Science* 23 (1): 37–58.

Pierson, Paul, and Theda Skocpol, eds. 2007. *The Transformation of American Politics: Activist Government and the Rise of Conservatism.* Princeton University Press.

Pine, Art. 1979. "IRS Softens Proposal Aimed At 'Segregation Academies.'" *Washington Post*, February 10. https://www.washingtonpost.com/archive/politics/1979/02/10/irs-softens-pro posal-aimed-at-segregation-academies/127aa5a4-5506-43e0-9da3-72ee8da321b3/.

Pinkovskiy, Maxim L. 2020. "The Impact of the Managed Care Backlash on Health Care Spend- ing." *RAND Journal of Economics* 51 (1): 59–108.

Plotke, David. 1989. "The Wagner Act, Again: Politics and Labor, 1935–37." *Studies in American Political Development* 3:104–56.

Poli, Robert E. 1982. "Why the Air Controllers' Strike Failed." *New York Times*, January 17. https:// www.nytimes.com/1982/01/17/business/business-forum-why-the-air-controllers-strike -failed.html.

Pomfret, John D. 1964. "Labor Opens Drive to Beat Goldwater; Platform Criticized." *New York Times*, August 4. https://www.nytimes.com/1964/08/04/archives/labor-opens-drive-to-beat -goldwater-platform-criticized.html.

Pooley, Eric. 2010. *The Climate War: True Believers, Power Brokers, and the Fight to Save the Earth.* Hachette Books.

Porter, Eduardo. 2019. "Ross Perot's Warning of a 'Giant Sucking Sound' on Nafta Echoes To- day." *New York Times*, July 9. https://www.nytimes.com/2019/07/09/business/economy/ross -perot-nafta-trade.html.

Prasad, Monica. 2018. *Starving the Beast: Ronald Reagan and the Tax Cut Revolution.* Russell Sage Foundation.

Preston, Julia. 2017. "How the Dreamers Learned to Play Politics." *Politico Magazine*, Septem- ber 9. https://www.politico.com/magazine/story/2017/09/09/dreamers-daca-learned-to-play -politics-215588.

Price, Todd A., Andrew J. Yawn, and Maria Clark. 2021. "What's behind the Wave of Pro- posed Laws Targeting Trans Youth in the South." *Tennessean*, February 16. https://www .tennessean.com/story/news/american-south/2021/02/16/south-states-proposed-laws-tar geting-transgender-youth-sports/6754838002/.

Purnick, Joyce. 1981. "Strike Is Hurting Businesses That Depend on Air Traffic." *New York Times*, August 6. https://www.nytimes.com/1981/08/06/nyregion/strike-is-hurting-businesses-that -depend-on-air-traffic.html.

Quilantan, Bianca. 2020. "Supreme Court Sidelines Case against Bathroom Access for Transgen- der Students." *Politico*, December 7. https://www.politico.com/news/2020/12/07/supreme -court-bathrooms-transgender-students-443434.

Quinn, Mattie. 2019. "Criminal Justice Reform Paves the Way for Welfare Reform." *Governing*, January 9. https://www.governing.com/archive/gov-welfare-felons-states-federal-ban-tanf -snap-pennsylvania.html.

Rabin, Roni Caryn. 2019. "Eager to Limit Exemptions to Vaccination, States Face Staunch Re- sistance." *New York Times*, June 14. https://www.nytimes.com/2019/06/14/health/vaccine -exemption-health.html.

Radcliffe, Marcy, and Kaleigh Rogers. 2023. "Red State Voters Support Anti-Trans Law. Their Lawmakers Are Delivering." FiveThirtyEight, April 18. https://fivethirtyeight.com/features /red-state-voters-support-anti-trans-laws-their-lawmakers-are-delivering/.

Ragusa, Jordan M., and Nathaniel A. Birkhead. 2020. *Congress in Reverse: Repeals from Recon- struction to the Present.* University of Chicago Press.

Raines, Howell. 1980. "Cuban Backlash Grows in Florida as Influx of Refugees Nears 30,000." *New York Times*, May 10. https://www.nytimes.com/1980/05/10/archives/cuban-backlash-grows-in-florida-as-influx-of-refugees-nears-30000.html.

Raskin, A. H. 1981. "The Air Strike Is Ominous for Labor." *New York Times*, August 18. https://www.nytimes.com/1981/08/16/business/the-air-strike-is-ominous-for-labor.html.

Rauchway, Eric. 2008. *The Great Depression and the New Deal: A Very Short Introduction*. Oxford University Press.

Reese, Ellen. 2005. *Backlash against Welfare Mothers: Past and Present*. University of California Press.

Reich, Robert. 2007. *Supercapitalism: The Transformation of Business, Democracy and Everyday Life*. Knopf.

Reichley, James A. 1981. *Conservatives in an Age of Change: The Nixon and Ford Administrations*. Brookings Institution Press.

Reilly, Mollie. 2016. "North Carolina Governor Signs Bill Banning Cities from Protecting LGBT People." *HuffPost*, February 23. https://www.huffpost.com/entry/north-carolina-lgbt-discrimination_n_56f2b7dbe4b0c3ef5217676c.

Rein, Lisa. 2022. "Senators Kill Sweeping Plan to Reshape Sprawling VA Health-Care System." *Washington Post*, June 29. https://www.washingtonpost.com/politics/2022/06/29/senators-kill-sweeping-plan-reshape-sprawling-va-health-care-system/.

Reinhardt, Uwe E. 1999. "The Predictable Managed Care Kvetch on the Rocky Road from Adolescence to Adulthood." *Journal of Health Politics, Policy and Law* 24 (5): 897–910.

Reis, Patrick. 2021. "The Last, Best Chance on Climate." *Rolling Stone*, March 22. https://www.rollingstone.com/politics/politics-features/biden-pass-climate-legislation-1140934/.

Rhodes, Jesse H. 2012. *An Education in Politics: The Origins and Evolution of No Child Left Behind*. Cornell University Press.

———. 2017. *Ballot Blocked: The Political Erosion of the Voting Rights Act*. Stanford University Press.

Rhodes-Purdy, Matthew Henry, Rachel Navarre, and Stephen M. Utych. 2021. "Populist Psychology: Economics, Culture, and Emotions." *Journal of Politics* 83 (4): 1559–72.

Richardson, George P. 1991. *Feedback Thought in Social Science and Systems Theory*. University of Pennsylvania Press.

Richardson, J. David, Lionel Olmer, and Paula Stern. 1994. "Trade Policy." In *American Economic Policy in the 1980s*, edited by Martin Feldstein, 627–58. University of Chicago Press.

Riotta, Chris. 2017. "GOP Aims to Kill Obamacare Yet Again after Failing 70 Times." *Newsweek*, July 29. https://www.newsweek.com/gop-health-care-bill-repeal-and-replace-70-failed-attempts-643832.

Ritchie, Melinda N., and Hye Young You. 2021. "Trump and Trade: Protectionist Politics and Redistributive Policy." *Journal of Politics* 83 (2): 800–805.

Roberts, David. 2020. "At Last, a Climate Policy Platform That Can Unite the Left." Vox, May 27. https://www.vox.com/energy-and-environment/21252892/climate-change-democrats-joe-biden-renewable-energy-unions-environmental-justice.

Roberts, Gene. 1966. "Civil Rights: A Turning Point." *New York Times*, September 19. https://www.nytimes.com/1966/09/19/archives/civil-rights-a-turning-point-politicians-uneasy-liberals-defect-or.html?searchResultPosition=1.

Robertson, David Brian. 2020. "Leader to Laggard: How Founding Institutions Have Shaped American Environmental Policy." *Studies in American Political Development* 34 (1): 110–31.

Robinson, Kenneth J. 2013. "Savings and Loan Crisis." *Federal Reserve History*, November 22. https://www.federalreservehistory.org/essays/savings_and_loan_crisis.

Robinston, Douglas. 1967. "Dr. King Presses Louisville Fight: Tells Negroes Fair Housing Battle Is at Crucial Stage." *New York Times*, May 4. https://www.nytimes.com/1967/05/04/archives /drking-presses-louisville-fight-tells-negroes-fair-housing-battle.html.

Rodrik, Dani. 2021. "Why Does Globalization Fuel Populism? Economics, Culture, and the Rise of Right-Wing Populism." *Annual Review of Economics* 13 (1): 133–70.

Rogers, Katie. 2016. "Transgender Students and 'Bathroom Laws' in South Dakota and Beyond." *New York Times*, February 25. https://www.nytimes.com/2016/02/26/us/transgender -students-and-bathroom-laws-in-south-dakota-and-beyond.html.

Romer, Thomas, and Barry R. Weingast. 1991. "Political Foundations of the Thrift Debacle." In *Politics and Economics in the Eighties*, edited by Alberto Alesina and Geoffrey Carliner, 175–214. University of Chicago Press.

Romero, Simon, and Timothy Williams. 2019. "When Sheriffs Say No: Disputes Erupt over Enforcing New Gun Laws." *New York Times*, March 11. https://www.nytimes.com/2019/03/11 /us/state-gun-laws.html.

Rosenbaum, David E. 1993. "Democratic Split over Trade Agreement Widens." *New York Times*, September 22. https://www.nytimes.com/1993/09/22/us/democratic-split-over-trade-agree ment-widens.html.

Rosenbluth, Frances McCall, and Margaret Weir. 2021. *Who Gets What? The New Politics of Insecurity*. Cambridge University Press.

Rosenthal, Brian M. 2015. "First-Time Texas Drug Felons to Be Eligible for Food Stamps Again." *Houston Chronicle*, August 20. https://www.houstonchronicle.com/politics/texas/article /Texas-drug-felons-to-be-eligible-for-food-stamps-6454029.php.

Rosentiel, Tom. 2011. "In Showdown with Air Traffic Controllers, the Public Sided with Reagan." Pew Research Center, February 22. https://www.pewresearch.org/2011/02/22/in-show down-with-air-traffic-controllers-the-public-sided-with-reagan/.

Roubein, Rachel. 2022. "Biden Still Hasn't Banned the Short-Term Health Plans He Called 'Junk.'" *Washington Post*, April 14. https://www.washingtonpost.com/politics/2022/04/14 /biden-still-hasnt-banned-short-term-health-plans-he-called-junk/.

Rovner, Julie. 1995. "Congress's 'Catastrophic' Attempt to Fix Medicare." In *Intensive Care: How Congress Shapes Health Policy*, edited by Norman Ornstein and Thomas E. Mann, 145–78. American Enterprise Institute and Brookings Institution.

Rubin, Bonnie Miller. 1996. "Bill Clinton Signs Health Care Bill." *Chicago Tribune*, September 27. https://www.chicagotribune.com/news/ct-xpm-1996-09-27-9609270212-story.html.

Rubio, Philip F. 2016. "Organizing a Wildcat: The United States Postal Strike of 1970." *Labor History* 57 (5): 565–87.

Rugaber, Walter. 1974. "Congress Clears Auto Safety Measure Eliminating Seat Belt Interlock System: Safety Advocate Defeat Arguments of Critics." *New York Times*, October 16. https:// www.nytimes.com/1974/10/16/archives/congress-clears-auto-safety-measure-eliminating -seat-belt-interlock.html.

Russonello, Giovanni. 2020. "What's Driving the Right-Wing Protesters Fighting the Quarantine?" *New York Times*, April 17. https://www.nytimes.com/2020/04/17/us/politics/poll -watch-quarantine-protesters.html?searchResultPosition=9.

Saad, Lydia. 2009. "Cost Is Foremost Healthcare Issue for Americans." Gallup.com, September 23. https://news.gallup.com/poll/123149/Cost-Is-Foremost-Healthcare-Issue-for-Americans.aspx.

———. 2017. "Gallup Vault: Nixon's China Visit Was a Game Changer." Gallup.com, February 17. https://news.gallup.com/vault/204065/gallup-vault-nixon-china-visit-game-changer.aspx.

Sabl, Andrew. 2002. *Ruling Passions: Political Offices and Democratic Ethics.* Princeton University Press.

Sachs, Susan. 1999. "Pressed by Backlog, U.S. Rethinks Citizenship Test." *New York Times,* July 5. https://www.nytimes.com/1999/07/05/nyregion/pressed-by-backlog-us-rethinks-citizenship-test.html.

Sakuma, Amanda. 2017. "Obama Leaves Behind a Mixed Legacy on Immigration." NBC News, January 15. https://www.nbcnews.com/storyline/president-obama-the-legacy/obama-leaves-behind-mixed-legacy-immigration-n703656.

Salmans, Sandra. 1985. "Bill Propose 25% Duty against Japan, 3 Others." *New York Times,* July 18. https://www.nytimes.com/1985/07/18/business/bill-propose-25-duty-against-japan-3-others.html.

Salmon, Daniel A., Matthew Z. Dudley, Jason M. Glanz, and Saad B. Omer. 2015. "Vaccine Hesitancy: Causes, Consequences, and a Call to Action." *Vaccine* 33:D66–D71.

Samuels, Alex. 2021. "How Democrats Became Stuck on Immigration." FiveThirtyEight, March 30. https://fivethirtyeight.com/features/how-democrats-became-stuck-on-immigration/.

Sanbonmatsu, Kira. 2008. "Gender Backlash in American Politics?" *Politics & Gender* 4 (4): 634–42.

Sanger-Katz, Margot. 2018. "Another of Obamacare's Unloved Provisions Is Gone." *New York Times,* February 9. https://www.nytimes.com/2018/02/09/upshot/obamacare-ipab-medicare-congress.html.

Schattschneider, E. E. 1935. *Politics, Pressures, and the Tariff: A Study of Free Private Enterprise in Pressure Politics.* Prentice-Hall.

Scheve, Kenneth F., and Matthew J. Slaughter. 2007. "A New Deal for Globalization." *Foreign Affairs* 86 (4): 34–47.

———. 2018. "How to Save Globalization: Rebuilding America's Ladder of Opportunity." *Foreign Affairs* 97 (6): 98–112.

Schickler, Eric. 2016. *Racial Realignment: The Transformation of American Liberalism, 1932–1965.* Princeton University Press.

Schickler, Eric, and Devin Caughey. 2011. "Public Opinion, Organized Labor, and the Limits of New Deal Liberalism, 1936–1945." *Studies in American Political Development* 25 (2): 162–89.

Schlozman, Daniel. 2015. *When Movements Anchor Parties: Electoral Alignments in American History.* Princeton University Press.

Schneider, Anne L., and Helen M. Ingram. 1993. "Social Construction of Target Populations: Implications for Politics and Policy." *American Political Science Review* 87 (2): 334–47.

———. 2019. "Social Constructions, Anticipatory Feedback Strategies, and Deceptive Public Policy." *Policy Studies Journal* 47 (2): 206–36.

Schneider, Elena and Holly Otterbein. 2022. "'THE central issue': How the fall of Roe v. Wade shook the 2022 election," *Politico.* December 19. https://www.politico.com/news/2022/12/19/dobbs-2022-election-abortion-00074426.

Schneider, Gregory S. 2019. "Virginia AG Herring: 'Second Amendment Sanctuary' Proclamations Have No Force." *Washington Post,* December 20. https://www.washingtonpost.com/local/virginia-politics/virginia-ag-herring-second-amendment-sanctuary-proclamations-have-no-force/2019/12/20/5f7adcb2-234b-11ea-a153-dce4b94e4249_story.html.

———. 2020. "Va. Governor Signs Gun-Control Laws, Delivering on Democrats' Campaign Promises." *Washington Post*, April 10. https://www.washingtonpost.com/local/virginia-pol itics/va-governor-signs-gun-control-laws-delivering-on-democrats-campaign-promises /2020/04/10/b3a8acec-7b4d-11ea-a130-df573469f094_story.html.

Schneider, Gregory S., and Michael Scherer. 2019. "In Virginia, Republicans Confront a Fearful Electoral Future." *Washington Post*, November 9. https://www.washingtonpost.com /politics/in-virginia-republicans-confront-a-fearful-electoral-future/2019/11/09 /2bbdc7aa-026b-11ea-8bab-0fc209e065a8_story.html.

Schneider, Gregory S., Laura Vozzella, and Scott Clement. 2019. "Poll Finds Virginia Voters Focused on Gun Policy Ahead of Pivotal Election." *Washington Post*, October 4. https://www .washingtonpost.com/local/virginia-politics/new-poll-finds-virginia-voters-focused-on -gun-policy-ahead-of-pivotal-election/2019/10/03/db034922-e472-11e9-a331-2df12d56a80b _story.html.

Schneider, Gregory S., Laura Vozzella, and Antonio Olivo. 2019. "Gun Debate Ends Abruptly in Virginia as GOP-Controlled Legislature Adjourns after 90 Minutes." *Washington Post*, July 9. https://www.washingtonpost.com/local/virginia-politics/gun-debate-hits-full-throttle -in-richmond-as-legislature-convenes/2019/07/09/caf20590-a1d4-11e9-bd56-eac6b b02d01d_story.html.

Schragger, Rich. 2020. "Second Amendment Sanctuaries and the Difference between Home Rule, Local Recalcitrance, and Interposition." *Second Thoughts: A Blog from the Center for Firearms Law at Duke University*, May 5. https://sites.law.duke.edu/secondthoughts/2020/05 /05/second-amendment-sanctuaries-and-the-difference-between-home-rule-local-recalcitrance -and-interposition/.

Schuck, Peter H. 2001. "Immigration Reform Redux." In *Seeking the Center: Politics and Policymaking at the New Century*, edited by Martin A. Levin, Marc K. Landy, and Martin M. Shapiro, 113–31. Georgetown University Press.

———. 2008. "Immigration." In *Understanding America: The Anatomy of an Exceptional Nation*, edited by Peter H. Schuck and James Q. Wilson, 341–74. Perseus.

Schulman, Bruce J., and Julian E. Zelizer. 2008. *Rightward Bound: Making America Conservative in the 1970s*. Harvard University Press.

Senate Finance Committee. 1979. *Tax-Exempt Status of Private Schools: Hearing before the Subcommittee on Taxation and Debt Management Generally of the Committee on Finance, United States Senate, Ninety-Sixth Congress, First Session*. U.S. Government Printing Office, April 27.

Serrin, William. 1981a. "A.F.L.-C.I.O. Defers Action to Back Up Air Controllers." *New York Times*, August 7. https://www.nytimes.com/1981/08/07/us/afl-cio-defers-action-to-back-up -air-controllers.html.

———. 1981b. "A New Breed of Striker Emerging: Young, Affluent and Angry." *New York Times*, August 10. https://www.nytimes.com/1981/08/10/us/a-new-breed-of-striker-emerging-young -affluent-and-angry-news-analysis.html.

Shanahan, Eileen. 1975. "Church Schools Get Racial Order." *New York Times*, May 23. https:// www.nytimes.com/1975/05/23/archives/church-schools-get-racial-order-irs-says-dis crimination-will-result.html.

Shao, Elena, and Lisa Friedman. "Ban Gas Stoves? Just the Idea Gets Some in Washington Boiling." *New York Times*, January 11. https://www.nytimes.com/2023/01/11/climate/gas-stoves -biden-administration.html.

Shapiro, Robert Y., and Tom W. Smith. 1985. "The Polls: Social Security." *Public Opinion Quarterly* 49 (4): 561–72.

Sharp, James Roger. 1993. *American Politics in the Early Republic: The New Nation in Crisis.* Yale University Press.

Shear, Michael D., and Helene Cooper. 2017. "Trump Bars Refugees and Citizens of 7 Muslim Countries." *New York Times,* January 28. https://www.nytimes.com/2017/01/27/us/politics /trump-syrian-refugees.html.

Shear, Michael D., and Zolan Kanno-Youngs. 2021. "In Another Reversal, Biden Raises Limit on Number of Refugees Allowed into the U.S." *New York Times,* May 4. https://www.nytimes .com/2021/05/03/us/politics/biden-refugee-limit.html.

Sheingate, Adam. 2020. "Policy Regime Decay." *Policy Studies Journal* 50 (1): 65–89.

Sheth, Sonam. 2017. "Trump's Decision to End DACA Sparks Backlash from Both Sides of the Aisle." *Business Insider,* September 5. https://www.businessinsider.in/trumps-decision-to -end-daca-sparks-backlash-from-both-sides-of-the-aisle/articleshow/60383072.cms.

Shipan, Charles R., and Craig Volden. 2008. "The Mechanisms of Policy Diffusion." *American Journal of Political Science* 52 (4): 840–57.

Shiver, Phil. 2021. "Facebook Permanently Bans Pro-Gun Group without Explanation: Report." Blaze, February 4. https://www.theblaze.com/news/facebook-bans-gun-group-without-explanation.

Sides, John. 2018. "The Extraordinary Unpopularity of Trump's Family Separation Policy (in One Graph)." *Washington Post,* June 19. https://www.washingtonpost.com/news/monkey-cage/wp /2018/06/19/the-extraordinary-unpopularity-of-trumps-family-separation-policy-in-one-graph/.

Sides, John, Chris Tausanovitch, and Lynn Vavreck. 2020. "The Politics of COVID-19: Partisan Polarization about the Pandemic Has Increased, but Support for Health Care Reform Hasn't Moved at All." *Harvard Data Science Review, Special Issue 1, COVID-19: Unprecedented Challenges and Chances.* https://doi.org/ 10.1162/99608f92.611350fd.

———. 2022. *The Bitter End: The 2020 Presidential Campaign and the Challenge to American Democracy.* Princeton University Press.

Sides, John, Michael Tesler, and Lynn Vavreck. 2019. *Identity Crisis: The 2016 Presidential Campaign and the Battle for the Meaning of America.* Princeton University Press.

Sinclair, Barbara. 1991. "Governing Unheroically (and Sometimes Unappetizingly): Bush and the 101st Congress." In *The Bush Presidency: First Appraisals,* edited by Colin Campbell and Burt Rockman, 155–84. Chatham House.

Skerry, Peter. 1980. "Christian Schools versus the IRS." *Public Interest* 61:18–41.

Skocpol, Theda. 1992. *Protecting Soldiers and Mothers: The Political Origins of Social Policy in the United States.* Belknap Press.

———. 2013. *Naming the Problem: What It Will Take to Counter Extremism and Engage Americans in the Fight against Global Warming.* Paper presented at the Symposium on the Politics of America's Fight against Global Warming, Cosponsored by the Columbia School of Journalism and the Scholars Strategy Network, February 14.

Skocpol, Theda, and Alexander Hertel-Fernandez. 2016. "The Koch Network and Republican Party Extremism." *Perspectives on Politics* 14 (3): 681–99.

Skocpol, Theda, and Vanessa Williamson. 2016. *The Tea Party and the Remaking of Republican Conservatism.* Oxford University Press.

Skrentny, John D. 2011. "Obama's Immigration Revolution: A Tough Sell for a Grand Bargain." In *Reaching for a New Deal,* edited by Theda Skocpol and Lawrence R. Jacobs, 273–320. Russell Sage Foundation.

Slaughter, Thomas P. 1986. *The Whiskey Rebellion: Frontier Epilogue to the American Revolution.* Oxford University Press.

Smialek, Jeanna, and Ana Swanson. 2020. "American Consumers, Not China, Are Paying for Trump's Tariffs." *New York Times,* January 6. https://www.nytimes.com/2020/01/06/business/economy/trade-war-tariffs.html.

Smith, David, and Tom Phillips. 2018. "Child Separations: Trump Faces Extreme Backlash from Public and His Own Party." *Guardian,* June 19. http://www.theguardian.com/us-news/2018/jun/19/child-separation-camps-trump-border-policy-backlash-republicans.

Smith, Mark A. 2000. *American Business and Political Power: Public Opinion, Elections, and Democracy.* University of Chicago Press.

Smithsonian National Postal Museum. 2010. "The 1970 Postal Strike." *Smithsonian,* March 17. https://postalmuseum.si.edu/the-1970-postal-strike.

Snyder, Jack. 2020. "Backlash against Naming and Shaming: The Politics of Status and Emotion." *British Journal of Politics and International Relations* 22 (4): 644–53.

Social Security. n.d. "Ratio of Covered Workers to Beneficiaries." Accessed March 19, 2021. https://www.ssa.gov/history/ratios.html.

Sommers, Benjamin D., Anna L. Goldman, Robert J. Blendon, and E. John Orav. 2019. "Medicaid Work Requirements—Results from the First Year in Arkansas." *New England Journal of Medicine* 381 (11): 1073–82.

Sontag, Deborah. 1992. "Across the U.S., Immigrants Find the Land of Resentment." *New York Times,* December 11. https://www.nytimes.com/1992/12/11/nyregion/across-the-us-immigrants-find-the-land-of-resentment.html.

Soss, Joe. 1999. "Lessons of Welfare: Policy Design, Political Learning, and Political Action." *American Political Science Review* 93 (2): 363–80.

Soss, Joe, and Sanford F. Schram. 2007. "A Public Transformed? Welfare Reform as Policy Feedback." *American Political Science Review* 101 (1): 111–27.

Sotomayor, Marianna, and Yasmeen Abutaleb. 2022. "Jayapal Draws Ire of Fellow Democrats over Bungled Ukraine Letter." *Washington Post,* October 27. https://www.washingtonpost.com/politics/2022/10/27/jayapal-ukraine-letter/.

Spitzer, Robert J. 2022. *The Gun Dilemma.* Oxford University Press.

Stack, Liam. 2020. "Backlash Grows in Orthodox Jewish Areas over Virus Crackdown by Cuomo." *New York Times,* October 7. https://www.nytimes.com/2020/10/07/nyregion/orthodox-jews-nyc-coronavirus.html.

Stanley-Becker, Isaac. 2021. "Anti-Vaccine Protest at Dodger Stadium Was Organized on Facebook, Including Promotion of Banned 'Plandemic' Video." *Washington Post,* February 1. https://www.washingtonpost.com/health/2021/02/01/dodgers-anti-vaccine-protest-facebook/.

Starr, Paul. 1982. *The Social Transformation of American Medicine: The Rise of a Sovereign Profession and the Making of a Vast Industry.* Basic Books.

———. 2011. *Remedy and Reaction: The Peculiar American Struggle over Health Care Reform.* Yale University Press.

———. 2017a. "The Next Progressive Health Agenda." *American Prospect,* March 23. https://prospect.org/health/next-progressive-health-agenda/.

———. 2017b. "The Republican Health-Care Unraveling: Resist Now, Rebound Later." *American Prospect* 28 (2): 5–7.

———. 2018a. "The Long Game on Taxes." *American Prospect* 29 (3): 1–6.

———. 2018b. "A New Strategy for Health Care." *American Prospect* 29 (1): 1–18.

———. 2022. "Conservatives Hope to Turn Back the Cultural Clock. Can They Succeed?" *Washington Post*, July 12. https://www.washingtonpost.com/opinions/2022/07/12/supreme -court-abortion-conservatives-laws/.

Stein, Jeff, Maxine Joselow, and Rachel Roubein. 2022. "How the Schumer-Manchin Climate Bill Might Impact You and Change the U.S." *Washington Post*, July 28. https://www.washington post.com/us-policy/2022/07/28/manchin-schumer-climate-deal/.

Steinmetz, Katy. 2016. "Why LGBT Advocates Say Bathroom 'Predators' Is a Red Herring." *Time*, May 2. https://time.com/4314896/transgender-bathroom-bill-male-predators-argument/.

Sterman, John D. 2000. *Business Dynamics: Systems Thinking and Modeling for a Complex World*. McGraw-Hill Education.

Stessin, Lawrence. 1973. "The Man from OSHA." *New York Times*, June 17. ProQuest, http:// search.proquest.com/docview/119876856/abstract/FAA263A453864F96PQ/1.

Stewart, James B. 2012. "How Broccoli Landed on Supreme Court Menu." *New York Times*, June 14. https://www.nytimes.com/2012/06/14/business/how-broccoli-became-a-symbol-in -the-health-care-debate.html.

Stimson, James A. 1991. *Public Opinion in America: Moods, Cycles, and Swings*. Westview Press.

———. 2012. "On the Meaning & Measurement of Mood." *Daedalus* 141 (4): 23–34.

Stokes, Leah C. 2016. "Electoral Backlash against Climate Policy: A Natural Experiment on Retrospective Voting and Local Resistance to Public Policy." *American Journal of Political Science* 60 (4): 958–74.

———. 2020. *Short Circuiting Policy: Interest Groups and the Battle over Clean Energy and Climate Policy in the American States*. Oxford University Press.

Suderman, Alan. 2019a. "Democrats Capture Virginia Legislature for First Time in Decades." *Christian Science Monitor*, November 6. https://www.csmonitor.com/USA/Politics /2019/1106/Democrats-capture-Virginia-legislature-for-first-time-in-decades.

———. 2019b. "Democrats Win Full Control of Virginia Statehouse." AP News, November 6. https://apnews.com/article/87ba998f09fd43359011e64fe0e68ad2.

———. 2020. "Virginia Senators Reject Gun Control Ban." *Arkansas Democrat-Gazette*, February 4. https://www.arkansasonline.com/news/2020/feb/04/virginia-senators-reject-gun -control-bi/.

Sullivan, Sean, Seung Min Kim, and Tyler Pager. 2021. "White House Announces It's Keeping Trump-Era Refugee Caps, Then Backtracks amid Furor." *Washington Post*, April 16. https:// www.washingtonpost.com/politics/biden-administration-to-keep-refugee-cap-at-trumps -level-far-less-than-what-it-proposed-to-congress/2021/04/16/02c099da-9ece-11eb-b7a8 -014b14aeb9e4_story.html.

Sulzberger, A. O., Jr. 1978. "Private Academies Protest Tax Plan." *New York Times*, December 11. http://timesmachine.nytimes.com/timesmachine/1978/12/11/110981415.html.

"Sweeping Thrift Bailout Bill Cleared." 1990. *CQ Almanac 1989*, 101st Congress, 1st Session, 117– 33. CQ Press. http://library.cqpress.com/cqalmanac/cqal89-1138219.

Swidey, Neil. 2017. "Trump's Anti-Immigration Playbook Was Written 100 Years Ago. in Boston." *Boston Globe Magazine*, January 31. https://apps.bostonglobe.com/magazine/graphics /2017/01/immigration.

Tarrow, Sidney G. 2011. *Power in Movement: Social Movements and Contentious Politics*. Cambridge University Press.

Taylor, Jeff. 2016. "City Council Votes 7-4 to Add LGBT Protections to Charlotte Non-Discrimination Ordinance." *Qnotes*, February 23. https://goqnotes.com/42016/city-council-votes-7-4-to-add-lgbt-protections-to-charlotte-non-discrimination-ordinance/.

Taylor, Stuart. 1983. "Tax Exemption Ruling: An Old Question Still Lingers." *New York Times*, June 14. https://www.nytimes.com/1983/06/14/us/tax-exemption-ruling-an-old-question-still-lingers-news-analysis.html.

Teles, Steven Michael. 2008. *The Rise of the Conservative Legal Movement: The Battle for Control of the Law*. Princeton University Press.

Temple-Raston, Dina. 2008. "House Rejects Bailout Bill; Wall Street Shudders." NPR, September 29. https://www.npr.org/2008/09/29/95180529/house-rejects-bailout-bill-wall-street-shudders.

Terry, Don. 1997. "Strong Blow Is Delivered to State Law on Aliens." *New York Times*, November 15. http://timesmachine.nytimes.com/timesmachine/1997/11/15/148393.html.

Tesler, Michael. 2021. "Republican Views on Immigration Are Shifting Even Further to the Right under Biden." FiveThirtyEight, August 17. https://fivethirtyeight.com/features/republican-views-on-immigration-are-shifting-even-further-to-the-right-under-biden/.

Thomas, Sue. 2008. "'Backlash' and Its Utility to Political Scientists." *Politics & Gender* 4 (4): 615–23.

Thompson, Darrel, and Ashley Burnside. 2022. "No More Double Punishments: Lifting the Ban on SNAP and TANF for People with Prior Felony Drug Convictions." CLASP: Center for Law and Social Policy, April 19. https://www.clasp.org/publications/report/brief/no-more-double-punishments/.

Thompson, Dennis F. 1993. "Mediated Corruption: The Case of the Keating Five." *American Political Science Review* 87 (2): 369–81.

Thomson-DeVeaux, Amelia. 2017. "The Christian Right Has a New Strategy on Gay Marriage." FiveThirtyEight, December 5. https://fivethirtyeight.com/features/the-christian-right-has-a-new-strategy-on-gay-marriage/.

Thrush, Glenn. 2009. "Boehner Banking on Cap-and-Trade Backlash." *Politico*, June 29. https://www.politico.com/blogs/on-congress/2009/06/boehner-banking-on-cap-and-trade-backlash-019472.

Tichenor, Daniel J. 2002. *Dividing Lines: The Politics of Immigration Control in America*. Princeton University Press.

———. 2009. "Navigating an American Minefield: The Politics of Illegal Immigration." *Forum* 7 (3): 000010220215408841325. https://doi.org/10.2202/1540-8884.1325.

———. 2012. "Splitting the Coalition: The Political Perils and Opportunities of Immigration Reform." In *Building Coalitions, Making Policy: The Politics of the Clinton, Bush, and Obama Presidencies*, edited by Martin A. Levin, Daniel DiSalvo, and Martin M. Shapiro, 75–118. Johns Hopkins University Press.

———. 2016. "The Demise of Immigration Reform: Policy-Making Barriers under Unified and Divided Government." In *Congress and Policy Making in the 21st Century*, edited by Jeffery A. Jenkins and Eric M. Patashnik, 242–71. Cambridge University Press.

———. 2021. "Populists, Clients, and US Immigration Wars." *Polity* 53 (3): 418–38.

Tikkanen, Roosa, and Melinda K. Abrams. 2020. "US Health Care from a Global Perspective, 2019: Higher Spending, Worse Outcomes?" Commonwealth Fund. https://www.commonwealthfund.org/publications/issue-briefs/2020/jan/us-health-care-global-perspective-2019.

Time Magazine / Cable News Network. 1989. *Yankelovich / Time Magazine / CNN Poll: Savings and Loan Crisis / Gun Control.* Edited by Yankelovich Clancy Shulman. Roper Center for Public Opinion Research. https://doi.org/10.25940/ROPER-31099203.

Tobias, Jimmy. 2017. "Trans Rights Weren't the Only Target of North Carolina's 'Bathroom Bill.'" *Nation,* March 31. https://www.thenation.com/article/archive/trans-rights-werent-the -only-target-of-north-carolinas-bathroom-bill/.

Tolbert, Jennifer, and Larisa Antonisse. 2017. "Listening to Trump Voters with ACA Coverage: What They Want in a Health Care Plan." KFF, February 22. https://www.kff.org/report -section/listening-to-trump-voters-with-aca-coverage-issue-brief/.

Tomasky, Michael. 2017. *Bill Clinton: The American Presidents Series: The 42nd President, 1993– 2001.* Macmillan.

Toner, Robin. 1994. "Collapse of Bill on Health Care Relieves Fears: Little Anger in Electorate over Health." *New York Times,* September 11. https://www.nytimes.com/1994/09/11/us /collapse-of-bill-on-health-care-relieves-fears.html.

———. 1995. "Angry Opposition Attacks the Process: Democrats Say Republicans Are Pushing Medicare Plan Too Fast." *New York Times,* September 22. https://www.nytimes.com /1995/09/22/us/the-104th-congress-the-democrats-angry-opposition-attacks-the-process .html.

Torriero, E. A. 2008. "Property Tax Wallop Spurs Backlash." *Chicago Tribune,* February 3. https:// www.chicagotribune.com/news/ct-xpm-2008-02-03-0802020352-story.html.

Toscano, David J. 2019. "The Gun Sanctuary Movement Is Exploding." Slate Magazine, December 11. https://slate.com/news-and-politics/2019/12/second-amendment-gun-sanctuary -movement-constitution.html.

Treaster, Joseph B. 1981. "13,000 Air Controllers Defy Reagan Dismissal Deadline; 72% of Flights In." *New York Times,* August 5. https://www.nytimes.com/1981/08/05/nyregion/13000-air -controllers-defy-reagan-dismissal-deadline-72-of-flights-in.html.

Tucker, Marc. 2016. "Tough-Minded Federal Accountability Is Dead: What Will the States Do Now?" *National Center on Education and the Economy,* February 19. http://ncee.org/2016/02 /tough-minded-federal-accountability-is-dead-what-will-the-states-do-now/.

Turner, James Morton, and Andrew C. Isenberg. 2018. *The Republican Reversal: Conservatives and the Environment from Nixon to Trump.* Harvard University Press.

Tversky, Amos, and Daniel Kahneman. 1981. "The Framing of Decisions and the Psychology of Choice." *Science* 211 (4481): 453–58.

United States Department of Labor. 2021. "Trade Adjustment Assistance for Workers Program: FY 2020 Annual Report." https://www.dol.gov/sites/dolgov/files/ETA/tradeact/pdfs/Annu alReport20.pdf.

UPI. 1981. "Many Flight Controllers Want to Reject New Contract." *New York Times,* June 25. https://www.nytimes.com/1981/06/25/us/many-flight-controllers-want-to-reject-new-con tract.html.

Valelly, Richard. 2016. "How Suffrage Politics Made—and Make—America." In *The Oxford Handbook of American Political Development,* edited by Richard Valelly, Suzanne Mettler, and Robert C. Lieberman, 445–72. Oxford University Press.

Valverde, Miriam. 2020. "Donald Trump's Immigration Promises: Failures and Achievements." *PolitiFact,* July 27. https://www.politifact.com/article/2020/jul/27/donald-trumps-immigration -promises-failures-and-ac/.

Van Cleave, Philip. 2019. "Virginia: Important Statement about VCDL Capital Lobby Day, Jan. 20th 2020." Ammoland Shooting Sport News, December 18, https://www.ammoland.com/2019/12/virginia-important-statement-about-vcdl-capital-lobby-day-jan-20th-2020/#axzz6m5foJcLO.

Vesoulis, Abby. 2019. "New Survey Shows Growing Support for Transgender Rights amid Federal Rollback of LGBTQ Protections." *Time*, June 11. https://time.com/5604398/growing-support-trans-rights/.

Vogel, David. 1983. "The Power of Business in America: A Re-Appraisal." *British Journal of Political Science* 13 (1): 19–43.

———. 1989. *Fluctuating Fortunes: The Political Power of Business in America*. Basic Books.

———. 1996. *Kindred Strangers: The Uneasy Relationship between Politics and Business in America*. Princeton University Press.

———. 1999. "The Triumph of Liberal Trade: American Trade Policy in the Postwar Period." In *Taking Stock: American Government in the Twentieth Century*, edited by Morton Keller and R. Shep Melnick, 35–53. Cambridge University Press.

———. 2001. "The Post-War Liberal Trade Regime: Resilience under Pressure." In *Seeking the Center: Politics and Policymaking at the New Century*, edited by Martin Levin, Marc Landy, and Martin Shapiro, 313–36. Georgetown University Press.

"Voters React More to Local Issues." 1991. *CQ Almanac 1990*, 101st Congress, 2nd Session, 901–3. CQ Press. http://library.cqpress.com/cqalmanac/cqal90-1112067.

Vozzella, Laura. 2020. "Why Northam's Assault Weapons Bill Never Really Had a Chance in the Virginia Senate." *Washington Post*, February 23. https://www.washingtonpost.com/local/virginia-politics/why-northams-assault-weapons-bill-never-really-had-a-chance-in-the-virginia-senate/2020/02/23/64e02b6c-5334-11ea-929a-64efa7482a77_story.html.

Wagner, Jennifer, and Jessica Schubel. 2020. "States' Experiences Confirm Harmful Effects of Medicaid Work Requirements." Center on Budget and Policy Priorities, November 18. https://www.cbpp.org/research/health/states-experiences-confirm-harmful-effects-of-medicaid-work-requirements.

Waldman, Paul. 2018. "The Liberal Backlash Is Coming." *American Prospect*, July 9. https://prospect.org/api/content/7eede446-d8e8-5a01-b321-5c1fce148b0e/.

Walker, Grace. 2016. "New Georgia Law Lifts Food Stamp Ban for Drug Felons." Red & Black, May 7. https://www.redandblack.com/athensnews/new-georgia-law-lifts-food-stamp-ban-for-drug-felons/article_e047283c-1413-11e6-ad63-6767de912a3e.html.

Walter, Stefanie. 2021. "The Backlash against Globalization." *Annual Review of Political Science* 24 (1): 421–42.

Wawro, Gregory J., and Eric Schickler. 2007. *Filibuster: Obstruction and Lawmaking in the U.S. Senate*. Princeton University Press.

Weaver, Amy M., and Amy E. Lerman. 2010. "Political Consequences of the Carceral State." *American Political Science Review* 104 (4): 817–33.

Weaver, R. Kent. 1986. "The Politics of Blame Avoidance." *Journal of Public Policy* 6 (4): 371–98.

———. 2000. *Ending Welfare as We Know It*. Brookings Institution Press.

———. 2010. "Paths and Forks or Chutes and Ladders? Negative Feedbacks and Policy Regime Change." *Journal of Public Policy* 30 (2): 137–62.

Weaver, Vesla M. 2007. "Frontlash: Race and the Development of Punitive Crime Policy." *Studies in American Political Development* 21 (2): 230–65.

Webel, Baird, Marc Labonte, Bill Canis, Ben Goldman, Jim Monke, Randy Schnepf, and Rachel Y. Tang. 2020. "Federal Assistance to Troubled Industries: Selected Examples." *CRS Report* R46277. Library of Congress, Congressional Research Service.

Weber, Lauren, and Joel Achenbach. 2023. "Covid Backlash Hobbles Public Health and Future Pandemic Response." *Washington Post*, May 8. https://www.washingtonpost.com/health/2023/03/08/covid-public-health-backlash/.

Weber, Max. 1987. "Politics as a Vocation." In *Selections in Translation*, edited by W. G. Runciman, 221–25. Translated by E. Matthews. Cambridge University Press.

Weinraub, Bernard. 1985a. "Reagan Orders Moves against Trade Partners." *New York Times*, September 8. https://www.nytimes.com/1985/09/08/world/reagan-orders-moves-against-trade-partners.html.

———. 1985b. "Reagan Rejects Shoe Import Curb." *New York Times*, August 29. https://www.nytimes.com/1985/08/29/business/reagan-rejects-shoe-import-curb.html.

Weir, Margaret. 2006. "When Does Politics Create Policy? The Organizational Politics of Change." In *Rethinking Political Institutions: The Art of the State*, edited by Ian Shapiro, Stephen Skowronek, and Daniel Galvin, 171–86. New York University Press.

Weisberg, Jacob. 2016. *Ronald Reagan: The American Presidents Series: The 40th President, 1981–1989.* Macmillan.

Wesleyan Media Project. 2018. "2018: The Health Care Election." October 18. https://mediaproject.wesleyan.edu/101818-tv/.

Wheaton, Brian. 2022. "Laws, Beliefs, and Backlash." UCLA, Anderson School of Management, June 27. https://www.anderson.ucla.edu/sites/default/files/document/2022-09/Laws%20Beliefs.pdf.

White, Joseph. 2020. "Costs versus Coverage, Then and Now." *Journal of Health Politics, Policy and Law* 45 (5): 817–30.

"White House Calls the Shots, as Illegal Alien Bill Clears." 1997. *CQ Almanac 1996*, 104th Congress, 2nd Session. CQ Press. http://library.cqpress.com/cqalmanac/cqal96-1092264.

Wicker, Tom. 1990. "Precedent for a Veto." *New York Times*, October 24. https://www.nytimes.com/1990/10/24/opinion/the-nation-precedent-for-a-veto.html.

Wildavsky, Aaron B. 1989. *Speaking Truth to Power: The Art and Craft of Policy Analysis.* Transaction Publishers.

Wilensky, Harold L. 2002. *Rich Democracies: Political Economy, Public Policy, and Performance.* University of California Press.

———. 2012. *American Political Economy in Global Perspective.* Cambridge University Press.

Williams, Timothy, and Sarah Mervosh. 2020. "Virginia Governor Declares State of Emergency ahead of Gun Rally." *New York Times*, January 17. https://www.nytimes.com/2020/01/15/us/virginia-gun-rights-rally.html?searchResultPosition=1.

Williams, Timothy, Sabrina Tavernise, Zolan Kanno-Youngs, and Sarah Mervosh. 2020. "Amid Tight Security, Virginia Gun Rally Draws Thousands of Supporters." *New York Times*, January 20. https://www.nytimes.com/2020/01/20/us/virginia-gun-rally.html.

Williamson, Vanessa, Theda Skocpol, and John Coggin. 2011. "The Tea Party and the Remaking of Republican Conservatism." *Perspectives on Politics* 9 (1): 25–43.

Willsher, Kim. 2018. "Macron Scraps Fuel Tax Rise in Face of Gilets Jaunes Protests." *Guardian*, December 5. https://www.theguardian.com/world/2018/dec/05/france-wealth-tax-changes-gilets-jaunes-protests-president-macron.

Wilson, James Q. 1973. *Political Organizations.* Basic Books.

Winkler, Matthew A. 2016. "What Were You Thinking, North Carolina?" *Bloomberg*, April 19. https://www.bloomberg.com/opinion/articles/2016-04-19/what-were-you-thinking-north -carolina.

Witkin, Richard. 1981. "Air Control Union Breaks Off Talks as a Strike Looms." *New York Times*, August 3. https://www.nytimes.com/1981/08/03/us/air-control-union-breaks-off-talks-as -a-strike-looms.html.

Witt, Emily. 2020. "A New Backlash to Gun Control Begins in Virginia." *New Yorker*, January 28. https://www.newyorker.com/news/dispatch/a-new-backlash-to-gun-control-begins-in-virginia.

Wlezien, Christopher. 1995. "The Public as Thermostat: The Dynamics of Preferences for Spending." *American Journal of Political Science* 39 (4): 981–1000.

Wlezien, Christopher, and Stuart N. Soroka. 2012. "Political Institutions and the Opinion-Policy Link." *West European Politics* 35 (6): 1407–32.

WRAL-TV (Raleigh). 2016. "Results of SurveyUSA Election Poll #22836." April 12. https://ww wcache.wral.com/asset/news/state/nccapitol/2016/04/12/15637752/PollPrint.pdf.

Wright, David. 2016. "North Carolina Moves toward Ending Transgender Bathroom Dispute." *CNN Politics*, CNN, December 19. https://www.cnn.com/2016/12/19/politics/charlotte -repeals-transgender-bathroom-ordinance/index.html.

WSLS10 (Roanoke). 2019. "Hundreds Attend Meeting in Pulaski County to Voice Support for Becoming Second Amendment Sanctuary." November 25. https://www.youtube.com/watch?v =DOwzBEqDY54.

Yang, Crystal S. 2017. "Does Public Assistance Reduce Recidivism?" *American Economic Review* 107 (5): 551–55.

Yglesias, Matthew. 2016. "How Max Weber Explains the 2016 Election." Vox, July 11. https://www .vox.com/2016/7/11/12053146/max-weber-hillary-clinton.

———. 2022. "Democrats Are Doing Far Better Than Expected. How Come?" *Guardian*, November 9. https://www.theguardian.com/commentisfree/2022/nov/09/democrats-did-far-better -than-expected-how-come.

Yoffie, David B. 1989. "American Trade Policy: An Obsolete Bargain?" In *Can the Government Govern?*, edited by John E. Chubb and Paul E. Peterson, 100–138. Brookings Institution Press.

Yoon-Hendricks, Alexandra, and Zoe Greenberg. 2018. "Protests across U.S. Call for End to Migrant Family Separations." *New York Times*, June 30. https://www.nytimes.com/2018/06/30 /us/politics/trump-protests-family-separation.html.

Young, Neil J. 2016. "How the Bathroom Wars Shaped America." *Politico Magazine*, May 18. https://www.politico.com/magazine/story/2016/05/2016-bathroom-bills-politics-north -carolina-lgbt-transgender-history-restrooms-era-civil-rights-213902.

Younis, Mohamed. 2020. "Americans Want More, Not Less, Immigration for First Time." Gallup. com, July 1. https://news.gallup.com/poll/313106/americans-not-less-immigration-first -time.aspx.

———. 2021. "Sharply Fewer in U.S. View Foreign Trade as Opportunity." Gallup.com, March 31. https://news.gallup.com/poll/342419/sharply-fewer-view-foreign-trade-opportunity.aspx.

Yurcaba, Jo. 2021. "N. Carolina Cities Begin Passing Historic LGBTQ Nondiscrimination Laws." NBC News, January 17. https://www.nbcnews.com/feature/nbc-out/n-carolina-cities -begin-passing-historic-lgbtq-nondiscrimination-laws-n1254539.

Zelizer, Julian E. 2010. *Jimmy Carter: The American Presidents Series: The 39th President, 1977– 1981*. Macmillan.

————. 2015a. "The Contentious Origins of Medicare and Medicaid." In *Medicare and Medicaid at 50: America's Entitlement Programs in the Age of Affordable Care*, edited by Alan B. Cohen, David C. Colby, Keith A. Wailoo, and Julian E. Zelizer, 3–20. Oxford University Press.

————. 2015b. *The Fierce Urgency of Now: Lyndon Johnson, Congress, and the Battle for the Great Society*. Penguin Press.

————. 2018. *The Presidency of Barack Obama: A First Historical Assessment*. Princeton University Press.

————. 2022. "Daniel Bell and the Radical Right." In *Defining the Age: Daniel Bell, His Time and Ours*, edited by Paul Starr and Julian E Zelizer, 111–32. Columbia University Press.

Zürn, Michael. 2021. "How Non-Majoritarian Institutions Make Silent Majorities Vocal: A Political Explanation of Authoritarian Populism." *Perspectives on Politics* 20 (3): 1–20. http://dx.doi.org/10.1017/S1537592721001043.

Index

Page numbers in italics refer to figures and tables.

Chicago Studies in American Politics

A series edited by Susan Herbst, Lawrence R. Jacobs, Adam J. Berinsky, and Frances Lee; Benjamin I. Page, editor emeritus

Series titles, continued from front matter

The Limits of Party: Congress and Lawmaking in a Polarized Era
by James M. Curry and Frances E. Lee

America's Inequality Trap
by Nathan J. Kelly

*Good Enough for Government Work: The Public Reputation Crisis in America
(And What We Can Do to Fix It)*
by Amy E. Lerman

Who Wants to Run? How the Devaluing of Political Office Drives Polarization
by Andrew B. Hall

*From Politics to the Pews: How Partisanship and the Political Environment
Shape Religious Identity*
by Michele F. Margolis

The Increasingly United States: How and Why American Political Behavior Nationalized
by Daniel J. Hopkins

Legislative Style
by William Bernhard and Tracy Sulkin

Legacies of Losing in American Politics
by Jeffrey K. Tulis and Nicole Mellow

Why Parties Matter: Political Competition and Democracy in the American South
by John H. Aldrich and John D. Griffin

Neither Liberal nor Conservative: Ideological Innocence in the American Public
by Donald R. Kinder and Nathan P. Kalmoe

Strategic Party Government: Why Winning Trumps Ideology
by Gregory Koger and Matthew J. Lebo

Post-Racial or Most-Racial? Race and Politics in the Obama Era
by Michael Tesler

The Politics of Resentment: Rural Consciousness in Wisconsin and the Rise of Scott Walker
by Katherine J. Cramer

Legislating in the Dark: Information and Power in the House of Representatives
by James M. Curry

Why Washington Won't Work: Polarization, Political Trust, and the Governing Crisis
by Marc J. Hetherington and Thomas J. Rudolph

Who Governs? Presidents, Public Opinion, and Manipulation
by James N. Druckman and Lawrence R. Jacobs